CW00545150

STALIN'S CLAWS

TATTERED
FLAG

Tattered Flag Press West Sussex

STALIN'S
CLAWS

FROM THE PURGES TO THE WINTER WAR
Red Army operations before Barbarossa 1937-1941

E.R. HOOTON

Published in Great Britain in 2013 by
Tattered Flag Press
PO Box 2240
Pulborough
West Sussex RH20 9AL
England

office@thetatteredflag.com
www.thetatteredflag.com

Tattered Flag Press is an imprint of Chevron
Publishing Ltd.

Jacket Design: Mark Nelson

Cataloguing-in-Publication Data for this book
is available from the British Library

ISBN 978-0-9543115-5-1

Typeset and design by Mark Nelson,
Sydney, Australia

Printed and bound in the UK by the MPG
Books Group, Bodmin and King's Lynn

For more information on books published by
Tattered Flag visit: www.thetatteredflag.com

CONTENTS

PREFACE

ON 22 June 1941 German troops invaded the Soviet Union and quickly smashed through the Red Army to occupy vast tracts of the country.

While Russian troops usually fought bravely, on this occasion the Red Army almost collapsed and months would elapse before it would be able to hold the invader. A major alibi for this defeat was the Purges of Soviet Society which reached a height of ferocity in 1937–1938 as the 'Ezhovshchina' and which killed or jailed thousands of officers and left many more on the reserve list in limbo.

Undoubtedly, the Purges had a major impact upon the Red Army, paralysing initiative and any form of liberal military thought and replacing experienced officers with men promoted far above their level of capability who were given no training for their new responsibilities. They also removed most of the senior Red Army leadership including those who had espoused the cause of making mechanised forces the core of the future army.

Yet this is only part of the reason for the Red Army's catastrophic performance, for the fundamental problem was a lack of trained staff officers. Unlike the German Army, it was the inability of the military radicals to turn their vision into reality which was a major military incentive for the Red Army's Purge; the leaders had not been given staff officer training to help them to identify and overcome the obstacles to combined-arms operations, command and control as well as logistics on the modern battlefield.

Until 1936 generals had to make do with a short command course, which certainly had no effect upon many such as future Marshal Semyon Budenny. It was Boris Shaposhnikov who foresaw the need for a staff college and many of the pre-war graduates, such as Georgii Zhukov, would mastermind the Soviet Union's forceful victories in the Second World War. Others would provide the intellectual infrastructure which was the foundation of these victories and there can be little doubt that by 1945 the Soviet General Staff were far better than the famed German General Staff.

Yet the Purges straddled the Ezhovshchina and continued well into the Second World War. This book attempts to tell the story of how the Red Army evolved against the background of the Purges and also how it conducted major operations between 1937 and 1940.

In doing so I have used not only published works but also exploited the vast range of reference material which is available on the World Wide Web. Much of this has been assembled by amateurs, such as myself, who are also military history enthusiasts and many have clearly had access to Soviet official files which would be difficult, or impossible, for foreigners to access even in this more liberal age. The Web also provides access to many published works, especially those published in the former Soviet Union, which might be difficult to access otherwise.

I have taken one liberty in attempting to personalise the story for the wider Western readership. Wherever possible I have referred to generals by their personal name, rather than using the usual initials: e.g. General D.G. Pavlov becomes Dimitri Pavlov while his friend G.I. Kulik becomes Gregorii Kulik. In addition, Japanese names are given in the Western fashion with personal names first.

I would like to thank Robert Forsyth, publisher at Tattered Flag Press, for the opportunity to write this book; Slough Library for obtaining various books; and my daughter, Jennifer, for her assistance with certain Russian words. I would also like to thank all those who took the time to reply to my questions. All errors of interpretation are, of course, my own.

E.R. HOOTON

AUTHOR'S NOTE

In order to distinguish Russian military units from non-Russian units, throughout the text I have used numerals (i.e. '24th') for Russian formations and have spelled out the numeral designations for non-Russian formations (i.e. 'Twenty-fourth').

E.R.H. 2013

GLOSSARY

Russian

Armikom Armiya Kommissar I/II Ranga – Army Commissar I/II Rank. Political officers similar to Komandarm

(AON) *Armiya Osobogo Naznachiya* – 'Special Purpose Army'

Brigkom Brigada Kommissar – Brigade Commissar. Political officer equivalent to a Kombrig

Dalyinevostochnyai Krasnoznamennaya Front – Far Eastern Red Banner Front

Divkom Divisiya Kommissar – Division Commissar. Political officer equivalent to Komdiv

Eshovshchina – 'Eshov's thing'. The term for the Purges under Ezhov

(GRU) *Glavnoye Razvedyvatel'noye Upravleniye* – Main Intelligence Directorate. Army Intelligence

Komandarm II Ranga Komandir Armia – Army Commander I Rank. Equivalent to General or Colonel General

Komandarm II Ranga – Army Commander II Rank. Equivalent to Lieutenant General

Kombrig Komandir Brigada – Brigade Commander. Equivalent to Brigadier General

Komdiv Komandir Diviziya – Division Commander. Equivalent to Major General

Komkor Komandir Korpus – Corps Commander. Equivalent to Lieutenant General

Korkom Korpus Kommissar – Corps Commissar. Political officer equivalent to Komkor

Narodnom Komissariate Oborony – Main Military Council

(NKVD) *Narodnyy Komissariat Vnutrennikh Del* – People's Commissariat for Internal Affairs

Osovogo Strelkobyi Korpus – Special Rifle Corps

Otdelynaya Krasnoznamennaya Armiya – Separate Red Banner Army

(OKDVA) *Otdelynaya Krasnoznamennaya Dalyanevosto Chnaya Armiya* – Separate Far Eastern Red Banner Army

(PVO) *Protivovozdushnaia Oboronoa* – Air Defence Troops

(RKKA) *Raboche-Krest'yanski Krasnoi Armiyy* – Red Army

Rezerv Glavnogo Komandovaniya – Main Command Reserve

(UR) *Ukreplennye Raiony* – Fortified Regions

Voenno Vozdushnye Sily-RKKA or VVS-RKKA (or just VVS) – Red Army Air Force

Japanese

Daihon'ei – IGHQ Imperial General Headquarters

Polish

(DOK) *Dowództwo Okr gu Korpusu Corps* – Area Commands

(KOP) *Korpus Ochrony Pogranicza* – Border Protection Corps

(ON) *Obrona Narodowa* – National Defence

A CARTOON BY DAVID LOW AS PUBLISHED IN THE PICTURE POST OF 24 FEBRUARY 1940.
(REPRODUCED COURTESY OF SOLO SYNDICATION/ASSOCIATED NEWSPAPERS LTD)

CHAPTER ONE

PARADE OF THE DAMNED

'Why do you need me to die?'
FROM A LETTER TO IOSEF STALIN BY NIKOLAI BUKHARIN

THE May Day Parade in Moscow was the Soviet Union's opportunity to display its military prowess to the world. The year 1936 was no exception, but the occasion would prove to be a watershed for two men standing on Lenin's Tomb.

For Iosef Stalin, officially General Secretary of the Soviet Bolshevik (Communist) Party, and for Marshal Mikhail Tukhachevskii, Deputy Defence Commissar and Inspector of Military Training, there was pride in the Five Year Plans which had industrialised the Soviet Union and produced the cornucopia of tanks, motorised troops and artillery which sped across Red Square. Behind them came Russia's traditional forces: cavalry, horse-drawn artillery and phalanxes of infantry, goose-stepping with fixed bayonets, while overhead flew squadrons of aircraft, among them a twin-engined TsKB-6 bomber which looped-the-loop and would be the prototype for the DB-3 (later Il-4) medium bomber.

The baby-faced Tukhachevskii had calculating eyes but was a cultured man; he played the violin and made the instruments in his spare time, which may have helped with his female conquests. He knew that despite the great progress, the armed forces' colossus had feet of clay; indeed the vehicles which rolled across Red Square were from a special parade formation which had priority for spares and mechanics to ensure the embarrassing breakdowns which had marred earlier parades were avoided, yet both of these were in short supply throughout the armed forces. Tukhachevskii was aware of other problems such as the quality of leadership, but he was confident that the Red Army (Raboche-Krest'yanski Krasnoi Armiyy – RKKA) would overcome these and be able to execute the radical new form of warfare as expressed in its Provisional Field Service Regulations 1936 (Vremennyy Polevoy Ustav 1936 or PU 36), and as demonstrated during the previous autumn's exercises to the astonishment of his contemporaries.[1]

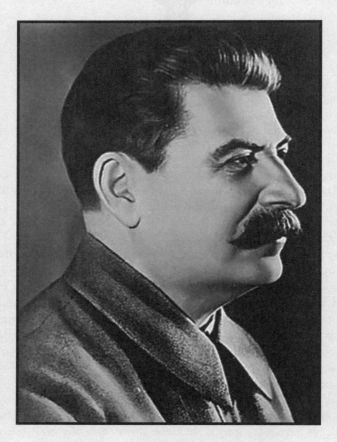

A PORTRAIT OF IOSEF STALIN FROM 1936 AS THE PURGES
BEGAN TO UNLEASH A HOLOCAUST UPON SOVIET SOCIETY.

What he could not anticipate was that Stalin, standing only a few feet from him, was preparing to unleash a holocaust upon the whole of Soviet society. He would purge it of people deemed 'hostile' to Communism and to the Soviet Union including thousands of Soviet officers, many of whom would follow Tukhachevskii into early graves. In doing so he would hamstring the Soviet Union's defences as they faced their greatest threat and almost bring about the destruction of Communist rule.

From its birth, the Bolshevik state faced enemies on all sides but defeated them in detail. Then, like the French, it tried to export the revolution at bayonet point, only to be rebuffed by the Poles in 1920. When hostilities against internal and external enemies ended in the early 1920s Russia was economically ruined, with the army rapidly demobilised from some 5.5 million to 10 per cent of that figure and armed with an eclectic mix of weapons and equipment, most obsolete.[2]

The country was too poor to maintain a large standing army and the reduced Red Army became a territorial militia organisation made up of 46 of 77 rifle divisions and one of 11 cavalry divisions. To provide some sinew in the west, work started in 1928 on four fortified regions (Ukreplennye Raiony - UR) to shield the western approaches, but when the new chief-of-staff, Boris Shaposhnikov, sought 40 million roubles for this requirement the Defence Minister (People's Commissar for Military and Navy Affairs), Kliment 'Klim' Voroshilov, could find only 24 million.[3]

Until the country was industrialised and rebuilt there was little the Red Army could do except dream and follow foreign developments, although secret agreements designed to test weapons forbidden to Germany under the Versailles Treaty gave it direct access to German military thought and technology from the mid-1920s until 1933. The Germans tested military aircraft, tanks, artillery and chemical weapons, closely observed by their hosts, the German anti-tank gun proving the basis of the Russian weapon, while German welding techniques were later incorporated into Russian tank construction.

Russian reflections on future war and developments in armoured vehicles began to synthesise into a radical doctrine which combined operational and technical experience into a form of warfare dreamed by only a few outside the Soviet Union. Conventional military doctrine after the First World War was shaped by the three-year impasse on the Western Front and repeated on the Isonzo and Salonika Fronts. The impasse reflected the increasing use of field fortifications which had begun in the later Napoleonic Wars and saw the shield gradually grow stronger than the sword.

Field fortifications became a key feature in the Tactical-Level (battalion to army corps) battlefield, restricting access to the ever-growing concentrations of artillery ('gun line') whose range, accuracy and lethality steadily increased until by the Great War it was truly, to use Stalin's phrase, 'The God of War', creating a wall of flame and steel through which, if unchallenged, no organised body of men could pass. From 1915 to 1917 artillery conquered the ground while infantry occupied it, but defenders responded with greater dispersal, the proliferation of automatic weapons and the shelter of concrete structures.

From late 1917 the impasse was broken by secretly concentrating overwhelming force upon a narrow part of the front, wrecking the defences with a short but intense bombardment, then outflanking the surviving strongpoints to threaten the 'gun line', withdrawal of which would cause the enemy to retreat. These tactics provided Tactical manoeuvre, although progress was often slow and methodical because it was impossible to neutralise every enemy automatic weapon and artillery piece exposing vanguards to enemy fire or to counter-attack. Sustained artillery support was essential to counter this but moving the gun line blocked roads and helped to restrict exploitation of Tactical success at the 'Operational' Level (army to army group).

At the Strategic Level (army group and above) the shield held firm because the defenders could exploit undamaged road and rail communications to re-establish defences in a more favourable position and with renewed artillery concentrations. The attackers, on the other hand, depended upon roads which were often damaged or blocked to slow the movement of reinforcements and supplies. The longest Allied advance on the Western Front in the latter part of the Great War was made by the British who took three months to travel the 135 kilometres from Amiens to Mons – an average of 1.5 kilometres a day, while even the German breakthrough in March 1918 saw a 70-kilometre advance from St Quentin to Amiens taking 15 days or 4.5 kilometres a day!

Most of the world's armies believed future operations would follow this pattern in general, although much would depend upon the strength of enemy artillery. As armies absorbed the lessons of 1918 they continued to worship at the 'God of War's' altar and nowhere was this better illustrated than in the French Army's 'Instructions sur l'emploi tactique des grande unités' of 1936. This envisaged a methodical, centrally-controlled battle (bataille conduite) with advances by combined arms forces in phases of 1–2 kilometres behind a shield of artillery fire.[4] The French infantry advance would be around 5 kilometres per day and would then halt for artillery to be moved forward, a process which could take up to 10 hours.[5]

'Firepower kills' as Pétain observed and as the Instructions noted: 'The attack is the fire that advances, the defence that halts (the enemy).' The gunners dictated all progress so that the attackers pounded the defences like a battering ram, chipping off the defences (the Russians called this 'gnawing away') until the enemy 'gun line' was forced to withdraw.[6] This period of withdrawal offered the best prospect of Operational-Level exploitation, or as the Instructions summarised the offensive: 'The offensive battle thus assumes the form of successive actions of force, preceded by indispensable delays for their preparation, and followed by periods of movement more or less long.'[7]

Conventional wisdom assumed a methodical advance would lead to Tactical-Level success; indeed the French regarded the defensive fortified regions as springboards for an offensive, but also assumed the continued dominance of the

Strategic-Level defensive as in the Great War. Even motorisation was believed to help the defence, allowing infantry and artillery to create rapidly a new defensive line, although air attacks could impede such movement.[8]

These conventional views were less appropriate on battlefields where concentrations of both men and materiel were weaker, such as the Eastern and Middle Eastern Fronts. Here, as with all the Soviet Union's western neighbours, it was easier to exploit Tactical success at both the Operational and even Strategic Levels. Once a breakthrough had been achieved, Tactically large cavalry forces had ranged deep into the enemy rear, threatening communications, forcing major withdrawals and creating strategic mobility. Significantly, Hans von Seeckt, the curious mixture of radical and conservative personality who shaped the *Reichsheer*, not only retained cavalry but also demanded they carry lances!

Experience in both the East and West meant the Germans did not blindly accept conventional wisdom. In the West, once the bombardment ceased, the Germans infiltrated the wrecked defences (a tactic ignored by the French) with combined arms groups and made directly for the 'gun line' spearheaded by 'mobile divisions' which conducted Operational-Level exploitation relying upon speed and mobility. In the immediate aftermath of the Great War, although they recognised the power of the defence, the Germans were still confident that such tactics would work purely with the traditional arms.[9]

The German command doctrine manual 'Truppenführung 1933' exploited this experience and noted: 'The objective of the combined arms in an attack is to bring the infantry into decisive action against the enemy, with sufficient fire power and shock action so that it is possible to drive through deeply and break down the final hostile resistance.' By again stabbing directly at the enemy 'gun line' the Germans aimed to undermine Tactical-Level defence and exploit this success at the Operational Level by continuously striking and leaving the initiative to forward commanders, who received as much artillery support as possible. Ultimately, the Germans believed they could push deep into enemy territory to break through, neutralising Strategic-Level defence and even making possible the encirclement of large forces.[10]

The key to Germany's new tactics were tanks, with even the most hidebound military traditionalist recognising the value of these new vehicles. The post-Great War years saw massive advances in automotive technology and greatly improved cross-country performance; more powerful and reliable engines (aided by lead additives in petrol), together with new transmission and suspension systems, would clearly influence warfare, but who would it benefit more: the defender or the attacker?

The radical commentators, like Basil Liddell Hart and John (J.F.C.) Fuller, favoured the sword and saw the battlefield mastered by massed armour dominating the action, Fuller even envisaging 'land fleets'. The bulk would be formed of 'cruiser' tanks, similar to the Vickers Mark E (6-ton), while the scouting 'destroyers' would be the automobile-sized tankettes (the first was built in a garage) such as the

Vickers Lloyd. At the heart would be land 'battleships' – heavy, multi-turreted vehicles such as the Vickers A1E1 Independent. The traditional arms, in this philosophy, were reduced to protecting the tanks' supplies and communications.[11]

Indignant that the infantry and artillery should be reduced to little more than 'hewers of wood and carriers of water', the conservatives continued to place their faith in the 'God of War' and the traditional arms. They recognised the value of the tank in Tactical operations supporting the traditional arms of infantry (heavy tank) and cavalry (light tank) and reluctantly recognised the value of motor-mechanised forces in helping to seal, but not exploit, breakthroughs at the Operational Level. Field artillery had proved the greatest battlefield threat to the tank ('shell-proof' tanks did not enter service until the mid-1930s), while they felt the proliferation of anti-tank guns and minefields would also restrict tank movements. It is worth noting that during the Second World War the German Army successfully converted French 75 mm field guns to the anti-tank role with dedicated ammunition for use against the Red Army.

Radicals and conservatives agreed that the tank should be used en masse. But the French believed it should operate within the artillery shield, supporting the infantry, and even when they created armoured divisions (Division Cuirassée de Réserve) very much as Liddell Hart and Fuller advocated to counter enemy tanks in support of the infantry. The mechanised cavalry divisions (Division Légère Mécanique) had the traditional cavalry role and were committed in the period after the enemy 'gun line' had been forced to move.[12]

German armoured warfare pioneers synthesised their own experience, foreign (especially British) military thought and in-depth studies of the problems, to persuade all but the most conservative that the speed of modern tanks accelerated a Tactical-Level breakthrough and made possible Operational-Level exploitation.[13] The Panzer division was essentially a Great War mobile division with a tank regiment replacing one of the three infantry regiments. *Truppenführung* noted: 'When closely tied to the infantry, the tanks are deprived of their inherent speed and may be sacrificed to hostile fire.' It added: 'The infantry must use the (shock) effect produced by attacking tanks to advance rapidly.'[14] However, conservatives in the German Army created mechanised cavalry divisions (Leichte Division) with many wishing to confine tanks to infantry support, and a consensus on the use of armour based upon the radicals' ideas did not really emerge until the mid-1930s.[15]

Although the Russians could not access '*Truppenführung* 1933', they appear to have been aware of its 1921 predecessor. The Russians absorbed the German experience and blended it with their own experience of the Great War and the post-Revolution Wars, seasoned with readings from foreign military thought, notably British theories, on armoured warfare. For the Soviet Union, the 1920s were spent largely in this form of reflection due to its industrial and economic weakness, which included gross exaggerations of the tank threat to its security. During the late 1920s Tukhachevskii, Vladimir Triandafillov and Konstantin Kalinovskii developed a concept known as 'deep battle' and similar to that of the

Germans which involved Tactical-Level breakthroughs and Operational-Level exploitation up to 200 kilometres at a time.

The concept would remain a dream until the new factories began production; the traditional rifle and cavalry divisions began to receive an abundant supply of equipment; the inventories of automatic weapons rose from 33,000 to 155,000 between 1928 and 1937 while those for vehicles rose from 2,750 to 41,000 between 1929 and 1935. In key weaponry 7,000 tubes of field artillery were delivered between 1928 and 1935, while 11,000 armoured vehicles were produced between 1930 and 1934 and air strength rose from 1,400 aircraft in 1928 to 6,672 in 1935.[16] By the end of the First Five Year Plan Russia had produced 5,644 tanks including 2,430 T-27 tankettes and 1,550 T-26 light tanks, based upon the Vickers 6-ton, and a Motor-Mechanisation Academy was opened in 1932.[17] While some of this equipment was modified from Imperial days, much of it was new – especially the armour, which benefited from studies of designs imported from Great Britain and the United States.

As divisions received more weapons, vehicles and signalling equipment, so they required greater professional support at all levels with the result that during the mid-1930s the territorial militia divisions were replaced with cadres of professionals who would be augmented by reservists in times of crisis. By 1938 this process was complete. As their capabilities increased, their role was also considered and most agreed that it should be offensive.

The Soviet Union followed the trend of most European powers in extending the frontier fortified regions with their concrete bunkers, casements and pill-boxes. Another nine were added to the western border and eleven to the eastern from 1933, both to shield vulnerable parts of the country (as with the Mannerheim Line) and to channel an anticipated attack, allowing the more economic use of manpower (like the Maginot Line). Indeed the original 13 fortified regions had 3,200 bunkers held by 25 machine gun battalions with 18,000 men,[18] yet the so-called 'Stalin Line' was also intended to provide springboards for offensive and the emphasis in Soviet military education institutions was upon the offensive. It was not until 1938 that a study, 'The Army on the Defensive', was produced.[19] But what form would the offensive take?

When Triandafillov and Kalinovskii were killed in an air crash in 1931 it was left to Tukhachevskii as Nachal'nik vooruzheniya (Chief of Ordnance) to try to implement 'deep battle' through large armoured forces which would conduct both breakthrough and exploitation. In this task he was assisted by his predecessor, Ieronim Uborevich, and his friend Grigol (also known as Servo) Ordzhonikidze, Chairman of the National Economy Supreme Council and later Commissar for Heavy Industry. In part this was because so many tanks were emerging from Ordzhonikidze's factories that they were able to meet the requirements both of the infantry and the cavalry, allowing the Russians to form five mechanised brigades by 1932 (the first in 1930), and 15 tank and 12 mechanised regiments together with 75 armoured battalions for the rifle divisions (most with tankettes but 15 with

A Red Army rifle regiment machine gun team trains with a Degtyrarova Pekhotny Model 1928 (DP 28) light machine gun. This was one of a series of robust, reliable weapons of all calibres and types which emerged from Soviet Russia's arms factories. It was reportedly nicknamed the 'Grammofon' (Gramophone) because of the disc-like 47-round magazine. (Nik Cornish at www.Stavka.org.uk)

tanks).[20] Even Semon Budenny, the Red Army's Joachim Murat, recognised that cavalry required an armoured element and by 1930–31 the principle of a battle deep in the enemy's rear beyond the 'gun line' was being accepted as 'deep operations'. By early 1933 it was accepted as the Red Army's official doctrine.[21]

Like any other army, the Red Army had its conservatives, but in this case they were also part of the so-called 1st Cavalry Army clique which had close personal associations with Stalin himself. Stalin's sole experience of military operations had been in the Civil War, leaving him with views which were increasingly archaic. For military decisions he relied upon a few close associates, especially Voroshilov and Budenny who both shared his views.

Stalin, known as 'Vozhd' ('The Boss') to his entourage, and as 'Khozyain' ('The Master') to the bureaucracy, was a pock-marked Georgian who smelled of tobacco, often puffing on a pipe he filled from torn-up cigarettes. He was mildly anti-Semitic, but a strong Polonophobe with a coarse turn of speech, often deliberate, and yet he was well read with a 20,000-volume library and he wrote with clarity. He also shared the Georgian (and Corsican) fondness for vendettas and wrapped grudges around him like a cloak, once observing: 'The greatest delight is to mark one's enemy, prepare everything, avenge oneself thoroughly and then go to sleep.'[22] To the end of his life Stalin kept in his desk the last letter from the purged Nikolai Bukharin, once one of the Party's leaders, who wrote from his death cell: '*Why do you need me to die?*'

Those of his intimates associated with the Red Army such as Voroshilov and Budenny, who addressed him by the familiar 'thou' (ty), were not known for profound military thought. Voroshilov looked like everyone's favourite uncle, but he was petulant, cruel, vain and stupid: according to one commentator 'Voroshilov rarely saw a stick without getting the wrong end of it'.[23] A former metal worker he became Stalin's friend in 1918 and 'The Boss' called him the 'Commander-in-Chief from the lathe' while he, in turn, referred to his master by his revolutionary code name 'Koba'. He was a man who moulded his views to fit those of Stalin to whom he demonstrated unquestioning and zealous obedience. On occasion, however, he would lose his temper publicly with his master who, nevertheless, usually celebrated the anniversary of the October Revolution in Voroshilov's Kremlin apartment, where 'Klim' could indulge his love of ballroom dancing. Voroshilov was a military lightweight with an inferiority complex to the cleverer generals and he demonstrated a total absence of any leadership quality or even capability, but his traits as a 'Yes' man and world-class toady ensured he remained nominally at the apex of Soviet power for a decade after Stalin's death.[24]

Budenny (his name is also shared with a Russian horse bred as a charger for cavalry officers) was a gallant cavalry regiment commander whose sole military education was a two-year course at the M. V. Frunze Military Academy completed in 1932, although he reportedly tried to extend his military expertise. His IQ seemed lower than his moustache size and in the debates on the future of the Red Army he tried to secure the place of his beloved cavalry, of which he was inspector from 1924. Indeed, future Marshal Ivan Konev would later observe: 'He was a man with a past, but no future, a man who hardly progressed in his thinking beyond the Civil War.' He had little capability and his character was probably summed up in his answer as an Imperial dragoon when asked his thoughts on the 1905 St Petersburg uprising: 'My job is to serve, your Excellency.' He too was an unquestioning supporter of Stalin.[25]

The Cavalry Army clique resented Tukhachevskii's criticisms of their operations during the war with Poland and when he became Army chief-of-staff in the mid-1920s, he frequently quarrelled with Voroshilov and his deputy, the equally inadequate Gregorii Kulik. Kulik, like Voroshilov, had met Stalin in 1918 and participated in 'The Boss's' 'victory' at Tsaritsyn (later Stalingrad) where he had been a gunner. Stalin would later say of Kulik: 'He understands artillery.'[26] Although not a member of Stalin's inner circle, Kulik was both a sycophant and a stiff-necked conservative who headed the Artillery Directorate from 1926 until 1929 when, like Budenny, he began a two-year course at the Frunze Academy from which he emerged as commander and commissar of the 3rd Rifle Corps. In 1936 he was sent to Spain's Madrid Front as a military advisor (as General 'Kuper' or 'Cooper') returning in May 1937.[27]

Eventually Stalin engineered Tukhachevskii's transfer to the Leningrad Military District and his replacement with Boris Shaposhnikov who probably did more than anyone else to hold the Red Army together professionally before the German invasion.[29] Shaposhnikov, the son of a distillery manager, was an anachronism: softly-spoken, exquisitely polite, schoolmasterish (he wore pince-nez) and with a face like parchment due to recurrent bouts of ill health, probably from the malaria contracted when he served in the Tsarist Army, he was the founder of the Red Army General Staff and professionally conservative. He called almost everyone 'dear fellow' (golubchik) rather than 'comrade' (tovarish) and his Tsarist gentility and old-fashioned approach fascinated Stalin, Shaposhnikov being the only military leader apart from Voroshilov who would call Stalin by his name and patronymic (Iosef Vassilievich) and the only one allowed to smoke in Stalin's office. One reason he remained in the top echelons was because Stalin knew his proposals were carefully considered: he signed nothing without checking it first, and if an alternative was selected not only would he not object but also he would strive to implement it. As head of the Frunze Academy from 1932 to 1935, he improved training to Operational Level and encouraged war games which exploited operational experience.

Shaposhnikov also sought to create a fully-trained General Staff, the 'Brain of the Army' as he called it in his key book of 1927, rather than rushing senior officers through a Frunze command course. There was strong opposition, notably from Budenny, but the General Staff was nevertheless established in 1935 and the following year the General Staff Academy opened its doors. Initially officers were reluctant to become staff officers because they feared being office-bound, but gradually there was a change in attitude and the brains behind the Red Army's victories in the Second World War would emerge from its classrooms. However, it appears there was less emphasis upon Strategy which was regarded as the prerogative of the political leadership.

But this military professional was also a courtier and, as a conservative, he was no friend of Tukhachevskii whom he denounced in the 1920s.[29] When Tukhachevskii wrote a memo to Voroshilov on 11 January 1930 advocating a mechanised army which would exploit the new technology to drive up to 200 kilometres into the enemy, Shaposhnikov responded by stating that the economy could not support the forces envisaged. Stalin, after seeing both memos, agreed with Shaposhnikov, describing Tukhachevskii's ideas as 'science fiction'.[30] Ironically, Shaposhnikov was purged in 1931 while commanding the Volga District, but within a year he became commander and commissar of the Frunze Academy (although he did not join the Party until 1930), was again investigated in 1933 and cleared (although described as being 'of weak character') and in 1935 became Komandarm I Rank (Army Commander 1st Class).

Stalin had been plotting against Tukhachevskii since 1930 and the mechanised forces were the issue at the heart of it but at that time he was, like a British Premier, 'first among equals' and lacked the political power to finish off the general. Aleksandr Egorov, a member of Stalin's 'court' who succeeded Shaposhnikov in 1931, together with the other western military district commanders, Uborevich in Belorussia and Iona Yakir in Kiev, as well as Ordzhonikidze, persuaded a reluctant Stalin to change his mind and, naturally, what he thought, as did Voroshilov. Reluctantly reversing his opposition to mechanisation, Stalin told Tukhachevskii: 'Now the question has become clearer to me, I have to agree that my remark was too strong and my conclusions were not right at all.'[31]

In January 1932 new plans emerged for massed tank units and within two months the first two mechanised corps were created as a consensus emerged on the future of warfare which was seen also to require a commitment from aviation, including airborne units.[32] The first units, 11th and 45th Mechanised Corps, were formed in the Leningrad and Kiev Military Districts during 1932 and in an apparent change of heart, in July 1933 Voroshilov sent Stalin and Vyacheslav Molotov (Chairman of the Defence Commission) a note calling for increased tank production, remarking that such a measure would meet the requirements of 'deep battle' to create an army capable of advancing up to 200 kilometres in a day. But it was, in fact, a copy of a request he had received from Egorov.[33]

Unfortunately for the 'Young Turks' the development of the new formations did not go smoothly and the later disputes undoubtedly contributed to the devastating Purge of the army. There were profound problems with command and control, as well as logistics and all-arm co-ordination, although there was more success with air support thanks to Yakov Alksenis, commander of the Red Army Air Forces (Voenno Vozdushnye Sily-RKKA or VVS-RKKA or simply VVS) who co-operated with Tukhachevskii to develop paratroop units as part of the 'deep battle' concept. One reason for the poor command and control was a lack of radios which was due to inadequate production; while the Germans learned to install them in even their lightest tanks, in the Red Army they were installed only in unit commanders' tanks with signals relayed by flags.

Exercises involving the larger armoured units, from mechanised brigades to mechanised corps, which were often understrength, revealed the scale of the problems. By the end of 1933 a level of disenchantment was obvious to Voroshilov for reports clearly demonstrated that there were serious problems, both of execution and support, which even Tukhachevskii recognised and he demanded studies to resolve them.[34] In part, these problems of command and control were due to the 'dual command' nature of the Red Army's decision-making process which required consensus of 'the military council', a structure extending to battalion level, comprising the commanding officer, his chief-of-staff, and the Party's political officer or commissar.

This last office was the Party's eyes and ears within the army and while possessing an expertise only in political matters, such as propaganda, and a limited understanding of military matters, the commissar could veto any decision by the professionals. Persuading him to support a course of action could be time-consuming and, to speed up decision-making, the military council was abolished in 1934 with operational decisions now the prerogative of the commander.[35]

But the 1934 manoeuvres were 'an abysmal failure' and although the 5th and 7th Mechanised Corps were created in the Moscow and Leningrad Districts (the latter replacing the 11th Mechanised Corps transferred to the Trans-Baikal District) this marked a temporary halt as the Red Army sought to get to grips with the problems, one solution being to reduce the corps' size. By the end of the year even an ardent supporter of 'deep battle', Egorov, seemed to be turning in the wind, advocating the primacy of infantry.[36] Changes brought improved performances in 1935 and during September manoeuvres were conducted involving 75,000 troops, 800 tanks and 500 aircraft by Yakir's Kiev District and Komkor Semon Turovsky's Kharkov District. But both Voroshilov and Shaposhnikov noted continued problems with command and control as well as co-ordination and the Red Army clearly had a long way to go before it perfected 'deep battle'.[37]

During 1935 there were major changes involving the Red Army's leadership. In the aftermath of the Revolution the traditional officer corps was replaced by 'commanders' and this term was incorporated in the rank structure from platoon commander (Komvzvoda) to army commander (Komandarm). From 22 September traditional terminology (e.g. lieutenant, captain) was restored but the term 'general' remained anathema so that ranks from Brigadier General upward still retained the old titles of Kombrig, Komdiv, Komkor and Komandarm, while on the same day the Red Army Staff was renamed the General Staff of the Workers and Peasants Red Army.[38] The decree gave the officer corps immunity to arrest by the civil authorities without Voroshilov's authority while the officers also received considerable benefits. Similar changes were enacted in the navy. Less than two months later, on 22 November, five of the most senior commanders were given the rank of Marshal of the Soviet Union: Budenny, Vasilii Blyukher, Egorov, Tukhachevskii and Voroshilov.[39]

By 1936 there were four mechanised corps, four heavy tank brigades, 15 independent mechanised brigades (several assigned to cavalry corps), six tank regiments in cavalry divisions, together with 83 tank battalions and companies in rifle divisions. But there was dissatisfaction about the mechanised 'deep battle' concept and on 21 May Voroshilov transferred the heavy tank brigades from the Avtobronetankovoye Upravleniy (Motor-Mechanised Directorate) to the Tankovii Rezerv Glavnogo Komandoraniya (High Command Tank Reserve), weakening the mechanised corps whose strength was augmented by independent mechanised brigades. Mechanised corps participated in the 1936 exercises in Uborevich's Belorussian Military District, with Uborevich trying to use them to exploit tactical success.

Following a major restructuring of the Red Army leadership in 1935, five of its most senior commanders were given the rank of Marshal of the Soviet Union. They are seen here following their appointment in November 1935 (from left to right): Mikhail Tukhachevskii, Semon Budenny, Kliment Voroshilov, Vasilii Blyukher and Aleksandr Egorov.

Voroshilov was unconvinced and again noted the failure to co-ordinate the arms. He criticised harshly the armoured forces during a review from 13-19 October, and demanded a rethink of tank tactics as well as improved command and control. He asked 'Why the hell do we need tanks?' and felt that infantry could take an objective with good artillery preparation. He thus doubted the need for an expensive tank force. The tank, he clearly felt, was best used to help infantry breach defences and in his final report on 3 November he made no mention of 'deep battle', indeed the terminology was disappearing from official publications throughout that year.[40] Yet on the penultimate day of 1936, amidst a growing belief that the tank's role should be to support the traditional arms, the mechanised 'deep battle' was formally adopted as Red Army doctrine in the Provisional Field Service Regulations 1936 (Vremennyy Polevoy Ustav 1936 or PU 36).

There was also growing concern about the impact upon 'deep battle' of the new generation of anti-tank guns, a feeling reinforced by experience in Spain where Kombrig Semon Krivoshein led a Russian tank force from October 1936 to January 1937, being replaced by Kombrig Dimitri Pavlov, who became a friend of Kulik. Reports from Spain led Kulik to observe that the anti-tank gun could sweep the battlefield of tanks as the machine gun swept it of infantry.[41] But a far greater internal threat to the Red Army had been developing over the previous two years.

Revolutionary movements, like all political ideals, are prone to factionalism and their leaders tend to respond by imposing orthodoxy and purging those who refuse to accept it. The Communist Party under Stalin was no exception, and was especially paranoid when it discovered after the Revolution that the Czar's secret police had many double agents in their ranks. From 1930 to 1934 there was a low-level Purge against Stalin's opponents on the Left (former supporters of Leon Trotsky) and the Right (Grigorii Zinoviev and Nikolai Bukharin) and against opponents of agricultural collectivisation. Some officers, such as Shaposhnikov, were caught in these events and a few were sentenced to be executed, but reprieved and reinstated.

The pebble which began the avalanche was the assassination of popular Leningrad Party boss Sergei Kirov in the Party offices in December 1934. Stalin had been close to Kirov and initially believed the Leningrad Party organisation needed purging by Genrikh Yagoda's Narodnyy Komissariat Vnutrennikh Del (People's Commissariat for Internal Affairs or NKVD) but, under torture, prisoners began to implicate people in Moscow, including army officers.[41] Those arrested included Komkor Gaia Gai, head of the military history department at the VVS N.E. Zhukovskogo Academy on 3 July 1935. Gai was a distinguished cavalry commander in post-revolution operations, but a *bête noire* of the Cavalry Army clique.

Gai's escape from jail and subsequent recapture aroused Stalin's suspicions of Yagoda. The NKVD chief had received a penitent letter from the general and in a rare moment of kindness sent a doctor to examine him. Stalin was told that Gai had died but there can be little doubt that Yagoda's successor, Nikolai Ezhov, told him the truth with inevitable consequences. After being rearrested Gai was held for 18 months then shot on 11 November 1937 for 'involvement in the anti-Soviet terrorist organisation.'[43] By contrast, Kombrig Ivan Kosoputskii who was arrested around the same time, appears to have been reinstated by the end of 1936.[44]

The pace picked up in 1936 with 13 generals arrested by Yagoda's men including two military district deputy commanders: Komkor Vitaly Primakov (Leningrad), once closely associated with Trotsky, and Semon Turovsky (Kharkov) were both shot on 12 June 1937, while the former military attaché to Great Britain, Komkor Vitovt Putna, was shot on 1 July 1937. More ominously, Yagoda was clearly moving into the Red Army's educational system, arresting two lecturers at the General Staff Academy established only that year, Komdivs Ivan Pauka and Vasilii Stepanov. The latter was shot by the end of the year, but the former appears to have been reinstated, as was Kombrig Ivan Nikitin, commander of the 5th Cavalry Division. Nikitin would later play a major role in defending the Ukraine from the Germans but was captured and died in a prisoner-of-war camp. Many of the nine senior commissars arrested that year were also in the training establishment with half coming from the Military-Political Academy. Yagoda also arrested one of Yakir's divisional commanders and a VVS staff officer who was a close friend of Yakir.[45]

The early Purges turned Stalin from first among equals to undisputed leader but beyond his immediate circle he became more paranoid and increasingly isolated, a process possibly accelerated by his wife's suicide. He felt many had lost their absolute 'faith' in the Party and he was especially angry with corruption within the leadership.[46] He rapidly lost confidence in Yagoda, a corrupt, hedonistic collector of pornography, and replaced him on 26 September 1936 with Ezhov. Yagoda's fall led many to feel the Purges had ended – but they had barely begun.[47]

The diminutive (he was only 5 feet tall) and amoral Ezhov had boyish looks and charm but like many short people compensated for his lack of height with force of personality and hard work. Unfortunately, in his case his compensation was sheer viciousness, demonstrated in March 1938 when his predecessor was executed in the basement of the Dherzinski building in Lubiana Square, Moscow. Ezhov had him stripped naked, savagely beaten then dragged into the execution chamber. During the later so-called 'Ezhov regime', (Ezhovshchina) he adopted a 'hands-on' – or more accurately 'fists-on' – approach, savagely beating many people in his office and proudly displaying his blood-stained shirt, hence his nickname 'The Poisoned Dwarf'. But he also suffered from a bipolar condition which led him into huge mood swings including deep depression.[48]

Increasingly, Stalin was widening the circle of the Purges and was especially suspicious of Tukhachevskii who, in 1930, had been accused of plotting a coup before being cleared by Stalin himself, although he nicknamed the future Marshal 'Napoleonchik.' However, Stalin was not a man to leave paper trails and instead would guide his political police chiefs with hints or by forwarding the concerns of the Central Committee, concerns he had previously arranged to be discussed. It appears that when votes were taken on death sentences for senior Party officials or military leaders, Stalin would leave his vote blank.

Budenny and Voroshilov had been urging Stalin to destroy 'enemies' within the Red Army for more than a year, and certainly Voroshilov was dropping poison in Stalin's ear about Tukhachevskii with whom he had furious arguments, leading him to exclaim in May 1936: 'Fuck you'.[49] This fed Stalin's suspicions of the military leadership and he informed his inner circle: 'It is time to finish with our enemies because they are in the army, in the staff, even in the Kremlin.' Budenny guessed that Tukhachevskii, Yakir and the Deputy Commissar for Defence and head of the Red Army Political Administration, Armykom I Yan Gamarnik, were in the firing line, but there is unlikely to have been a formal order for such a purge although Stalin undoubtedly discussed it in private with Ezhov.

The 'Dwarf' began to build a case against Tukhachevskii for treason with the Germans. Voroshilov noted that at the last meeting of the two sides in September 1933 when the Germans were winding up their covert facilities in the Soviet Union, Tukhachevskii expressed the wish that Germany might have 2,000 bombers to extract herself 'from her difficult political situation'. Voroshilov underlined the passage three times.[50] To find 'evidence' Ezhov began arresting junior officers to implicate the senior ones, and in a Plenary Meeting of the Communist Party's

Central Committee between February and March 1937 Molotov, as Chairman of the Council of People's Commissars, demanded a more thorough exposure of 'wreckers' in the Red Army, for they 'had already been found in all segments of the Soviet economy'.[51]

Molotov had been the driving force in merging all the Soviet Union's farms into collectives in a process which had seen hundreds of thousands exiled and millions die of starvation. He would also prove an enthusiastic supporter of the Purges, signing many death warrants, witnessing torture and being one of the few people with whom Stalin discussed the Purges. It was during this Plenary meeting in February that Ordzhonikidze committed suicide following the arrest of his deputy, Grigori Pyatakov, losing Tukhachevskii – his last friend in Stalin's court.[52]

Yagoda was arrested on 9 March and his position as Commissar for Posts and Telegraphs was assigned to one of Tukhachevskii's closest associates, Komandarm II Rank Innokentii Khalepskii, head of motor mechanisation in the Red Army since 1929 and an ardent supporter of mechanised 'deep battle'.[53] Also, during a show trial on 2 March, Tukhachevskii's name came up as a potential plotter and it was clear to The Great and The Good that the Marshal was a dead man walking, as even he recognised.

Yet he attended the 1937 May Day Parade although snubbed by everyone else on Lenin's Tomb, including Egorov and his fellow Deputy Commissar for Defence, as well as Gamarnik. Perhaps Tukhachevskii wished to see the fruits of his labours for one last time as he did not remain on the podium for the civilian parade but walked off with his hands in his pockets. He had been scheduled to attend the Coronation of George VI in London but, on 4 May, the British Embassy was informed that he had been taken ill and a visa was no longer required.[54] The same day the former commander of the Moscow District, Komkor Boris Gorbachov, was arrested in the Urals District barely two months after the previous Urals District commander, Komkor Ilya Garkavy, had been arrested.

On 11 May the prelude to the military Purges sounded when the commissars regained authority over military matters and there were wholesale changes in the leadership; Egorov became First Deputy Commissar of Defence and was replaced by Shaposhnikov; Tukhachevskii's friend, Komandarm I Rank Yakir, was transferred from the Kiev to the Leningrad Military District; while Komandarm I Rank Uborevich was relieved of the Belorussian District. Worse, Tukhachevskii was demoted from Deputy Defence Commissar to become commander of the backwater Urals Military District. The following day Komandarm II Rank Avgust Kork, head of the Frunze Academy, was arrested but the day after that Stalin met Tukhachevskii for the last time and promised him he would soon be back in Moscow – but not how. On 15 May Gorbachov's deputy, and Tukhachevskii's friend, Komkor Boris Feldman, was arrested, the doomed Marshal telling a visiting general: 'What a grand provocation!'

Feldman was apparently the key used by the NKVD, being beaten into submission and then implicating the others for which his incarceration was eased

May Day 1937 and the political and military elite of the Soviet Union stand on top of Lenin's tomb to review the May Day parade in Moscow. At top, from left, Stalin, Lazar Kaganovich (Railways Minister), Ivan Akulov (the Soviet Union's Procurator), Andrei Andreev (Politburo member), Georgi Dimitrov (the Bulgarian General Secretary of Comintern), Nikolai Ezhov (NKVD chief), Anastas Mikoyan (at that time a Politburo member), Vyacheslav Molotov (Chairman of the People's Commissars), Vlas Chubar (Molotov's deputy) and Mikhail Kalinin (Chairman of the Central Executive Committee of the USSR). The military men in the lower row are Marshal Mikhail Tukhachevskii, Komandarm Ivan Belov (Belorussian Military District commander), Marshal Kliment Voroshilov, Marshal Aleksandr Egorov and Marshal Semon Budenny. Both politicians and military leaders ignored Tukhachevskii when he appeared with them. He was arrested 11 days later and executed a month later. Akulov, Belov, Chubar and Egorov all fell victim to Ezhov's executioners, while the wives of Molotov and Kalinin, as well as several others who were on the rostrum, were arrested and sent to the Gulags or executed. (Bettmann/Corbis)

and he even received biscuits.[55] Tukhachevskii was arrested on 22 May while en route to take up his new appointment as commander of the Urals District, which became a waiting room to the execution chamber, and on the same day similar fates befell Komkor Nikolai Efimov, head of the Artillery Administration (he was replaced by Kulik), then Yakir and Uborevich on 28 and 29 May respectively. Ezhov took personal control of Tukhachevskii's interrogation and soon his blood-stained confession was presented to Stalin by the triumphant 'Dwarf'.[56]

Stalin revealed the 'plot' to 160 commanders who were gathered in the Kremlin on 1 June, claiming that some beautiful German Mata Hari had recruited Tukhachevskii in Berlin. Voroshilov proclaimed: 'I never trusted Tukhachevskii, I never particularly trusted Uborevich… they were scoundrels.' He added: 'They were degenerates. Filthy in their private lives.' During the meeting several officers were arrested including one general, Komkor Mikhail Sangurskii, Deputy Commander of the Far Eastern Army.[57] Interestingly, although there was considerable post-war discussion of an agreement between SS *Obergruppenführer* Reinhard Heydrich, the amoral head of the Nazi Party's own intelligence organisation, the *Sicherheitsdienst*, and the NKVD to forge documents showing

'…Tukhachevskii's dealings with the Germans', none of this was presented either then or at Tukhachevskii's 'trial'.[58]

Stalin was determined to humiliate the army leadership and decided to establish a military tribunal to try the accused. Two Marshals, Blyukher and Budenny, were selected although the former was reluctant and discussed the matter twice with his old friend Gamarnik. Then, on 31 May, the NKVD visited Gamarnik, informed him he had been dismissed and his deputies arrested, and he shot himself after they left, fearing he would be on the wrong side of the tribunal.[59] Kulik would be given Gamarnik's Kremlin apartment while Shaposhnikov acquired his dacha.[60]

The tribunal met at 09.00 on 11 June and included Shaposhnikov (Red Army chief-of-staff from 11 May), Alksenis, Komandarm I Rank Ivan Belov, the new Belorussian District commander, Komandarm II Rank Pavel Dybenko, the new Leningrad District commander, Komandarm II Rank Nikolai Kashirin, head of combat training and Komdiv Elisei Goryachev, the Kiev District Deputy Commander. The generals were clearly bemused to be facing their former colleagues: Tukhachevskii, Yakir, Uborevich, Putna, Primakov, Kork, Feldman and Komkor Robert Eideman, head of the Obshchestvo druzhei oborony I aviatsionno-khimicheskogo stroitel'stva (Osoaviakhim) (the Society to Support Aviation and Chemical Defence), who had been arrested on 22 May; Belov later commented, 'Tomorrow I'll be in the same place.'[61]

Few of the generals, possibly including Budenny, believed that the defendants had plotted with the Germans and planned a coup (although all had been involved in establishing the secret German organisation in Russia); the club used to beat them was mechanisation, or rather its failure. Indeed Budenny accused the defendants of 'wrecking' the Red Army by creating mechanised corps. Tukhachevskii remarked of the accusations: 'I feel I am dreaming', but had written on his blood-stained confession: 'I confess my guilt, I have no complaints.' Ezhov later informed his master: 'Only Budenny took an active part, the rest were silent for the most part. Alksenis, Blyukher and perhaps Belov asked one or two questions.' The accused, who had all been beaten, may have been promised clemency in return for confession, and admitted their 'guilt' including trying to wreck the Red Army by driving through its mechanisation at the expense of the cavalry.

Just after lunch the tribunal found the accused guilty and hours later they were all shot. Stalin, having been given the list of proposed sentences, did not even glance at them before stating simply, 'Agreed'.[62] Most sent appeals for mercy, Feldman apparently believing almost to the last that this would be granted, but there was none. On Yakir's appeal for mercy Stalin scrawled, 'Swine and prostitute', to which the toady Voroshilov added gloatingly: 'A perfectly precise definition', while Lazar 'Iron Lazar' Kaganovich, who replaced Ordzhonikidze and was Yakir's best friend, wrote: 'The only punishment for the scoundrel, riffraff and whore is the death penalty.'[63]

For the condemned there would be no heroic death before a firing squad. Instead, Ezhov had replaced the timber-lined execution chamber in the basement of the Lubianka, the NKVD's Moscow headquarters, with a purpose-built one in the courtyard of the building next door. The victims were driven there in limousines from the Lubianka in the first hour of 12 June, the sentence was read out and they were then ordered to strip to their underwear. Two guards would take their arms and lead or drag them in and the executioner would shoot them once through the back of the head with a pistol, the blood draining through a specially designed depression. The body would then be dragged out and taken for immediate cremation or burial in a distant site, often with others, the cadavers stacked in trucks like firewood or in metal coffins.[64]

Budenny's active role in the 'trial' earned him the command of the Moscow District whose arrested leaders were not replaced for a month as a precaution against an army reaction, although there is no evidence that any officer even considered this. He assumed his new post on 6 June having told Stalin: 'I will try to justify your trust.'[65] Yet shortly afterwards the NKVD arrived in his office and allegedly tried to arrest him, only to be held at bay with a pistol as Budenny frantically telephoned Stalin who cancelled the arrest. However, Budenny's wife Olga would later end up in a cell and go mad in solitary confinement. When Budenny's staff were arrested he went to complain to Voroshilov who told him to take the complaint to Stalin. Budenny did so asking: 'If these are the enemy, who made the Revolution?' Stalin laughed: 'What are you saying Semon Mikhailovich? Are you crazy?' Stalin called Ezhov: 'Budenny here claims it's time to arrest us.' Budenny claimed that Ezhov did release a few officers.[66]

The tribunal's lack of enthusiasm condemned all save Budenny and Shaposhnikov. Kashirin was arrested on 19 August and shot on 14 June 1938; Alksenis, Belov and Dybenko were arrested between November 1937 and February 1938 and all were shot on 29 July, together with another three, Komandarm II Rank Ivan Dubovoi of the Kharkov District, Aleksandr Sedyakin, head of the air defence organisation (Protivo-Vozdushnaya Oborona - PVO), and Mikhail Velikanov, commander of the Trans-Baikal District, while Goryachev, promoted to Komkor, committed suicide on 12 December. The Ezhovshchina now went into top gear against the armed forces and during the year 11,034 officers (9.6% of the 114,300-strong officer corps) were dismissed and mostly arrested, including 276 generals (Kombrigs and above) as well as 152 army commissars of equivalent rank (see Table 1-1).

Those arrested faced constant interrogation (known as 'the conveyor belt') and beatings with clubs and truncheons, the victim sometimes lying face down, which may be why the NKVD called it 'French wrestling' (francuskaya borbu), as well as sleep deprivation. The process was sometimes witnessed by Politburo members such as Molotov and Anastas Mikoyan, a friend of Uborevich, and one of the few who sought to protect victims.[67] A few died 'under interrogation', such as the commander of the 63rd Mountain Rifle Division, Komdiv Fedor Buachidze, the day after he was arrested on 30 July.

Table 1-1: Army leadership (including VVS and PVO) arrested or dismissed in 1937

	Senior	Komkor	Komdiv	Kombrig	Korkom	Divkom	Brigkom	Total
Jan	-	-	-	1	1	-	1	**3**
Feb	-	-	-	1	-	1	4	**6**
Mar	-	1	-	4	-	-	-	**5**
Apr	-	1	3	3	1	1	1	**10**
May	6	15	17	14	2	2	2	**58**
Jun	2	5	20	17	2	4	9	**59**
Jul	1	4	11	20	1	9	12	**58**
Aug	2	3	1	16	4	2	7	**35**
Sep	1	-	3	11	-	1	5	**21**
Oct	2	1	7	8	-	6	7	**31**
Nov	7	6	6	7	3	5	4	**38**
Dec	2	1	11	17	3	5	14	**53**
u/k	-	-	7	25	1	7	11	**51**
Total	**23**	**37**	**86**	**144**	**18**	**43**	**77**	**428**

Senior: Marshals, Komandarm, Armikom. u/k: date unknown.

Source: Based upon Dmitry Churakov's *Red Army Soldiers Repressed* in Aleksandr Kiyan's the Workers' and Peasants' Red Army (RKKA) website (rkka.ru) and Parrish, *Sacrifice of the Generals*.

Stalin was well aware that torture was routinely used and when Ezhov asked in December 1937 for authority to conduct a 'severe interrogation' of one unfortunate, Stalin scrawled, '*Beat him, beat him*' across the request.[68] On another occasion he told Ezhov about the investigation of another individual: 'Isn't it time to squeeze this gentleman and force him to report on his dirty little business? Where is he, in a prison or a hotel?' He also counter-signed death warrants – 357 lists with some 40,000 names – and ignored pleas for clemency such as in the poignant case of Dybenko who denied being an American spy. 'I don't even speak American', Dybenko protested, concluding: 'Comrade Stalin, I beg you to look again at all these facts and to remove the badge of shame from me, as I do not deserve it.' Stalin simply noted: 'For Voroshilov.'[69]

Voroshilov and Lev Mekhlis, the head of the Red Army's Political Administration, worked closely with the NKVD in the Purges. The Defence Minister was an enthusiastic accomplice of the Purges who demanded that the NKVD arrest 300 officers, boasting on 29 November 1938 that 40,000 had been arrested and 100,000 promoted, and yet the NKVD had assembled a dossier on him as a contingency. Mekhlis was a fanatic who was nicknamed 'The Shark' or 'The Gloomy Demon' and was described as working in a 'neurotic, blood-curdling frenzy'.[70]

Because of these attitudes the Military Collegium of the Supreme Court of the USSR tried 3,816 members of the armed forces in 1936, 8,681 in 1937 and 8,360 in 1938.[71] Between 1937 and 1938, 34,000 officers were discharged, of whom

11,596 were reinstated by 1940, but 7.7 per cent of the officer corps dismissed in 1937 for political reasons was never reinstated, dropping to 3.7 per cent in 1938. When a man fell, so did his family: 18,000 wives and some 25,000 children were taken away with adults, including Tukhachevskii's wife and two brothers, who were shot. Others were jailed, children being either imprisoned or placed in orphanages. Gamarnik's widow was arrested and died in a labour camp while his daughter, who was 12 at the time of her father's death, was jailed when she reached 16, a pattern frequently repeated. Some families waited 20 years before being reunited while many never saw their loved ones again.[72]

Those who escaped the executioner often faced 'sitting', (the Russian slang verb for imprisonment was 'sidet' [to sit]), for long periods in labour camps where many died. Every arrested officer of Komkor rank and above was shot, while only two of 85 Komdivs and eight of 144 Kombrigs are known to have been reinstated, one of the former being future Marshal of the Soviet Union, Konstantin Rokossovsky, who returned to command the 5th Cavalry Corps minus his front teeth and finger nails. The slaughter of the commissar corps was even higher, reflecting the fact that the vast majority of the army leadership was also Party members, with only one Korkom, two Divkom and one Brigkom known to have been reinstated. The lower the rank, the greater the chance of escaping, but of 7,402 captains dismissed, 24 per cent (1,790) were arrested.[73] The victims of the Purges were bewildered by their fate – one minute in the audience and the next in the arena.

The Great Terror, as it has also been called, was like a tornado, with everyone aware of its presence but with no one certain where the twister would land to bring death and destruction. During 1937 alone, seven district commanders, some 16 district deputy commanders or chiefs-of-staff, the entire top command echelon of the nation's air defences, 22 commanders of corps and 42 commanders of divisions, were arrested together with many of the senior officers in the staff and educational organisations, while Red Army intelligence lost its leader, Armikom II Rank Yan Berzin, on 28 November together with at least seven department heads, their assistants and several experienced agents. Their deaths were approved often by friends who felt compelled to launch hysterical denunciations to save themselves, Egorov writing of one: 'All these traitors to be wiped off the face of the earth as the most hostile enemies and disgusting scum.'[74]

The impact upon the offensive spearhead forces was devastating: all the mechanised corps lost their commanding officers (Kombrig Aleksandr Grechanik of 5th Mechanised Corps was transferred to the Motor-Mechanisation Academy and later arrested), three lost their chiefs-of-staff and commissars,[75] while operations officers were also lost.[76] Within the corps of eight mechanised brigades, the commanders of six were arrested (two commanders of the 5th Corps' 14th Mechanised Brigade and three commanders of the four Rifle and Machine Gun Brigades), while nine commanders of the 15 independent mechanised brigades were arrested. Significantly, in the politically less contentious independent heavy tank brigades the commander of only one of the four units was arrested.

In addition, eight corps commanders in seven cavalry corps were relieved together with two chiefs-of-staff. The 4th Cavalry Corps had three successive commanders arrested or dismissed: Komdiv Ivan Kosogov on 26 May, Kombrig Arkady Borisov on 11 July and Komdiv Yakov Sheko on 10 August. Only Borisov was reinstated after nearly three years in jail and he was killed in action in 1942. In the 5th Cavalry Corps Konstantin Rokossovsky's successor, Kombrig Dmitri Vainerkh-Vainyark, was dismissed on 2 February 1938, arrested two days later and ultimately shot, as was the commander of the 7th Cavalry Corps, Komdiv Petr Grigorev (arrested on 24 July 1937), while his successor, Colonel Vinogradov Syseov, was dismissed in March 1938. Out of 34 cavalry divisions, 17 divisional commanders were dismissed or arrested, the 3rd, 9th and 20th Divisions losing two each. Where divisional commanders were unscathed, the chief-of-staff usually fell into the NKVD's clutches and 57 cavalry division staff officers were victims.[77]

Yet Komdiv Georgii Zhukov's 6th Cavalry Corps was apparently shielded by his patron Budenny, despite Zhukov coming into the NKVD's sights. Some time in the late summer of 1937 Zhukov was summoned to meet the new district commander, Komdiv Valentin Moulin, but instead found himself facing the new district commissar and future head of Military Intelligence, Armikom Filip Golikov, who asked him whether any of his friends or relatives had been arrested. Zhukov rolled off a list of Red Army colleagues, including Rokossovsky, and (according to his own account) praised them, leading to a warning from Golikov not to praise 'enemies of the people'.

Golikov then studied Zhukov's file which included reports from the corps commissar accusing him of a 'brutal' attitude to his subordinates and a failure to appreciate the role of the commissars. Zhukov replied that he had been 'brutal' to those who had neglected their duties and he fully appreciated the importance of commissars. At this point Moulin arrived, dismissed the reports and offered Zhukov command of 3rd Cavalry Corps, although this took some weeks to come through as Golikov, influenced by the corps commissar's reports, had opposed it.[78] Zhukov later said he was glad for the delay as he could observe the NKVD witch-hunt on senior commanders and had no desire to end up in one of their basement rooms. When he arrived he discovered that the corps commissar who had made the adverse report about him had himself been removed.[79]

As commander of the 6th Cavalry Corps, Zhukov was informed that he would be denounced at the meeting of the corps' Party members. Zhukov admitted he was 'a little nervous' when he arrived for the meeting, in which several division commanders and commissars denounced him for harshness and rudeness to them amounting to sabotage, as well as friendship with 'enemies of the people' such as Uborevich. He admitted being rude, apologised and then asked how he was to know they were 'enemies of the people'. The meeting decided not to expel him from the Party, but it was galling for Zhukov that the mob was led by his former commissar, Sergei Tikhomirov, with whom he had worked for four years and apparently had good relations. After the meeting he rounded on Tikhomirov and tongue-lashed him so that their future relationship would be icily professional. When the commissar tried to mend fences twenty years later, Zhukov ignored his letters.[80]

Seven months after assuming command of 6th Cavalry Corps, Zhukov was finally transferred to command of 3rd Cavalry Corps in February 1938. He replaced Komkor Goryachev who, like Belokoskov, had been accused of associating with 'enemies of the people', had been relieved on 25 January and subsequently shot himself on 12 February.[81] It was only after Zhukov was replaced by another future Marshal, Komkor Andrei Eremenko, who arrived after graduating from the Frunze Academy, that Zhukov's corps assistant commander, Kombrig Aleksandr Gorbatov, was arrested. In two of three divisions a regimental commander was dismissed while in the 29th Cavalry Division, Kombrig Vladislavovich Pavlovski was dismissed some time in 1938 together with two regimental commanders.

This indicates the fearsome randomness of the terror process with arrests driven by suspicion and denunciation. Suspicions expressed by Party leaders often began the process which was undoubtedly fuelled by an element of 'payback' for past disputes and slights, certainly by both Budenny and Voroshilov, although both may have been genuinely concerned about the direction of mechanised 'deep battle' which neither comprehended. A racist element emerged in concern over those with 'foreign motherlands' i.e. those who were not pure Slav, so that anyone of Polish (Rokossovsky), Baltic State (Alksenis) or Jewish (Feldman) origins were suspect. In the case of Tukhachevskii, his investigator, F.F. Ushakov, revealed that he first arrested Feldman who refused to confess any charge. Ushakov then read his file and discovered he was linked to other generals and locked himself in his office with Feldman in order to beat out a 'confession', implicating the others. Tukhachevskii faced similar treatment and was 'singing' within a day.[82]

Ushakov later told a rehabilitation commission: 'Taking hardly any sleep, I dragged out of them more and more facts and more and more names of plotters. Even on the day of the trial, I managed to get some additional testimony out of Tukhachevskii which implicated Apanasenko and others in the conspiracy.'[83] The last name is interesting, for while Volkogonov gives it in the index of his book as 'I.P. Apanesenko', although no general of that name was arrested, the only other candidate was Komdiv Iosef Apanasenko, deputy commander of the Belorussian District, a former 1st Cavalry Army man and a staunch Stalinist who would continue to hold senior positions and would act as Far Eastern plenipotentiary with great success between 1941 and 1943.

Denunciation pushed many men onto 'the conveyor belt' and became a way of life, often inspired by personal jealousy and ambition. The North Caucasus District commander, Semon Timoshenko, denounced Budenny who repaid the compliment, while Nikita Khrushchev, regarded as one of The Inseparables with his close friend of Ezhov and the plump, moon-faced bureaucrat Georgii

Malenkov, later claimed to have saved Timoshenko. The threat of denunciation made officers and even non-commissioned officers afraid to impose discipline, causing major problems within units. The fear of arrest was such that before a Party meeting, the 27th Cavalry Division Commander, Komdiv Vasilii Belokoskov, prepared a suitcase.[84]

Many turned to denunciation to save themselves, but even this did not always succeed; Kombrig Yan Zhigur, a senior lecturer in major unit tactics at the General Staff Academy, wrote to Stalin on 7 November 1937: 'I request you, Comrade Stalin, to check up on the activity of Marshal Egorov as head of the General Staff, as he bears responsibility for the errors committed in training for the operational-strategic deployment of our armed forces and their organisational structure.'[85] Six weeks later Zhigur was himself arrested and shot on 22 August 1938 but, like many semi-educated men, the paranoid Stalin had a near biblical belief in the written word and had received similar complaints from others.

He handed the matter to Ezhov who, predictably, soon reappeared with 'confessions' and it was also decided that Egorov's film star wife (with whom Stalin had flirted five years earlier) was a Polish spy which further damned him. Stalin discussed the matter with Molotov and Voroshilov and during a meeting of the Central Committee between 28 February and 2 March 1938, Egorov was removed from the committee and the matter referred to the NKVD, Stalin leaving his voting slip blank as usual.[86] Egorov, who had once refused the offer of a dacha which had belonged to one of his executed comrades, was officially transferred to the Trans-Caucasus District where he was arrested on 28 April and shot on 23 February 1939.

Another factor in the Purges of the army was Stalin's determination to control corruption within the leadership. Yakir, for example, used to rent out dachas, while some military leaders' wives, notably Olga Budenny and her best friend Galina Egorov, wore expensive, flashy and smart Western clothes. Stalin always regarded women as security risks and on 20 June 1937, he warned Budenny that his wife (who was flirting with Polish diplomats and who had had an affair with a singer) was 'conducting herself dishonourably', adding ominously: 'You must be brave.' She was soon arrested and jailed, a heartbroken Budenny sobbing at her fate, but he later remarried. Egorov's wife, too, was arrested and shot even before her husband.[87]

Once their names were damned with a spot, the officers would be isolated and arrested when they least expected it. Generals were often sent to the Volga or Urals Districts, while for commissars it appears to have been visits to the Military Collegium of the Supreme Court in Leningrad where six were arrested between October 1936 and June 1937, five of them heads of faculty of the N.G. Tolmachev Military-Political Academy. By the end of August all were dead.

Gorbatov's experiences were typical.[88] He was serving in the Kiev District's 7th Cavalry Corps when he was shocked to learn of Yakir's arrest and the new district commissar, former tailor and Cavalry Army clique member, Korkom Efim

Shchadenko, was openly suspicious of everyone.[89] When the corps commander, Grigorev, was urgently summoned to Kiev, Gorbatov, an old friend, went to visit him and his wife and found them understandably apprehensive. He tried to cheer them up but the worst happened.

A public meeting of Gorbatov's 2nd Cavalry Division heard that Grigorev had been arrested as 'an enemy of the people' and Gorbatov was given the first opportunity to denounce his old friend. Instead he went against the flow of the meeting to defend him and a month later he was relieved of his command and expelled from the Party. He was reinstated into both army and Party in March and became Zhukov's deputy. This may have followed one of Stalin's frequent informal meetings with officers, many of whom discussed superiors. During one a Komdiv Kulikov from the Kiev District told Stalin:

'Gorbatov is now worried.'
Stalin responded: 'Why should he worry if he is an honest man?'
Kulikov replied: 'I wouldn't say he is pure. He is clearly connected.'
Stalin asked: 'Is he scared?'[90]

Nothing happened at first, but in September Gorbatov learned that his requisition for winter clothing had been rescinded and the following day he was transferred to the reserve. Gorbatov went to Moscow to discover the reason and was awakened in the early morning of 22 October 1938 by a knock at the door of his hotel room and told there was a telegram which he thought was from his wife. When he opened the door there were three men in uniform who told him he was under arrest and when he demanded to see the warrant he was told: 'You can see for yourself who we are.'

He was driven to NKVD headquarters in Lubianka, sharing a cell with seven other officers and officials who quickly removed any illusions he might have had of an error. His captors left him to stew for four days before he was taken to an office and invited to write down his 'crimes'. He refused on several occasions, despite verbal abuse, and was then transferred to Lefortovo prison and placed in solitary confinement.

His treatment at Lubianka was repeated, then the beatings started with prolonged gaps for contemplation and by the third round he just wanted to die. But he would not sign a confession and in May 1939 he appeared before a military tribunal which, after a five-minute trial, sentenced him to 15 years – a terrible shock for Gorbatov who had expected freedom. He was sent to Far Eastern labour camps where he almost died but was eventually reinstated on the eve of the German invasion in June 1941, being warmly welcomed by Timoshenko and given time to recover as well as receiving back pay for the two-and-a-half years he was imprisoned.[91]

Few stories had such happy endings and many of the officers whom Gorbatov encountered were either shot or died in the camps. His story also indicated the long memories of the secret police, illustrated by the fates of Komdiv Sergei

Lukirsky and Kombrigs Aleksandr Baltiiskii, Nikolai Saposhnikov (no relation
to the chief-of-staff) and Aleksandr Verkhovski. All had come under suspicion in
1930–1931 and all but Baltiiskii arrested, Verkhovski actually being sentenced to
death. The jailed men were released in return for volunteering for operations in the
Far East and apart from Lukirksy, who became a scientific editor on the board of
the Military Encyclopedia, all became lecturers at the Frunze Academy.
Shaposhnikov was dismissed from the army on 19 June 1937 while the remainder
were arrested by March 1938 and shot during the year.

The unpredictability of the Ezhovshchina was demonstrated by the fate of
Komandarm II Rank Ioakim Vatsetis, head of the Frunze Academy's military
history faculty. The Latvian officer had joined the Academy in 1922 and played a
major role in shaping the Red Army in the late 1920s.[92] He was giving a two-part
lecture on 29 November 1937, but during the break the class commissar
announced: 'Comrades! The lecture will not continue. Lecturer Vatsetis has been
arrested as an enemy of the people.' He was shot on 28 July 1938. The strain was
such that throughout Soviet society many, such as Timoshenko, turned to vodka
and this applied even to the investigators![93]

The Terror continued throughout 1938 but with fewer victims – 6,742
including at least 243 generals (see Table 1-2) or their political equivalent, although
their survival rates improved with 45 generals known to have been ultimately
reinstated together with a dozen commissars. But by the end of the year, the Red
Army's accumulated losses are known to have amounted to three out of five
Marshals of the Soviet Union, 13 Komandarm I/II Rank, 53 Komkor, 134 Komdiv,
244 Kombrig, 16 Armikom (one suicide), 29 Korkom, 76 Divkom and 107
Brigkom. Another 48 generals (three Komkor, five Komdiv and 40 Kombrig) and
44 commissars (10 Divkom and 34 Brigkom) were probably victims in this period
but no detailed information is available. Of 90 Komkor only six survived and 36
of 180 Komdiv.[94]

The sudden changes in leadership also disrupted training and, despite the Purges,
there were frequent complaints about this during major conferences between
November 1937 and June 1938. It also affected discipline for in the paranoia of the
era, an unhappy soldier could denounce his superior while even friendships between
officers were placed under strain; no one knew who might next be denounced and
face scrutiny from the NKVD because of an association with 'an enemy of the
people'. Above all, there was an atmosphere of fear, with few willing to accept sole
responsibility for actions in case they were then held to account.

The impact on one key district was revealed by Komandarm I Rank Ivan
Fedko who succeeded Yakir in the Kiev District. He noted that from June to
20 November 1937 his district had purged 1,894 men, of whom 861 had been
arrested, with the district headquarters losing 75 per cent of its staff together with
90 per cent of the corps commanders, 84 per cent of the division commanders and
37 per cent of the regimental commanders. He also noted that the District was
now led by young men since 3,000 new officers, political workers and

administrators were brought in as replacements.[95] Fedko himself would be arrested on 7 July 1938 and shot on 26 February 1939. Zhukov noted that nearly all the corps commanders in the Belorussian District had been arrested and their replacements lacked the knowledge and experience to meet their responsibilities.[96] As Habeck observed: 'Many commanders would spend the purge years trying to stay out of official notice, hide from responsibility for any decisions, and generally do nothing controversial or radical.'[97]

Some officers escaped because their superiors quietly posted them to remote locations while others had near miraculous escapes including future Marshals of the Soviet Union, Konev and Rodion Malinovsky, and Marshal of Tank Troops Pavel Rybalko. Konev praised Uborevich rather than denouncing him, but was himself denounced to Mekhlis who took no further action. Malinovsky served in Spain with some 900 other officers and, unlike many of them, he was not arrested when he returned to Russia. Rybalko was even more fortunate for he served as an aide in the Motor-Mechanised Directorate and became an advocate of mechanised 'deep battle', but from 1937 to 1939 he was Military Attaché in Poland and displayed a profound antipathy to his hosts before later assuming the same position in China.[98] It is worth noting that six generals who were military attachés with major powers were arrested and shot.

Table 1-2: Army (including VVS and PVO) leadership arrests 1938

	Senior	Komkor	Komdiv	Kombrig	Korkom	Divkom	Brigkom	Total
Jan	1	2	8	11	3	3	2	**30**
Feb	2	6	11	19		8	6	**52**
Mar			7	22		1	1	**31**
Apr	1	1	2	4		3	2	**13**
May		1	3	9	2		1	**16**
Jun			2	7	2	6	2	**19**
Jul	1	1	4	9	2	2	2	**21**
Aug			3	4		2	1	**10**
Sep		1	1	1	2	3	1	**9**
Oct	1	1	1	1				**4**
Nov		2				1		**3**
Dec		1				1		**2**
u/k			6	13		3	12	**34**
Total	**6**	**16**	**48**	**100**	**11**	**33**	**30**	**244**

Senior: Marshals, Komandarm, Armikom. u/k: date unknown.
Source: Based upon Dmitry Churakov's *Red Army Soldiers repressed* in Aleksandr Kiyan's the Workers' and Peasants' Red Army (RKKA) website (rkka.ru) and Parrish, *Sacrifice of the Generals*.

Russian historians have tried to underplay the impact of the Eshovshchina, claiming it has been exaggerated by some historians and that the 1938 figures amounted to either only 3.7 per cent of the officer corps (which had expanded 56 per cent to 179,000) or a total 17,776 amounting to 6 per cent of the officer corps. In addition, 16,525 officers and commissars were dismissed from the army and these provided most of the 11,596 men who had been reinstated by May 1940. However, the remaining two thirds (22,705) were either lying in unmarked graves or in labour camps from which few emerged. The Purges carried away the more experienced officers, all of whom had been serving in 1937 and on this basis, then, the Red Army lost 15.5 per cent of its officers. The purged generals included more than 150 senior staff officers or specialised experts as well as more than 100 senior members of the educational and training infrastructure.

These were the cream of the Red Army and the expansion of the officer corps in 1938 occurred using only junior officers. The need to replace the lost leadership meant rapid promotions and many came from the first course of the newly-opened General Staff Academy. Only a quarter of the 137 men in this course, which would include four future front commanders, actually completed it because 68 of the most promising students during August to November 1937 were drafted to plug the gaps caused by the Eshovshchina. Colonel Aleksandr Vasilevsky, who would become Chief of the General Staff during the war, would become responsible for operational training of senior officers; Colonel Nikolai Vatutin became an assistant chief-of-staff, then a district chief-of-staff; Colonel Matvei Zakharov became Leningrad District chief-of-staff and then joined the General Staff responsible for organisation and mobilisation; while Kombrig Alexei Antonov (who would succeed Vasilievsky at the end of the war) became Budenny's chief-of-staff in the Moscow District and the following year an instructor at the Frunze Academy.[99]

Timoshenko became a Red Army senior troubleshooter during the late 1930s. The son of a peasant and a one-time barrel maker, this shaven-headed conservative with a powerful voice and flinty grey eyes would at least prove competent. When Yakir was arrested Timoshenko was deputy commander of the Kiev District, but in June 1937 he assumed command of the North Caucasus District, then the Trans-Caucasus District in September, before returning to Kiev as the commander in February 1938. In March 1938 he signed a document boasting about purging the district.[100]

The impact of these changes upon the Soviet air and air defence forces was especially severe and of 13,000 officers in 1937, 36 per cent, 4,724, was purged.[101] The VVS and PVO commanders, Alksenis and Aleksandr Sedyakin, were both purged together with their chiefs-of-staff (Komkor Vasilii Lavov's replacement in the VVS, Komdiv Semon Testov, was arrested six months later), the air commanders in Kiev, Moscow (two of them), Volga, Central Asia, Siberia and the Far East together with the PVO commanders in Baku, Belorussia, Kiev, Leningrad and the Far East (Baku and the Far East losing successive commanders), while the head of training, Komkor Aleksandr Todovsky, was also a victim. Alksenis had created a 900-strong strategic bomber force based upon the Armiya Osobogo Naznachiya – AON ('Special Purpose Army') of which there were three subdivided into two or three brigades of two regiments. The NKVD hammered this organisation with the two AON commanders, Komkor Vasilii Khripin (AON 1) and Felix Ingunns (AON 2), as well as eight brigade commanders, being arrested.[102] Alksenis's replacement, Komkor Aleksandr Loktionov, was appointed only on 28 November 1937 and was a former rifle unit commander who had four years' experience as assistant VVS commander in the Belorussian and Kharkov Districts and arrived from commanding the Central Asia District.

The impact of the Purges upon Red Army doctrine was predictable but it went beyond the decapitation of the mechanised arm. Everyone had been assessing the experience of fighting in Spain which broke out in July 1936 and concluded in March 1939. This appeared to confirm the views of the sceptics that armoured forces would have great difficulty forcing their way through fortifications augmented by anti-tank guns and that ultimately their role would be support of the infantry, a view which grew even as the mechanised warfare exponents were being rounded up. Kulik's friend Pavlov, who had commanded the tank brigade in Spain and in October 1938 took over the Motor-Mechanised Directorate, certainly supported this view. By November 1937 armoured breakthroughs ceased to be part of Red Army doctrine and were replaced with system attacks by infantry supported by tanks and artillery. Even Egorov, who had once supported the revolutionary concept, had completely swung in the other direction.[103] Curiously, none of those who so strongly opposed mechanised 'deep battle' commented on the fact that J.F.C. Fuller, one of the most influential theorists of mechanised warfare, was a prominent member of the British Fascist Party.

There was an absence of common armoured doctrine throughout 1938 and Pavlov tried to resolve the situation while avoiding 'the harmful theory' of independent tank action described in PU 36.[104] In an attempt to begin resolving the situation and between March and August 1938, all mechanised units were designated tank units, underlining their infantry-support role (see Table 1-3) with the mechanised brigades becoming light tank brigades. The 5th, 7th, 11th and 45th Mechanised Corps became respectively the 15th, 10th, 20th and 25th Tank Corps each with 12,364 men and 660 tanks, and in action they were to be augmented by the four heavy tank brigades, eight new light tank brigades, six tank regiments (in cavalry divisions), and 23 light tank/tankette battalions to support the rifle divisions.

The new units reflected Pavlov's belief that tank units themselves did not require infantry or artillery and he was enthusiastically supported by Voroshilov, although Shaposhnikov was more cautious. Pavlov also argued that the tanks should be tied to the apron strings of the infantry and artillery and here he had Shaposhnikov's support. The concept of mechanised units breaking through enemy defences and exploiting victory had now been consigned to the scrapheap by the Red Army's new leaders and the change to contemporary conservative views on the employment of armour was complete by the end of 1938, with the tank part of the combined arms group gnawing its way through the enemy defences. The only independent

Table 1-3: Redesignation of mechanised units 1938

Mechanised Brigade	Light Tank Brigade	Notes
1	11	
2	42	
3	36	
4	32	
5	2	5 MC/15 TC
6	8	11 MC/20 TC
8	29	
9	18	7 MC/10 TC
10	27	5 MC/15 TC
11	35	
12	24	
13	37	
14	34	
15	38	
16	22	
17	23	
18	25	
19	1	7 MC/ 10 TC
21	6	
22	26	
23	3	
31	13	7 MC/ 10 TC
32	15	11 MC/20 TC
133	4	45 MC/ 25 TC
134	5	45 MC/ 25 TC

Source: Eugene Drig's website 'Mechanizirovannieye Korpusa RKKA' http://mechcorps.rkka.ru.
MC = Mechanised Corps TC = Tank Corps

action permitted was for tank groups to strike into the enemy rear, either when the terrain was favourable or poorly defended.[105]

For the conservatives like Voroshilov, Budenny and Kulik, the removal of the 'wreckers' and the restoration of military orthodoxy ended the imperative for purging the Red Army and there are reports that some of the leaders, including Kulik, discreetly began to suggest this. The need to end the merry-go-round of arrests and appointments, in the west if not in the east, was underlined by the deteriorating international situation in Europe. During the summer Germany loudly began to demand control of parts of Czechoslovakia where large numbers of ethnic Germans lived – notably the Sudetenland.[106]

Moscow and Paris both had military assistance treaties with Prague and as the crisis developed, the Belorussian and Kiev Districts became Special (osobyi)

Districts on 26 July 1938, allowing them to be brought close to a war-footing and to form armeskie gruppy (army groups). Shaposhnikov drew up a partial mobilisation plan which was discussed twice by the Politburo and on the evening of 21 September the Kiev District was ordered to mobilise the Volochinsk-Prokurov (later Khmelnitskii), Kamenets-Podolskii and Vinnitsa Army Groups. Reservists were called up to provide each rifle division with 8,000 men, the 2nd Cavalry Corps was moved closer to the Polish frontier and the district air force was mobilised and reinforced by three fighter regiments, three fast bomber regiments and a heavy bomber regiment.

District commander Timoshenko was able to report within 24 hours that this had been achieved and a command post established at Prokurov. Shortly before midnight on 23/24 September the Belorussian District was also ordered to mobilise its Polotsk, Lepel and Minsk Army Groups and this too was achieved within 24 hours. During the day engineer battalions were mobilised. The total force mobilised appears to have been 30 rifle and 10 cavalry divisions, three tank corps, seven tank and motor-rifle brigades and a dozen aviation brigades together with much of the western PVO. To maintain strength units were allowed to retain draftees whose time was due to expire.[107]

Plans were then made to expand the Red Army and on 29 September it was decided that the Belorussian, Kiev, Leningrad and Kalinin Districts would form another 17 rifle divisions, three tank corps headquarters, 22 tank and three motor-rifle brigades while internal districts would create a Second Echelon of 30 rifle and six cavalry divisions, two tank corps and 15 tank brigades (see Table 1-4 for rifle unit background). However, geography proved the insurmountable hurdle to support for the beleaguered Czechs for the Red Army would have to cross some 175 kilometres of Polish territory or 275 kilometres of Rumanian territory.

Table 1-4: Red Army Rifle Units

Divisions	1 January 1937	1 January 1938	1 January 1939
Active	53	52	84
Territorial	35	34	-
Mountain	9	10	14

Source: Glantz, *Soviet Mobilisation in Peace and War*, Table 2.

The lack of a direct rail link across Rumania meant this route was impractical, but the excellent communications across Poland were blocked by Warsaw's refusal to give permission for the Red Army to cross its territory. A party of VVS officers flew to Prague in late September to organise the reception of 700 aircraft in Slovakia. Voroshilov stated on 28 September that he could despatch 548 aircraft by the end of the month including 246 SBs, but Rumania denied air space access so that throughout the crisis Moscow could only rattle a sabre. The Western

Powers' ultimate abandonment of the Czechs angered Stalin who felt that by handing over Czechoslovakia to the Germans, London and Paris were setting a dangerous precedent.

In 1934 Stalin had told the 17th Party Congress that there was a possibility of an agreement with Nazi Germany and he turned increasingly to this option over the coming months while Shaposhnikov revised strategic deployment plans in the light of the new strategic situation and the Third Five Year Plan. The new plan, approved in principle by the Main Military Council on 13 November, assumed that Germany had allied itself with the Poles and had entered Lithuania and Latvia with the allies assembling 130-140 infantry, four motorised and 12 cavalry divisions with 8,500 guns, 6,380 tanks and 4,136 aircraft. These would face 90 Belorussian District Divisions as well as the Minsk and Polotsk Fortified Regions which would be reinforced from the interior within 20 days of mobilisation. They would smash the enemy. A second version anticipated an attack upon the Kiev District which would go on the defensive in the Proskurov Salient (Novogrod-Volynsk and Letichev Fortified Regions) to shield assembly of a counter-offensive force.[108]

Stalin now decided that the Purges needed to become more selective and that Ezhov should be replaced, especially as the stress of frequent 'interrogations' of people he knew had left him physically and emotionally exhausted. The defection of a senior NKVD officer to the Japanese (see next chapter) was a key element and Stalin authorised the execution of some of Ezhov's protégés. The hysterical NKVD chief, fearing his own torture chambers, was only too aware how easy it was to become a victim and he began executing any who might incriminate him. He had few friends, Andrei Zhdanov the Leningrad Party boss being a special enemy, and as early as 22 August, Stalin appointed fellow Georgian, Lavrenti Beria, as Ezhov's deputy to 'assist him' with his workload.[109]

Beria was a curious mixture of contrasts: a devoted husband and a sexual predator, a wit and a torturer, obsequious to his superiors and arrogant to his subordinates. Yet he was well educated, a point he highlighted by wearing pince-nez, but with clear glass and no lenses, and he would run the Soviet equivalent of the Manhattan Project, demanding precision and punctuality.[110]

Immediately, he began to undermine Ezhov who sought solace in drink and sexual excess – with both sexes – and when Ezhov appeared in his office, he was clearly the worse for wear. The Poison Dwarf's position deteriorated: on 23 October, in Stalin's presence, he had to listen to a complaint by writer Mikhail Sholokhov; then on 14 November, Stalin ordered a Purge of the NKVD, giving Beria the opportunity to remove hundreds of Ezhov's cronies and clients, while the following day the Politburo ordered an end to cases being investigated by military tribunals.

Just over a week later Ezhov tendered his resignation as head of the NKVD and Beria moved smoothly into his seat, but Ezhov remained nominal Water Transport

Commissar. This marked the formal end of the Ezhovshchina, but Ezhov himself remained under a cloud and in March Stalin asked him publicly whether or not he was organising a conspiracy.

A desperate Ezhov later denounced fellow Inseparable Malenkov (head of the Communist Party Cadre Directorate) in an attempt to save his own skin, but on 10 April he was ordered to report to Malenkov for an investigation into the charges. He arrived to discover Malenkov had removed his portrait; then Beria appeared and arrested him. He was executed in the early hours of 3 February and it is reported that Beria, in a moment of poetic revenge for Yagoda, had him stripped naked and beaten savagely before the weeping 'Dwarf' was dragged into the execution chamber.[110/111]

ENDNOTES

1. For Tukhachevskii see Shimon Naveh's entry in Shukman pp.255-273 and Simpkin pp.3-13.
2. See Tyushkevich pp.160-163.
3. Short p.9. For the Soviet fortifications see Niel Short *The Stalin and Molotov Lines*, and also Kaufmann & Jurga, *Fortress Europe* pp.349-370.
4. The most comprehensive study of French doctrine is in Doughty, *The Seeds of Disaster*. Only when Germany was weak in the 1920s did French plans envisage a rapid advance. Doughty p.33.
5. Op. cit. pp.101-102.
6. Op. cit. pp.3-12, 91-95.
7. Op. cit. pp.92-93.
8. Op. cit. pp.33-34, 52, 74, 96, 105, 108-109.
9. Habeck pp.20, 21-24.
10. Doughty pp.4, 86, 105, 109, 159-160.
11. I am very grateful to Professor Richard Ogorkewiecz for his comments on doctrine. All errors of interpretation are my own.
12. Doughty pp.152, 167-173, 176.
13. Habeck pp.72-76, 190-194, 208-213, 218-226, 233-241, 250-254, 270-273.
14. Doughty p.160.
15. Habeck pp.52-70, 99-103, 139-143, 188-189, 209, 220-226, 237-241.
16. Tsushkevich pp.186-191.
17. Habeck p.196.
18. Short, *The Stalin and Molotov Lines* pp.6-10; Tarleton article.
19. See Gerard's article.
20. Habeck p.167 f/n 38.
21. Op. cit. pp.152-157, 180.
22. Sebag Montefiore pp.86, 88, 205.
23. Op. cit. p.46.
24. For Voroshilov see Sebag Montefiore pp.46-47, 126; Service p.291; Shukman pp.313-324.
25. For Budenny see Sebag Montefiore pp.11, 58 f/n, 294, 304; Shukman pp.57-65.
26. Sebag Montefiore p.295.
27. The only biography of Kulik is in Parrish, *Sacrifice of the Generals* (hereafter *Sacrifice*) pp.203-207.
28. For Shaposhnikov see Shukman pp.217-237; Sebag Montefiore pp.356-357.
29. Sebag Montefiore states that he also once denounced a cook for over-salting meat.
30. Habeck pp.126-127, 132.
31. Sebag Montefiore pp.51-52.
32. Habeck pp.167-170. It was Stalin's flirtation with Egorov's wife during a party at Voroshilov's flat that led to the suicide of Stalin's wife, Nadya, in October 1932.

33. Habeck pp.196-197.
34. Op. cit. pp.133-135, 156, 176-179, 197-199, 201-205. See Simpkin and also PU 36 Para 7.
35. Tyushkevich p.195. Future Marshal of the Soviet Union, Ivan Konev started his career in the Red Army as a commissar who, at Kork's suggestion, turned from 'the dark side' and spent two years at the Frunze Academy and became an officer. See Shukman pp.92-93.
36. Habeck pp.213-218.
37. Op. cit. pp.226-231. Turovsky would be arrested in September 1936 and shot in July 1937.
38. Kombrig, Komdiv etc were army designations; commissars were Brigkom, Divkom, Korkom and Armikom.
39. Erickson, *Soviet High Command* (hereafter *Command*) pp.391-393.
40. Habeck pp.241-244.
41. Zaloga p.26.
42. See Sebag Montefiore pp.99-100, 126-127, 131-141.
43. Rayfield pp.265-266.
44. Details of purged general-rank officers from the Aleksandr Kiyan's website and Dmitry Churakov's 'Red Army Soldiers repressed' section.
45. Watt's article.
46. Sebag Montefiore pp.1-18, 45-50, 55, 80-81, 97, 113-115, 124 f/n, 186-187. Molotov would later comment about Purge victims: 'The main thing was that, at the decisive moment, they could not be depended on', Sebag Montefiore p.216.
47. Op. cit. pp.178-179.
48. For Ezhov see Sebag Montefiore pp.150-153, 218, 241. Ezhov inherited from Yagoda two gruesome trophies – the bullets which executed Zinoviev and Kamenev, and which he kept in his desk.
49. Sebag Montefiore p.197.
50. Habeck pp.184-185.
51. Stalin also dropped hints. See Getty & Naumov p.170.
52. For the Great Terror and the armed forces see Erickson, *Command* pp.471-509; Getty & Naumov pp.169-174; Volkogonov pp.316-329. For pressure on Ordzhonikidze from 1936 see Sebag Montefiore pp.180-181, 185, 188-189.
53. He was arrested on 13 November 1937 and shot on 29 July 1938.
54. Erickson, *Command*, pp.458-459.
55. Rayfield p.314.
56. See Main's article on Tukhachevskii's arrest and confession.
57. Sebag Montefiore pp.199-200.
58. Erickson, *Command* pp.379, 433-436. Sebag Montefiore p.201.
59. For his daughter's account see Volkogonov pp.321-322.
60. Sebag Montefiore pp.230-231, p.615 f/n 7.
61. Op. cit. p.200.
62. Volkogonov pp.321-324.
63. Rayfield, pp.315. Sebag Montefiore p.200 says Kaganovich wrote: 'For this traitor, bastard and shit, there is only one punishment - execution.'
64. Sebag Montefiore pp.200, 219.
65. Shukman p.61.
66. Sebag Montefiore p.201. There is no doubt the attempt to arrest Budenny was an elaborate charade to keep him 'loyal', for if Stalin had wanted him arrested the Marshal would not have been able to telephone his office.
67. Getty & Naumov p.3; Sebag Montefiore pp.198, 218.
68. Sebag Montefiore p.218.
69. Volkogonov p.325.
70. Parrish: Lesser Terror pp.26-27; Sebag Montefiore pp.201-201, 209, 213.
71. Parrish: Lesser Terror p.32.

72. Sebag Montefiore pp.196, 207, 610 f/n 13; Volkogonov p.322. It is worth noting that Stalin caused the arrest of the wives of President Mikhail Kalinin and even his own private secretary, Aleksandr Proskrebyshev, whose wife was executed!

73. Rayfield p.315.

74. Sebag Montefiore p.199.

75. Divkom Petr Feldman was transferred to the Black Sea Fleet and later arrested.

76. The Leningrad-based 7th Mechanised Corps appears to have suffered the least. Information on mechanised and tank units from Eugene Drig's website, Mechanizirovannieye Korpusa RKKA at http//:mechcorps.rkka.ru.

77. For Russian cavalry see website Kavaleriiskie Korpusa RKKA at http//:rkka.ru/Cavalry.

78. Moulin would be arrested in February 1938 and shot four months later.

79. Zhukov pp.147-149. These events must have taken place in the late summer and probably in September because Rokossovsky was not arrested until August 1937 and Golikov was not appointed to the Belorussian District until September. Because of this encounter and the failures of Soviet Military Intelligence in 1941, Zhukov possessed an understandable antipathy to Golikov. See Shukman pp.77-88.

80. Op. cit. pp.154-157.

81. During exercises he worked with Mikhail Potapov, a tank brigade commander who served at Khalkin Gol. Zhukov pp.152-153.

82. Volkogonov p.323.

83. Op. cit.

84. Sebag Montefiore pp.203, 219, 225-226, 277; Zhukov pp.149-151. After he was dismissed in the 1950s Zhukov kept a suitcase in his hall for the moment he was arrested.

85. Volkogonov p.326.

86. Op. cit. pp.326-327. Stalin had also turned on the foreign Communists in his country and Ezhov executed 110,000 of the 144,000 Polish Communists in the Soviet Union. Sebag Montefiore p.204.

87. Sebag Montefiore pp.205, 213-214.

88. See Gorbatov, Gody I Voiny, Chapter 5.

89. He would later become head of the Red Army's Cadre Directorate which made him head of personnel.

90. Sebag Montefiore p.201.

91. Op. cit. See also Pleshakov pp.31-34.

92. See biography in Erickson, Command p.846.

93. Sebag Montefiore p.241.

94. Rayfield p.315.

95. Habeck pp.261-262.

96. Zhukov p.154.

97. Habeck p.277.

98. Shukman pp.93-94, 118, 210-211.

99. Op. cit. pp.277, 289, 331.

100. Op. cit. pp.240-241.

101. See Reina Pennington's article on Russian air power from 1922 to 1941 in Russian Aviation and Air Power in the Twentieth Century p.47.

102. Yet AON 3 was created at Rostov in May 1938.

103. Habeck pp.257-258, 261, 264-265, 266-267.

104. Op. cit. p.277.

105. Op. cit. pp.279-280, 285.

106. For the Soviet Union and the Munich Crisis see Ragsdale.

107. For Red Army plans see Ragsdale pp.111-122; Rukkas; see also Tarleton's article.

108. For the new plan see Tarleton's article. By the end of 1938 the Red Army had 98 rifle divisions and 5 rifle brigades.

109. Sebag Montefiore pp.210, 244.
110. Op. cit. pp.244–246.
111. For the fall of Ezhov see Sebag Montefiore pp.246–248, 262–263, 288; Service pp.368–369; Parrish's article *The Downfall of the 'Iron Commissar'*.

CHAPTER TWO

FACING THE RISING SUN

'A Japanese shell got you, didn't it?'
COLONEL ISAMU CHO TO KOMANDARM II GRIGORII SHTERN, 11 AUGUST 1939

IF the Red Army leadership was concerned about the impact of the Purges in the West as conflict loomed in 1938, it did nothing to inhibit the Ezhovshchina which tore through the forces in the East even as they were engaging the enemy.

Since 7 August 1929, the Soviet Union's eastern provinces of Ussuri, Amur and Trans-Baikal had been under a semi-autonomous military command, Otdelynaya Krasnoznamennaya Dalyanevosto Chnaya Armiya (OKDVA) or Separate Far Eastern Red Banner Army, under future Marshal Blyukher with his headquarters at Khabarovsk. Peasant's son and factory worker Blyukher spent most of the Civil War in the Far East, became military advisor to China's Kuomintang forces from 1924 to 1927, had a brief sojurn in Kiev, and then returned to the Far East.

Initially he faced the Imperial Japanese Army on the narrow Korean border and on Sakhalin Island, which the two countries shared. The rest of the long, winding border, most of it Manchuria, faced Chinese warlord armies which Blyukher had bested in a fierce clash in 1929, and so the OKDVA's six rifle divisions (four of them territorial units) and two cavalry brigades organised into the 18th and 19th Rifle Corps were more than adequate for purpose. But in 1931 the strategic situation changed radically.

The Japanese Kwangtung Army (Kantohgun) held the former Russian naval base of Port Arthur in Manchuria but, with army political support in Tokyo, it occupied the whole of Manchuria to secure economic resources for the Homeland islands. The Kwangtung Army grew from two divisions and 30 aircraft with 64,900 troops in 1931, to four divisions, 180 aircraft and 164,100 troops by 1935, and by 1937 it had six infantry divisions, a cavalry brigade and a tank brigade comprising some 205,000 troops, 170 tanks and 340 aircraft. The puppet kingdom of Manchukuo, established by Japan, had its own army – little more than a border guard and gendarmerie, originally with 110,000 men, but reduced in August 1934 to 72,000 when it was restructured into five divisional-sized district armies organised into mixed and cavalry brigades.

From Manchuria the Japanese threatened the whole of the Soviet Far East and its resources, causing a steady expansion of Blyukher's forces which were augmented by an estimated 40,000 NKVD frontier troops.[1] Between 1932 and 1934, three divisions were converted from territorial to active status and one was transferred from the Siberian District. In 1933 a Special Military Construction Corps with 15,000 men was established to operate in the Far East and began work the following year on 11 fortified regions with numerous bunkers in order to shield vulnerable terrain and make more efficient use of the rifle formations.[2] On 7 May 1935 the forces east of the Urals were reorganised and the Trans-Baikal Group of Forces became a Military District under Komkor I.K. Griazev while OKDVA became the Far Eastern Military District but reverted to its original designation on 2 June 1935.[3]

Between 1936 and 1937 six rifle divisions were created or converted from territorial formations while three divisions of Kolkhoz (collective farm) workers and part-time soldiers were also converted into active formations bringing the total to 15. The Kolkhoz Cavalry Division also became an active formation and joined another unit raised from a cavalry brigade. Blyukher's two cavalry brigades had earlier been expanded into divisions, all of which had a mechanised regiment, and by July 1937 OKDVA had 83,750 troops, 890 tanks and 946 guns.[4]

Mechanised forces were not neglected: a brigade was created in 1932, two more were transferred from Europe to ODKVA in 1933 and 1934 and in October 1934 placed under 11th Mechanised Corps headquarters, although this corps lacked a rifle-machine gun brigade until May 1938. The corps operated within the Trans-Baikal District, created in May 1935. In August 1937 a mechanised brigade was transferred to the 57th Osovogo Strelkobyi Korpus (Special Rifle Corps) in Mongolia, only to be replaced less than a month later so that by July 1938 the 11th Mechanised Corps alone had some 500 tanks.[5] VVS strength was also steadily increased to 766 aircraft and augmented by the 5th Heavy Bomber Brigade, a formidable force far from the Soviet Union's industrial and agricultural heartland and facing an ever-growing threat.

Reportedly Blyukher tolerated little political interference in OKDVA's operational life and it is claimed that he clashed with Stalin over collectivisation and was also at loggerheads with Voroshilov.[6] His remoteness from Moscow inevitably provided him with a great deal of autonomy, one aspect being the near feudal corps with three rifle divisions and a cavalry brigade whose troops lived in collective farms. However this formation became the 20th Rifle Corps in 1936 and the units were converted to a conventional organisation, albeit with a large cadre. To reduce OKDVA's dependency upon the industrial heartlands of European Russia, the economy of the Far East was strengthened with new factories and greater economic resources were provided while thousands of people were forcibly relocated to increase Blyukher's manpower. This overall strengthening of OKDVA may be the reason that Blyukher was made a Marshal of the Soviet Union.

Although Blyukher was forced to sit on the tribunal which 'judged' Tukhachevskii, this was no endorsement and he is reported to have commented: 'It'll be my turn next.' Indeed arrests began within OKDVA during 1937; the most senior officer was Komandarm II Rank Mikhail Velikanov, the Trans-Baikal District commander arrested on 20 December following the detention of his chief-of-staff, Komdiv Yakov Rupinov; the commander of the 11th Mechanised Corps, Komdiv Yakov Davidovskii, and district motor-mechanised chief, Kombrig Vasilii Mernov. The NKVD also struck the district's political organisation and arrested the District Commissar, Korkom Viktor Shestakov, Political Department head Divkom Gregorii Krolevetskii, and five Brigkom. By 5 October 1938, all had been hustled into the execution chamber while Shestakov's deputy Divkom, G.F. Nevraev, had committed suicide.

The Maritime Group of Forces in Ussuri also suffered as of 15 May: Divkom F. Levenzon, the group's head of construction; the district chief-of-staff, Komdiv Aleskeii Balakirev; the Group's VVS commander, Komdiv I.S. Florovskii; as well as the OKDVA air defence chief, Kombrig Pavel Rybkin, arrested on 3 July. The VVS suffered badly too: OKDVA air commander, Komkor Albert Lapin, was one of the first arrested on 17 May followed shortly afterwards by the commander of the 5th Heavy Bomber Brigade, Komdiv Vladislav Kokhanskii. Kombrig G.K. Kisch, who succeeded Lapin, was arrested on 9 October, a month before Ingaunns, the 2 AON commander who had been Lapin's predecessor.

Blyukher also began to feel the hot breath of the NKVD on his neck; his deputy commander and old friend, Komkor Mikhail Sangurskii, was arrested on 1 June; his Inspector of Cavalry, Kombrig Ivan Nikulin, on 13 June and his artillery chief, Kombrig Vladimir Leonovich, during September. The political organisation did not escape, with the head of the OKDVA Political Department, Divkom Isidor Vayneros and his deputy, Brigkom Yan Draiman, in jail during the first week of October, while the secretary of the OKDVA Party Committee, Brigkom Ivan Sadovnikov, followed on 23 November. Only Sadovnikov escaped execution and he was jailed for 10 years in August 1939. Blyukher also saw three rifle corps commanders (including Komkor Mikhail Kalmyakov, the former Kolkhoz Corps commander) and two corps' commissars arrested, together with 11 division and fortified region commanders as well as four of their political officers. Only one fortified region commander would be reinstated, the rest either killed or condemned to a living death. The NKVD also arrested and executed Komkor Edvard Lepin and Komdiv Ivan Rink, the Military Attachés to China and Japan respectively, while several senior agents familiar with China and Japan also perished.

There were more victims in 1938 including the new commander of the Maritime Group, Komandarm II Rank Mikhail Levandowski, Blyukher's new chief-of-staff and his deputy, Komdivs Vladislav Vasentsovich and Ehrman Mago, although the last two were subsequently reinstated. There was no such happy ending for Kombrig Petr Tiit, the PVO commander, who was arrested on 12 March, while the chief of the OKDVA Political Department, Divkom Ivan Kropachev, who was arrested in April, was jailed. Tiit's deputy, Komdiv Gregorii Vorozheikin, who was arrested on 14 May would be reinstated and become VVS chief-of-staff in 1941-1942, but the head of military construction, Komkor Andrei Sazontov, was shot, as was Maritime Group commissar, Korkom Semon Skvortsov. Yet of nine Kombrigs arrested from May, including the OKDVA head of motor-mechanised forces, Mikhail Solomatin, all but one were reinstated. The Trans-Baikal District again suffered badly, losing the commissar Korkom Avgust Bitte; the district deputy commander, Komkor Nikolai Lisovski; the assistant chief-of-staff, Kombrig Vladimir Turkhan; together with the commanders of two rifle divisions, although one was later reinstated.

By the beginning of May Blyukher's command was a quivering ruin, and on 1 July Mekhlis arrived at Kharbarovsk, accompanied by Ezhov's deputy, Mikhail Frinovsky, to drive into the wreck. Mekhlis was a former shoemaker who could cobble together treason from the most innocuous circumstances and wildest coincidences, a true witch-hunter, but his purpose was not, as has been previously thought, to purge OKDVA – indeed, relatively few of the survivors were arrested under his authority – but, rather, to complete the Purge and bring Blyukher to account.[7] Blyukher tried to protect his subordinates and had Voroshilov's support – indeed Mekhlis would complain to Stalin that the Defence Commissar had ordered a trial cancelled.[8]

Mekhlis's arrival saw another three Komdivs arrested but they would be reinstated 14 months later. His presence seems to have been to act as the Party's watchdog on Blyukher, whose wings were quickly clipped. On 28 June, the OKDVA became the Far Eastern Red Banner Front (Dalyinevostochnyai Krasnoznamennaya Front) and was subdivided into the 1st (Ussuri) and 2nd (Amur) Red Banner Armies (Otdelynaya Krasnoznamennaya Armiya), the former under Komdiv Kuzma Podlas (who was transferred to the Kiev District as deputy commander on 1 September) and the latter under Komdiv Yakov Sorokin. Meanwhile, the Far Eastern and Trans-Baikal Districts were placed under Voroshilov's direct control.[9] Konev would take over 2nd Army on 4 September 1938 despite receiving an extremely adverse report from the NKVD. He was saved by the Director of the Army Political Department, Armikom I Rank Petr Smirnov, in a letter of 25 December 1937 and although Smirnov, by then the Navy Commissar, was arrested on 30 June 1938, Mekhlis did not pursue the matter because he had bigger fish to fry.[10]

By now the Far Eastern forces were expanded to 105,800 men but, in addition to Mekhlis, another set of eyes was watching Blyukher – his new chief-of-staff, Komandarm II Grigorii Shtern.[11] Shtern was very much Voroshilov's man; he had conducted many assignments for him in the early 1930s including acting as chief military advisor to the Spanish Republican government from January 1937 to April 1938 and, before coming to the Far East, initially as an army chief-of-staff.

His presence may be explained as preparation by Voroshilov for Blyukher's replacement with his own experienced man whose presence might help offset the inexperience of the Red Army's leadership in the region.

Mekhlis's arrival helped to trigger Blyukher's downfall, and possibly Ezhov's. Since the end of July 1937, the NKVD's Far Eastern head was Commissar of State Security, III Rank Genrikh Lyushkov, who had investigated Kirov's assassin and the first senior victims of the Great Terror, Zinoviev and Lev Kamenev. He was then sent east on the personal orders of both Stalin and Ezhov, with 200 staff. However both his predecessors had been purged and when he received a summons to Moscow he feared the same fate, a fear Ezhov apparently encouraged.

Early on the morning of 13 June 1938 Lyushkov defected, fearing he would be purged just like his predecessors. He crossed the border into Manchuria, taking documents which showed that the OKDVA was far stronger than the Kwangtung Army had imagined. The Kwangtung Army now believed it would be outnumbered 5:1 in the event of a conflict and hastily revised its plans, including increasing its air strength by a third, with Lyushkov serving it as an advisor until the Russians invaded Manchuria in August 1945, when his new masters shot him. His defection terrified Ezhov, to the extent that he asked Frinovsky to accompany him when he reported to Stalin: 'On my own, I don't have the strength.'

Less than a month after Lyushkov's defection the Japanese intercepted a coded message to Blyukher's headquarters in Khabarovsk from a command post on the extreme south of the Manchurian border where it overlapped the Korean border. This disputed frontier ran along the valley of the river Tumen, which runs to the Sea of Japan. Some 10 kilometres from the coast the river bends westwards for about 6 kilometres to avoid high ground beside Lake Khasan, which was adjacent to the Russian frontier, then regains its southward course after some three kilometres. There had been great tension and numerous incidents along the border throughout 1938.[13]

The area enclosed by the looping river as well as the marshy, narrow strip to the north, belonged to Manchukuo, the Japanese puppet regime in Manchuria, and was based upon two heights on the north-western side of the enclosed territory which dominated the valley to the east. On the far side of the valley lay the Soviet frontier, but it was disputed whether this was based upon the Bezymyannya Heights (also described as Shachaofeng or the Nameless Heights) in the north and the Zaozernaya Heights (also called Changkufeng) a kilometre to the south and some 150 metres high, the latter extending into Manchurian territory, while Japanese-occupied Korea lay on the western bank of the Tumen. The Zaozernaya gave good views over the southern part of the border down to the sea and also permitted observation of the port of Najin as well as the Korean-Manchuria railway, while the heights were extremely defensible because of their steep slopes – up to 85 degrees on the western (Japanese) side and up to 45 degrees on the eastern (Russian) side. An agreement between the Russian and Chinese Empires of 1886 agreed that the border ran west of Lake Khasan and that the

Russians could occupy 'some' territory to the west, although there was no definition of 'some' and from early July the 59th (Posetskogo) Border Sector command was pressing to establish a permanent and fortified border post by occupying Zaozernaya.[14]

The Japanese intercepted a message on 6 July and the same day a Russian advance party moved onto the western slopes of the Zaozernaya.[15] Within two days they were reinforced and began to fortify the heights with trenches and barbed wire entanglements as well as obstacles, while a company of 119th Rifles/40th Rifle Division waited in support near Lake Khasan. Blyukher was well aware of the level of tension with Japan and was especially concerned about conflict on his extreme left. On 22 April he had placed the local 39th Rifle Corps (Kombrig V.N. Sergeev) area on alert.[16]

For the Japanese this was a critical time: to end the increasingly costly war in China, Tokyo had committed 700,000 men (equating to 16 out of 24 divisions,) including forces scheduled for use against the Soviet Union, but the Kwangtung Army was reluctant to commit troops for fear of undermining Manchurian security. The Japanese sought to resolve the crisis through diplomacy but, on 15 July, the Russians rejected a demand for the withdrawal of their troops and Tokyo discussed its response.

The same day a Japanese border guard was shot dead and there was a dispute over whose territory it had been that he had fallen. Imperial General Headquarters (Daihonei), or IGHQ, decided to use the lower quality Korea Corps (Chosengun) under General Kuniaki Koiso, a man with a fiery temper who had kept very tight control of the border and focused upon exploiting natural resources but who was being retired. His replacement, from 18 July, was General Kotaro Nakamura, an extremely experienced officer and a former War Minister. Nakamura began to concentrate the Nineteenth Division (Lieutenant General Kamezo Suetaka) on the banks of the Tumen, but just a week later Tokyo vetoed escalation of the incident and was otherwise content simply to monitor the situation.

The Korea Corps was essentially a gendarmerie and frontier guard force lacking an operations officer, heavy artillery and a supply organisation, although it did have three air regiments (60-100 aircraft) and its other major formation, Twentieth Division, had been sent to China. With the army committing large forces in a drive towards Wuhan in central China and the navy preparing for a major amphibious operation to take Canton, IGHQ wanted no distractions. However, the Kwangtung Army would egg on Korea Corps and threaten to intervene if its colleagues did not act. The remaining Nineteenth Division was under Suetaka, an infantryman galled at the fact that his division had not been deployed to China and determined to make it so battle-worthy it would be sent to the front. He was a combination of martinet and stern father and he whipped his division into shape.

On 19 July, the Posetskogo border guards, claiming that the Japanese were openly talking of regaining the disputed heights, requested Blyukher to bring up the support company, receiving his agreement the following day with the proviso that the border guards would not fall victim to 'provocations'. Tokyo still sought a diplomatic solution but with the refusal of Moscow to abandon the disputed heights, the options were reduced and the military option became favoured. On 24 July Blyukher ordered Podlas to reinforce Sergeev's 39th Corps, with Colonel Vladimir Bazarov's 40th Rifle Division ordered to send reinforced battalions from both the 118th and 119th Rifles as well as a cavalry squadron. In addition, the regional air defence system was placed on alert. The division was something of a slender reed having seen its previous commander, commissar, chief-of-staff, artillery and medical chiefs arrested.

Yet Blyukher was no sabre rattler and ordered a commission to investigate the situation, pointing out that the border was ill-defined and that the border guards might have exceeded their authority and constructed positions in Manchurian territory. The border guard leaders were furious, stating that any errors were extremely small, barely a metre, yet Blyukher, without informing Mekhlis, still sent a telegram to Voroshilov on 26 July demanding their arrest and urged a negotiated solution. However, the border guard commander, Colonel Grebennyuk, sent another to Ezhov and Beria stating that he would hold the ground. Consequently, a second commission of inquiry sent by Blyukher on 27 July was sent packing.[17]

The tense stand-off ended on the morning of 29 July when the Russians began digging in on the Bezymyannya Heights. Suetaka decided to attack, although pretending to heed his superiors' calls for restraint. A small force drove the Russians off Bezymyannya, killing five of the 11 defenders, including the commander, and wounding the remainder. An ad hoc platoon of border guards quickly counter-attacked and by the evening had driven the Japanese down the hill, the two Japanese battalions losing a quarter of their officers, half their non-commissioned officers and 10 per cent of their men – a total of 178 casualties.[18]

Blyukher alerted his forces and brought Bazarov's division to a war footing. That evening the Japanese began shelling the two heights. Two battalions of the 118th Rifles were moved nearer the heights while Suetaka decided to commit a larger force. On the night of 31 July/1 August, a regimental battle group of two infantry battalions with artillery and engineers under the commander of the Seventy-Fifth Infantry, Colonel Kotoku Sato, crossed the river. By the morning it had driven the Russians from Bezymyannya Heights then pushed 4 kilometres into Soviet territory, the 94 defenders suffering 83 casualties (13 killed). Anticipating a counter-attack, Suetaka wished to reinforce Sato but Nakamura considered that the operation had ended the incident and on 4 August Tokyo approached Moscow about talks to resolve the situation. Despite this, Suetaka brought up his Seventy-Third and Seventy-Sixth Infantry as well as the rest of his Twenty-Fifth Mountain Artillery.[19]

The immediate Red Army response was weak because the 118th Rifles had little ammunition and most men carried only wooden training grenades. One company lost 24 dead in an abortive counter-attack on 1 August as the Far Eastern Front leadership (including Mekhlis) was despatched to inspect the situation. From just after noon the VVS began appearing over the battlefield, bombing and strafing not only the Japanese positions north of the Tumen but also targets south of the river, including passenger trains, and disrupting enemy logistics by forcing the civilians bringing up supplies to flee on their ox carts. In response, the Japanese strengthened their air defences in northern Korea and placed their fighters on alert but IGHQ was determined to restrict the conflict and apart from a two-fighter mission covering reinforcements being railed northwards, Japanese aircraft were grounded throughout this conflict. Meanwhile Shtern became the first senior Soviet officer on the scene and immediately cancelled the hastily organised counter-attacks.

Bazarov was given a day to prepare a more coherent response and attacked on 2 August, the 119th and 120th Rifles striking from the north and the 118th Rifles with the division's 32nd Tank Battalion from the south. The operation was hastily prepared and the execution was fragmented, with one regiment having to wade Lake Khasan. It also lacked artillery support, despite the presence of two artillery battalions, for fear shells would explode across the border. Only toeholds were established on the eastern slopes at great cost. The other attack was made across a narrow strip of marshy land within the Soviet border and suffered heavy losses, anti-tank guns picking off the tanks. The meagre gains were abandoned the following day, at which point Mekhlis appeared and began his usual solution of drumhead courts-martial, four luckless gunners being the first victims; he had already been criticising Blyukher for his failure to adopt a 'gung ho' attitude. Meanwhile, with exquisite timing, the 2nd Mechanised Brigade's leadership was purged three days before it was deployed to the front.[20]

As a result of the debacle and because of Blyukher's perceived lack of enthusiasm for the fight, Voroshilov instructed Shtern to take over 39th Rifle Corps on 3 August. In addition to his corps' 32nd, 39th and 40th Rifle Divisions, Shtern could call upon the 2nd Mechanised Brigade which had 94 BT-5/7s and 5 KhT-26 flame-thrower tanks together with 1st Army resources, giving him 32,860 troops. The 32nd Division (Colonel N.E. Berazin), the mechanised brigade (under its new commander, Colonel Aleksei Panfilov, who would later distinguish himself in the defence of Moscow), three artillery regiments (27 batteries) and 250 aircraft (180 bombers, including TB heavy bombers) were assigned to regaining the heights and on 5 August Voroshilov authorised them to cross the borders to strike the enemy flanks.[21]

Shtern's plan was for the 32nd Rifle Division to attack from the north, regaining the Bezymyannya, while 40th Rifle Division regained the Zaozernaya by striking from the south. Each division had a tank battalion (40th Division received one of Panfilov's battalions) to support the infantry while the rest of Panfilov's armour, with 63 tanks, was kept in reserve. The bad weather which plagued the battlefield – mist, fog, rain and wind – meant that the Russians were unable to exploit their total air superiority and flew only 700 sorties in five days against an enemy devoid of air cover, while in the days before the assault the rain turned the roads into mires.

Just before midnight on 2/3 August the Japanese Army General Staff, responding to IGHQ orders, instructed Nakamura to contain the situation by merely securing the border with reinforcements. Suetaka deployed two battalions of the Seventy-Sixth Infantry (Colonel Sanji Okido) to the western sector. But with Nakamura's approval he planned a counter-offensive and for this his Thirty-Seventh Brigade assumed command of the Tumen bridgehead on the evening of 3 August, although arguments within the Korea Corps staff meant that Nakamura refused to release Suetaka's Seventy-Fourth Infantry to him. The brigade commander was Major General Nobuki Morimoto, who was transferred from a Kwangtung Army brigade and he reached the battlefield on 2 August. The Russian aerial and artillery bombardment had continued for days and it was obvious that the Japanese lacked the means for counter-battery work. Nakamura thus requested heavy artillery from the Kwangtung Army, but the Army waited until the evening of 6 August before despatching two 150 mm guns and two 100 mm rail guns which arrived the following day

The Russian counter-offensive began on 6 August in fog, which delayed the attack until 14.00 hrs, the bombardment commencing and firing wildly at 13.15 hrs. The VVS was unable to reach the battlefield until 16.00 hrs when it dropped 122 tonnes of bombs on 'enemy terrain' with indifferent accuracy although it again disrupted Japanese supplies, causing shortages of food and ammunition. The marshy ground severely restricted movement of the tanks and of 43 tanks supporting the 95th Rifles/32nd Division, only 10 reached the enemy defences while anti-tank guns picked off the vehicles with impunity leaving the Russian riflemen to charge unsupported into the Japanese defences, suffering heavy losses in the process. The 118th Rifles redeemed itself by reaching the Zaozernaya around midnight of 6/7 August and securing them by 9 August in the teeth of intense enemy fire and numerous counter-attacks, which frequently degenerated into bombing contests with grenades.[22]

Each side brought up reinforcements, Nakamura assembling the Seventy-Fourth Infantry on the southern bank of the Tumen (it crossed the river on the night of 9/10 August) while moving up Thirty-Eighth Brigade headquarters, the new commander of which, Major General Nobuaki Ono, did not reach the front until 8 August. Anti-aircraft and heavy artillery were also deployed to support the bridgehead bringing the Japanese commitment to 12 battalions and 37 guns while, as a precaution, on 10 August, IGHQ ordered the Kwangtung Army's Hundred-and-Fourth Division, assembling at Dairen, to join the Canton landing force as a pretext for moving it to the Manchukuo/Korea/Soviet border. Japan reopened negotiations on 10 August and with IGHQ support Tokyo decided to close down the battle and a ceasefire went into effect at noon on 11 August. Half-an-hour beforehand the Russians suddenly began a massive bombardment as if in revenge for the Japanese attack. When Shtern, his head bandaged, rode up to negotiate the truce, the Japanese chief negotiator, the commander of the Seventy-Fourth Infantry, Colonel Isamu Cho, asked: 'A Japanese shell got you, didn't it?'[23]

The Japanese had shown a tenacity in defence which would become a feature of their operations in later years, while the Russian infantry had displayed heroism. Poor tactical training at company level and below was all too obvious and the failures to co-ordinate the various arms as well as the shambles of a logistics system had cost the Russians dearly. Of 32,860 Russian troops, 4,071 (12.4 per cent) were casualties with 717 killed, 2,752 wounded and 75 missing, some of whom were captured. Of the dead, 191 (more than a quarter) were junior infantry officers or non-commissioned officers while another 527 went down either from malaria in the marshy conditions or from the effects of drinking poor water. The Russians also lost nine tanks destroyed and 76 damaged, of which 39 were repaired.[24] The Japanese committed some 7,300 troops and suffered 1,439 casualties (19.7 per cent), including 526 dead and it was clear that the Red Army remained a formidable opponent. Suetaka's division suffered 863 casualties including 313 dead, the Seventy-Fifth Infantry losing nearly half its men. Nevertheless tensions remained and during the spring of 1939 there would be several minor clashes in this area of the border.

From 16 August Tokyo began defusing the crisis: eight days later the General Staff ordered Nakamura to return the reinforcements he had received and not to aggravate the situation. On 9 November 1938 Suetaka became commander of Twelfth Corps, essentially a training command in China, and 10 months later he was appointed to command Kwangtung Army's Third Corps. The Kwangtung Army leadership was furious that Tokyo had appeared to let the Russians off the hook and it assumed operational responsibility for the Changkufeng sector a few months later. In March 1939 its survey team discovered alleged Soviet violations of the border and wanted to attack, but Tokyo rejected the request and the new deputy chief-of-staff, General Tetsuzo Nakajima, on the instructions of his superior, Prince Kanin, sent a personal letter to Kwangtung Army commander, General Kenkichi Ueda, ordering him to scrap plans to regain the heights. This fed what has been described as a border defence neurosis in the Kwangtung Army and added to the deteriorating relations between the Army and the General Staff.[25]

It was Blyukher's swansong and, while there have been many tales of rows between him and Mekhlis, the last straw for Stalin was the failure to make better use of air power.[26] Apparently in a telephone conversation on 6 August, Stalin asked Blyukher why he had ignored Voroshilov's order to bomb enemy forces on Soviet territory including the heights. Blyukher replied that the take-off had been delayed by bad weather, but that he had ordered Kombrig Pavel Rychagov, his air commander (like Shtern, a Spanish Civil War veteran) to take off 'regardless of anything'. He added: 'The planes are now taking off, but I am afraid it is inevitable that we'll be hitting our own units as well as Korean settlements.'

Stalin replied: 'Tell me honestly, Comrade Blyukher, do you really want to fight the Japanese? I don't understand your concern about hitting Korean settlements and also your fear that the air force won't be able to do its duty because of the fog... Why worry about the Koreans when our people are shooting at the

Japanese? What's a bit of fog to Soviet aviation when it really wants to defend the honour of the Soviet motherland?'[27]

Mekhlis, whose sole tactical idea consisted of suicidal frontal assaults, had been criticising Blyukher's indecisiveness and in Stalin's mind the exchange confirmed it. After Lake Khasan, Blyukher told his wife: 'The sharks have arrived. They want to eat me.' The 'Shark' (Mekhlis) arrested four of Blyukher's staff and had them shot out of hand.[28]

Blyukher was summoned to Moscow on 18 August, possibly flown back by Stalin's personal pilot, for a 'review of the operations' with Stalin, Voroshilov, Molotov and Shaposhnikov. Inevitably, most of the blame was placed upon Blyukher for failing to assign formation officers who could lead, for failing to purge 'enemies of the people' from his ranks and, perhaps the most damning, for questioning the legality of the frontier force actions.[29] Following the review Voroshilov drew up a formal criticism of Blyukher on 4 September.

Blyukher and his family, including a six-month-old baby, were arrested on 22 October. Beria beat the Marshal savagely every night in Lefortovo prison: indeed, when Blyukher's wife, Galina, saw his swollen face with one eye hanging out of its socket she said he looked as if 'a tank had driven over him'. Apparently Beria got carried away, possibly hoping to have a confession in time for the anniversary of the October Revolution, for the Marshal's injuries proved fatal and he died on 9 November without signing anything. Stalin ordered an immediate cremation upon learning the news.[30]

As Voroshilov may have hoped, Shtern replaced Blyukher but the Purges continued. The commander of the 2nd Army, Sorokin, was arrested and either died or was shot by the end of the year, being replaced by Konev. Between 1936 and 1939, 432 officers were 'repressed' and more than 70 per cent were shot, the remainder rotting in prison camps; but the brother of Stalin's wife, Nadya, the Motor-Mechanised Directorate commissar, Pavel Alliuyev, returned to Moscow on 1 November 1938 with evidence that most of the victims were innocent. He was horrified to discover that most of his department

The military conservative Kliment Voroshilov, along with Gregorii Kulik and Lev Mekhlis, would be the driving force of the Purges of the Red Army and Navy. One issue involving the purged radicals was over armour, with Voroshilov once asking, 'Why the hell do we need tanks?'

had been arrested and that afternoon he died suddenly, possibly having been poisoned.[31]

For the Kwangtung Army there was unfinished business and the Russians were to face a far sterner test along the 700-kilometre Mongolian frontier which the Japanese had been probing steadily since they had occupied Manchuria.[32] A Mongolian salient stuck into Manchuria and China with the town of Tamsag-Bulak (also written as Tamtsag-Bulak and Tamsak-Bulak) at its base. One hundred kilometres beyond the town, the Khalkin Gol (Khalkin River) secured the ill-defined border in a region which had been home to nomads for centuries. The Khalkin (or Halha) valley ran north-east to south-west, but turned due south shortly before it was joined by its eastern subsidiary, the Khailastyn Gol (also called the Holsten), at the top of whose valley was the village of Nomonhan.

Here the Khalkin was a largely swampy valley, some 3 kilometres broad in a deep, 100-metre depression and some 700 metres above sea level, the steep-banked river flowing at up to a metre per second. The river itself was up to 130 metres wide and up to two metres deep in places but there were several fords. The Khailastyn ran through a narrow (1-2 kilometre) ravine and was 5-10 metres across and a metre deep but, as with the Khalkin, there were fords during the summer. The swampy valleys were breeding grounds for mosquitoes which behaved with voracious neutrality and the saline water often contaminated the region's few wells.

A broad, low, ridge runs for 750-760 metres in a gentle arc north-west and west of Nomonhan and the Bain-Tsagan Heights, at some 740 metres, dominating the upper valley on the western bank while south of the Khailastyn is a lower ridge, mostly about 740 metres, but with a line of hills over running for 750 metres roughly east to west. Where the river turned south-east was Khamar Daba (or Hamar-Daban or Hamar-Duaban), a 752-metre height with good views along the upper valley and the ground on the western side was slightly higher than the eastern. On the eastern bank of the Khalkin a belt of sand dunes, some 50 metres high, began 4 kilometres north of the confluence and extended some 10 kilometres long and up to 3 kilometres wide, while 3-4 kilometres south of the Khailastyn, and within the bend of the Khalkin, lay three smaller parallel lines of dunes running north-south.

The desert steppe terrain had short, coarse grass covered by up to 10 centimetres of fine sand in places but was usually firm enough to take armoured vehicles. Drifting sand, due to the strong winds of the region, occasionally covered roads. The weather was extremely changeable during the summer, with cloudless skies and temperatures up to 40°C (104°F) in the day to 18°C (60°F) at night, but the great heat led to thunder storms and heavy rain while mornings frequently brought fog which dispersed quickly.

The Mongolians, backed by the Russians, claimed that the border with China/Manchukuo was some 20 kilometres east of, and parallel with, the Khalkin but the Japanese claimed that it ran along the Khalkin Gol. The Japanese surveyed the area from 1934 yet remained undecided on the issue and there was a series of raids fuelled by a traditional antipathy between the Manchurians and the Mongolians, of whom the Kwangtung Army had a low opinion.[33]

Outer Mongolia (The Mongolian People's Republic) underpinned the defence of the Soviet Union's Far Eastern territories with their ill-defined borders and consequently was the first Soviet satellite. From November 1934 Moscow and Ulan Bator had an understanding that the Red Army would support Mongolia if Japan invaded. Following major clashes on the Mongolian/China/Manchukuo border during 1935 the two nations concluded a mutual assistance pact in March 1936 leading the Russians, in September 1937, to establish the 57th Corps under the Trans-Baikal District but in Mongolian territory, as well as providing 'advisors' to the 50,000 strong Mongolian Army. The first commander was Konev who had initially the 36th Motorised Rifle Division, one (later three) motor-mechanised (motobronevaya) brigades and an aviation brigade with a regiment each of fighters and light bombers.[34]

Mongolia also suffered severely from Purges conducted with Russian NKVD 'assistance' in a power struggle between the head of state, Khorloogiin Choibalsan, a Stalinist disciple, and Premier Anandyn Amar. The Purges claimed up to 35,000 victims, some 4 per cent of the population, of whom half were Buddhist lamas (many accused of spying for the Japanese). Choibalsan eventually had Amar arrested in March 1939, tried in Moscow and executed in July 1941.[35]

The Purges swept through both armies in Mongolia; in July 1937 Divkom Gevork Safrazbekyan, the chief political instructor of the Mongolian People's Army (MPA) and cavalry brigade commissar, Brigkom Anatolii Lebedev, were both executed, while the advisor to the MPA commander, Komkor Leonid Vainer, was arrested the following month. During 1938 the NKVD arrested the 57th Corps' commissar, Korkom Arkhip Prokfiev, who was shot 16 months later, and Konev's chief-of-staff, Komdiv Vasilii Malyshkin, who was later reinstated as the 36th Rifle Division commander and the chief-of-staff. The first chief military advisor, Kombrig Ivan Nikitin, was recalled in October 1937 due to his lukewarm support for the Purges and transferred to the reserves.[36]

By the spring of 1939 the forces in Manchuria consisted of 57th Corps, under Komdiv Nikolai Feklenko since October, with a motorised rifle division, a tank, a cavalry and three motor-mechanised brigades – in all a total of 30,000 troops with 265 tanks and 280 armoured cars as well as the 100th Aviation Brigade with 84 Russian and 23 Mongolian combat aircraft.[37] Feklenko's command was of mixed quality, Colonel Kalinychev's 100th Aviation Brigade having very low morale due to poor accommodation and assessments later describing the regimental and squadron leadership as 'disgraceful'. Discipline received the lowest rating while only 55 per cent of the fighters was serviceable. The strike regiment was converting from R-5Sh light assault biplanes to the new SB twin-engined bomber. Feklenko also controlled the MPA's eight brigade-size (1,600 men and

4 field guns) cavalry divisions with a total of 50,000 troops, of which the 6th Division was responsible for the Tamsag-Bulak Salient.[38]

Friction on the Manchurian-Mongolian frontier increased during 1939 with more than a dozen border clashes in the first five months, especially in the Khalkin valley and from 11 May Mongolian border guards began moving in strength east of the river despite determined Manchurian resistance.[39] This led to the involvement of the Japanese Army's nearest unit, the Hailar-based Twenty-Third Infantry Division under General Michitaro Komatsubara. Komatsubara was, for a Japanese, a tall officer at 5 feet 7 inches and very experienced; he had fought the Germans in 1914 and the Red Army in 1922, then taken an intelligence path acting twice as Military Attaché in Moscow before later running spying from Hailar. When news arrived of the Mongolian actions, Komatsubara happened to be briefing his subordinates on the new Kwangtung Army regulations for solving border disputes, which gave local commanders a great deal of initiative including authority to cross the border.[40]

Feklenko appears to have anticipated problems and on his own initiative – a brave thing to do in the circumstance – created, on 3 March, a small 1,200-man battle group with eight T-37 reconnaissance tanks based upon the 11th Tank Brigade at Tamtsak-Bulak to support the 6th Mongolian Division.[41] Meanwhile, Komatsubara despatched a battle group based upon Twenty-Third Reconnaissance Regiment, led by Lieutenant Colonel Yaozo Azuma, complete with air support. As this formation drove westwards the Mongolians fell back across the Khalkin. With the situation 'restored' the Japanese returned to Hailar on 16 May but the following day the 6th Mongolian Division re-crossed the river and established a position in the hills on the eastern bank.[42]

Komatsubara now sent a larger force under Colonel Takemitsu Yamagata, the Sixty-Fourth Infantry Regiment commander, with an infantry battalion, the reconnaissance regiment and support weapons comprising some 1,600 Japanese, and the First, Seventh and Eighth Manchukuo Cavalry Regiments totalling 4,500 men. The infantry battalion ensured that Yamagata's mission would not be 'here today, gone tomorrow', his orders being to seize the confluence of the two rivers. Both Komatsubara and Yamagata were aware of the proximity of Russian troops, and Russian aircraft began operating in the area from 18 May; but both officers chose to ignore all the Kwangtung Army's hints about not aggravating the situation, Yamagata departing on 28 May with all the confidence of General Custer at Little Big Horn. Learning of the Japanese concentration, on 16 May Voroshilov ordered Feklenko to secure the Khalkin and the following day the 149th Rifles (Major Ivan Rezmizov) and 9th Motor-Mechanised Brigade set out, although Rezmizov's unit had to drive 1,060 kilometres and did not arrive until the 28th, while the latter had to cover 700 kilometres and arrived the following day.[43]

On 28 May Azuma's regiment returned under a cloudless sky and drove south along the Khalkin's eastern bank towards its confluence with the Khailastyn, overrunning a Mongolian regimental headquarters and threatening to isolate it in dunes near the river. Meanwhile the first of Rezmizov's battalions crossed the river in the early evening and attacked the reconnaissance regiment which was left to fight alone, the Japanese infantry battalion acting as spectators, driven back and partly isolated. Azuma led a desperate banzai charge breakout from which only four men emerged, before the regiment retreated having lost 63 per cent of its men (with 105 killed, including Azuma). The Russians then attacked the rest of Yamagata's force, but were alarmed by the sudden arrival of another of Komatsubara's infantry battalions and withdrew to the western bank, allowing the Japanese to claim success before they too withdrew on 1 June having lost 290 out of 2,082 men. For their part, Communists lost some 370 men (including 171 dead and missing) out of 2,300 (1,257 Mongolian). Russian field artillery, aggressively led and facing only light infantry support guns, proved decisive but the lack of a sector leader meant the success was not exploited.[44]

Both sides pondered the future, Tokyo fearing the incident might become a full border war, despite the Kwangtung Army's repeated assurances that this would not happen, although it did not believe the border was secure. Komatsubara was determined to return to the fray so, as often happened in the 1930s, the Japanese Army tail wagged the dog with junior officers driving events. Indeed, while the Kwangtung Army was reassuring Tokyo, its Operations Department was preparing plans for a major offensive, involving the Seventh Division, a substantial armoured force and most of its air force, exploiting an efficient rail system serving railheads at Arshaan and Hailar and two good earth roads from Hailar to the battlefield.

These plans were shown to Kwangtung Army chief-of-staff, Lieutenant General Rensuke Isogai, who wished to secure approval from the General Staff, but the Operations Department impatiently dismissed his caution and pressured him to present it to the one-legged General Kenkichi Ueda, commander of the Kwangtung Army and former commander of the Korea Corps. Ueda was a strong supporter of the Strike North (Hokushin-ron) or anti-Russian strategy and modified the plan to incorporate elements of Seventh Division in a mechanised task force under First Tank Group commander, Lieutenant General Masaomi Yasuoka. This plan was approved on the morning of 20 June and Komatsubara received it with tears of joy.[45]

When the General Staff in Tokyo learned of the unilateral move it was concerned, but Japanese society abhors personal confrontation and the Operations Department was unwilling to interfere, despite concerns about the quality of forces and equipment. Offers of help from neighbouring commands were dismissed, partly because the Kwangtung Army intelligence severely underestimated the Communist forces in the combat zone at 1,000 men, 10 guns and 10 armoured vehicles. In fact the Communists had some 13,000 troops, having despatched more troops from 36th Rifle Division and 11th Tank Brigade together with the 8th and 9th Motor-Mechanised Brigades, a heavy artillery battalion and 100 aircraft, while the Mongolians brought up their 8th Cavalry Division from the south, support being underpinned by three bridges thrown across the confluence of the two rivers.[46]

The May battles undermined Moscow's confidence in Feklenko, who had succeeded Konev barely seven months earlier and appeared out of his depth, as did his chief-of-staff who had been in his post only two months longer. Voroshilov and Shaposhnikov decided they needed a steadier hand at the plough and they opted for Zhukov, deputy commander of the Belorussian District, who was training mobile forces (cavalry and armour) and who had just completed war games on 1 June when summoned to Moscow. No doubt with some trepidation, he met Voroshilov the next morning and was briefed on events at Khalkin Gol before being told to fly out that afternoon and submit a report to the General Staff upon his arrival.[47]

Zhukov arrived at 57th Corps headquarters, which had been moved to Tamsag-Bulak, on 5 June. A grim-faced figure with icy-blue eyes which seemed to bore through those he met, Zhukov was a perfectionist: failure in his eyes would earn a tongue-lashing and, indeed, he was known to threaten to horsewhip cowering subordinates. He demanded clarity, tidiness and certainty in action and was not impressed with Feklenko or his staff who failed even to establish a landline communications net and had only the vaguest idea of the overall situation. Zhukov toured the battlefield in an armoured car and through a combination of instinct and judgement, augmented by briefings from the Defence Ministry and Shtern's staff, produced a plan based upon an active defence of the bridgehead followed by a counter-offensive. He recommended the removal of both Feklenko and his chief-of-staff, but retained the commissar, Regkom M.S. Nikishev, and the following day Zhukov became corps commander with Kombrig Mikhail Bogdanov as his new chief-of-staff. Feklenko was recalled to Moscow. Zhukov in the meantime demanded reinforcements including aircraft, at least three rifle divisions and an armoured brigade, which Moscow approved on 7 June.[48]

Japan's Provisional Air Task Force (Rinji Hikotai) had established air superiority when the conflict began with four squadrons or Chutai (32 aircraft) operating from bases around Hailar, some 160 kilometres from the battlefield. Many Kwangtung Army airmen were veterans of the China Incident, where some had fought Russian pilots while, in opposition, Kalinychev's airmen were demoralised, poorly trained and flying obsolete aircraft in poor condition, with the brigade headquarters remaining at Bain Tumen, 300 kilometres from the battlefield. On 21 May the Trans-Baikal District transferred Major Kutsevalov's 23rd Air Brigade to Bain Tumen with 101 aircraft but during that month the Russians lost 21 aircraft – 10 per cent of their air strength including 17 machines to enemy action; the Japanese lost one aircraft. The Japanese had air superiority and this was strengthened by transferring another six squadrons (50 aircraft) to the area. On 27 May Feklenko had what is described as a 'hard-hitting' telephone conversation with Voroshilov who 'expressed great dissatisfaction'. The following day Feklenko told Shaposhnikov that unless Moscow intervened he would have to abandon the eastern bank. In fact Soviet intelligence consistently overestimated Japanese air strength, claiming the Japanese had 180 aircraft on 27 May when in reality they had about 50, with the result that the Russians outnumbered their enemy throughout the conflict.[49]

Moscow reacted promptly on 29 March, despatching three Douglas DC 3 transports, one flown by Stalin's personal pilot and carrying 48 combat veterans from Spain and China under VVS deputy commander, Komkor Iakov Smushkevich (known in Spain as General 'Douglas'). The plan was to send some 270 aircraft. Smushkevich's delegation arrived on 2 June, together with fighter reinforcements, and dispersed to airfields to begin training crews. There was a lull in air operations, apart from reconnaissance missions. The first big fighter sweep, 105 aircraft on 20 June, was a disaster with 14 Soviet aircraft (13 per cent) shot down and 11 pilots killed, while the Japanese lost five. But the Russians now had more than 300 aircraft to cover the battlefield, including 135 twin-engined SB bombers which made their debut on 24 June. The Kwangtung Army moved Lieutenant General Tetsuju Giga's Second Air Division (Hikoshidan) to Hailar which had three air brigades (Hikodan) with 16 squadrons (128 aircraft). Giga launched a pre-emptive strike against enemy airfields with 104 aircraft (including 30 bombers) on the morning of 27 June and while the Russian early warning organisation failed to alert some units in time, the attacks were poorly co-ordinated, destroying just 18-19 aircraft (148 were claimed!) for the loss of four. The General Staff was furious at the Kwangtung Army's defiance and Operations Chief, Colonel Masazumi Inada, tongue-lashed the Kwangtung Army chief-of-staff despite the fact that they were friends. As a result relations between the two organisations never recovered. On 29 June IGHQ sent Ueda a directive to localise border conflicts and banned air attacks east of the Khalkin.[50]

Meanwhile, Zhukov prepared – often using a cool Mongolian yurt as his headquarters. He arrived together with the rest of 11th Tank Brigade, which had to drive 800 kilometres, with many tanks damaged through spontaneous fires due to a combination of the heat and leaking petrol, a problem experienced throughout the campaign.[51] On 3 July 57th Corps headquarters was upgraded to 1st Army Group and two days later it came under a Front Group organised at Chita under Shtern which controlled all Soviet forces from the Trans-Baikal District to Vladivostok. But this was no resurrection of the OKDVA; Shtern was regarded as a safe pair of hands and his front command not only provided nominal oversight of Zhukov but also a separate headquarters ready to meet a larger threat if it should develop. Mekhlis was also on hand to ensure Moscow's rule was obeyed to the letter, while Shaposhnikov 'supervised' from Moscow.[52]

The changes came as Komatsubara prepared to storm the Khalkin with 15,000 troops, 73 tanks and 14 tankettes, supported by 20 guns which faced 12,541 troops with 186 tanks and 86 field and heavy guns.[53] Komatsubara led several task forces of which the largest, under Major General Koichi Kobayashi, had the Seventy-First and Seventy-Second Infantry supported by Colonel Shinichri Sumi's Motorised Offensive Unit, (the motorised Twenty-Sixth Infantry) as well as the remnants of the Twenty-Third Reconnaissance Regiment. On his left would be

Yasuoka's detachment, two tank regiments augmented by Sixty-Fourth Infantry and an engineer regiment. In reserve were an infantry battalion and an engineer regiment. The tank brigade proved a mixed blessing, for the tracks of the tanks churned up the roads making them almost impassable to the soft-skinned vehicles which focused their attention on moving men rather than supplies.[54]

Komatsubara's forces reached their jump-off points by dawn on 2 July for a two-pronged attack: Kobayashi would cross the Khalkin some 20 kilometres west of Nomonhan and some 3 kilometres north-west of the sand dunes to seize the steep-sided Bain-Tsagan Heights (which the Japanese called the Hara Heights), some 40 kilometres from the border recognised by the Russians, then sweep down the western bank to the confluence with the Khailastyn, with Sumi ready to exploit any success. Yasuoka would strike the enemy eastern bridgehead between the dunes and the Khailastyn from the north-east. Komatsubara was especially anxious to strike because intelligence wrongly believed that the Communists were abandoning the eastern bank when, under Shtern's prodding, Zhukov was strengthening his defences.

Zhukov was aware in general terms and was expecting an attack due to the intensification of enemy air attacks, but his supply lines suffered because the railhead was some 645 kilometres away at Borziya and it was an earth road to Tamtsak-Bulak. The 6th Mongolian Cavalry Division held the left flank underpinned by the 11th Tank Brigade and 7th Motor-Mechanised Brigade. The 36th Motorised Rifle Division's 149th Rifles held a bridgehead on the eastern bank, north of the Khailastyn, with the 9th Motor-Mechanised Brigade, the tank brigade's machine gun battalion being south of the Khailastyn, and the 8th Mongolian Cavalry Division secured the right while the 36th Division's 24th Rifles was in reserve. Zhukov expected the main blow to come like the others against the eastern bridgehead and had assembled a counter-attack force consisting of the 11th Tank Brigade (Colonel M.P. Yakovlev), 7th Motor-Mechanised Brigade (Colonel A.L. Lesovoi) and the 24th Motorised Rifles (Lieutenant Colonel Ivan Fedyuninsky).

In a spectacular lightning storm which preceded a rainy morning, Kobayashi began crossing in the early hours of 2/3 July and, having secured the western bank, assembled the Kwangtung Army's only pontoon bridge, across which the main body began to surge during the morning. A senior MPA advisor, Colonel Ivan Afonin, who came to inspect 6th Mongolian Division at dawn on 3 July, found it engaged in a bitter battle having been driven north-west from the Bain-Tsagan Heights. He drove immediately to Zhukov's headquarters to report. The surprised Zhukov acted promptly, ordering a heavy artillery battalion to engage the enemy, Soviet aircraft to strike the crossing point and his counter-attack forces to smite the northern threat immediately.

A piecemeal response saw Yakovlev strike with 127 tanks at 09.00 hrs joined nearly two hours later by Lesovoi, the armour making numerous cavalry-style charges and firing wildly on the move, without support, to keep the enemy off balance. Yakovlev's tanks flared into flame, sometimes through overheating and sometimes because of petrol-filled bottles crashing on the engine compartments, and the battlefield was marked by black plumes of smoke, the brigade losing 72 tanks (56.6 per cent) as well as half of its 10 KhT-26 flame-thrower tanks.[55] Shtern had wanted Yakovlev to wait for Fedyuninsky, but Zhukov was adamant that he had to strike immediately and Shtern would later agree it was the right decision. Fedyuninsky's infantry appeared later in the day, having assembled in the wrong location and lacking contact with either Zhukov or Yakovlev, whose operations were plagued by unreliable radios. Eventually Zhukov's aide arrived at Fedyuninsky's headquarters with a map upon which Zhukov had personally drawn the direction of the regiment's attack.

Meanwhile, lack of traffic control brought anarchy to the Japanese bridgehead, while the rickety 35-year-old pontoon bridge was not strong enough to carry loaded trucks. Even artillery had to be broken down, with engineers clearing the bridge every half-hour for emergency maintenance. The confusion wrecked hopes of a rapid advance, and with Russians pounding the Japanese formations, Kobayashi reluctantly dug in. Komatsubara, on a tour of inspection, was almost killed by one of these wild charges and was saved only by an artillery battery holding off the tanks, but he quickly recognised that with his bridgehead overlooked from the Bain-Tsagan Heights, it was untenable and should be evacuated.

The withdrawal began that night (3/4 July), but Lesovoi, Yakovlev and Fedyuninsky maintained pressure, isolating and wiping out a battalion of the Twenty-Sixth Infantry. Kobayashi grimly held the peak of the Bain-Tsagan Heights as the Russians fought their way up the slopes in a fierce and confused struggle. By the evening of 4 July the bridgehead was some 5 kilometres long and only 2 kilometres wide and under constant artillery and air bombardment, the Twenty-Third Division command post being hit and the division chief-of-staff, Colonel Tsutoma Ouchi, killed. During the night of 4/5 July, the bridgehead was finally evacuated and the pontoon bridge blown up, ending Japanese hopes of striking on the western bank. Kobayashi's three infantry regiments lost some 10 per cent of their men – 671 casualties including 220 dead and missing, and many officers fell, with the Twenty-Sixth Infantry losing most of its regimental staff, two battalion- and half the company commanders.

Yasuoka's attack upon the Russian eastern bridgehead went wrong almost immediately. Rezmizov's 149th Rifles and 9th Motor-Mechanised Brigade held a strong position with secure flanks with strong artillery support and were alerted by an increase in vehicle movements. The attack began at the same time as Kobayashi's, but facing a storm of both rain and shells as well as numerous counter-attacks, the Japanese infantry advanced slowly in a grinding battle. On the first night, Colonel Yoshio Tomada of Fourth Tank Regiment used his initiative to launch a nocturnal attack and overran the eastern bank gun line, but without infantry support was unable to exploit the success. The defence owed much to the favourable terrain and the replacement of linear fortifications with strongpoints organised in depth supported by obstacles.[56]

Komatsubara returned across the Khalkin believing, wrongly, that Yasuoka was within five kilometres of Russian bridges and so to exploit the 'success' he brought Kobayashi with him, leaving only two battalions of Seventy-First Infantry and Manchurians south of the river Khailastyn. He renewed his assault in rain on the evening of 7/8 July, surprising Rezmizov and driving back two of his battalions. The Japanese reached the regimental headquarters some 4 kilometres from the river and in the fighting which followed, Rezmizov was killed while the Russians were so shaken that during that night several rifle companies fired upon each other. Ignoring weak Japanese counter-battery fire, the defenders contained the threat although on the morning of 7 July artillery fire forced Zhukov and Nikishev to abandon their dugout command post and drive off, only to be strafed by a Japanese aircraft which forced them to take cover in an abandoned trench.[57]

To provide some shelter from the remorseless Russian guns, the Japanese switched to night attacks which made slow progress and on 11 July they took Hill 733, overlooking the confluence. In the confused fighting Yakovlev was killed by a sniper. Neither side's armour was handled well, often operating in small, unsupported formations which roamed the battlefield blazing away, consuming fuel and ammunition, before withdrawing for replenishment. The Japanese tanks frequently fell victim to deadly anti-tank guns, while the Russian armour, often dug in, proved to have superior anti-tank ammunition compared to Japanese rounds which often bounced off enemy armour.

By now Zhukov had reinforced the bridgehead, putting Fedyuninsky's 24th Rifles on the left of 149th Rifles, the 5th Rifle Machine Gun Brigade on its right. The Russians held a perilously small bridgehead some 4 kilometres wide and 7 kilometres deep; indeed, Japanese raiding parties harassed the bridge defenders, but Komatsubara had lost a quarter of his men – 2,122 casualties including 585 dead and missing – and a fifth of his guns. He decided to consolidate his forces, withdraw the most exposed units and bring up more artillery, leading to a relative lull which lasted 10 days.

Ueda decided to finish off the bridgehead the traditional way, with artillery. To preserve his armour he disbanded the Yasuoka detachment on 9 July and withdrew the tank regiments. Yasuoka was furious, believing his men were on the verge of victory, claiming to have destroyed 66 tanks and 20 armoured cars, and to have captured 11 armoured vehicles and other materiel. He had lost 139 men and only 40 per cent of his armour remained available: 13 tanks and two tankettes were destroyed, 14 tanks and a tankette suffered major damage but were repaired, while 17 tanks and four tankettes suffered minor damage.

Russian reinforcements were pouring into the Trans-Baikal District which conducted a partial mobilisation to form 93rd and 114th Rifle Divisions and on 31 July received the Moscow District's 37th Tank Brigade. From the west the 37th and 46th Rifle Divisions were sent east of the Urals during the summer.[58]

In May the District also created Kombrig P.F. Fedorovich's 82nd Rifle Division from the 244th Rifle Regiment but it proved a somewhat slender reed and 20 per cent of its troops were poorly armed raw recruits. Its 603rd Rifles, followed by the 602nd Rifles, took positions on the quieter front south of the Khailastyn on 12 July after marching 300 kilometres, but two days later collapsed under a Japanese attack. Its men fled in panic throwing away their weapons and those who kept them used them on commissars and officers who tried to stop the rout. Mekhlis would complain on 16 July about 'cases of extreme indiscipline and crime' including hundreds of cases of self-injury. He rounded up the men and applied his usual remedy for 'indiscipline', even shooting several commanders before ranks of sullen troops.[59]

To the Japanese, the expulsion of the Communists had become a matter of prestige and they despatched the new Third Heavy Artillery Brigade under Major General Yuzaburo Hata with 38 heavy guns. The brigade was placed under Major General Eitaro Uchiyama together with an artillery locator regiment and began to arrive on the battlefield from 18 July with some 245 tonnes of ammunition which, along with field artillery rounds, absorbed 70 per cent of the Kwantung Army's artillery ammunition. Beginning on 21 July Uchiyama concentrated upon counter-battery fire and harassing enemy movements, but rain washed away these hopes until 23 July. The bombardment began in temperatures so high that at least one Japanese gun was destroyed by the shell detonating in the breech. The Japanese Air Force was also involved, dropping 148 tonnes of bombs from 128 bombers on the Russian bridgehead and gun lines. It quickly became apparent that although nominally out-gunned with 76 to 82 tubes, the Russians had better weapons and greater stocks of ammunition, while the VVS blinded the Japanese gunners by harassing their spotter aircraft and even shooting down an observation balloon. The Japanese also had little training in indirect fire and were woefully unprepared for counter-battery operations, while the Russians proved painfully accurate, destroying 16 tubes (19.5 per cent) including half the 100 mm guns, although Hata's men did manage to neutralise 13 heavy guns including eight 122 mm and four 152 mm howitzers.[60]

In the face of heavy artillery fire, the exhausted Japanese infantry, many of whom were suffering from dysentery, showed an uncharacteristic but understandable reluctance to attack and would frequently take cover. With little progress and heavy losses totalling 4,400 by 25 July including 1,413 dead and missing, Ueda called a halt on 30 July, withdrawing Uchiyama's headquarters to leave Hata as artillery supremo.

The Japanese went on to the defensive but fortifying their positions was difficult, many men being the flotsam left by the tide of the offensive and exposed to enemy fire. A timber shortage made it difficult to create wire entanglements and when Russian stakes were exhausted, the men had to use wood from ammunition and ration boxes while the sandy soil made it impossible to dig deep trenches or foxholes. Serious shortages of materiel reflected the parlous state of the Kwantung Army's motor transport; although Komatsubara had support from up to 1,000 trucks, a quarter of them were unserviceable. Only half his losses had been replaced, preventing the digging of anti-tank trenches, a serious problem when there were few anti-tank guns. Intelligence reported that the enemy was having supply problems, but radio traffic suggested the possibility of a Soviet attack at some time between 5–10 August.[61]

Russian probes into the area south of the Khailastyn led Komatsubara to reinforce the sector with Colonel Riei Hasebe's regimental-sized Eighth Border Garrison Unit which stabilised the situation. More ominously, Japan's military attaché to Moscow, who had returned along the Trans-Siberian Railway in early August, reported it full of troop trains. Japanese intelligence amended its appreciation to expect an attack by 14 August. Although this failed to materialise, forward commanders, especially in the north, were aware that the enemy was assembling forces. Yet when Japanese aircraft spotted Russian troops moving up late on 19 August, the news failed to interest either Ueda or Komatsubara.

Komatsubara's troops were all deployed forward with few reserves, supported by Hata's gunners; from north to south he had Sixty-Fourth and Seventy-Second Infantry in line north of the Khailastyn with Twenty-Sixth Infantry in reserve, while the Twenty-Eighth and Seventy-First Infantry were to the south. His flanks were anchored by two lightly armed battalions: in the north, Lieutenant Colonel Eiichi Ioki's reinforced 23rd Reconnaissance Battalion on Hill 721 (Fui Heights), which he planned to reinforce, and in the south by Colonel Iwao Yotsuya's lightly armed 6th Independent Garrison Unit. The Sixth Corps under Lieutenant General Ryuhei Ogisu was scheduled to take over the line and bring up Lieutenant General Noboru Kunisaki's Seventh Infantry Division, but on the day of the Russian offensive Ogisu was in Hailar and his headquarters did not arrive until 23 August, with Seventh Division's Fourteenth Brigade reinforced by an Independent Garrison Unit.

Zhukov worked late night after night, dining on occasion with his deputy, the impassive, thin-faced Kombrig Mikhail Potapov, who was very popular because of a fund of witty stories and the fact that he was a good listener. The two had met in Belorussia when Potapov's tank brigade had supported Zhukov. When the pair dined there were strict instructions that they were not to be disturbed. On 31 July Zhukov was promoted to Komkor and celebrated the next day by sitting on the parapet of a trench near his headquarters playing the accordion and singing.[62]

But events during the last Japanese attack had underlined how tenuous was his success for he attracted Beria's attention who now read his file. The Japanese crossing of the Khalkin and the tank charges which followed gave Beria the excuse to drop poison down 'The Boss's' ear with claims that Zhukov had 'betrayed' Mongolia by allowing an enemy incursion. Stalin despatched a committee to investigate the matter: it included the Red Army's Armour and Artillery chiefs, Pavlov and Komkor Nikolai Voronov, but was headed by Kulik (see Chapter One).

The abusive, self-important Kulik, with a moustache like an afterthought, threw his weight around. He demanded the abandonment of the eastern bridgehead, but once again Voroshilov shielded his protégé, Zhukov, and on 15 July recalled Kulik to Moscow, confirmed Zhukov's actions and permitted Pavlov and Voronov to remain as 1st Army Group's specialist assistants. But no sooner had Kulik departed than another bird of ill omen, Mekhlis, appeared having been advised by Beria to 'check this man'. However, he too found no reason for criticism. Yet the threat was all too real; the chief Red Army military advisor to Mongolia, Komdiv N.N. Livinov, who was arrested on 3 July, remained in a labour camp until July 1946, while the original chief-of-staff of 57th Corps, Kombrig Aleksandr Kushchev, was arrested some time during the Khalkin Gol battles and remained in a prison camp until reinstated in 1943.[63]

The defensive battles had displayed the glaring weaknesses in Red Army staff work, especially in terms of all-arms co-ordination and supply. Zhukov's prime objective now was good management, both of his subordinates and their men, with detailed preparation which ensured that they would have the maximum support to ensure they took their objectives.[64] The first requirement was to expand his forces and provide adequate supplies; indeed, he requested 55,000 tonnes of supplies but with the railhead far from the battlefield, Zhukov had to rely on motor transport. His staff carefully assessed the supply requirements and discovered they would need 3,500 trucks and 1,400 bulk liquid carriers for fuel and water, but to 14 August Zhukov had only 1,724 and 912 respectively, although he then received another 1,250 trucks and 375 tankers.

For the first fortnight Zhukov used every available vehicle, including those of the artillery regiments even though this left the guns immobile, and he organised the supply route in two stages; firstly, from the border village of Solovyovsk to Bain Tumen and from there to Tamsag-Bulak, a route subdivided into 30-50 kilometre sections with rest stations where the drivers, who often drove two nights without sleep, could get something to eat or drink while their vehicles could receive minor servicing or repairs. The vehicles moved at night, with drivers making five-day round trips of up to 1,400 kilometres, following the tail lights of the vehicle ahead. If a vehicle broke down, nomads would lend assistance or other vehicles would tow them.

The trucks brought in 18,000 tonnes of artillery ammunition, 6,500 tonnes of aircraft ammunition, 15,000 tonnes of lubricants, 4,000 tonnes of food, 7,500 tonnes of fuel and 4,000 tonnes of miscellaneous supplies. Zhukov also demanded, and received, substantial reinforcements, including 57th Rifle Division and the 20th Tank Corps' 6th Tank Brigade, both of which arrived on 5 August – the latter with 245 BT-7s, a regiment of the 152nd Rifle Division, the battalion-strength 212th Airborne Brigade, a long-range battery, two communication battalions and a pontoon battalion which raised the number of bridges across the Khalkin to 12.[65] The heat and sand caused major problems for the Russian gunners during early August, with 37 guns out of action between the 6th and the 20th, 60 per cent

Soviet infantry carrying hand grenades and with their rifles fitted with bayonets, follow behind Bystrokhodny (Fast Tank) Mark 7 (BT-7) tanks as they attack Japanese positions at Khalkin Gol in August 1939. The BT-7, which used the American-designed Christie chassis, was fast and highly mobile and, like most Russian tanks, well armed with a 45 mm gun. But these tanks were vulnerable to field gun fire and their petrol-driven engines made them prone to fires, several at Khalkin Gol bursting into flame when petrol evaporated then ignited in the desert heat. This led to a requirement for a better armoured and better armed vehicle with a diesel engine, and Mikhail Koshkin's design, retaining the Christie chassis, became the famous T-34.

of them the heaviest pieces (122 mm and 152 mm), but by 20 August, 1st Army Group had 280 guns (sixty-four 76 mm field guns, thirty-six 107 mm guns, sixty-eight 122 mm howitzers, four 122 mm guns, twenty-four 152 mm howitzers and twelve 152 mm guns augmented by 162 short-range 76 mm regimental infantry support guns.[66] They would support 57,000 men, including 3,000 in the rear echelons, 2,260 Mongolians and 438 tanks.

Zhukov planned a double envelopment from the north and south, exploiting the open Japanese flanks and their lack of armour. The Southern Group, led by Potapov, would deliver the main blow using Colonel Ivan Galanin's 57th Rifle Division, half of 11th Tank Brigade, 6th Tank and 8th Motor-Mechanised Brigades and reinforced 8th Mongolian Cavalry Division – a force with some 265 tanks. It was to drive directly to Nomonhan, bypassing enemy centres of resistance and link up with Northern Group to turn eastwards heading along both sides of the Khailastyn to destroy the enemy piecemeal. The Northern Group would be led by Colonel I.V. Shevnikov with the remainder of 11th Tank Brigade, the 601st Rifles of the 82nd Rifle Division, 7th Motor-Mechanised Brigade and 6th Mongolian Cavalry Division with some 100 tanks to destroy the forces shielding the Japanese right, then driving to Nomonhan after which it would mop up in the north-west. Kombrig Daniil Petrov's Central Group would hold the enemy in place along a

23-kilometre front, the 36th Rifle Division having moved into the northern sand dunes, leaving the 5th Rifle Machine Gun Brigade holding the line to the Khailastyn, while the rest of the 82nd Rifle Division held the line south of the river and would cover Potapov's bridgehead on his left. The army reserve, consisting of 9th Motor-Mechanised Brigade, 212th Airborne Brigade and a battalion of 6th Tank Brigade with some 50 vehicles, was 6 kilometres west of Khamar Daba, where Zhukov had his headquarters.

Counter-battery and anti-reserve preparation was to be effected by the Central Group with 90 guns ranging from 76 mm to 152 mm, augmented by 77 regimental guns. Although the Southern Group would benefit from this concentration, it had only 40 pieces of field artillery and some 60 regimental guns for its preparation.[67] The bombers were to strike enemy reserves and artillery. Artillery preparation would last 165 minutes with the last 15 minutes focusing upon the enemy positions and the offensive would be launched at 09.30 hrs.

There were serious efforts made to achieve surprise, with Sunday 20 August selected for the offensive because Japanese officers often left the front for the weekend. Only Zhukov, Potapov, the chief-of-staff and commissar knew the overall plan, while a dozen specialists (including Voronov and Smushkevich) worked out details, all the documentation being produced by a single typist. Commanders were expected to conduct reconnaissance and Zhukov set an example, changing into a private's tunic when he inspected the terrain either from a staff car or, to the delight of his Mongolian allies, on horseback.[68] There was also a great deal of effort made to conceal Russian intentions, with radio instructions on construction work broadcast in easily crackable codes during the first half of August to deliberately mislead the Japanese. Movements of armour and vehicles were covered, as in the First World War, by aircraft noise augmented by artillery fire, while trucks with their silencers removed roared up and down the front for a fortnight to provide audio camouflage. The VVS flew in such a way that its routine was recognised and ignored by the Japanese. No movements were permitted until 18 August and breaches in security were dealt with by Zhukov's usual harshness.

Most senior officers learned details of the plan on 17 August when they sat down to an al fresco lunch, at a table with a white tablecloth, outside Zhukov's headquarters. They were then given a few hours to complete their own preparations before Zhukov arrived the following day to inspect them. Shevnikov's inspection was a disaster and an apoplectic Zhukov replaced him with the 11th Tank Brigade commander, Colonel I.P. Alekseenko.[69] That night the reinforcements began to move forward, concealed by heavy rain, regimental commanders receiving detailed instructions barely three hours before the assault. Two political department trucks with record players and loudspeakers covered Southern Group activity by loudly playing sounds of engineering works.

The Russians now exploited their numerical superiority to control the air through a bitter battle of attrition for which the Japanese were unprepared.

At the beginning of July the Russians had 280 aircraft, including 132 SB bombers, and, with the establishment of 1st Army Group, the VVS established a headquarters at Tamsag-Bulak under Kombrig Aleksandr Gusev. The SBs were extremely active during July and towards the end of the month began striking enemy airfields with some success, but the Japanese still had more experienced pilots and in a month of fierce air battles Moscow lost 88 aircraft, 79 to enemy action. The Russians introduced the I-153 Chaika (Seagull) fighter from 7 July and that night TB-3 heavy bombers transferred from Trans-Baikal made their combat debut with three of them dropping 1.6 tonnes of bombs. The Japanese appear to have lost 28 aircraft and in mid-July they reorganised their forces, withdrawing one air brigade and two squadrons of Fiat BR 20 bombers, then dividing the remaining 14 squadrons of 133 aircraft to create a fighter and a bomber/reconnaissance brigade.[70]

By the beginning of August the VVS had 532 aircraft, air strength dropping just before Zhukov's offensive partly due to fierce battles which cost 77 aircraft during the month and partly due to the need to withdraw the Chaikas temporarily due to mechanical problems. But reinforcements arrived including, on 18 August, a detachment of five I-16s carrying the new RS-82 unguided air-to-ground rocket and a Mongolian R-5 light bomber squadron for night attacks. By the time of the offensive Russian air strength had risen to 587, including 211 bombers of which 23 were heavy bombers. One fighter squadron was based near Zhukov's command post for urgent tactical reconnaissance and shortly before the offensive all the SB regiments were placed under the operational control of 100th Fast Bomber Regiment. By contrast, Japanese air strength rose by only five squadrons (28 aircraft) which arrived from China, although Russian intelligence estimated it at 450 aircraft. The Russians began striking enemy airfields and IGHQ reluctantly permitted retaliatory strikes. However, due to declining rates of serviceability and crew exhaustion, the new policy was not implemented. Japanese losses mounted and the Kwangtung Army decided to conserve its strength for one major blow scheduled for 24 August.

The night of 19/20 August was quiet, broken only by the occasional crackle of machine gun fire and lit by the odd flare. As dawn broke, the river valleys were covered with a mist. After three hours' sleep, Zhukov was awoken by his aide, Vorotnikov, with a cup of tea. He shaved and went calmly to the observation post, joining his command team and visitors such as Shtern, Voronov and Smushkevich. Then he sat at his table with a box of red and blue pencils.[71] The bombardment began at 06.15 hrs and began to tear apart the flimsy Japanese defences aided by two bombing attacks involving 205 sorties upon reserves and gun positions, while the I-16s used the air-to-ground rockets for the first time. The artillery and air bombardments stunned the defenders whose guns did not reply for 90 minutes as the Russians achieved total surprise. The Kwangtung Army headquarters did not learn of the offensive for more than 24 hours![72]

At 09.30 hrs red flares soared into the air and the assault troops moved out, Potapov's to the strains of 'The Internationale' which was played at full blast by the two propaganda trucks.[73] His advance swept forward like a wave, broken by the breakwaters of the dunes. The Mongolians and Colonel V.A. Mishulin's 8th Motor-Mechanised Brigade swept along the outer flank to cover the frontier, with the latter establishing positions across the Khailastyn from Nomonhan, the former being aided by a sudden mutiny by 3,000 Manchurian infantry on the easternmost flank, most of them then defecting or deserting.

The spearhead, 80th and 127th Rifles of Galanin's 57th Rifle Division, advanced between the two outermost dune fields and Division's 293rd Rifles with 82nd Division's 603rd Rifles advanced between the innermost dunes. Two battalions of 11th Tank Brigade covered the left, while 80th Rifles was to have been supported by Colonel M.I. Pavelkin's 6th Tank Brigade. Unfortunately, the pontoon bridge assigned to the brigade was not strong enough to carry the tanks and they had to ford a rain-swollen river. Pavelkin's crews spent most of the day plugging openings in their armour with rags and mud as well as finding pipes which would keep exhaust gases above the river. They drove through the Khalkin later in the day with hulls almost submerged to support 80th Rifles by evening as it pushed towards the frontier through the dunes. Galanin's division broke through the Infantry's defences and advanced beyond the dune zone, but the 80th Rifles' move created a gap which had to be plugged by the divisional reconnaissance battalion.

Over the next two days, Potapov's mechanised forces drove towards the border, outflanking the southern force. Mishulin's 8th Brigade reached the border south-east of Nomonhan on 23 August, isolating the enemy south of the Khailastyn, the outer ring strengthened by the arrival of 127th Rifles. Meanwhile, the main force drove deeper into the defences, wiping out local reserves and overrunning artillery, strongpoints being blasted at point-blank range by artillery and later by flame-thrower tanks.

The Northern Group was less successful against Ioki, whose positions on what was described as 'a raised pancake', pointed to the Khalkin and earned the Russian nickname 'The Finger'. Ioki's stubborn resistance surprised the Russians whose artillery support was inadequate, partly due to Shevnikov's bungling and, instead of bypassing the strongpoint, the Northern Group was sucked into a bitter and bloody battle. Anticipating problems, but apparently not overruling the original plan, Zhukov reinforced the 82nd Division's 601st Rifles under Major I. Zander with another tank battalion (splitting Alekseenko's tank brigade in half) and artillery, but the 800 defenders were in a strong position as the approaches were devoid of cover.

The Mongolians established a frontier screen north of Ioki while 7th Motor-Mechanised Brigade isolated the position from the south, but Zander's infantry had to fight for every inch of ground. Although Zander was killed by the end of the day, there was stalemate. On 21 August, Komatsubara sent a battalion of Twenty-Sixth Infantry north as well as trucks with supplies to Ioki, but they failed to get through and on 23 August an exasperated Zhukov sent an airborne brigade to

Northern Group. In the face of overwhelming odds Ioki, now down to 200 exhausted men and running short of ammunition, withdrew on his own initiative during the night of 24/25 August and the survivors reached safety the following day. Meanwhile the 9th Brigade outflanked Ioki and advanced along the border towards the Khailastyn and, by accident rather than design, drove through Komatsubara's supply network and over his hospital, reaching Nomonhan on 22 August where two days later it met 8th Brigade.

Petrov's Central Group, which included 17 tanks attached to 82nd Division, faced the bulk of Twenty-Third Division and made heavy weather of pushing through the Japanese defences, advancing barely a kilometre on the first day despite artillery firing over open sights and the fact that regiments had been ordered to infiltrate the enemy strongpoints and then strike them from the rear. Because of the stubborn resistance, on 23 August Zhukov gave Petrov the airborne troops from Northern Group and two border guard companies and they gradually pushed back the Japanese into a pocket. As the temperature reached 40°C on 24 August, plaguing both sides with thirst, Zhukov's subordinates sought a brief rest for their tired men, but he rejected anything which would lose the initiative.

By mid-morning of 20 August, Komatsubara recognised the main threat was in the south but remained unaware of the scale of it. He decided to strip his defences north of the Khailastyn and to launch a counter-offensive, but then the Sixth Corps chief-of-staff, Major General Fujimoto Tetsukuma, arrived and ordered the Seventy-Second Infantry to be kept in line. Ogisu agreed with Komatsubara about a counter-offensive south of the Khailastyn – although he had an ulterior motive in seeking the Seventh Division as reinforcements and the counter-offensive provided the excuse to have it transferred with a strong force of anti-tank guns on 23 August – but it was too late to make any difference.

The counter-offensive was plagued by a lack of resources and protracted arguments between Ogisu's and Komatsubara's staffs, causing the intervention of War Minister General Shunroku Hata who agreed with the corps commander on the afternoon of 23 August that the forces north of the Khailastyn should be stripped to create an assault force of nine battalions, nearly half Komatsubara's force. Ogisu and Hata ignored the fact that Komatsubara's men were exhausted and short of food, water and ammunition and would have to traverse a battlefield dominated by enemy air and artillery forcing piecemeal movement, so the attack on 24 August was a disaster. It struck 80th Rifles and 8th Motor-Mechanised Brigade with weak artillery support, the Russians had superior observation posts for their guns, and the exhausted infantry had to attack across open terrain led by sword-wielding officers in what American troops would later call 'Banzai charges'. Once pinned down they were subjected to tank attacks and, to make matters worse, Japanese bombers accidentally hit Komatsubara's headquarters as the Russians began overrunning his gun line north of the Khailastyn. Within three days every battery was lost.

Renewed Japanese assaults over the following two days also failed and Ogisu was forced to recognise that he needed reinforcements. However, although Seventh

Division had finally arrived, the Kwangtung Army was reluctant to commit further forces for fear this would weaken the defence of Manchuria. On 26 August the Kwangtung Army finally learned the full scale of the Russian offensive thanks to a captured map. It ordered Fourth Division and almost every divisional anti-tank battery and heavy artillery regiment to the front.

On 25 August the Russians began reducing the southern pocket after an hour-long bombardment during which the VVS dropped 96 tonnes of bombs, but resistance remained so fierce that Shtern urged caution, recommending a temporary delay of one or two days. Again Zhukov refused because it would allow the enemy to recover. The following day the assault force was reinforced with 293rd Rifles of 152nd Rifle Division. This unit punched through the Twenty-Sixth Infantry, seizing high ground which offered an uninterrupted view for 12 kilometres to the east. The Japanese response was piecemeal and during the day's fighting they lost half their men. On 27 August Zhukov began to finish off the enemy south of the Khailastyn and had largely succeeded by dusk, although Hasebe's three border guard battalions continued to hold the Noro Heights (Hill 742) despite facing three rifle regiments. Hasebe was eventually ordered to withdraw and succeeded in doing so that night while the Japanese pulled back their force south of the Khailastyn to the border and by 28 August the last strongpoint was stormed.

Zhukov now focused upon the northern pocket which was assaulted from the west on 27 August by 149th Rifles and 5th Machine Gun Brigade, from the north by Fedyuninsky's 24th Rifles and 601st Rifles, and from the east by 9th Motor-Mechanised Brigade and 127th Rifles, the last of these units crossing the Khailastyn by dusk to encircle Sixty-Fourth Infantry. Meanwhile Northern Group plus 36th Division struck from the west and north after a three-hour artillery bombardment. During intense fighting the following day and after 57th Division had committed 293rd Rifles, the Japanese were encircled. On the night of 27/28 August, Komatsubara led 1,000 survivors of his division, ostensibly to relieve Yamagata's Sixty-Fourth Infantry, but actually on a death-before-dishonour mission.

Accidentally striking between Central and Southern Groups against sleeping troops, the Japanese had initial success but they were soon stopped by fierce Russian artillery fire, forcing withdrawal the following night. The withdrawal degenerated into a rout during which Yamagata and the Thirteenth Field Artillery commander, Colonel Takuhide Ise, shot themselves, although some 240 Yamagata's men were fortunate enough to escape. On the evening of 28 August, Fedyuninsky was ordered to destroy the enemy and had succeeded in doing so by morning; during the night some 400 Japanese attempted a breakout through 293rd Rifles on the northern bank of Khailastyn, but these troops were annihilated in the process. Komatsubara was not among them; the dithering Ogisu had finally ordered him to withdraw on 30 August and, after attempting suicide, the divisional commander obeyed, returning with some 400 exhausted and demoralised survivors, having abandoned his wounded. Meanwhile the defence collapsed and on 31 August

Zhukov reported to Moscow that the Japanese west of the frontier were either dead or in prison camps.

Both sides' air forces were extremely active, the Japanese dropping 23.5 tonnes of bombs on 20 August alone, and flying 51 bomber sorties against Russian airfields the following day escorted by 88 fighters, with losses of six aircraft. Between 23 August and 1 September the Japanese dropped more than 50 tonnes of bombs in a desperate effort to help their troops, while the exhausted fighter pilots fought a bloody battle of attrition which saw their Ki-27 fighters shot down faster than the factories could produce them, forcing Tokyo to despatch 23 obsolete Ki-10 biplanes on 26 August. Total Japanese losses in August amounted to 64 aircraft (five on the ground) of which 43 occurred during Zhukov's offensive, while VVS losses for the whole of the month were 77 incurred in massed bomber and fighter missions, the bomber losses declining sharply as the fighters' efforts bore fruit.

Although Japanese forces were now north of the original border, Ogisu thirsted for revenge and was receiving reinforcements – two brigades, a regimental battlegroup and virtually all the Kwangtung Army's armoured and artillery reserve. In addition, on 1 September, the Joint Air Command (Koku-Heidan) under Lieutenant General Eijiro Ebashi arrived from Japan IGHQ, relieved Second Air Division on the night of 5/6 September, absorbing its squadrons and adding Major General Makoto Sasa's Second Air Brigade with nine squadrons from China. This gave Ebashi 255 aircraft by 13 September. Ebashi launched a two-day counter-air campaign on 14 September, but with only 13 medium bombers it had little effect and during the September battles the VVS lost 18 aircraft and the Japanese, 28.

Ogisu harboured visions of a grand operation, but Tokyo decided on 30 August that while Manchuria would be reinforced this would be only to secure the existing border and not to regain ground, IGHQ drafting an order to this effect. On 6 September, the day after diplomatic negotiations began, the Kwangtung Army was banned from launching a counter-offensive. Some ambiguity in the instructions gave Ogisu sufficient leeway to launch attacks on his flanks during the night of 8/9 September and despite border bickering lasting until 11 September, the Russians contained the threat.

As early as 18 July Tokyo had decided it would avoid an all-out war with Russia, and the Kwangtung Army was told to 'grin and bear it'. But efforts to seek a negotiated solution collapsed when, as a result of the stunning news of the Russo-German Treaty of August 1939, Kiichiro Hiranuma's government collapsed on 28 August. His successor, General Nobuyuki Abe, also acted as Foreign Minister and with Germany's subsequent invasion of Poland, Tokyo realised that Moscow also wished to avoid all-out war.[74]

Tokyo began discussions with Molotov on 9 September, but it was only on 14 September, the day the Russians informed Berlin that they were now ready for military operations in Poland, that Molotov (who was aided by Russian agent, Richard Sorge, and his 'Ramzai' spy ring) agreed to a ceasefire and to create a joint border commission. The agreement came into effect on 15 September and although the Russians were fuming over Ebashi's air offensive, they did not change their minds; indeed on 12 September Smushkevich and 20 veteran pilots were flown to the Western Districts to support operations in Poland. The 1st Army Group was disbanded on 16 September but Zhukov and his staff remained on the battlefield until the end of October, at which point they were then transferred to Ulan Bator where Zhukov remained with his wife and daughters until he was appointed commander of the Kiev District in May.[75]

For its part Tokyo decided to bring the Kwangtung Army to heel with its own purge of both its leadership and that of the Army General Staff, Nakajima being relieved by the Fourth Division commander, Lieutenant General Shigeru Sawada. The Kwangtung Army's commander, chief-of-staff, deputy chief-of-staff and operations chief were all retired or transferred, the new army commander being Lieutenant General Yoshijiro Umeza who arrived on 8 September.

The Red Army lost 8,694 dead and missing with 15,952 wounded and sick during the action while its allies suffered 165 dead and 391 wounded.[76] Materiel losses were also heavy and during the campaign the Red Army lost a third of its guns, 96 tubes, of which 88 were destroyed and eight damaged, although during Zhukov's offensive the materiel losses were only seven pieces of field artillery, seven regimental guns and 139 vehicles.[77] By the end of August the two tank brigades, which had begun the offensive with 307 serviceable tanks, had only 84 operational with 44 destroyed and 158 damaged (up to 75 per cent by anti-tank guns) of which 86 were repaired. On 25 August alone the 11th Brigade lost 61 out of 88 tanks, of which 60 were burnt out.[78] The VVS lost 488 aircraft, 83 per cent (406) to enemy action in the air and on the ground during the whole campaign.

The Japanese also suffered severely and out of 75,738 men committed, some 17,700 were casualties (23 per cent), including 8,630 dead, while 202 Manchurians also died. In fact, the Twenty-Third Division lost 10,880 men, or 68 per cent of its total complement of 15,975 men, including 5,425 dead and missing, while a further 1,340 were taken ill. The Seventy-First Infantry suffered 93.5 per cent casualties! The Seventh Division lost 3,357 or 32.5 per cent of its 10,308 men including 1,506 dead. The ferocity of the struggle may be gauged by the fact that the prisoner-of-war exchange involved only 88 Japanese, 87 Russians and 50 Manchurians.[79] The shame of capture meant that many Japanese prisoners chose to remain with their captors, while two Japanese officer airmen were badgered into committing suicide, as were Ioki and Colonel Hasebe.

The air battles were the greatest the VVS had ever fought, sometimes involving more than 200 aircraft, flying 20,524 sorties of which 70 per cent (14,458) were in August and September. More than 90 per cent were mounted by fighter units which lost 317 aircraft to enemy action (a 1.7 per cent loss rate), while the bombers flew 2,015 and lost 88 (a 4.4 per cent loss rate). The Russians claimed 646 victories. Personnel losses were 174 dead (six on the ground) and 113 wounded. The Japanese, who claimed 1,260 victories (98 on the ground), lost 156 combat aircraft with 218 damaged while their personnel losses were 152 dead and 66 severely injured, two key fighter regiments losing 55 per cent and 70 per cent of their pilots, many of them combat veterans. The VVS had focused upon the battlefield, flying only 188 sorties (less than 1 per cent) against enemy reserves and communications, and expended 1,298 tonnes of bombs while the Japanese used 970 tonnes.[80]

Khalkin Gol was a crushing victory for the Red Army and a terrible shock for the Japanese Army, especially the Kwangtung Army. For the first time Tokyo had encountered a war of materiel for which its industry, the best in Asia, was totally inadequate and, for all the propaganda hype, it was clear that Japan was no match for the Soviet Union. An expansion of Japanese industry and forces began with the army paying greater attention to mechanised forces – the units which had performed so badly in Mongolia. For Stalin, the conclusion was a pleasing one: despite the Purges the Red Army had performed well, but there remained ominous signs that the perennial problem of inter-arm co-ordination remained exacerbated by the decimation of the officer corps and the future of mechanised forces remained unresolved.

In truth, Zhukov's use of armour was conventional in Red Army terms, with light mechanised forces making deep penetrations and the heavier armour largely supporting the infantry. The one clear lesson was that the tanks were too lightly armoured and their reliance upon petrol made them horrifyingly vulnerable to fire. What was especially remarkable about Zhukov's performance was that he achieved a spectacular result with limited resources; his divisions were under strength with very little artillery (the 36th Division deployed with only two field batteries) and limited armour, and it appears that up to a quarter of his tanks were unserviceable.[81] Voronov returned from Khalkin Gol to emphasise the need for greater artillery densities to break through enemy defences. He also recommended a more rapid change to mechanical, rather than equine, traction for the guns and these lessons would be underlined by the surge of activity in the West.[82]

ENDNOTES

1.   Erickson, *Command*, p.451 (hereafter Erickson).
2.   See Tarelton article.
3.   See Mil'bakh article *Repression in the Red Army in the Far East* (hereafter *East*).
4.   Erickson, pp.399–400, 414–415. Erickson p.451 claims OKDVA became the Far Eastern Red Banner Front in February 1937, but it appears that it did not become a front until June 1938.
5.   Shishkov pp.440–441.
6.   Erickson, p.397; Shishkov p.441.
7.   Erickson, pp.492–494. Most of the officers whose arrest Erickson links with Mekhlis's arrival were already undergoing interrogation.
8.   Mil'bakh, *East*; Montefiore pp.247, 617 f/n 13.
9.   Shishkov p.440 claims Konev was commanding 2nd Army but this did not occur until 4 September 1938 according to Mil'bakh, *Repression in the 57th Special Corps* (hereafter *57 Corps*). See also Rzheshevsky in Shukman p.94. Podlas was arrested on 22 April, but was reinstated and died commanding 57th Army during the abortive Kharkov campaign of 1942.
10. See Mil'bakh, *57 Corps*.
11. Shishkov p.441. The Japanese calculated Russian strength at 370,000. Coox, *Small War* p.22 (hereafter Coox).
12. Coox p.11 and article *The Lesser of Two Hells*; Montefiore p.221; Shishkov pp.439–440. The Japanese executed Lyushkov on 20 August 1945.

13. Coox pp.3–10; Shishkov pp.432–434.
14. Shishkov pp.442–443. For the Japanese background see Coox pp.12–24.
15. For the Lake Khasan/Changkufeng conflict see Coox; Erickson pp.494–498; Shishkov pp.432–468. For Soviet armour in this battle see Drig, *Battles in Lake Hasan* in his mechcorps.rkka.ru website. Shishkov p.447 states Lyushkov crossed the border near this sector but into Manchukuo. See Coox p.15. This might explain why the NKVD was so anxious about the sector.
16. Shishkov p.441. For border guards' experience see Tereshkin.
17. Shishov pp.447–448.
18. Coox, pp.83–94; Shishkov pp.449–451.
19. Coox pp.95–172, 187–204; Shishkov pp.451–453.
20. For the first Russian counter-attack see Coox pp.204–216; Shishkov pp.454–457.
21. Berazin would end the Second World War as Commandant of Berlin, but died there in a traffic accident in 1945. Coox p.393.
22. Russian counter-offensive Coox pp.217–286, 320–323; Shishkov pp.460–463. For diplomatic moves see Coox pp.297–319.
23. Coox p.333. Suetake claimed he selected the colourful Cho to lead the negotiations because he had not taken part in the fighting and had the cleanest uniform. Coox pp.332–334.
24. Russian losses. Kirovsheev pp.47–51; Shishkov p.472.
25. Coox pp.352–353.
26. Erickson p.497.
27. Volkogonov pp.327–328.
28. Montefiore p.247.
29. Habeck p.278.
30. Mil'bakh, *East*; Montefiore p.253; Pleshakov pp 32–33. The baby went into an orphanage and vanished.
31. Mil'bakh, *East*; Montefiore p.256.
32. Coox, Nomonhan pp.148–163 (hereafter Coox).
33. For the background see Coox pp.142–147; Shishkov pp.473–477, 482.
34. Vorotnikov pp.10–11.
35. For the Mongolian Purges see Montefiore p.204 f/n; Shagdariin Sandag; Shishov pp.477–478; Vorotnikov pp.10–11, 13–14; Kaplowski's article and websites *Stalinist Purges in Mongolia* and *Stalinist Repression in Mongolia*. Curiously, Shishov blames Beria, who was in Georgia at this time, for the Mongolian Purge, although the Georgian was certainly responsible for Amer's fate.
36. Based upon Kuznetsov, *The Soviet Military Advisors in Mongolia* and Mil'bakh, 57 Corps. Mil'bakh gives the 36th Division commander as Kombrig Emlin but no record of such an officer can be discovered.
37. Kondratyev p.5.
38. For the Red forces in Mongolia see Kondratyev pp.5–7. RKKA in World War II website, 'Battles 1938–1940, Khalkin-Gol Battle (Nomonhan Incident).'
39. Coox pp.167–192.
40. Coox pp.175–192; Shishov pp.478–480, 482–483.
41. Shishkov pp.480–481 and RKKA in World War II. According to Novikov, Richard Sorge, Moscow's top agent in Tokyo reported a build-up in western Manchukuo after a tip from a British Embassy contact.
42. Coox pp.192–200; Shishkov pp.482–483.
43. Coox pp.200–203; Shishkov pp.482–486.
44. Coox pp.203–250; Erickson pp.518–519; Vorotnikov pp.14–15, 18; RKKA in World War II.
45. Coox pp.250–255, 257–262. Ueda lost his leg in Shanghai to an assassin's bomb.
46. Coox pp.255, 262–264; Erickson p.519.
47. Zhukov pp.161–162.
48. Shishkov pp.490–492; Vorotnikov pp.22, 24–29; Zhukov pp.162–163. Vorotnikov became Zhukov's aide and remained close to him until Zhukov's death, his account of Khalkin Gol providing much needed personal information to give this fearsome leader a human perspective. Feklenko would hold important roles in the armoured forces fighting the Germans.

49. For May air battles Kondratyev pp.6-10; Shishkov pp.486-487. Kondratyev provides the most comprehensive account of air operations over Khalkin Gol incorporating Sekigawa's articles.
50. For the June air battles Coox pp.256-257, 266-269, 273-278; Kondratyev pp.10-17; Shishkov pp.487- 489, 492.
51. Vorotnikov p.22.
52. Op. cit. p.78.
53. Shishkov p.493.
54. For the July battles see Coox pp.284-489, 490-548, 640-641 f/n 21; Erickson pp.520-521; Kondratyev pp.18-26; Shishkov pp.492-501; Vorotnikov pp.39-53, 67-68; Zhukov pp.165-168; Novikov.
55. Data from website: rkkaww2.armchairgeneral.com.
56. Vorotnikov p.33.
57. Op. cit. p.46.
58. Shishkov p.500, Anmekary website article and Drig's Mechanizirovannieye Korpusa entry on mechcorps.rkka.ru website, as well as Crowfoot's divisional histories. In August-September two light armoured tank brigades were created in the east.
59. Shishov p.499. The Khalkin-Gol Battle in rkkaww2.armchairgeneral website.
60. Mil'bakh, *Red Army Artillery… on the Khalkin-Gol* (hereafter *Artillery*). Between 12 July and 6 August the Red Army lost 64 guns including six 152 mm, twenty-six 122 mm, four 107 mm, sixteen 76 mm and 12 anti-tank guns.
61. For early August see Coox pp.549-571, 573-590, 660 f/n 32 & 35; Erickson pp.532-534; Kondratyev pp.26-29; Shishkov pp.503-504; Vorotnikov pp.69-81, 84-85, 93-94; Novikov.
62. Vorotnikov pp.36, 55-57, 90-91, 183-184. Potapov would command 5th Army with distinction during the 1941 frontier battles with Fedyuninsky as one of his corps commanders. Potapov was captured but was regarded as a hero and escaped Stalin's vengeance.
63. Shishkov pp.500; Vorotnikov pp.50, 53. It is unclear when Kulik's committee arrived, but it appears to have been around 11-12 July.
64. Vorotnikov pp.30-31
65. Tank strength from rkkaww2.armchairgeneral.com website.
66. Mil'bakh, *Artillery*.
67. For artillery see rkkaww2.armchairgeneral.com website.
68. Vorotnikov pp.81, 92. Apparently Zhukov wore spurs even when he was driven.
69. Vorotnikov p.82 suggests Shevnikov was reduced to the ranks and fought in a tank crew.
70. The Russians estimated Japanese air strength in early July at 312 aircraft.
71. Vorotnikov p.95.
72. For Zhukov's offensive see Coox pp.663-778; Erickson pp.534-537; Kondratyev pp.26-29, 29, 31-38; Shishkov pp.504-511; Vorotnikov pp.69-105; Zhukov pp.168-176.
73. Kondratyev p.31.
74. For the negotiations see Coox pp.885-913.
75. Vorotnikov p.186.
76. Kirovsheev pp.51-57. Shishkov p.515 says 9,703 dead.
77. Mil'bakh, *Artillery*.
78. Tank loss date from Soviet Losses in the Khalkin-Gol Battle, see rkkaww2.armchairgeneral.com website.
79. For casualties see Coox pp.914-979, Appendices J-L.
80. Air force data from Kondratyev pp.40, 52.
81. Tank data extrapolated from tank brigade loss data in rkkaww2.armchairgeneral.com website.
82. Voronov p.132.

CHAPTER THREE

BLOWS TO THE WEST

'Watch out, bad times are coming...'
COMMENT BY SOLDIER OF THE UKRAINIAN FRONT TO POLISH CIVILIANS, SEPTEMBER 1939

S TALIN'S need to wind down the Far Eastern conflict reflected the alarming success of Nazi Germany's armoured spearheads which were rushing towards the Soviet border following one of the most striking volte-faces in modern political history. Ironically, the Panzer Divisions' success in 1940 came as the Red Army conservatives finally achieved the mechanised forces they had always sought.

Beria's appointment made the Purges more selective and efficient: indeed the 6th Tank Brigade, which had supported Zhukov's Southern Group at Khalkin Gol, saw its commissar, Brigkom Stepan Bondarenko, arrested and executed by the end of the year.[1] The most prominent victim was Navy Minister Komandarm I Rank Mikhail Frinovsky who was arrested on 6 April 1939 and shot on 4 February 1940. The head of VVS training, Komkor Aleksandr Todovsky was arrested in May 1939 but later released, as was the head of the Trans-Caucasus District supply network, Komdiv Grigorii Zusmanovich, who would be captured holding a similar position with 6th Army during the Battle of Kharkov in May 1942 and would die in German captivity. The only other European Komdiv to fall was A.G. Orlov, head of the Military Academy's foreign language facility, who was arrested on 30 April 1939 and shot within a year. Three European Kombrigs were arrested, one being shot and the others dying in labour camps.

In fact Beria, having executed 413 senior officers condemned by his predecessor between 24 February and 16 March 1939, suggested ending the Purge because there was no one left. Stalin responded: 'I think we're well and truly rid of the opposition millstone.' Yet on 9 November 1939 Mekhlis sought more arrests in the army 'for lack of revolutionary loyalty'. Stalin described the officers' 'errors' as due to misunderstandings and replied to Mekhlis: 'I propose to limit ourselves to an official reprimand.'[2]

Yet the NKVD was relentless and in March 1939 it re-arrested Korkom Ivan Petukhov, head of the Defence Ministry secretariat, barely a month after he was released following a seven-month incarceration. He would die in a labour camp two years later, as did Korkom Martin Apse, the Trans-Caucasus District commissar. Beria also continued Ezhov's work of eliminating the leadership of the Red Army's intelligence service including Divkom Pavel Kolosov, the acting Operations Chief who remained in a labour camp until 1944 but who rejoined the army in 1955, as well as department heads Brigkom Arto Artashes and Vladimir Volya, the latter being shot in March 1940, while Brigkom Mark Shneiderman, an operative in Europe, America and Asia, was arrested in March 1939 and not released until December 1946. Another six Divkoms, including M.N. Polyakov of the Kiev District, were removed. Two of them were shot and another died in a labour camp, while another Brigkom was arrested in April 1939 and shot a year later. Nevertheless, the hurricane of the Purges was blowing itself out and within the army there was a sign of some easing. Nikitin, who was recalled from Mongolia in 1937, was cleared and became commander of the Western District's 6th Cavalry Division.

Voroshilov and Kulik continued to exert their malign conservative influence, the latter remaining as head of the Main Artillery Directorate and, therefore, weapons development. His arrogant incompetence would have a significant impact upon the Red Army; he opposed the development of sub-machine guns, the Katyusha multiple rocket launcher and land mines. In a society where abuse of subordinates was the norm, Kulik was notorious, being considered even by his colleagues as a 'murderous buffoon'. His command style, probably modelled on Stalin's, was to order a course of action and then shout 'Jail or Medal!' at the unfortunate, meaning promotion and decorations for the successful, the Gulag for the unsuccessful.

The new leadership busied itself redrafting Red Army doctrine which appeared in December 1939 as document PU 39. Although there were obvious similarities with its predecessor, this was a very different document, literally reflecting the Party line. Whereas PU 36 (see Chapter One) had been divided into chapters on General Principles, Operational and Material Support for Combat Operations, Political Work, Principles of Command, Encounter Battles, Offensive, Defensive, Night, Winter and Special Condition Battles, Troop Movements and Troop Accommodation/Security, the new doctrine followed General Principles with Army Organisation and then featured a chapter on Political Work. Army Management, Operational and Maintenance Support for Combat Operations, Offensive, Counter-Attack and Defensive Battle chapters were followed by chapters on Winter, Special Conditions then two on co-operation with Riverine and Fleet forces while the last two dealt with Army Movement and, as with PU 36, Troop Accommodation as well as Security.

The difference between the two appears from the opening chapter: 17 paragraphs in PU 36 and 23 in PU 39, replacing concise concepts with political rhetoric. Where PU 36 begins to outline the principles in the second paragraph,

PU 39 begins only on the 12th and the overall succinct precision of the original is replaced by wordy generalisations and exhortations, although some paragraphs, such as No 16/PU 36 on the economic use of ammunition, appear to be repeated in No 20/PU 39. What is missing from the first chapter of PU 39 is any definition of the advantages and the roles of tanks, although the same may also be said of both infantry and artillery. Chapter Seven, dealing with Offensive Battles (including night attacks) in 92 paragraphs (compared with 61) provides far greater detail than its predecessor and emphasises repeatedly combined arms operations.

Chapter Two stated that the infantry was the prime arm, deciding the battle in co-operation with other arms (Paragraph 25), while the basic role of the tank was as direct support of the infantry. However, once the enemy had been defeated, tanks could be used for the deeper attack, destroying enemy artillery, staffs and headquarters: 'In this case they can play the decisive role in environment and destruction of enemy (Paragraph 27).' This paragraph notes that armour could be used for independent operations in large groups, together with motorised infantry and artillery with aviation support. Yet this was no return to the glory days of Tukhachevskii's vision of mechanised warfare, but rather a squaring of the circle with advances achieved by task forces based upon augmented motorised rifle and cavalry divisions.

The Purges had taken Tukhachevskii's supporters, including the Motor-Mechanised Directorate head, Komandarm II Rank Khalepskii, who was arrested on 13 November 1937 and shot on 29 July 1938. There were temporary successors until Pavlov's appointment in October 1938.[3] Shot with Khalepskii was Central-Asia District commander, Komkor Ivan Gryaznov, the directorate's former deputy director, who had been arrested five months earlier.[4] Pavlov himself noted in November 1938 that 62 members had been arrested that year alone and that in July, against an establishment of 196 men, leaving only 80 and despite 'extraordinary' efforts to plug the gap, his directorate was only 73 per cent of establishment. Only one of the original tank brigade commanders was still in the post; the remainder, as well as all the tank corps commanders and 80 per cent of tank battalion commanders, had been 'relieved'.[5]

Mikhail Tukhachevskii was the leading military radical in the Red Army espousing the causes of large mechanised and airborne forces. The failure of the Red Army to master the problems of large mechanised forces would be the prime reason that would cost the music-loving Marshal his life.

The discussion of mechanised doctrine became a free-for-all, with those considering emulating Tukhachevskii's ideas restricted by fear of the NKVD. Kulik's friend, Pavlov, was a conservative, reinforced by his experiences in Spain, and he railed against ideas that tanks were omnipotent and capable of independent action, a concept he described as 'harmful'.[6] At a meeting of the Narodnom Komissariate Oborony (Main Military Council) between 21-29 November, Pavlov proposed stripping the tank corps of its motorised rifle brigades and engineers and giving the infantry more tank units. The first idea was supported by Voroshilov but opposed by Shaposhnikov, who also opposed Pavlov's proposals for shackling tank movement to ensure infantry and artillery support. There was general agreement with Voroshilov that tanks could no longer be divided into infantry support and breakthrough groups, yet he refused to endorse the idea that tanks should simply accompany the infantry. He believed that having invested so much in mechanised units, the Soviet Union needed to find the best way of using them.[7]

Voroshilov's orders on Red Army training, published on 11 December 1938, merely stated that mechanised formations should improve co-operation with other arms including the VVS, something that was qualified by the main text book on armoured forces, *Avtobronetankovye Voiska*, which appeared about the same time. This publication emphasised close co-operation between tanks and infantry, which would direct the armour, although armoured groups could be used to 'beat up' the enemy rear provided they were not too far from the riflemen.[8] Within six months the leash on the tanks had been pulled tighter with the new armoured forces text book, *Broetankovye Voiska* of July 1939 which emphasised infantry support aided by the artillery. There was no mention of breakthrough groups and only passing mention of raiding the enemy rear, although the tanks were permitted to go slightly ahead of the riflemen, but not too far for fear of annihilation by enemy artillery and anti-tank guns. They might even be permitted to strike deeper into enemy territory if the defences were weak or the terrain could be exploited.[9]

A report of 16 November 1939 to Pavlov on the performance of armour at Khalkin Gol was a masterpiece of deducing the 'right' results. It focused on the extemporised tank counter-attacks upon the Japanese bridgehead in July noting that, unsupported or weakly supported, such counter-attacks had failed to destroy the enemy defences, suffered heavy losses and were unable to hold ground. But 6th Mechanised Brigade's attack with strong infantry and artillery support had been successful. Curiously, the report did not mention the fact that the mechanised forces had isolated the main Japanese forces for defeat in detail.[10]

In August 1939 Kulik was appointed head of a commission to investigate the future of armoured forces, with the purge-long debate brought to a head by the tactical and supply weaknesses shown at Lake Khasan. For three weeks the commission reviewed armoured organisation and, while it confirmed the view that mechanised units should work closely in a combined arms framework, it rejected Pavlov's call to disband the tank corps. They would be retained to support breakthroughs with infantry and cavalry, although if the enemy was routed, they might act independently. Yet simultaneously they were to be emasculated with the removal of rifle-machine gun brigades and rifle-machine gun battalions of the tank brigades.

The commission opted for the development of two types of tank brigade; one for infantry support and the other for independent operations. The Main Military Council discussed the report in November and concluded that operations in Poland had '...demonstrated the difficulty of command and control during operations of tank corps as well as their cumbersome size' and that '...separate tank brigades operated better and were more mobile.'[11] Therefore, there was no requirement for tanks corps, and Defence Ministry directive No 4/2/54008 of 7 December 1939 ordered their disbandment beginning with 25th Tank Corps (2 January), followed by the 15th Tank Corps (9 January), 20th Tank Corps (15 January) and 10th Tank Corps (17 January), the last delayed because of operations in Finland. The 20th Corps was reorganised into 65th and 109th Motorised Rifle Divisions, but the others were reduced simply to tank brigades, creating a total of 54 tank brigades and 10 companies (see Table 3-1 for details of the expansion of the Red Army). The tank corps would be replaced by motorised rifle divisions which might be augmented with armour to become mechanised divisions, and on 21 November it was decided to create up to 15 motorised divisions by the first half of 1941 each with 275 tanks.[12]

Table 3-1: Red Army expansion June 1938 – September 1939

Formation	1 June 1938	1 September 1939
Rifle corps	27	25
Regular rifle divisions	71	96
Territorial rifle divisions	35	-
Motorised rifle divisions	-	1
Cavalry corps	7	7
Cavalry divisions	32	30
Rifle brigades	-	5
Tank corps	4	4
Tank brigades	26	38
Strength	1,513,000	1,520,000

Source: Glantz, *Soviet Mobilisation in Peace and War*, Table 2.

The stubborn determination to keep the tanks reined to the infantry indicated the malign influence of Voroshilov, Kulik and Pavlov who could not have been ignorant of the dramatic events developing upon Europe's battlefields, events in which they participated following one of the most remarkable somersaults in diplomatic history. In the aftermath of the Munich Crisis, Stalin began re-evaluating his diplomatic and strategic options with Germany.

In the late 1920s and early 1930s the Soviet Union, under Jewish Foreign Minister Maksim Litvinov, sought to avoid military conflict through diplomatic efforts and in February 1929 the Litvinov Pact saw the Soviet Union, Estonia, Latvia, Poland and Rumania promise not to use force to settle disputes. Litvinov, one of the first Central Committee members to wear a suit, sought good relations with Great Britain (his wife was English) and France as the foundation for collective security against the rising power of Germany, persuaded Washington to recognise the Soviet Union in 1933, and the following year he took the Soviet Union into the League of Nations. But the profound suspicion of the Soviet Union among the Establishments and many voters in Western Europe, together with fear of war, meant Litvinov was unable to exploit his diplomatic successes.

Munich underlined this, although the refusal of conservative, Catholic and nationalistic Poland to allow the Red Army to cross its territory in order to support the Czechs proved the insurmountable hurdle. Hopes of the post-Munich Pact peace which existed at the beginning of 1939 dissipated on 15 March when the Germans occupied the remainder of the Czech Republic (the eastern half, Slovakia, having seceded the previous day) and a week later Berlin forced Lithuania to cede the port of Klaipeda (Memel).

Yet the Western Powers, aware of German economic weaknesses, remained optimistic and in March 1939 Chamberlain's government began a deterrent policy designed to prevent, or at least delay, war – buying time until military expenditure brought Berlin's economy to the verge of collapse and leading to the overthrow of the Nazi regime. Britain and France guaranteed the independence of Poland, Belgium, Rumania, Greece, and Turkey and a week later London and Warsaw agreed in principle to turn that guarantee into a military alliance. This alliance, or mutual assistance treaty, was regarded by London merely as a diplomatic marker, but on 28 April Hitler seized on the earlier agreement to denounce both the 1934 German-Polish Non-Aggression Pact and the 1935 Anglo-German Naval Agreement.

German propaganda was now railing against Poland, ostensibly over the port of Danzig (Gdansk), an autonomous German city under overall Polish control at the end of a finger of Polish territory which divided East and West Prussia. Many Germans loathed the Poles for taking Second Reich (Imperial Germany) territory at the end of the Great War and Hitler regarded this as a pretext for a war which would annihilate the Polish nation. London, which was slow to recognise the scale of Hitler's plan, urged Warsaw to concede Danzig to prevent a war from flaring up, but despite overt and covert pressure, the Poles refused while Berlin misinterpreted the British actions as groundwork for another Munich-style sell-out. To further his master's ambitions, German Foreign Minister Joachim von Ribbentrop undermined efforts to reach a diplomatic solution, recalling the German Ambassador to Warsaw and refusing to meet the Polish Ambassador, with Polish obstinacy on concessions playing further into his hands.

The German tide was clearly lapping eastwards as Stalin pondered his options in the great 'poker game' as he described it.[13] As early as 1934 he had hinted at an agreement with Hitler despite the mutual antipathy between Nazi Germany and the Soviet Union. There are indications he was seeking some form of agreement with Hitler through low-level (and thus deniable) approaches throughout the 1930s, with the possibility of a world war and an Allied naval blockade of Germany presenting him an opportunity. Hitler feared a blockade could strangle the Third Reich, as it had the Second Reich; he wanted food and raw materials from eastern Europe, while Stalin wanted technology for the third Five Year Plan, which began in 1938, and in March trade talks provided the pretext for negotiations.

Stalin had publicly attacked Litvinov, but the Foreign Minister bravely challenged him and 'The Boss' backed down, also vetoing Beria's plan to murder the Litvinovs in a fake car accident. But he did decide to replace Litvinov and on the night of 3/4 May, the NKVD surrounded the ministry, which was neighbour to Lubianka. Litvinov was visited by Molotov, Beria and Malenkov who informed him he had been sacked.[14] Litvinov's dismissal and replacement by Molotov signalled a significant change in Soviet foreign policy, as Litvinov later observed: 'Do you really think that I was the right person to sign a treaty with Hitler?'

Beria soon arrested many of Litvinov's closest workers, none of whom provided incriminating 'evidence' and, after the German invasion, Litvinov would be appointed deputy Foreign Minister and Ambassador to the United States where he secured agreements on lease-lend material. Molotov himself, like most of the Soviet leadership, was hard-working, but this was a new type of responsibility and he often went into blind rages against staff.

As German and Russian negotiators danced their diplomatic minuet, Stalin kept open his options as Britain and France continued their policy of containing Hitler by seeking a military agreement with the Soviet Union. In an exchange for a military agreement, Stalin wished for a free hand in the Baltic States to prevent German 'indirect aggression'. Estonia and Latvia were pressured by Germany into signing 'friendship pacts' during June, but this aroused Allied fears that Moscow was seeking to intervene in the Baltic States and Finland. By mid-July political negotiations between the Soviets and the Western Powers had stalled, but on the 25th the Allies accepted the Soviet proposal to send a military delegation – although it took three weeks to arrive because the international situation was too delicate to send a warship, forcing the delegation to sail in a liner.

The Allies' much maligned representatives had distinguished war records. Admiral Sir Reginald Aylmer Ranfurly Plunkett-Ernle-Erle-Drax (often referred to as Reginald Plunkett or Drax) was an experienced officer who had been the first post-war director of the Naval Staff College and he held medium-level positions including Commander-in-Chief, Plymouth. In 1939 he would become the first Commander-in-Chief, The Nore, until he reached mandatory retirement age, whereupon he became a convoy commander. General Joseph Edouard Doumenc was a motor transport specialist who had organised the vehicles supplying Pétain's army at Verdun, and he later helped to create France's tank force. After the Great War he worked in North Africa, rising slowly in the ranks to become a member of the Conseil Supérieur de la Guerre in 1938. He would later become head of France's anti-aircraft forces and was accidentally killed in the Alps in 1948.

The delegation lacked detailed knowledge of Allied plans, forcing it to refer frequently to London and Paris and preventing it from concluding a military treaty.[15] By contrast, the Soviet delegation was on its home ground and consisted of Voroshilov, Shaposhnikov with his deputy, Komkor Ivan Smorodinov, VVS commander Loktionov, and former Pacific Fleet commander, now Navy Minister Flag Officer II Rank Nikolai Kuznetsov. Shaposhnikov informed his guests that the Soviet Union would deploy 120 rifle divisions and 16 cavalry divisions, supported by up to 5,000 heavy and medium guns, up to 10,000 tanks and up to 5,500 fighters and bombers. When asked what it would deploy, Major General Thomas Heywood (the military attaché to France) said Britain would provide a mechanised division and five infantry divisions, a figure Moscow regarded as ridiculous. Yet once again, despite every effort by the British and French, it was the refusal of the Poles to allow the Red Army onto their soil which ultimately undermined the Allied effort and Stalin now considered the unthinkable – an agreement with Nazi Germany – although British Foreign Minister Lord Halifax had warned the Cabinet of the possibility in May.

By early August the planned German-Soviet economic agreement was almost complete and negotiations turned towards political issues which rapidly became a non-aggression treaty. The trade agreement was signed on 19 August and two days later Berlin assured Moscow it would approve secret protocols to the proposed non-aggression pact, placing Poland east of the Vistula River, Latvia, Estonia, Finland, and Rumania's province of Bessarabia within the Soviet Union's sphere of influence. The Russians promptly suspended military talks with the British and French as Stalin indicated he would sign the agreement and he then invited Ribbentrop to Moscow.[16]

Ribbentrop, the Anglophobic former Ambassador to Great Britain, was advising Hitler that Britain would not go to war over Poland and was boosted by the deciphering of British diplomatic codes which showed London urging Warsaw to make concessions. Similar sources showed the British military attaché to Warsaw arguing that his country could not save Poland if Germany attacked because the Poles could hold out only with Russian military support. Upon receiving Stalin's message, Hitler ordered the Wehrmacht to mobilise for a campaign solely against Poland believing that if he could keep Moscow neutral then he could avoid world war which, in turn, would undermine British expressions of support for Warsaw.

Unlike his rivals, Ribbentrop promptly flew out to Moscow on 23 August using Hitler's personal Focke-Wulf Condor four-engined transport aircraft and was surprised to be met by Stalin, who participated in the talks. Originally Germany proposed that only northern Latvia, to the river Daugava (also known as the Western Dvinsk or the Düna), would be in the Soviet sphere of influence. But this sole obstacle was overcome when Hitler conceded the whole country to Stalin, and within 13 hours the details of the non-aggression pact had been worked out.

The 10-year pact included the provision of neutrality if either went to war against a third power and pledged that neither would join an organisation 'which is directly or indirectly aimed at the other', although Germany made no effort to leave the anti-Soviet Anti-Comintern Pact signed with Japan in November 1936 and joined a year later by Italy. More important were the Secret Protocols, which divided a conquered Poland placing the eastern part (east of the rivers Pisa, Narev, Vistula and San) within the Soviet sphere of influence, together with Finland, Estonia and Latvia. Germany also pledged not to interfere with the Soviet Union if it decided to reoccupy the Rumanian province of Bessarabia. Some 200,000 square kilometres of Poland, inhabited by 13.5 million people, were to come under Russian influence, together with the former western Belorussia and Western Ukraine, areas where the Poles formed 40 per cent of the population, Ukrainians 34 per cent and Belorussians 9 per cent.[17] These territories had been taken by the Poles during the Polish-Soviet War (1919-1920), which had poisoned relations between Stalin and Tukhachevskii, and had been ceded by the Soviet Union in the Treaty of Riga in 1921. The new border agreed between Berlin and Moscow was essentially that proposed by Lord Curzon in 1919 as Poland's eastern border, a proposal rejected by Lenin's government.

Upon hearing of the signing, Hitler promptly set 26 August as the date for the offensive on Poland. He told a meeting of Wehrmacht commanders that Britain and France would not go to war over the issue, adding: 'My only fear is that at the last moment some Schweinhund will make a proposal for mediation'. Göring was less optimistic and frantically tried some backdoor diplomacy in a vain attempt to avoid war, especially when London signed a mutual assistance treaty with Warsaw on 25 August. But it was too late to save the Anglo-French policy, especially in the Balkans where Turkey, which would have had to underwrite the policy, recognised that it was fatally flawed without Soviet support and refused to make any military commitment.

Nevertheless, London's actions and Mussolini's refusal to join Germany in military action did give Hitler time to reflect and he postponed the invasion for nearly a week to 1 September. On 30 August Berlin issued an ultimatum, the demands of which were made deliberately impossible to meet. When Ribbentrop refused to give the British Ambassador, Sir Neville Henderson, a copy of those demands that night, the two almost came to blows as the scales fell from the eyes of the shocked British diplomat. Following incidents engineered by the SS on the border with Poland, Germany went to war rejecting Mussolini's offer of mediation based upon a ceasefire. London and France immediately issued an ultimatum demanding German withdrawal from Poland and when this did not occur, they declared war on 3 September, leading a visibly shocked Hitler to ask Ribbentrop: 'Now what?' But by then, of course, the die was cast.

Armed forces reflect their societies and Poland's was no different. The rural economy and conservative nature of the nation shaped an army which depended upon landline communications, moved largely by train, and on muscle power, human and equine, with little motorisation and even less armour, together with an air force which at one time foreswore bombers! Strategic planning until 1936 had focused on a war with the Soviet Union and her other Slavic neighbours, and made no provision for the growing threat of strategic envelopment after March 1939. As the scale of the threat became apparent, Warsaw adopted a defensive posture for 'Plan West' (Zachód) which was underwritten by promises of its old ally, France, to begin an offensive on Germany's western defences – although France would take 21 days to mobilise and another 17 before the Wehrmacht faced a serious threat there.

The Polish leadership believed the Franco–British ultimatum alone would cause an uprising to overthrow the Nazi regime, but a fatal miscalculation was the assumption that the war would escalate in stages, beginning with an assault to take Danzig/Gdansk. Thus when mobilisation was announced on 29 August to begin the following day, it was delayed under intense Franco-British diplomatic pressure for 24 hours and consequently nearly a third of Poland's infantry battalions (139 out of 455) had not been mobilised when the Germans attacked. By contrast both neutral Belgium and the Netherlands, which faced less of a threat, mobilised their forces on 23 August and 28 August respectively.[18]

Four active divisions and two brigades had been mobilised on 23 March while the Polish reservist motorised brigade was assembled for 'exercises'. On 23 August six of the eight Corps Area Commands (Dowództwo Okręgu Korpusu – DOK) alerted their active units (15 divisions and seven brigades) and the two in the southeast of the country followed suit four days later. But by the end of the month shortages of motor transport and rolling stock crippled movement and by 1 September only 21 infantry divisions (including two reserve) and 12 brigades were under the operational command of the seven corps-sized 'armies' ready to defend the frontiers; four divisions were assembling near the frontiers or being railed to them, while 14 divisions (including six reserve) were still assembling. The army was augmented by the local territorial National Defence units (Obrona Narodowa – ON), mostly consisting of trained reservists under reservist leadership but, in reality, no more than poorly armed infantry, and the Border Protection Corps (Korpus Ochrony Pogranicza – KOP), most of whose lightly armed battalions were along the eastern border.

The Poles decided to defend the whole of their frontier rather than concentrating behind one of the great natural river barriers which divided the country and a third of their forces were in or around the Polish Corridor. 'Plan West' anticipated a slow withdrawal behind these barriers but it remained a general concept and when detailed planning work did begin on 4 March 1939, it focused only on the initial stages of the conflict. The Poles believed they could fight on for six months, twice their allies' estimates, but it was expected that it would be a slow moving, conventional struggle in which the Poles would exploit their frontier fortifications.

Within hours the German invasion tore up the plans of London, Paris and Warsaw due to two factors no one had considered: the Luftwaffe and what the Wehrmacht described as 'Mobildivisionen'. Since 1934, the Luftwaffe had been shaped to strike throughout the enemy's 'Operational' depth and while failing to annihilate the Polish Air Force, it set to with a will, using its bombers to strike railways, roads, communications centres, barracks and supply dumps. With landlines cut, the Polish High Command quickly lost touch with its 'armies' at the front and with their roads and railways suffering a rain of bombs, the movement of men and supplies was slowed to an uncertain trickle.

The Mobildivisionen (comprising Panzer, Leicht Panzer and Motorisiert formations) exploited this situation, striking deep into Polish territory, outflanking major centres of resistance and aiming for communications hubs, the loss of which further disrupted Polish resistance. The relationship between the two arms was symbiotic with each assisting the other so that within a week German spearheads had advanced up to 225 kilometres to the banks of the Vistula and the San, isolating Warsaw and thousands of troops. The capital came under attack from 9 September and the following day the Polish Commander-in-Chief, Marshal Edward Rydz-Smigly, ordered a retreat south-east, hoping to establish a bridgehead on the Rumanian frontier. Behind the German lines however, there was anarchy as large numbers of Polish troops sought escape or launched brave, but futile, attacks.[19]

Berlin had expected the Red Army to join the fray almost immediately; on 1 September the Luftwaffe sought to use Minsk Radio as a navigation beacon, while the following day a delegation of five Soviet officers secretly arrived in Berlin to co-ordinate operations with the Wehrmacht.[20] Fearing the unravelling of his agreement if German troops entered eastern Poland, Ribbentrop urged the German Ambassador in Moscow to alert Molotov in a hope that the unsubtle hint would prod the Red Army into moving. Stalin's sloth was partly due to his own sense of caution because there was the prospect that if the Red Army and the Wehrmacht did make contact in Poland they would come to blows, snaring the Soviet Union into a war the pact was supposed to avoid. Only on 9 September did Molotov respond to confirm the Red Army's imminent move into eastern Poland as Moscow became alarmed by the speed of the German advance which was entering Polish territory allocated to the Soviet Union. Yet Stalin also feared the threat of a two-front war with Japan and only with the Nomonhan Incident ceasefire did these fears disappear.

On 2 September it was decided to expand the Red Army from 96 to 173 rifle divisions and add more Rezerv Glavnogo Komandovaniya-RGK (Main Command Reserve) artillery regiments.[21] The following day Voroshilov ordered that the Belorussia, Kiev, Leningrad, Moscow, Kharkov, Orel and Kalinin Districts be brought to combat readiness, retaining for a month 1937 class conscripts who were scheduled to return home on 20 September. All leave was cancelled to retain

310,632 men while 26,014 specialists were called up. Three days later districts were ordered to conduct 'large-scale training exercises' – a secret mobilisation – but these were poorly organised and took some districts up to three days to complete.

A premature German report on the fall of Warsaw led Molotov, Voroshilov and Shaposhnikov to draft orders on 9 September for the Belorussian and Kiev Districts to begin a secret concentration on Poland's frontier with a view to an attack two days later; Molotov activated the Vitebsk, Brobruisk and Minsk Army Groups (later 3rd, 4th and 11th Armies) and Shaposhnikov the Zhitomir, Vinnitsa and Kamenets-Podolski Army Groups (subsequently redesignated Northern, Eastern and Southern) which later became the 5th, 6th and 12th Armies respectively.[22] In addition, the Moscow District created a 10th Army which had arrived at the frontier by 15 September just as the Ukrainian District activated the Odessa Army Group (later 13th Army). The long-range bomber force (AON 1, 2, 3) moved to western airfields. Simultaneously, Molotov also ordered the regional administrations to provide the Red Army with motor vehicles, horses and carts for transport, while on the evening of 12 September the railways were placed under control to support the build-up.[23]

On 11 September the two districts became the Belorussian and Ukrainian Fronts under Komandarm II Rank Mikhail Kovalev and Timoshenko respectively, with their boundary being the river Pripyat and the surrounding marshes, also known as the Polesie Swamps. However, their planned advances were to be mirror images; Kovalev's Front contracted because of neutral Latvia and Lithuania while Timoshenko's expanded to give him responsibility for two thirds of Russian-occupied Poland, the demarcation line to be reached by 14 September. Kovalev's right would march through the great, heavily forested plain of the Naliboki Wilderness (Puszcza Nalibocka), the flank secured by Komkor Vasilii Kuznetsov's 3rd Army advancing from Polotsk which would cut the Polotsk-Lida railway near the border then move down the river Dzisna, along the Lithuanian border. Kovalev's advance would assist Komkor Nikifor Medvedev's 11th Army thrusting from Minsk, taking Vilna and Lida in order to secure the northern bank of the Nieman. Komkor Ivan Boldin's Cavalry-Mechanised Group (followed by Komkor Ivan Zakharin's 10th Army) would secure the southern bank of the river, bypassing Baranowicze (Baranovichi) to advance along the Minsk-Bialystok railway to Grodno, while Komdiv Vasilii Chuikov's 4th Army south of the railway would move through the northern edge of the Pripyat Marshes and take the great fortress city of Brześć nad Bugiem (Brest-Litovsk or Brześć Litewski).

Timoshenko's 36th Rifle Corps would shield his right, as it moved through the Pripyat Marshes together with Komdiv Ivan Sovetnikov's 5th Army which would operate north of the Avratynsk Hills, taking Rovno and Dubno. Sovetnikov would then drive westwards to Luck (Lutsk). Komkor Filip Golikov's 6th Army would take south-eastern Poland, the former Austrian province of Galicia and the most highly developed region in the east of the country, sweeping the hills and taking Lwow (Lvov or Lemberg), while Komandarm II Rank Ivan Tyuleniev's 12th Army would try to prevent Polish forces escaping into Rumania and would advance westwards through Tarnopol and Stanislawow (Stanislau) and then to Stryj to cut the rail links.

But the mobilisation (publicly revealed on 11 September) encountered many problems. Lacking experienced units, the two districts, hastily formed during the second half of August 1939, numbered 17 rifle divisions created from regiments of existing divisions, as well as three light tank brigades – but they were not ready by mid-September. The imminent harvest led the civil authorities to delay transferring vehicles, many of which, in any case, were worn out due to lack of maintenance. Even the mechanised forces had just half their establishment; on 11 September the 25th Tank Corps had only 373 trucks instead of 812, and 10 tractors out of 230. Poor maintenance and a chronic shortage of spares meant that tanks frequently broke down and tank brigades had to be deployed by rail. But the rail system had lost too many key staff to the Purges and could not cope. Troops often waited hours to embark on- or disembark from trains. In the Kiev District the 44th Rifle Division's artillery and the 23rd Corps Artillery Regiment failed to arrive in time, as did the 10th Tank Brigade which had only 70 T-28s, instead of 98, and it proved impossible to bring down 10th Tank Corps from the Leningrad District. The few roads leading to the front saw massive jams due to inadequate traffic control which drivers often ignored.

These problems forced the Red Army to attack in echelon with the first consisting of 617,588 men, 4,733 tanks (1,308 or more than 27 per cent with rifle and cavalry divisions), 4,959 guns and 3,298 aircraft (see Table 3-2) organised into 16 cavalry and 39 rifle divisions, two tank corps and 11 tank brigades – a force more than adequate to crush the Polish defenders who were outnumbered at least 10:1. These forces were steadily expanded and by early October they constituted 2,421,300 men, 6,096 tanks, 5,467 guns, and 3,727 aircraft. They were organised into 60 rifle divisions, 13 cavalry divisions, two tank corps and 18 tank brigades, including 15 RGK artillery regiments (360 heavy and medium guns) of which Timoshenko would receive the lion's share (11 regiments). Stalin was a man who considered all the options and this massive force was clearly intended less to conquer eastern Poland and more to insure that the conquered territory remained in Russian hands. However, when he issued his orders for an offensive on 12 September his forces were simply not ready; Timoshenko, for example, had a second echelon of some 535,000 men, 500 tanks, and 3,500 guns.

While commissars were appointed on 11 September to supervise the movement of supplies and to release 500 tonnes of coal for mobilisation purposes, the Front orders were not distributed because Moscow learned the truth about Warsaw as the French began probing the West Wall in the semblance of an offensive. This, combined with the mobilisation problems, as well as continued negotiations with the Japanese, led the Kremlin to postpone the offensive into Poland until the Far East was secure. On the afternoon of 10 September, Molotov summoned the German Ambassador, Friedrich von Schulenburg, and informed him that because Moscow was surprised

Table 3-2: Soviet First Echelon Forces in Poland – 17 September 1939

Belorussian Front

Command	Men	Guns	Tanks (In divisions)
3rd Army	121,968	752	743 (273)
11th Army	90,000	520	265 (17)
Cavalry Mechanised Group	65,595	1,234	864 (269)
10th Army	42,135	330	28 (28)
4th Army	40,365	184	508 (100)
23rd Rifle Corps	18,547	147	28 (28)
Total	**378,610**	**3,167**	**2,436 (715)**

Source: Meltyuhov, Table 7 p.119 Amended with Porter p.23.

Guns includes anti-tank and infantry support.

Note: 11th Army men and guns estimated.

Ukrainian Front

Command	Men	Guns	Tanks
5th Army	80,844	635	522 (221)
6th Army	80,834	630	675 (179)
12th Army	77,300	527	1,100 (193)
Total	**238,978**	**1,792**	**2,297 (593)**

Source: Op. cit. Guns includes anti-tank and infantry support.

by the rapid progress of the Wehrmacht it was not ready to attack Poland. He also revealed the Party line that Moscow would wait until Poland was nearer collapse and then declare it was coming to the aid of Belorussians and Ukrainians threatened by Germany! He admitted this would simply be a pretext so that, in the eyes of the masses, the Soviet Union would not appear to be an aggressor.

The fronts did not receive their new orders until 14 September, when the symbolic French offensive ended and the mobilisation was completed. The following day the armies were alerted to begin the offensive at dawn on Sunday, 17 September. That day, Molotov informed Schulenburg that the offensive would begin sooner than he had earlier claimed, but Moscow did not want to act until Warsaw fell, and inquired when that would happen. Yet as Molotov spoke the fronts took operational control of NKVD border guards whose tasks were to destroy Polish border guard troops and to prevent Polish refugees entering the Soviet Union. On 15 September Ribbentrop reported the imminent fall of Warsaw (which did not finally surrender until 28 September), confirmed the planned division of Poland and sought detailed timings of the Russian invasion to co-ordinate Wehrmacht operations.

The following day the Polish Ambassador in Moscow was informed that the treaties between the two countries were void because Poland had ceased to exist.

In a stupefying piece of hypocrisy, the Russians stated this was creating a situation which might threaten the Soviet Union and in view of this Moscow would no longer be neutral. Russian forces would cross the border to protect the lives and property of the Belorussians and Ukrainians in Poland. Other embassies received the same message with the reassurance that the Soviet Union remained neutral in any conflict, which was hardly reassuring to Moscow's immediate neighbours. Molotov was unable to inform Schulenburg exactly when the Red Army would strike, but at 02.00 hrs the following morning Stalin informed him that Red Army troops would cross the border in four hours. Even as he spoke, the NKVD rail protection organisation within the seven western districts was reinforced '…to ensure the smooth operation of the railways'.

The Red Army would advance through the flat countryside of a region so backward, compared with western Poland, that it was often called Poland 'B', being 81 per cent agricultural with a largely illiterate population including many Ukrainians, Belorussians and Jews who would welcome the Red Army as liberators.[24] Warsaw had begun military planning against the Russians before the ink was dry on the Treaty of Riga, aided by the fact that the forests of the Puszcza Nalibocka as well as the Pripyat Marshes provided some natural obstacles on the 1,412-kilometre-long frontier, while former Galicia was shielded by the river Zbrucz, a tributary of the Dnienster (Dnestr), which had been the boundary with the Austrian Empire before the Great War.

'Plan East' ('Wschod') was updated by February 1939 but was based upon two false assumptions: that Poland's industrial and population centres to the west would not be threatened and that her traditional ally, Rumania, would join her. However, the Poles had deduced the general axes of the Russian threat essentially along the Minsk-Warsaw, Kiev-Lublin and Vinnitsa-Lwow rail lines. Warsaw recognised that the Red Army of the 1930s was a very different creature from the one it had defeated in 1920 and that Poland would have to rely upon a mobile resistance. Recognising that the Red Army would be split by the Pripyat Marshes, Poland aimed to destroy it in detail with frontier forces exploiting fortifications to fight a delaying action and eroding enemy strength until reserves assembled around Brześć nad Bugiem (Brest-Litovsk) launched a counter-offensive.[25]

New fortifications were built around Wilno from 1924, to secure the city from Lithuania, while two years later work began on fortifications along the Soviet border — mostly command bunkers, and anti-armour and anti-infantry measures such as steel rails and wire obstacles. Six sectors were constructed: Wilno, Lida, Baranowicze, Polesie, Wolyn and Podole (south-eastern Poland). The Polesie sector, covering the Pripyat Marshes, (as did most of the Wolyn), was the most extensive sector with work starting in 1934 and scheduled for completion by 1940. Fortifications were planned for the Marshes region to compensate for reduced manpower and it was aimed to have some 660 pillboxes, bunkers and casements (114 with artillery) at three locations, while dams and weirs were built to create water obstacles. In fact, only 800 of the 1,400 obstacles were completed and 188 out of 358 planned structures at Sarny, on the rail line to Kowel, intended for the greater threat from Germany, meant priority was switched to the west.

'Plan East' anticipated the Poles being outnumbered 3:1 but envisaged 18 infantry divisions and eight cavalry brigades initially deployed in the east with reserve forces of 11 infantry divisions, three cavalry and one mechanised brigade, all shielded by the Polish Air Force. In addition, there would be the KOP para-military frontier guards, established in the mid-1920s to prevent Communist guerrillas making cross-border raids which were ended by the 1932 Non-Aggression Pact. With the German invasion, Warsaw mobilised 24 KOP battalions (22 infantry and 2 fortress) and in eastern Poland 10 ON infantry battalions, but the only manned fortifications were at Wilno and Sarny, while some KOP units were sent westward and others stripped of officers. A few major towns had nominal garrisons augmented by depot troops, reserve units, recruits and small numbers of ON troops, including the 'Dzisnienska' Demi-Brigade in the far north.

But by 17 September the Wehrmacht had ground into the dust most of the 'Plan East' divisions, leaving the survivors fleeing eastwards or to Rumania in the south-east, while the air force consisted of a dwindling number of machines trying, desperately, to protect the troops in skies dominated by the black cross and the Swastika. Rydz-Smigly anticipated a major French offensive on 17 September and a week earlier decided Warsaw and Modlin would be held while the bulk of the Polish forces retreated to a bridgehead on the border with Rumania with headquarters at Kolomyja (Kolomea).

The strategy was further compromised when German General der Kavallerie Ewald von Kleist's 22nd Mountain Corps reached the outskirts of Lwow on 12 September. Within two days Rydz-Smigly lost contact with the surviving forces as the Germans began to isolate both Lublin and Cracow. Soon the Germans were 100-150 kilometres from the Soviet-Polish border and had occupied or isolated more than 40 per cent of the country. But the need to reduce enemy pockets combined with exhaustion and battle casualties was slowing their advance which increasingly involved grim battles of attrition.

Some retreating units would enter the eastern battlefield to provide nominal support but the only cohesive force in the East consisted of 18 KOP battalions with some 12,000 lightly armed men, while the Third KOP Regiment was being sent south by rail from the East Prussian border. On 9 September, the KOP forces in the Marshes, plus garrison and depot troops from Brześć nad Bugiem (Brest-Litovsk), Drohiczyn, Jasiolda and Kobryn, were consolidated into the Samodzielna Grupa Operacyjna Polesie or SGO Polesie (Polesie Independent Operational Group) under General Franciszek Kleeberg who created Sixtieth 'Kobryn' Infantry Division by combining the Jasiolda and Kobryn garrisons. The other two garrisons would be merged as Fiftieth 'Brzoza' Infantry Division from 22 September, while Kleeberg also created two cavalry formations from elements of his command: the 'Zaza' Cavalry Division (formed from elements of SGO Narew's 'Suwalska' and 'Podlaska' Cavalry Brigades) and the 'Podlaska' Cavalry Brigade, ultimately raising its strength to 17,000 with some 30 guns, although it was fragmented and never succeeded in forming a cohesive command. They would be augmented by stragglers, retreating units, police and civilian volunteers, but it seems the total number that faced the Russians was not the 100,000-150,000 claimed by Polish sources, but perhaps 50,000. There were, however, many arms and supply depots in the east bringing hope of refitting the units.

The invasion was spearheaded by the VVS which struck airfields, claiming 10 aircraft on the first day while Polish fighters shot down one or two raiders, but on that day Russian bombers accidentally struck a Red Army column destroying two fuel trucks and causing 11 casualties.[26] The VVS would use no more than 1,000 of its aircraft and even on the first day the Ukrainian Front flew only 618 sorties including 194 sorties by SBs and light bombers on the enemy rear and 81 SB sorties on enemy troops. There were 88 reconnaissance sorties, mostly by fighters, while the defence of key locations involved 59 sorties.[27]

Air activity was reduced over the next few days but on 22 September nine Ukrainian Front SBs bombed retreating Poles near Borovichi. Two days later bombers struck enemy concentrations 10-15 kilometres south-east of Kamen-Kashira, but the regimental commissar's aircraft was lost to ground fire. The only other incident of note occurred on 30 September when the Luftwaffe accidentally attacked artillery of the 5th Army's 44th Rifle Division, wounding eight men.

There was little air combat as the Polish Air Force was staging through Dubno, Luck and Kowel en route to the Rumanian bridgehead where it hoped to receive modern British aircraft. Rumania would receive some 300 former Polish military and civil aircraft, some of which it used to equip its own squadrons. Another 40 trainers and civil light aircraft flew to Latvia, where they were later seized by the Russians. The Ukrainian Front would claim to capture 116 combat and 138 civil and training aircraft together with 368 aero-engines, but it seems likely the majority of the aircraft were wrecks.[28]

On the ground Soviet Frontier Guard detachments struck many KOP guard posts along the frontier and executed many captured KOP personnel, yet the Russians continued to operate their frontier controls for documents and goods for months after Poland's occupation. Red Army troops drove past the shot-up guard posts accompanied by nine NKVD combat units each of 50-70 men (five with the Ukrainian Front) which had been formed on 8 September in order to seize communications centres and public property, as well as to arrest 'reactionary elements'.[29] News of the Soviet invasion created great confusion among the Poles, many of whom believed initially that they were coming as allies, leading President Ignacy Moscicki and Prime Minister Felicjan Slawoj Skladkowski to persuade Rydz-Smigły to rescind his initial instruction to the eastern border forces to resist.

That afternoon he ordered the troops to withdraw and to engage the Russians only in self-defence, but the commander of the KOP, Brigadier General Wilhelm Orlik-Ruckemann, did not receive the orders and told his men to fight. Rydz-Smigly tried to accelerate the withdrawal towards Rumania in an attempt to preserve as much as possible of the army for a potential evacuation to France. The Polish government entered Rumania on 18 September. In fact, the Soviet invasion and the advance to the Rumanian border by both Russian and German troops made it impossible for most of the the Polish Army to join the government, although it was German actions which prevented most commands from escaping. The largest force, the 'Krakow' Corps, near the Rumanian border, surrendered to the Germans on 20 September.

The Belorussian Front's 3rd Army under Kuznetsov faced especially weak opposition, although it suffered from supply problems for it lacked logistics units and those that there were, were short of vehicles. Yet within two days Kuznetsov overcame resistance from KOP units and volunteers to clear the northern part of the Polish province of Wilno. He then advanced upon the city of Wilno (also Vilna and Vilnius). The garrison commander, Colonel Jaroslaw Okulicz-Kozaryn, had only 14,000 troops of which 6,500 (mostly KOP) were armed, supported by 15 pieces of light artillery and anti-tank guns, and augmented by volunteers and armed stragglers. Okulicz-Kozaryn ordered the unarmed men to stay out of the fight as he shielded an evacuation of Polish civilians to Lithuania.

The Russians prepared to envelop the city with Kuznetsov assigning the task to Kombrig Pyotr Akhlyustin's Lepel Group which was equipped with more than 300 tanks. The Lepel Group was to attack from the north-east while 11th Army under Medvedev ordered Kombrig Semon Zybin's 36th Cavalry Division and 6th Tank Brigade, with 170 tanks, to strike from the south-east. The Russians hoped to take the city by dusk on 18 September, but supply problems delayed the assault until the following morning by which time Okulicz-Kozaryn was withdrawing. He sent a Lieutenant Colonel Podwysocki to inform the Russians he would not defend the city, but Podwysocki was unable to get through the lines and on his own initiative decided to defend the city.

During the day the Russians fought their way into the city centre, although tanks and cavalry were far from ideal for urban warfare. Their deployment forced Kuznetsov to commit elements of 4th Rifle Corps and it took the Russians 13 hours to secure the city. The 11th Army alone lost 13 dead and 24 wounded as well as five tanks, but the booty included 97 railway locomotives and 1,443 items of rolling stock, including many loaded freight wagons.[30] Meanwhile the remainder of 3rd Army bypassed the city and advanced to the Lithuanian border while mobile elements of 11th Army's 16th Rifle Corps took Lida.

To the south, the 800 tanks of Boldin's Group, with the tank corps on the right, the cavalry corps in the centre and the rifle corps, made steady progress along the railway to Baranowicze. Kombrig Mikhail Petrov's 15th Tank Corps crossed the border with 528 BT light tanks, augmented by 105 T-28 mediums of the 21st Tank Brigade, and took Slonim on 18 September, drove some 15 kilometres to the west of the city, but ran out of fuel the following day leaving the cavalry to continue.

The experiences of Komkor Andrei Eremenko's 6th Cavalry Corps were typical, with a rapid advance on the first day and one division covering

100 kilometres to take Novogrudok a day ahead of schedule. However fuel shortages the following day disrupted the advance, which was renewed only by draining petrol from a third of the tanks to fill the remainder while Polish columns retreating northwards across the corps' axis of advance also posed problems. The advance on 19 September was made through high winds and drizzle with the impetuous group commissar and Eremenko at one point almost taken prisoner by Polish troops. They were rescued when Russian tanks clattered up the road.[31]

The tank corps resumed its advance on 20 September but, with Eremenko's 4th Cavalry Division, it was sent north to Grodno, entering its southern outskirts during the evening. Grodno had been the headquarters of General Jozef Olszyna-Wilczyński's DOK III, responsible for north-eastern Poland, and then of the Grodno Operational Group, but this was disbanded after the German breakthrough and its units retreated to Lwow accompanied by the general to Pinsk. He then returned to Grodno where he helped suppress a Communist rising and, with the mayor, organised a defence against Petrov's 15th Tank Corps using troops, police, volunteers and even Boy Scouts. They were joined that evening by half of General Waclaw Przezdziecki's Wolkowysk Reserve Cavalry Brigade. But the defenders were woefully short of weapons and had only 24 machine guns, forcing many to rely upon Molotov Cocktails. They held out for two days, the Russians losing two tanks destroyed and 17 damaged.[32]

As the garrison began withdrawing towards Lithuania, General Olszyna-Wilczyński with his wife and aide followed in a staff car, but they were stopped by troops of the 2nd Tank Brigade near Sopockinie and after a brief interrogation, the two officers were shot, although the driver and Olszyna-Wilczyński's wife were allowed to continue. The 11th Army moved its headquarters into the city, the capture of which had cost some 200 casualties (about 50 dead), while the defenders reportedly lost 644 dead and 1,543 captured (including 66 officers), with only 514 rifles and 146 automatic weapons. Some 300 defenders were later shot, which included 29 officers from a column of 80 prisoners marched out of Grodno by 4th Rifle Division on 22 September, the survivors then being marched back.

The 4th Cavalry Division was ordered to drive towards Augustow and Suwalki, with the tank corps' 2nd Tank Brigade pressing on westwards with the remainder of Boldin's Group. However the Russians were unable to prevent Przezdziecki's cavalry breaking through at Kodziowce and moving towards the Augustow Forest, one regiment fighting a fierce action at Kodziowce on the night of 22–23 September before escaping into Lithuania.[33]

On 22 September the rest of Eremenko's corps reached Bialystok in the Soviet zone, but the city had been taken by the Germans who, reportedly, requested that a detachment of Colonel Issa Pliev's 6th Cavalry Division officially take over.[34] Eremenko was especially glad to take the airfield which was used to fly in much needed fuel for his tanks.[35] On the same day the Germans handed over Brześć nad Bugiem (Brest-Litovsk) to the 4th Army and a joint parade was held in front of General der Panzertruppe Heinz Guderian, commander of Nineteenth Motorised Corps and the commander of 29th Tank Brigade, Kombrig Semon Krivoshein.[36]

The 3rd and 11th Armies swept along the Latvian and Lithuanian borders, which were soon assigned to the NKVD which used some of the 15 detachments created on 21 September. They reached the East Prussian border by 27 September, 15th Tank Corps' 27th Tank Brigade having taken Suwalki on 23 September. Two days later Voroshilov warned Kovalev that he might face stubborn resistance from the remnants of the Polish Army. To pre-empt this, Boldin's Group crossed the river Bug, but was then ordered to stop for two days to await a German delegation. Afterwards the corps headquarters and 6th Cavalry Division moved to Bialystok.[37]

Chuikov's 4th Army, covered by 16th Rifle Corps on its right, used the 29th Tank Brigade to take Baranowicze and its unoccupied defences. The brigade then raced ahead and by the end of the following day it was south of Slonim with 32nd Tank Brigade. They were supported by 8th Rifle Division, although this division, together with 143rd Rifle Division which operated south of the railway, did not reach Baranowicze (on the northern edge of the Marshes) until 18 September. With the capture of Pinsk by 23rd Rifle Corps, the advance accelerated and during the evening armoured spearheads took Kobryn and were closing on Brześć nad Bugiem (Brest-Litovsk), while the following day the 5th Army's 45th Rifle Division took Kovel.

Kleeberg's SGO Polesie was too weak to hold back 4th Army and retreated for 450-500 kilometres along the northern bank of the Pripet. On 19 September General Orlik-Ruckemann arrived and assumed command of the group and of KOP Regiment 'Sarny' to the south and ordered all troops to concentrate at Kowel, but it was clear that the Russians would reach it first. He decided to make for the Bug at Wlodowa. As Orlik-Ruckemann retreated he absorbed remnants of SGO Narew which had been driven back from Grodno. There were minor clashes with Soviet vanguard and Communist Fifth Column troops as the KOP forces 'periodically bounced off superior enemy forces'.[38] Yet farcical situations developed at Tarnopol and Luck as Russian and retreating Polish columns marched side-by-side and took turns to give way to the other at intersections.[39]

The retreat was made as Poland 'B' collapsed into anarchy. The Polish masters there faced spontaneous risings by Ukrainian nationalists and Belorussian Communist revolts, some Belorussian areas having long been Party strongholds.[40] Some of the Communist revolts were spontaneous and some were organised by Soviet 'sleepers' and other agents despatched across the border to ensure friendly receptions for the Red Army. Many communities, anxious to be on good terms with the Red Army, prepared welcoming arches and flags, but when retreating Polish forces discovered these, they assumed the communities were pro-Russian. This led to reprisals with excecutions and the burning of buildings. As a precaution, some Polish commanders released ethnic minority reservists to prevent them from infecting their own units.

Both sides of the ethnic divide indulged in tit-for-tat reprisals as the Polish withdrawal created a power vacuum, the Red Army sometimes encouraging the minorities to pay off old scores not only against the Poles, but also the Jews. The commander of the Ukrainian Front's 234th Corps Artillery Regiment told people in the village of Mazow, near Wolyn, to take back what was theirs, assuring them that the Red Army would support them. To protect their communities, the Poles organised Citizens' Guards (Straz Obywatelska) units. Some of these remained in place after the arrival of the Russians, but in Lwow, for example, the Russians arrested the leaders at the end of September. The Red Army fanned the flames by shooting potential opponents as well as encouraging many Communists and poor people to form militias which became the de facto police force.

Even the most enthusiastic Communists were startled by the poor condition and behaviour of the Red Army. Their uniforms were often torn and dirty, the men often stank like toilet disinfectant, some cavalrymen lacked saddles, while troops were seen without boots, their feet wrapped in cloth, or with rifle slings made of string. The condition of Red Army horses was so bad that many units simply stole those of the peasantry or exchanged them, and there was much pilfering and outright theft as well as some rape. Behind the Red Army came Soviet officialdom and, as one Ukrainian Front soldier told local people: 'Watch out, bad times are coming.'[41]

The retreating Poles' major opponent was Zakharin's 10th Army, a Second Echelon formation which crossed the frontier on 18 September, then slowly followed the spearheads to consolidate the Soviet hold. On 28 September 52nd Rifle Division took Szack (now Shatsk in the Ukraine), some 75 kilometres south of Brześć/Brest and 50 kilometres north-west of Chelm, temporarily barring the Poles' way to the Western Bug. The Poles broke through, overrunning the divisional headquarters. The Russian commander, Colonel I. Russiyanov, was severely wounded and nine tanks of the 411th Tank Battalion which had been supporting him were destroyed. The following day Orlik-Ruckemann ambushed Chuikov's 143rd Rifle Division. During the night the Poles pushed back 52nd Rifle Division, isolating part of its 112th Rifles until the morning, but a counter-attack that afternoon smashed the Poles and reduced their main body to 3,000 men, who crossed the Bug the next day in a desperate effort to reach Warsaw or Modlin.[42] On 1 October they encountered the 5th Army's 45th Rifle Division near Wytyczno and this regular unit held them, forcing the Poles to disperse, with the largest group, under Kleeberg, continuing westward. However, on 5 October, near Kock, they encountered a German motorised division to which they surrendered after a four-day battle.[43]

The swatting of the irritating SGO Polesie brought to an end Sovetnikov's brief moment of glory protecting Timoshenko's right. After this he disappeared until September 1941 when he was transferred to the Far East, from where he returned in 1943 to resume his career as an army commander until the end of the war.[44] His 36th Tank Brigade (300 tanks) took Luck on 18 September and, by the end of the day, it controlled the lateral railway line running from Sarny to Dubno. However, the Sarny Fortified Area (Sarnenski Rejon Umocniony), which consisted of 170 kilometres of bunkers and trenches on both sides of the river Sluch, running to a depth of 5 kilometres, proved a formidable obstacle to 60th Rifle Division (31 tanks including 19 T-37s) which faced 4,000 well-trained troops of KOP Regiment 'Sarny', supported by an armoured train.

Although reinforced by two extra corps artillery regiments, flame-thrower tanks and border guard support, there was fierce fighting and every bunker had to be reduced individually. Fearing encirclement, the defenders were ordered to withdraw on 20 September although some failed to receive the order and held out until the 25th of the month.[45] The battle shackled Sovetnikov's progress and he reached the Bug only in the evening of 22 September. He then sent his 36th Tank Brigade across the river towards Chelm, but it was left virtually isolated and had to be rescued by the 44th and 87th Rifle Divisions.

Golikov's 6th Army made steady progress, its 17th Rifle Corps and 5th Cavalry Division taking Tarnopol against light resistance and with 40 casualties by the evening of the first day. Timoshenko ordered Golikov to make a forced march to Lwow but, as his horses were tired, he put 600 dismounted cavalry on the 35 tanks of the 24th Tank Brigade, and sent it westward towards the city. The Russians were unaware that the German Fourteenth Army was also racing for the town, and by 18 September the unlikely allies had surrounded it on three sides and were launching probing attacks while seeking a capitulation of the garrison, which was under the command of Major General Wladyslaw Langner (commander of DOK VI).

Early in the morning of 19 September the 24th Tank Brigade entered Lwow, where the defenders responded vigorously. The situation became more complex when a German mountain infantry regiment swept into the city from the south-east, neither of the allies being aware of the other. Inevitably there was a short, sharp firefight which killed three Germans and wounded nine, and killed four Russians and wounded three. The Germans lost three anti-tank guns, the Russians one or two tanks and two armoured cars. Recognising their error, both sides moved from 'war, war' to 'jaw, jaw', each demanding the other to withdraw. But then Hitler intervened when he ordered the Wehrmacht to pull back on the evening of 20 September.

The Russians planned to storm the city but Langner had decided to surrender to them, believing that fellow Slavs would help the Poles to fight the Germans. His chief-of-staff, Colonel Kazimierz Ryzinski, who negotiated the surrender, had not heard the radio and was told by the Russians that they would fight the Germans, but first needed to enter the city.[46] Golikov's 14th Cavalry Division did fight its way through the northern outskirts but on the morning of 22 September Langner surrendered and that afternoon the Red Army occupied the city.

The officers were allowed to flee to Rumania while the men went home, but the NKVD then reneged on the agreement and arrested many officers.[47]

The only other resistance that Golikov faced came from Colonel Zajaczkowski's Third KOP Regiment which had set out by rail for the Rumanian bridgehead on 13 September, but had detrained near Rowne when the Soviets invaded. The border guards retreated westwards in front of 5th and 6th Armies, clashing with Fifth Columnists and the Russian spearheads, but they appear to have given the 87th Rifle Division (5th Army) a bloody nose on 21-22 September when its 16th Rifle Regiment reportedly lost 230 dead and missing as well as 221 injured. Additionally, a reconnaissance company reportedly lost 29 dead, the casualties being the heaviest suffered by a single Red Army division in the campaign.[48] On 29 September Zajaczkowski crossed the river San south of Lublin and faced both the advancing Germans and the pursuing Russians, surrendering to the latter on 1 October.

Tyuleniev's 12th Army advanced rapidly and the seizure of Kolomea, headquarters of the Rumanian bridgehead, by its 13th Rifle Corps on 20 September dashed Polish hopes of continuing the struggle against the Germans, although some 202,000 Polish troops escaped to the south. This action saw the only tank battle of the Russian campaign when BTs of 23rd Tank Brigade encountered Polish 7TP (Vickers 6-ton Type A) tanks from the tank training centre, destroying one and damaging another which was burned by the crew.[49] The Russians pressed on to the river Stry, meeting little resistance; indeed, Colonel Ivan Yarkin's 25th Tank Corps lost only 12 of its 449 tanks with 15 damaged and 31 human casualties (seven dead). Tyuleniev met with forward elements of the German Fourteenth Army which had taken Stanislawow (Stanislau) in the Russian sector and transferred the town to Soviet control on 22 September. Meanwhile, Tyuleniev's 13th Corps completed its occupation of the tri-border (Poland-Hungary-Rumania) area, with 9th Cavalry Division exchanging fire with Hungarian troops, who had briefly crossed the frontier on 26 September, and using armour to push them back.

The following day the 4th Cavalry Corps' 34th Cavalry Division and 26th Tank Brigade clashed with, and defeated, 3,000 Polish cavalry of the 'Modlin' Corps under Brigadier General Wladyslaw Anders at Krukienice, between Przemysl and Lwow, and north of Sambor.[50] The 5th Cavalry Corps reached the upper river San and Hungarian border on 28 September but not before 120,000 Polish troops had escaped into friendly Rumania, some via Hungary, while another 20,000 reached temporary sanctuary in the Baltic States of Latvia and Lithuania.

When Soviet troops crossed the border, the military situation in central Poland was chaotic; the German Third and Fourth Armies were pushing towards Grodno, a motorised corps was east of Brześć nad Bugiem (Brest-Litovsk) while the German Fourteenth Army had nearly reached the Bug, having made substantial penetrations beyond the Curzon Line boundary. Early on 17 September, the Oberkommando der Wehrmacht (OKW) issued a directive to units outlining the

Wehrmacht's eastern boundary limit as the line Bialystok - Brześć nad Bugiem (Brest-Litovsk) - Lwow and prohibiting moves beyond it.

Three days later Hitler established the 'definitive line of demarcation' which followed the Narew, the Bug, the Vistula and the San, to which all troops in the east would withdraw by the following day. The same day, following 980 hours of continuous negotiation, Voroshilov and Shaposhnikov hammered out an agreement on the withdrawal with a German delegation consisting of Generalleutnant Ernst-August Köstring and Oberstleutnant Heinrich Aschenbrenner (the Military and Air Attachés in Moscow respectively) and the monocled Oberstleutnant Hans Krebs (Army Command representative and Köstring's predecessor). Under the terms of this agreement, the Red Army would move forward in 25-kilometre leaps from the morning of 23 September until the new frontier was reached on 3 October.[51]

But on the afternoon of 21 September the German delegation forwarded a message from Generaloberst Walter von Brauchitsch, the German Army Commander-in-Chief, requesting a 24-hour delay because fighting in Warsaw and west of Lwow had created a confused situation and the Wehrmacht needed to reorganise before withdrawing.[52] The Russians, no doubt reluctantly, accepted this, but that morning Voroshilov ordered Kovalev and Timoshenko to stop on the river lines they had reached and consolidate. That night both generals were informed of the modified agreement, although apparently too late to prevent a clash between German mechanised forces and 8th Rifle Division on the evening of 23 September which saw two Russian dead and two wounded.[53] On 29 September the two fronts were ordered to reach the frontier by that evening and to withdraw any units west of the line from 5 October. In another marathon session Voroshilov, Shaposhnikov and the German delegation agreed this would be completed by 12 October.

The Red Army in Poland 'B' had risen by 2 October to 2,421,300 men, 5,467 medium and heavy guns, 6,096 tanks and 3,727 aircraft in 56 rifle and 13 cavalry divisions, 18 tank and two motorised brigades – enough to hold territory and face down the Wehrmacht. On 14 November the two fronts reverted to Special Military Districts, but as the Ukrainian Districts now had such a long line of responsibility, the Odessa Military District was created on 23 October using the 13th Army forces, boosted from 1 November by the neighbouring 12th Army.[54]

Moscow would claim that it had captured more than 900 guns with a million shells, 10,000 machine guns and 300,000 rifles with 150 million rounds of ammunition (see Table 3-3) and 'up to' 300 aircraft.[55] The 5th Army alone claimed the capture of 64 railway locomotives and 2,174 pieces of rolling stock, while Timoshenko claimed to have captured 3,491 tonnes of petrol, oil and lubricants. Timoshenko's figures were certainly inflated, possibly because front commissar, Nikita Khrushchev, was seeking to make political capital with 'The Boss' and in terms of both personnel and infantry weapons they were certainly swelled by civilian arms and probably by anti-tank rifles.

Table 3-3: Booty captured in Poland

Front	PoW (Officers)	Rifles	Machine guns	Artillery	Tanks
Belorussian	60,202 (2,066)	29,254	17,232	134	45
Ukrainian	394,498 (16,723)	291,183		606	28
German	588,354 (11,446)	208,273	7,681	1,596	111
Total	1,043,054 (30,235)	528,710	24,913	2,336	184

Note: The Belorussian Front 'rifles' excludes carbines. 'Artillery' excludes anti-tank and anti-aircraft. 'Tanks' includes tankettes. German figure includes armoured cars. The Russians claimed to capture 64 armoured cars.

Timoshenko's haul of prisoners was certainly swelled by uniformed civilians such as police, firemen, rail and postal workers as well as land owners and officials; indeed by 2 October the Red Army reported capturing 99,149 troops while the 60,202 Belorussian Front prisoners included only 57,892 troops. Russian historians state that the vast majority of prisoners were freed but they admit the NKVD retained 125,400. The Red Army is believed to have inflicted up to 13,500 casualties on the Poles (3,500 dead) while the Germans inflicted 199,000 (66,000 dead), German losses being 44,300 (13,981 dead and missing). Soviet casualties totalled 2,383 (996 dead and missing) with 381 injured, the majority suffered by Timoshenko.[56]

In materiel terms figures are available only for the Ukrainian Front which lost 220 vehicles, two aircraft and five guns (11 were damaged). It is known that the Russians lost 138 tanks destroyed, two thirds from divisional units, many of which were equipped with the T-37/T-38 reconnaissance tank which weighed less than 4 tonnes. By 2 October the independent tank units, which began operations with 3,551 serviceable vehicles, were left with 3,071, of which 480 were reported damaged and 52 destroyed. More may have broken down.

The large number of Polish prisoners created supply problems which were cited by Kulik on 21 September when he proposed releasing Ukrainian and Belorussian members of the Polish Army. Kulik may have had a soft spot for the Poles and so did Kushchev, whose wife was Polish; he had rescued her parents who had remained in Poland in 1920.[57] Voroshilov and Shaposhnikov approved the mass release on 23 September, but it was reversed by Stalin three days later following an appeal by Mekhlis. Subsequently, Voroshilov and Shaposhnikov got 'The Boss' to confirm the original decision on 4 October.

The Red Army's performance had been less than glowing and while armoured and cavalry forces leading the advance superficially reflected Tukhachevskii's ideas, their actions actually underlined the new reality which would be encapsulated in

PU 39. This allowed mobile forces, and especially tanks, to clear the way against a disorganised defence and to overcome obstacles ahead of the infantry. But the pre-Purge criticisms of Voroshilov, Budenny and even Shaposhnikov about command, control and supply were also underlined, fuel being a key problem, while the number of vehicle breakdowns was alarming. The chaotic mobilisation, itself a reflection of the lack of experienced officers due to the Purges, aggravated the situation, leaving many soldiers short of food and equipment.

This undermined discipline and many Red Army troops proved to be exploiters rather than liberators, with numerous examples of petty theft. Even Poland 'B' was a cornucopia of consumer goods compared with the Soviet Union and officers were seen to rip the leather upholstery off motor cars and carry off tyres while requisitioning large supplies of sugar and flour.[58]

The Russian reaction to 'instances of arbitrary action, looting, lynching, requisitions, etc' was itself capricious. Although the Russians claim the perpetrators were 'usually suppressed' the Polonophobe Stalin sometimes took a benign view of theft and, when informed that Red Army troops had stolen treasures from a Prince Radziwill, said: 'If there's no ill-will they can be pardoned.'[59] Rape appears to have been a capital crime, where the individual was identified, while on 2 October the commissar of the 5th Cavalry Division's 131st Cavalry was shot for summarily executing seven Polish landowners. This, despite the fact that the 14th Cavalry Division shot four captured Polish officers on 22 September and the same day the Ukrainian Front tried 28 Polish soldiers and police of 'counter-revolutionary' crimes, executing 13 of them. This front claimed that from 15 September to 1 October it sentenced 49 troops for counter-revolutionary statements, robbery, assault, desertion (to German-held territory or Rumania), failure to comply with orders, looting, neglect, and violation of guard duty rules, with eight individuals executed.[60]

As the Russians consolidated their hold and, following Soviet-style elections, Poland 'B' sought to join the Soviet Union, Ribbentrop returned on 27 September. Both sides were jubilant with Stalin stating he would not allow Germany to be 'thrown to the ground' and promising to come to her aid if she was strongly pressed. The following day he received amendments to the Secret Protocols, with Ribbentrop agreeing all of Lithuania as coming within Moscow's sphere of influence in return for a financial indemnity and more Polish territory around Warsaw and Lublin. During the discussions Stalin stated that he planned to put pressure on the Baltic States to ensure they complied with Moscow's wishes.[61] On 31 October, Molotov reported to the Supreme Soviet: 'A short blow by the German Army, and subsequently by the Red Army, was enough for nothing to be left of this ugly creature of the Treaty of Versailles.' For the next year Germany's dependence upon Russian economic resources gave Stalin a strong negotiating position, leading him ultimately to overreach himself. Initially, however, he edged into the Baltic States of Estonia, Latvia and Lithuania which, with Finland, had emerged from the Russian Empire when revolutionary chaos removed the last barrier to nationalist feeling, but bloody civil wars followed because some of their people followed the Bolshevik creed. Their post-war independence, reluctantly recognised by the Soviet Union which concluded non-aggression treaties with them in 1932, was underpinned by the Western European powers; Latvia was Anglophile, Lithuania was Francophile, while Estonia (with Finland and Sweden) was Teutophile.[62]

Nevertheless, they remained uneasy about their more powerful neighbour's intentions and accommodated Moscow to avoid any pretext for intervention. Their uneasiness increased during the early 1930s and as Soviet mechanised power grew with the implied threat of a rapid invasion, the Estonian general staff grew especially pessimistic.[63] Finland, Estonia and Latvia had considered an alliance with Poland, but after the Poles seized Vilnius (Wilno), Lithuania had no diplomatic relations with Warsaw from 1920 to 1938; and this remained the insurmountable obstacle to united action which was confined to a diplomatic triple alliance or Entente in September 1934.

The Baltic Nations had cause for concern because in a Soviet General Staff war game held in April 1936, Tukhachevskii concluded that in the event of war with Germany and Poland, the Red Army should immediately occupy the Baltic States as a pre-emptive move. The Politburo did not agree and opted to cow the Baltic States into permitting Soviet troops onto their territory and a few weeks after the war game, Egorov invited the three chiefs-of-staff to see Soviet military power for themselves. Curiously, Tukhachevskii continued pursuing the invasion concept while in his prison cell, allegedly drafting a plan.[64]

On 23 March 1939 Germany forced Lithuania to cede Memel (Klaipeda) and insisted that the country sign a non-aggression pact with her. Six days later, Litvinov called on the Latvian and Estonian Ambassadors and warned them that any agreement, whether voluntary or under duress, which compromised their independence would mean the end of their non-aggression pacts with the Soviet Union. Despite this, on 7 June Estonia and Latvia also signed non-aggression pacts with Berlin.[65] For the Soviet Union the four states were always a potential threat; German troops had aided anti-Communist forces in Finland and Latvia both officially and unofficially, and their close links to Western European states made them potential bridgeheads to anti-Soviet forces.[66] From 1936 German and Estonian military intelligence co-operated. Two years later the German Navy was proposing to occupy Latvia, while during the 1930s the Baltic States became pseudo-Fascist autocracies.[67]

When the Red Army crossed into Poland on 17 September, Lithuania ordered a general mobilisation, but militarily the Baltic States were weak; even if fully mobilised they would have only 15 infantry and the equivalent of one cavalry division with 373,000 men supported by 800 guns, some 90 tanks and 150 combat aircraft, with no medium bombers. Estonia and Latvia had a military alliance from July 1921, but a proposal in 1934 to extend this to Finland and Latvia received short shrift, while Estonia had a secret agreement with Finland from 1930.

But the States held few joint exercises and made little attempt at joint procurement, while most of their military equipment dated back to the Great War, with Estonia having Russian and German weapons, Latvia having British and Lithuania also having German.

The Russian scheme for occupying these states would follow a well-oiled plan; the foreign ministers would be invited to discuss details of a trade agreement – Estonia's Karl Selter on 22 September, Latvia's Vilhelms Munters on 2 October and Lithuania's Juozas Urbsys on 3 October – only to receive a proposal for a mutual assistance pact involving the stationing of Soviet forces on their territory. At some point Stalin would meet the ministers, and his words to Munters were typical: 'I tell you frankly, a division of spheres of interest has already taken place. As far as Germany is concerned we could occupy you.' All too aware they were isolated from their Western European patrons, the three states reluctantly agreed, usually obtaining favourable trade treaties, with detailed arrangements made by the Red Army's district commanders.

Simultaneously, military pressure on the Baltic States increased, beginning as early as 13 August when Voroshilov ordered the Leningrad District to activate the Novgorod Army Group (Komdiv Ivan Khabarov) – renamed 8th Army on 14 September with headquarters at Pskov near the southern shore of Lake Peipus – and be ready to operate against both Estonia and Latvia. Khabarov was assigned 1st Rifle Corps and four, later five, rifle and one cavalry divisions, two tank brigades and the 10th Tank Corps. On 25 September, the 7th Army under Komandarm II Rank Vladimir Yakolev which had covered the Belorussian Front's right on the Latvian-Lithuanian border, was ordered to concentrate on the Estonian-Latvian border south of the Western Dvina within four days, with eight rifle and one cavalry division, as well as two tank brigades. It was assigned to the Kalinin District under Boldin, who had just returned from the Belorussian Front's Cavalry Mechanised Group (see Table 3-4). On the same day Russian aircraft began reconnaissance flights over Estonia while the Independent Rifle Corps deployed north of Lake Peipus on the Narwa–Leningrad road to attack Estonia.

Table 3-4: Forces deployed along the Baltic States 28 September – 6 October 1939

Command	Men	Guns	Tanks
Indep Rifle Corps	35,448	402	243
8th Army	100,797	1,133	1,075
7th Army	169,738	1,225	759
3rd Army	193,859	1,378	1,078
Total	**499,842**	**4,138**	**3,155**

Source: Metelyuhov Table 13 p.181. Guns probably includes infantry support and anti-tank.
Note: 4th Rifle Corps transferred from 7th Army to 3rd Army but the statistics are not duplicated.

Moscow selected Estonia as its first target for it knew that Tallinn and Helsinki had an agreement which made them gatekeepers of the Gulf of Finland and the approaches to Leningrad. Co-operation between the two Finno-Ugric states, separated by a narrow body of water, was natural but was stimulated by a mutual fear – shared with Sweden which had ruled Finland until 1809 – of the Soviet Union and its Baltic Fleet. Much of the Tsarist Fleet had gone to the scrapyard, but even in 1930 it had two dreadnought battleships and a light cruiser for training, as well as many destroyers and submarines which threatened the upper Baltic, while Stalin's announcement in 1936 of a major expansion of the Soviet Fleet further exacerbated fears in the region.

Encouraged by the Swedish General Staff, Stockholm and Helsinki negotiated an agreement in 1929 to blockade the Gulfs of Finland. The Swedes even offered to send troops to support this move.[68] In February 1930, following unofficial Swedish proposals, the Finnish General Staff proposed co-operation with their Estonian cousins and the first war games were held in 1933. On the Gulf, Finland had six 305 mm (12 in), eighteen 254 mm (10 in), four 203 mm (8 in) and fifty 152 mm (6 in) guns while the Estonians maintained three fortress complexes around Tallinn with four 305 mm, three 234 mm (9 in), thirteen 152 mm, three 130 mm and seven 120 mm weapons augmented by 17 mobile weapons (6 x 152 mm, 11 x 76 mm) upon mobilisation.[69]

The two sides refined their arrangements to include joint fire control and minelaying, while Finland modified its artillery coverage so that at the time of the first joint military exercise in 1936, Fort Mäkiluoto in Finland and Fort Naissaar in Estonia could cover the Gulf with 305 mm guns. The guns and mines were augmented by submarines: Finland acquired five between 1930 and 1934 while in July 1933, Estonia sold two destroyers to Peru to pay for two British-built submarines delivered in the spring of 1937 and equipped with jointly procured torpedoes and mines after Helsinki helped train Estonian crews.

But it was a Polish submarine which provided the pretext for Russian action when Poland's ORP *Orzel* arrived in Tallinn on 14 September with mechanical problems and a sick commander. The neutral Estonians interned the boat, removing most of its torpedoes and all of its charts, but four days later the submarine's crew made a daring escape to Great Britain.[70] The Russians loudly proclaimed Estonian collusion in the *Orzel*'s escape and expressed fears she would attack Soviet shipping, Molotov stating on 19 September that Moscow would hold Tallinn responsible for any losses.[71]

After receiving the demand for a mutual assistance treaty, Selter returned to Tallinn where the Baltic Fleet imposed a de facto blockade while ostensibly searching for the *Orzel*. Russian 'fears' appeared justified when the freighter *Metallist* (968 grt) was allegedly torpedoed and sunk in Narva Bay on 26 September with the loss of five lives, although there are doubts that this incident ever occurred and certainly no Polish submarine was involved.[72]

A Main Military Council directive was immediately sent to the Leningrad District to be ready to invade Estonia by 29 September. Voroshilov, apparently not anticipating a formal declaration of war, demanded that the Leningrad District's Komandarm II Rank Kirill Meretskov deliver '…a powerful and decisive blow to the Estonian Army' using 8th Army to stab upwards towards Tallinn while the Independent Corps would move westwards. Meanwhile, the 7th Army was to cover the southern flank while the Baltic Fleet destroyed the Estonian Navy. The Fleet had conducted a war game in March involving operations against both Finland and Estonia following a border incident involving the sinking of a ship by a submarine, and its August manoeuvres included fire support for troops operating in Estonia.[73]

Estonia's Army had only two infantry and one cavalry regiments and a dozen independent infantry battalions totalling 15,900 troops, while the air force had only 16 combat aircraft (four fighters), confining it to a defensive strategy, although from 1937 Tallinn seemed more concerned by a threat from Latvia. Their military alliance of 1923 had gradually dissolved due to personal and national differences, as well as growing doubts about Latvian commitment to resisting a Soviet invasion. A score of bunkers shielded Narva but plans for fortifying the southern borders had barely been completed and no significant work had begun because the Estonians faced a daunting 136,245 men.[74] On 25 September, as Russian reconnaissance aircraft appeared, the Estonians conducted a partial mobilisation and made a vain appeal for Finnish and Latvian military support. In these circumstances Tallinn was forced to accept Russian demands and Selter flew back to Moscow on 27 September to find Stalin celebrating the amended agreement with Molotov and Ribbentrop. After a convivial dinner, Stalin and Molotov met Selter and good-humouredly agreed to reduce the troop numbers from 35,000 to 20,000, with the Baltic Fleet having the use of Tallinn naval base temporarily for two years. The agreement was signed on 28 September.[75]

Meretskov made the detailed arrangements involving Komdiv Ivan Tyurin's 65th Special Rifle Corps (the former Independent Rifle Corps) with 16th Rifle Division as well as the VVS Special Group (15th, 38th Fighter, 7th, 53rd Long-Range Bomber, 35th, 52nd Fast Bomber Regiments) totalling 21,347 men, 283 tanks, 78 guns and 255 aircraft, but a lack of airfields slowed the air build-up. The troops entered from 18 October with great care taken to secure rail bridges, but Polish observers in Estonia were not impressed, noting that staff work was indifferent, no troops being available to use the six trains they had requested for 18 October. As in Poland, troop movement was poorly organised and slow, vehicles breaking down with alarming regularity while fuel supplies were infrequent and second-line troops seemed poorly clothed and shod. On 28 September the Baltic Fleet was ordered to be fully operational by the following morning and, tellingly, to seize both Estonian naval bases and the small fleet to prevent it from fleeing to Finland or Sweden.[76] In Tallinn the Russians quickly stationed four destroyers, 19 submarines, three patrol boats and two floating docks, while a task group was briefly stationed there before moving into Latvia.

Meanwhile, preparations were under way to occupy the other two Baltic States, Shaposhnikov ordering 8th Army on 1 October to regroup on the Latvian border while Voroshilov ordered air reconnaissance. The invasion of Latvia might have given the Russians pause for thought because they always rated Latvian troops highly and during the Second World War Latvian ground and air units would fight both for, and against, the Germans. The Latvian regular Army had four infantry divisions and 25,200 troops, but could be doubled in strength (with 143,000 men) and upon mobilisation would be supported by 400 guns, 27 tanks/tankettes (five dating from the Great War) and 60 combat aircraft, including 28 fighters and three light bombers.[77]

Facing them were Yakolev's 7th Army with nearly 170,000 men quickly supported by 100,000 of 8th Army. The Latvian war plans were to resist the Russians (Plan 'A') and Germans either separately or combined, but co-operation with the Estonian Army was the key to the first. This envisaged a retreat to a fortified position with some 50 bunkers in central Latvia (along the rivers Pededze, Lubans and Aiviekste), but with Estonia being occupied, no hope of any foreign military support and orders for modern equipment including 98 howitzers not yet completed, Riga had no choice but to surrender. On 5 October Munters signed the agreement, allowing the Russians to station a garrison of 25,000 in the country using bases at Liepaja, Ventspils and Pitrags until 1949 and stating that his government would also build airfields for the Soviet Air Forces, the agreement being ratified on 14 October.

A Baltic Fleet task group formed of the new heavy cruiser *Kirov* with the destroyers *Smetliviy* and *Stremitelny* and four minesweepers sailed into Liepaja (Libau) on 23 October as Boldin began talks. On Sunday, 29 October the Red Army followed with the 2nd Special Rifle Corps (67th Rifle Division and corps troops) as well as the 18th Air Brigade (21st, 148th Fighter, 31st Fast Bomber Regiments), totalling 21,559 troops.[78]

Tallinn and Liepaja proved a poisoned chalice for the Soviet Navy. Navy Minister Kuznetsov sent Fleet Flagmen II Rank Lev Galler (his deputy) and Ivan Isakov (Baltic Fleet commander) to tour the facilities and to evaluate the fleet's performance. They discovered the fleet was unready for operations with poor leaders and planning, no minesweeping exercises, slow modernisation, numerous accidents and few repair or storage facilities. Since the Revolution the Baltic Fleet had sought to regain freedom of action and now it had done so it was stretched to breaking point by the need to fit out and refurbish the new bases and to dredge deeper channels for the cruisers and battleships.[79]

From Lithuania Moscow initially demanded the right to station 50,000 troops, but steadily reduced this first to 35,000 and then to 20,000. Because Lithuania had had no border with the Soviet Union it was concerned only about threats from Poland and Germany, especially the former which had seized Vilnius (Wilno) in 1920 leaving both states in a formal state of war until 1938. Consequently the three plans were: 'L' (Lenkija) against Poland, 'V' (Voietija) against Germany and

'VL' against both. Each envisaged a defensive strategy, augmented by guerrilla operations using the border covering battalions. Mobilisation on 17–18 September expanded the army from 22,500 in three divisions to some 125,000 troops in four divisions, each of four or five regiments, supported by some 170 guns, 54 tanks (including 12 Great War Renault FT 17) and some 70 combat aircraft – but they faced the Russian 3rd Army with some 193,000 men.[80] The overwhelming force meant that on 10 October Lithuania agreed to accept a Russian garrison and the loss of a strip of territory to Germany but, in compensation, it received 6,739 square kilometres of former Polish territory including the city of Wilno (Vilnius). The Russians received Memel in exchange as another naval base.

Kovalev arrived on 22 October to negotiate the location of the bases and five days later it was agreed the Russians would receive four bases around Kaunus, the agreement being concluded as Lithuanian troops marched into Wilno. The bulk of the Russian troops began to arrive on 3 November and, within a fortnight, 18,786 troops were in the country forming 16th Special Rifle Corps and 5th Rifle Division with 2nd Tank Brigade, and the 10th Fighter and 54th Fast Bomber Regiments.[81]

Moscow loudly denied any plans to turn the three nations into Soviet states and on 25 October Voroshilov warned the garrisons that they were not to interfere in their 'hosts'' internal affairs, while any talk of 'Sovietisation' was to be ruthlessly suppressed. Yet Moscow did nothing to dissuade the hopes of local Communist parties.[82] On 27 November, Voroshilov's deputy and the VVS commander, Komandarm II Rank Loktionov, was given overall responsibility for the Soviet forces in the Baltic States (see Table 3-5) as the Finnish Foreign Minister was invited to Moscow on 5 October for 'trade talks'. They were to be words which Stalin would regret.

Table 3-5: Distribution of forces 17 November 1939

District	Corps			Divisions		
	Rifle	Cavalry	Tank	Rifle	Cavalry	Tank Brigades
Leningrad	5	-	1	17	1	5
Belorussian	7	2	1	22	5	5
Ukrainian	7	3	1	22	8	7
Odessa	2	-	-	8	-	1
Total	**21**	**5**	**3**	**69**	**14**	**18**

Note: Based on Kiyan, Drig's and Kavaleriiskie Korpusa RKKA websites.

ENDNOTES

1. Montefiore p.247.
2. Op. cit. pp.261–262, p.619 f/n 10.
3. Pavlov had been Deputy Director from June 1937, becoming a Komkor on 20 June 1937.
4. A letter from Pavlov on 20 November 1938 suggests Gryaznov succeeded Khalepskii although the on-line biographic data on Purge victims does not confirm this. See Habeck p.276.

5. Habeck p.276.
6. Op. cit. p.277.
7. Op. cit. pp.279-280.
8. Op. cit. p.280.
9. Op. cit. p.285.
10. Op. cit. pp.286-287.
11. Kolomiets article.
12. Habeck pp.287, 289. Details from Drig's Mechanizirovannieye Korpusa RKKA website.
13. Montefiore p.268.
14. Op. cit. pp.267-269.
15. A meeting to provide the delegation with detailed instructions was not held until 2 August. See UK National Archive WO 106/5860 'Negotiations with Russia'.
16. For the negotiations see Montefiore pp.272, 273-276; Rees pp.7-20.
17. Rees p.22.
18. For the Polish forces see Zaloga, Poland 1939, and also discussions on the 'Axis History Forum' website — Poland, 'The Rapid Collapse of the Polish Army'.
19. For the German campaign see Kennedy and Zaloga.
20. Gross pp.9-10.
21. Details of strength in Elisseva's article and Glantz article 'Soviet Mobilisation'.
22. The Ukrainian District Army Groups switched to numerical designations after the start of the campaign, but the numerical ones are retained in this account.
23. For Red Army preparations see Meltukhov pp.109-115 and Rukkas on the Kiev District mobilisation. The Kiev District's Second Echelon forces were formed only on 27 September. Kovalev was a typical product of the Purges; a divisional and corps commander until 1937, he became deputy commander of the Kiev District until taking over the Belorussian District in 1938. He was joined by his friend, Voronov, whose campaign ended when he was involved in a head-on collision which left him with concussion and broken ribs. Voronov p.134.
24. Gross pp.3-8.
25. For details of the plan see Szubanski and Kaufmann & Jurga pp.264-282. Fortifications with underground passages in Polesie website (http):forteca.w.activ.pl/polesiee.html. A résumé of Szubanski is in website (http):en.wikipedia.org/wiki/Plan_Wschod.
26. For the Russian campaign see Czeslaw, Kampania; Gross pp.17-18, 20-25, 28-32, 34-45, 48-49; Meltukhov pp.119-121; Porter p.23; Rees pp.23-29; Voronov pp.132-134; Zaloga pp.78-85; Henrik Krog's Soviet invasion of Poland 1939 website. The Hronos has a useful diary of Soviet operations. Article by Lukinov. For air operations see Wawrzynski.
27. Wawrzynski, Table 8 p.79. VVS casualties to enemy action up to 25 September were six aircraft and eight dead.
28. From 17 September the Black Sea Fleet deployed 10 submarines to watch Rumanian and Bulgarian ports.
29. It was probably they who liberated 64 Wehrmacht prisoners of war on the first day.
30. For Wilno see Czesław, Wilno-Grodno-Kodziowce.
31. Eremenko pp.16-23.
32. These were bottles of kerosene or petrol with a chemical or burning rag fuze used against armour. They were first developed in Spain and gained their name in Finland during the Winter War.
33. For Grodno and Kadziowice see Czeslaw; Eremenko pp.23-26. Drig's Mechanizirovannieye Korpusa RKKA website, 15th Tank Corps entry. Eremenko was apparently wounded in this battle.
34. Pliev would be the leading Red Army cavalry man during the Second World War. Decades later he would command Soviet ground forces in Cuba.
35. Eremenko p.26.
36. Krivoshein had led Russian tanks in Spain from 1936 to 1937. He would become a Hero of the Soviet Union and lead troops to Berlin in 1945. His assistant chief-of-staff, Major I.D. Kvass, who made the arrangements in 1939, would be killed in Brześć nad Bugiem (Brest-Litovsk) on 23 June 1941.

37. Eremenko pp.23-27.
38. Gross p.18.
39. Op. cit. p.23.
40. Ukrainian attacks began on 10 September. Some would fight the Red Army at Chodorow and Lwow.
41. Gross p.49.
42. The Russians lost 265 men, including 81 dead, and were reported to have killed all the Polish officers and non-commissioned officers they captured.
43. Orlik-Ruckemann escaped to England.
44. He would command 34th and 4th Armies.
45. Most of the 30 Russian border guards killed to 25 September probably died in this battle.
46. Gross p.22 f/n.
47. Langner managed to escape and reached England where he died in 1972.
48. Other sources state that the division had 236 casualties including 99 dead.
49. See Shpakovskyy and Saneev article: 'Bronetehnika i tankovye voiska Polshi'.
50. Anders was taken prisoner three days later. The Russians asked him to form a Polish exile Army under their command, but he took most of the surviving prisoners to join the British.
51. Krebs would be the last Chief of the Army General Staff.
52. The Germans had begun transferring troops from Poland to the West the previous day.
53. Two days later the division crossed the Western Bug.
54. Kiyan's Workers' and Peasants' Red Army (RKKA) website.
55. The Ukrainian Front claimed to have captured 135,903,977 rounds of rifle calibre ammunition and 803,040 shells, as well as 5,785 vehicles.
56. Kirovsheev pp.57-60. Higher figures are given by other sources.
57. Montefiore p.277.
58. Gross pp.46-47.
59. Montefiore p.278.
60. Meltyuhov Table 8 p.133; Hronos website.
61. Rees pp.29-34.
62. For Baltic military history Anderson is extremely valuable. I benefited from an English summary kindly provided by my good friend, Alex Vanags-Baganskis. See also his Anderson's article and Šèerbinskis, as well as Salo's dissertation available on the web.
63. Salo p.39.
64. Salo pp.40-41.
65. Dyke p.5.
66. German tank pioneer Guderian was wounded outside Riga in 1919.
67. Salo p.43.
68. See Amosov and Pochtarev for a detailed account of the blockade arrangements. At that time there were three dreadnoughts in the Baltic Fleet but one was transferred to the Black Sea that year.
69. Details kindly provided in response to my query by Mr Toomas Hiio in an e-mail of 17 October 2011.
70. She was lost, probably mined, in June 1940.
71. For the occupation of Estonia and its background see Metelyuhov pp.179-180; Montefiore pp.278-280; Tannberg & Tarvel.
72. Some sources suggest *Metallist* was sunk by the Baltic Fleet submarine *Sch 303* on the orders of Leningrad Party boss, Andrei Zhdanov, who was very close to the Baltic Fleet, to provide an excuse for the invasion. An alternative story is that she was damaged by *Sch 303* and finished off by the Project 39 class 'Guard Ship' (frigate) *Tucha*, while others suggest she was scuttled. The same submarine is reported to have attacked, but missed, another Soviet freighter. It is worth noting that a freighter with the same name was reported operating in the Azov Sea and a 1,375 grt transport would be sunk by Finnish coast defence guns in July 1941.
73. Salo pp.63-64.

74. For Estonian defensive planning see Salo pp.47–49, 56–63, 70. The mobilised army would have had 16 infantry regiments which were distributed between the three pre-war divisional sectors for a total of 105,000 troops and 250 guns.
75. Montefiore pp.278-280. The Estonians ratified the agreement on 4 October.
76. For the move into Estonia see Metelyuhov pp.180-181, 186-187. Salo pp.63-64. Website Documents on the Soviet Military Occupation of Estonia. The Estonian Fleet consisted of the two submarines, a First World War torpedo boat, eight gunboats and a few minesweepers. A planned advance into Estonia abandoned following the Estonian capitulation was codenamed 'Vulkan'.
77. For the Latvian Army see Anderson and also Salo pp.47–49, 54-55 including plans. For Russians see Metelyuhov pp.183-184.
78. Metelyuhov pp.186.
79. Dyke pp.4, 12-14.
80. For Lithuanian forces and plans see Salo pp.50, 55-56. For Russia see Metelyuhov pp.185-186. See extract from Urbšys's memoirs in article.
81. Metelyuhov pp.186-187.
82. Op. cit. p.188.

CHAPTER FOUR

THE WINTER WAR: DISASTER IN THE SNOW

'We enter Finland not as combatants, but as friends and liberators...'
KIRILL AFANASIEVICH MERETSKOV, COMMANDER OF THE LENINGRAD MILITARY DISTRICT, 30 NOVEMBER 1939

'Come and help us or we will all die here.'
KOMBRIG STEPAN KONDRATIEV, 34TH TANK BRIGADE, 25 FEBRUARY 1940

O Stalin and his creatures, the summons issued to Finland's Foreign Minister for 'trade talks' in Moscow on 5 October 1939 must have appeared a formality, given the way the Baltic States were succumbing to Russian pressure; but Finland was a very different case.

Finland worried Moscow because her independence received much German support, including an expeditionary force under General Rüdiger Graf von der Goltz. Indeed the Finnish Army's leadership, apart from its leader, General Carl Gustav Mannerheim, was drawn from members of the Prussian 27th Jäger Battalion and Finnish territory was used for devastating British raids on the Baltic Fleet's Kronstadt base outside Leningrad.[1] Mannerheim's troops also brutally suppressed the Finnish working classes and he remained a key defence figure throughout the inter-war years, sometimes hosting Goltz's personal visits to the country. The 1920 Treaty of Tartu (Dorpat) split the Karelian Isthmus north of Leningrad between Finland and the Soviet Union with the border some 32 kilometres from Leningrad. It ensured that some Finnish islands in the Gulf of Finland were demilitarised and gave Finland the ice-free port of Petsamo as well as nearby iron and nickel deposits which were of great interest to Germany and Great Britain.[2]

Post-war social policies improved the working classes' standard of living, but there were fears that Finland might follow the Baltic States and turn to a right-wing autocracy. These were fuelled by a farcical mutiny by the Suojeluskunta or Civil Guard (descendants of the anti-Bolshevik White Guard), while in 1932 right-wing demagogue, Kurt Wallenius, tried to kidnap the Finnish president in a coup which was quickly crushed. With the banning of the Finnish Communist Party in 1931 and the right-wing Academic Karelian Society speaking of reclaiming a 'Greater Finland' extending east to the Urals and south into Estonia, Moscow misinterpreted Finnish actions and Stalin believed the country to be a hotbed of

Fascist plotters and class antagonism. However, in January 1932, Moscow signed a non-aggression pact in Helsinki, the Russian signatory being the future Soviet Ambassador, Ivan Maiskii, who left shortly afterwards for Tokyo and then London.[3] The agreement included a conciliation commission for any future disputes, and with these pacts in place and confirmation of traditional Scandinavian neutrality, Helsinki looked confidently to the future.

But in April 1938 the Intourist Chief (NKVD Rezident) at the Soviet Embassy, Boris Yartsev, began a series of discussions with senior members of the Finnish government which excluded the Russian Ambassador. He sought guarantees that Helsinki would not allow Germany to use Finnish territory to attack the Soviet Union and would seek Russian military aid if Berlin struck. But, ominously, he also sought territorial concessions, including permission for a Red Army presence, and details of Finnish–Estonian plans to blockade the Gulf of Finland. Neither Yartsev nor Moscow would go into details and repeated Finnish pledges of neutrality were ignored.[4]

The talks continued throughout 1938 with Moscow offering the carrot of a favourable trade treaty in return for an air base in Finland as well as control of key Finnish defences. These demands were rejected however, because they violated the nation's independence and neutrality. Helsinki also feared they would compromise ultimately vain discussions with Sweden on military co-operation and possibly joint defence of the Ålands Islands at the entrance to the Gulf of Bothnia, which led to the iron ore deposits so important to both nations.

From March 1939 Moscow's demands for Finnish territory became more strident and Helsinki became more obstinate. The Finnish politicians rejected the initial proposal to lease some islands in return for some of Russian Karelia, although Mannerheim, who knew the weakness of the Finnish armed forces, supported the plan. During the abortive Anglo-French-Soviet negotiations in August 1939, Moscow sought a guarantee that the Baltic States and Finland would accept its military support if Germany attacked, but pressure from Finland and Sweden thwarted any such plans.[5]

Against this background Moscow summoned the Finnish Foreign Minister, Elias Erkko, for talks on 5 October, but some grit entered the well-oiled operation. Helsinki refused to send Erkko and despatched instead Juho Paasikivi, the former Ambassador to Stockholm, who spoke Russian and had helped to create the 1920 agreement. Stalin was present when the two sides eventually met on 12 October. The Soviet negotiators demanded firstly that the border be moved within 20 kilometres of Viipuri, then the ceding of islands in the Gulf of Finland, together with the Rybachi Peninsula near Petsamo, and the leasing of the Hanko Peninsula near Helsinki.[6] The Finns refused because moving the border would destroy the Karelian fortifications, while the other demands would herald the absorption of the country by Russia. They did offer minor concessions, which Molotov rejected on 23 October blustering: 'Is it your intention to provoke a conflict?' Paasikivi replied: 'We want no such thing, but you seem to.'

The discussions were clouded by mutual suspicion. The Russians had genuine strategic concerns but, as Khrushchev later observed about Soviet military action in Finland: 'Of course we didn't have any legal right. As far as morality was concerned, our desire to protect ourselves was ample justification in our own eyes.'[7] But what Stalin regarded as the malign influence of Germany in Finland actually represented the acutely nationalistic view of a newly-independent nation determined to maintain territorial and political integrity.

Erkko believed the Russians were bluffing about military action but Mannerheim, now chief military advisor to the government, disagreed. This led to an acrimonious dispute although the Karelia Army Commander, Lieutenant General Hugo Österman, agreed with Mannerheim when separately asked his opinion. The Finnish Cabinet confirmed Paasikivi's decisions, but asked him to return to Moscow to seek room for manoeuvre, leading to another fruitless round of talks there. As he departed the Kremlin on 3 November, Molotov observed: 'We civilians can see no further in the matter: now it is the turn of the military to have their say.' Yet at Moscow railway station on 9 November Stalin bizarrely shook hands with the departing members and wished them 'all the best'.

Mannerheim twice begged the government to re-open discussions, the second time on 26 November, when he argued that the army was in no condition to fight. When the government rejected his advice, Mannerheim tendered his resignation as Chairman of Finland's Defence Council and de facto Army Commander-in-Chief, although this was not formally accepted. The Finnish government remained desperately optimistic throughout November as the Soviet Press stepped up its campaign of vilification. Soviet reconnaissance aircraft violated Finnish air space and there were ominous reports of Russian forces massing near the borders combined with the construction of new roads and railways. Yet the Finns were cautious enough to evacuate their cities and close their schools although, when nothing happened, the evacuees returned and it was at least planned to re-open the schools.[8]

Until 1936 Red Army planning for Finland was 'mainly defensive', involving no more than six rifle divisions, but by 1937 it involved ten rifle and one mountain rifle divisions, and two tank brigades together with three supreme command reserve artillery regiments. On 19 April 1939 the Leningrad District submitted a plan involving six divisions and three tank brigades which would strike along the Karelian Isthmus with five more divisions operating north of Lake Ladoga.[9] At the end of June Shaposhnikov produced a contingency plan which envisaged a massive offensive in the Karelian Isthmus lasting several months and using substantial forces in order to reduce the Mannerheim Line, but it was not to Stalin's taste.

He summoned Meretskov, the Leningrad District commander, to Moscow and informed him he was to prepare a 'counter-offensive' in case Finland might become a springboard for an offensive against the Soviet Union. He also met one of the leading Finnish Communists, Otto Kuusinen, who was to act as his advisor on Finnish matters.[10] Specially trained troops were to be kept near the frontier as a contingency and the fortified zone was to be strengthened, but this was to be done in secret.

Having inspected his forces with Leningrad Party boss Zhdanov, Meretskov returned in mid-July with a plan envisaging an advance along the Karelian Isthmus and north of Lake Ladoga, involving 69 per cent of his forces in a campaign planned to last no more than 15 days. This met Stalin's approval in terms of timescale and he pledged full Soviet resources to support it. With these provisos the Main Military Council rubber-stamped the plan by the end of July. Zhdanov strongly believed that the Finnish 'masses' would rise up in support of the Red Army when its troops crossed the border, a view based upon the reports of the Soviet Ambassador; these reports influenced Meretskov.[11]

The Main Military Council reconsidered the plan on 14 October after the first round of negotiations. Shaposhnikov again advocated his own proposals as the basis for future operations, but 'The Boss', delighted at the Red Army success in Poland, rubber-stamped Meretskov's outline adding: 'The Leningrad Front is commissioned to conduct the entire operation against Finland. The General Staff is not to have a hand in this; it is to concern itself with other matters.' Almost everyone believed the forthcoming operation would be a walkover, taking little more than a fortnight, and Meretskov was concerned his spearheads might accidentally cross the Swedish border.

Detailed planning began on 29 October, Voroshilov ordering Meretskov to ensure the main thrusts enveloped and annihilated the Finnish Army, while diversions were made all the way north to Murmansk. To facilitate this task Meretskov constructed supply depots, roads and rail lines along the Leningrad-Murmansk railway to assist deployment in the northern wilderness. The train carrying the last Finnish delegation had barely crossed the border when, on 15 November, Stalin ordered Meretskov to accelerate his preparations and despatched Voronov (whom Meretskov had known in Spain) on a tour of inspection with Meretskov and Zhdanov. On 20 November they met Voroshilov to complete planning and assigned Yakovlev's 7th Army to the Isthmus and Komdiv Ivan Khabarov's 8th Army to thrust north of Lake Ladoga.

Surprisingly, Meretskov had little information on the Mannerheim Line and believed the weakest defences were on the eastern side of the Isthmus. This ignorance is astonishing given that the GRU had been beavering away for years: by 1938 it had produced a seven-page report with numerous photographs, some from defectors and others from Russian agents using miniature cameras, while further information had arrived via the German military attaché in Helsinki in September. According to Kushchev, the GRU had detailed information on the Mannerheim Line but the Leningrad Military District did not seek its help.[12]

Meretskov ordered Yakovlev to break through at Taipale using 19th Rifle Corps (Komdiv Filip Starikov) and 50th Rifle Corps (Kombrig Filip Gorelenko) which were to meet Khabarov at Hintola, seize the Finnish Army headquarters at Antrea and Viipuri, then march down the Simola-Lakhti Highway to Helsinki – a total advance of some 250 kilometres in about 10 days.[13] Just before the invasion, Voronov visited Meretskov to discuss artillery preparations and found Kulik and Mekhlis there. Asked to estimate the gunners' requirements he said he needed to know how long the campaign would last. When they replied 10-12 days he warned them the Red Army would be lucky if it did not take two or three months, earning him 'derisive gibes' from Kulik who ordered him to base his estimates on no more than 12 days.[14]

Meanwhile, Flagman Vladimir Tributs's Baltic Fleet, alerted by Kuznetsov on 3 November, was to control the Gulf of Finland by destroying Finland's two coast defence ships before they escaped to Sweden and to seize islands in the west while its Northern and Southern Defence Regions were to provide fire support for the army.[15] On 12 November Tributs created the Special Detachment under Captain Semon Ramishvili to seize the islands. When Meretskov assumed operational control of the fleet on 21 November, Ramishvili was ordered to take the islands, being reinforced with a rifle regiment for an amphibious assault.[16] The Fleet also had a substantial air role with 61st Fighter Brigade (177 fighters) responsible for air defence of the Leningrad area, while the 8th Bomber Brigade struck enemy airfields, coast defence batteries, bases and industry.

From 3 November Moscow began a war of words against the Finns whose border guards reported on 26 November hearing Russian artillery fire. Molotov claimed Finnish guns had shelled Russian Karelia, killing some border guards, although long after the event Khrushchev stated that the shellings were arranged by Kulik using an NKVD battery.[17] Moscow demanded that the Finns apologise and withdraw their forces 20-25 kilometres from the border. It also rejected Helsinki's attempts to invoke conciliation arrangements. Meretskov, who had anticipated a week's preparation before his 'counter-attack', now found it slashed to four days, apparently because Zhdanov wanted to offer Finland to Stalin as a 61st birthday present on 18 December. Molotov, using the usual Communist tortuous logic, now claimed that Finland no longer abided by the Non-Aggression Pact which Moscow now abrogated and, without awaiting a response, on 29 November broke off diplomatic relations.

Stalin had already decided that Finland would have a new government, removing the excuse for a declaration of war, and selected Kuusinen, a poet and Party hack, as its head. The post was offered originally on 13 November to Finnish Communist General Secretary, Arvo Tuominen, who was living in Sweden, but patriotism replaced ideology and after telling Communist cells in Finland to follow their own conscience, he went underground in Sweden.[18]

The new administration had its own 'army' with the formation on 11 November of the 106th Karelian National Rifle Division, also known as 1st Finnish Rifle Corps, with a nominal 14,000 men, but in reality it was 6,000, most probably made up of Soviet citizens of Finnish extraction. It never went into the field and only 16 Finnish prisoners of war would join it. Both administration and army vanished like the morning mist when they ceased to be an asset to Stalin, although the division was re-formed on 16 July 1940 as a Red Army formation.[19]

Meanwhile Meretskov hastily assembled Red Army formations and, following reports of Norwegian naval activity in the north, created Komdiv Valerian Frolov's 14th Army on 27 November, ordering it to take Petsamo and the Rybachii Peninsula, while Kuznetsov alerted Flagman Valentin Drozd's Northern Fleet. Both men were warned that hostilities might break out with Norway, but they were not to cross the frontiers.[20]

On the evening of 29 November, Stalin was dining in his apartment with Beria, Khrushchev, Molotov and Zhdanov, when it became clear that the Finns would not bend to Russian pressure. Casually, Stalin said: 'Let's get started today.' Just after midnight Voroshilov ordered Meretskov to begin the invasion that morning. Meretskov sent out a proclamation to his forces stating: 'We enter Finland not as combatants, but as friends and liberators, freeing the Finnish People from the clutches of the landowners and capitalists. We are not against the Finnish People, but against the Cajander-Erkko government, clutching the Finnish People and provoking war with the Soviet Union.'[21]

The advance began with a 70-minute bombardment starting at 06.50 hrs. Meretskov had nearly a quarter of the active Red Army – 450,000 men in 23 rifle divisions supported by 2,000 tanks and 1,000 aircraft. But his strategic reserve was still assembling on 30 November with only four of nine first-echelon divisions available due to mobilisation problems and because of the sudden setting of the invasion date. The Red Army had little intelligence, inaccurate maps, flat-trajectory field guns rather than howitzers for use in forests, and many anti-tank guns to be deployed against a nation with few tanks. Many trucks were carrying posters for post-occupation propaganda, and even bands, but there was little winter clothing and none of the troops was ski-trained; indeed, the vehicles were not even painted white to conceal them. Worse still, the absence of a formal declaration of war meant that for a fortnight the regional rail network remained on the slower peacetime schedule.[22]

With no official declaration of war and, in an age terrified about the threat from the air, the Russians committed a major propaganda error. As Russian troops crossed the border in an event which Erkko had earlier described as 'too terrible to contemplate', bombers from the new bases in Estonia made surprise attacks upon Helsinki and other towns. The Russians were aiming at military targets, but they were incredibly inaccurate, striking the Soviet Legation as well as offices and apartment blocks to kill some 200 people.[23]

Mannerheim drove through the bombed streets to Parliament, withdrew his resignation and was confirmed Commander-in-Chief. This was part of a major change in leadership with Premier Aimo Cajander's Finance Minister, Väinö Tanner, a bête noir of the Russians, engineering the resignation of both Cajander and Erkko on 1 December. They were replaced with a government of national unity under Risto Ryti, with Tanner becoming the Foreign Minister. The reshuffle was designed to prepare the way for negotiations using a direct radio appeal by Tanner, but it was ignored by the Russians.[24]

Helsinki sought the support of the League of Nations which was informed by Molotov that his government recognised only Kuusinen's administration (the Democratic Republic of Finland), which had been quickly established in the village of Terijoki. As for the League of Nations, its swansong was to condemn and to expel the Soviet Union while urging the despatch of military aid to Finland. Between December and February 1940 Helsinki acquired from Belgium, France, Great Britain, Italy and Sweden a considerable arsenal including 328 field-, 206 anti-aircraft- and 68 anti-tank guns, 100 anti-tank rifles, 216 mortars, 77,300 rifles, 3,425 light and 100 heavy machine guns as well as 164 aircraft (131 combat), while at least four 'non-combatant' aircraft were used in action, including a DC 2 airliner used as a bomber.[25] The quality and deliveries of this materiel were uneven, but they certainly eased the Finnish burden. In addition, more than 12,000 volunteers from Scandinavian countries, the Baltic States and Hungary would offer their services, although the majority arrived too late to fight. Aid was also received from partially-occupied Estonia where 150 volunteers crossed the Gulf of Finland, while the country's armed forces sent a stream of intelligence material to their former colleagues.

Much of this material reached Finland with Swedish support, which included the escort of convoys, while from 17 February an ice road was built across the Gulf of Bothnia between Sweden and Finland in order to ease the flow of supplies. The Russians did not learn of the road's existence until after the war via a German newspaper report.[26] Moscow was, however, concerned about Swedish intervention, intelligence having monitored activity in Finland and Estonia, and as early as 6 November Tributs began sending submarines from the Baltic bases to watch naval movements as a precaution against raids. By 30 November Tributs had 10 submarines off the Swedish coast while a task group consisting of the heavy cruiser *Kirov* and two destroyers, was sailing the Baltic. More submarines were scheduled to patrol the Swedish coast, although Meretskov delayed their departure.

Within two days of the Soviet invasion it became clear that the Royal Swedish Navy was planning defensive rather than offensive operations, by escorting convoys to Finnish ports and laying mines at the entrance of the Gulf of Bothnia.[27] Within hours the Kirov task group was ordered to bombard enemy coast defences.[28] To counter the Finnish Navy the Baltic Fleet had five torpedo boats and six submarines which were also to interdict coastal traffic. Then, all the submarines were recalled to ensure that a German ship evacuating Soviet embassy personnel from Helsinki was not threatened and a week elapsed before they could be redeployed.

The blockade of Finland's coast, announced by Moscow in the Kuusinen government's name on 8 December, and the simultaneous Finnish submarine campaign, were restricted by the gradual icing of the Baltic. The last Russian submarine tied up on 19 January. Initially, Russia deployed 11 submarines and 28 seaplanes, of which up to a third were unserviceable, with the boats interdicting traffic and laying mines – as did one Finnish submarine off Tallinn which sank a schooner.

The Russian campaign sank five ships (7,766 grt) at the cost of one boat lost to mines and a Finnish escort vessel lost in bizarre circumstances on 13 January when a depth charge exploded prematurely. Unrestricted operations were banned, forcing the boats to surface to identify potential victims, and armed German merchantmen frequently fired upon them. Torpedoes proved unreliable and officers had few navigation skills while the new bases lacked both communications facilities and supplies to support the offensive. Indeed, the lack of a formal declaration of war meant that the Russian Navy was unable to use wartime stores for several weeks. The bombers of the Baltic Fleet had more success in regular attacks upon ports, with the two coast defence ships augmenting the anti-aircraft defences of the main port of Turku. The navy bombers sank seven freighters (some 9,000 grt) and severely damaged an icebreaker but it was only from 29 January that Baltic Fleet bombers began a minelaying offensive.[29]

Despite Swedish support, Helsinki was disappointed by Stockholm's response. For more than a decade Sweden's military leadership had sought secretly to organise a forward defence against Russia through unofficial discussions with their opposite numbers in Finland and Estonia. The Finnish and Swedish General Staffs had a close working relationship, the latter keeping Helsinki informed about plans to deploy forces along the frontier; but Swedish society was divided on the issue of Suomi-Swedish relations. The liberals, who increasingly dominated Parliament, were sympathetic to the Soviet Union and, along with the Foreign Ministry, damned Helsinki's domestic politics while regarding Swedish conservative desires for closer relations with suspicion. Even when Finland adopted liberal policies and began to support a neutral foreign policy, most liberals remained intransigent. Molotov's foreign policy did lead the Swedes increasingly to question their stance, but it proved no Road to Damascus and, on 12 October, Stockholm had confirmed Parliament's decision in June to reject plans for joint defence of the Åland Islands.

Still hoping for Swedish military support, Tanner approached the Swedish Premier, Per Albin Hansson, but the Swedish Parliament was against any sort of direct involvement. On 27 November Hansson agreed only to provide military equipment, food and diplomatic support. Swedish public and political opinion remained divided during the Winter War and Helsinki formally sought Swedish military intervention on three occasions. But Stockholm denied them each time. On 19 February, King Gustav publicly rejected the last Finnish plea in an attempt to force the Finns to accept Soviet terms, but also to quell interventionist moves in his own country. In both aims he succeeded, but it would create great bitterness in his eastern neighbour.

The ghost at the banquet was Sweden's armed forces, severely neglected over the previous decades and with a rearmament programme agreed only in 1936. The army had only 16 light tanks and some tankettes, twenty-four heavy batteries, many with obsolete weapons, 76 heavy anti-aircraft guns, including 24 obsolete weapons – most of them static – and 154 static and 24 mobile light (40 mm) anti-aircraft guns. Conscription had been reduced to four months in 1924 and extended only in 1936, but it was not until the German invasion of its western neighbours in April 1940 that enlistment was extended to 15 months. The cutbacks in the late 1920s had reduced training, especially winter training, and there had been few exercises for major formations. The air force had only 130 combat aircraft (54 fighters, the most modern being 36 Gloster Gladiators) and the outbreak of the Second World War made it extremely difficult to re-equip from abroad – although in February it was announced that two fighter wings (Flottiljer) with six squadrons would be formed as well as another two reconnaissance squadrons.[30]

With the Russian invasion of Finland, Stockholm decided to secure the Finnish frontier by mobilising the Second Corps on 2 December, which comprised initially the Sixth Division reinforced by two infantry regiments (one from Fifth Division) and a mechanised cavalry battalion, but which was followed by the rest of Fifth Division on 17 December. Since these formations were raised largely in the more populous parts of central and southern Sweden, they needed winter training and became operational only on 25 February with some 26,600 men.

The corps was initially under General Archibald Douglas who believed in a forward defence along the Kemi River in Finland. Rather than offer a hostage to fortune however, the government replaced him by bringing out of retirement General Oscar Nygren, who had been the last Chief of the General Staff before it became the tri-service Defence Staff in 1936. Nevertheless, friendly Swedish Army personnel allowed equipment to cross the border while the supply base at Boden became a reliable source of materiel for the Finns.[31]

However, there remained a groundswell of support among Swedish people for their neighbour's heroic battle and a volunteer brigade, the Svenska frivilligkåren (SFK) was formed from 4 December under Major General Ernst Linder, a friend of Mannerheim, with Lieutenant Colonel Carl-August Count Ehrensvärd as his chief-of-staff. The corps would have some 8,260 men (including 125 Norwegians) and would include a squadron of F 19 raised from Swedish Air Force volunteers.

Meanwhile the Red Army discovered Finland's forces to be alert and with high morale, despite shortages of equipment due to under-funding and earlier 10 per cent cuts in the defence budget in 1932 and 1933 – which meant that the small arms ammunition factory had not been expanded even when defence budgets increased later in the decade.[32] Much old equipment was not replaced during the administration of the pacifist, cost-cutting Cajander and, despite the long winter nights, there were few torches, flare pistols or pyrotechnics. Mannerheim sought greater funding but was ignored and, like the rest of the armed forces, was forced to replace brawn with brain. He reorganised the reserves, which originally had simply filled out regular units, into territorially-based units led by regular officers which could quickly expand the army.

The Finnish defence plan, codenamed 'Venäjän Keskitys' ('VK' - Russian Concentration) had been updated in 1934, but the growth in Soviet military power meant two options in 1939: VK 1 and VK 2. VK 1 assumed that a Suomi-Soviet conflict was part of a wider struggle in which major Red Army forces were committed along the western borders and that an enemy thrust into the Karelian Isthmus would be stopped by a fortified line officially designated 'Pääpulustusasema' (Main Defensive Position) abbreviated to Pääsema. Later this became known popularly as the Mannerheim Line. The Finns would then stage a counter-offensive to regain the frontier or to secure better defence terrain in Russian territory, while forces north of Lake Ladoga would counter-attack spearheads, driving them across the borders to fight in Soviet territory.

But by 1939 the changing strategic situation meant VK 2 was the only practical option. This called for a purely defensive struggle in Karelia based upon the Mannerheim Line fighting against an anticipated force of 10 divisions until new allies or the League of Nations intervened to provide a negotiated settlement. The passive approach was strongly criticised by the Finnish Army leadership and there was concern that Cajander had been reluctant to fund further construction of the line. Certainly, in the first month of the war, the Finnish Army leaders in the Karelian Isthmus hoped to implement VK 1 in some form, while the active elements of VK 1 were encouraged north of Lake Ladoga where no more than four enemy divisions were anticipated.

Helsinki began preparations as negotiations reached an impasse in Moscow and, on 11 October, Mannerheim proposed a partial mobilisation. This was approved the following day as 'Ylimääräiset harjoitukset' (YH - 'an extra rehearsal' exercise) to avoid international notice. Further YH orders issued on 7 and 12 November expanded the 33,000-man regular army to 260,800, including 100,000 reservists with 100,000 para-military Civil Guard.[33] Manpower problems were eased through the Lovta Svärd, the Civil Guard's women's auxiliary, whose 100,000 members provided clerks, cooks, nurses and 'hotel services', thereby freeing scarce manpower. The expanded army and border guard force, the Suojeluskunta and the Lattas, meant that 14 per cent of Finland's population was under arms.[34]

The initial YH order created the Kannaksen Armeijan Esikunta (Karelian Isthmus Army) with 133,000 men (representing 42 per cent of the armed forces) and including the air defence units under Österman with two corps – Lieutenant General Harald Öhquist's Second on the western side with Fourth, Fifth and Eleventh Divisions, and Lieutenant General Erik Heinrichs' Third Corps with Eighth and Tenth Divisions in the Mannerheim Line. To prevent the Russians from outflanking the line, Major General Juho Heiskanen's Fourth Corps was deployed with 40,000 men north of Lake Ladoga comprising the Twelfth and Thirteenth Divisions, while in the Arctic wastes to the north was the North-Finland Group led by Major General Viljo Tuompo. The strategic reserve consisted of the Sixth Division in Luumäki and the Ninth Division in Oulu, ready to exploit the network of roads leading to the northern front, but the latter lacked artillery. In addition there were a cycle battalion, an artillery training regiment, a few battalions of poorly trained and lightly armed reservists, as well as the Field Replacement Brigade with nine battalions raised from supply troops.

There were desperate material shortages however, and department stores would be raided to provide the troops with greatcoats. Mannerheim's headquarters calculated that the army was short of 40 per cent of its machine guns, 10 per cent of light machine guns and 15 per cent of rifles, even with weapons transferred from the Civil Guard. Artillery was a major problem, although training and tactics devised by Lieutenant General Vilho Nenonen were generally superior to the Russians. As a captured Russian artillery officer asked: 'Your artillery hits almost every time with the first shots, but why don't you shoot more?' The answer was a shortage of tubes and ammunition, for while most Russian divisions had seventy-eight 76 mm and 122 mm guns, a Finnish one had only thirty-six, often of Great War vintage, the army having a total of 489 guns of which 77 were so old they lacked recoil systems. There were only 43 heavy 150-152 mm howitzers and 107 mm guns, while artillery ammunition was in short supply, totalling 271,300 rounds, of which 22,000 were for heavy weapons; with anticipated consumption at 640,500 rounds per month there was sufficient for three weeks of intense operations. With limited artillery ammunition, Finnish gunners paid great attention before the war to precision targeting and had mapped and ranged much of the Karelian Isthmus.

There was a general shortage of anti-tank and anti-aircraft guns: many of the former arrived from Sweden shortly before the Russian attack, and they were able to crack even the T-35 heavy tanks, while only 60 of an order for 134 German Rheinmetall 20 mm anti-aircraft guns had been delivered at the time of the invasion and Germany refused to complete the order.[35] The Finns had the advantage of 24 excellent short-range 81 mm mortars in each division and 4,000 Suomi KP/-31 (Suomi-konepistooli or Finland sub-machine gun).[36]

There was enough small arms ammunition for 60 days of operations, although distribution was very uneven. There was barely three weeks worth of shells for the field artillery and even less for heavy and coast defence artillery. There was enough petrol and oil to support the army for 60 days, but the air force had enough fuel for only 30 days. However, the Finns had excellent communications intelligence (comint) which used radio interception vehicles. They detected coded signals and sent them back to data collection centres where the messages were decrypted and sent to forward commanders often within four hours. This system would play a key role, especially in the northern operations.[37]

It was north of Lake Ladoga that the Finnish Army secured its greatest success and inflicted a series of humiliating defeats upon the Red Army, inflicting 141,300 casualties or slightly more than its opponent's total strength! The region consisted of forests which grew denser as they neared the Arctic Circle, the only habitation consisting of scattered farms and logging towns within clearings. Communication was by narrow roads, often little more than tracks capable of taking a horse-drawn wagon, and when the snow fell the only way of travelling between the roads was on skis.

Immediately north of the lake was Heiskanen's Fourth Corps with two divisions and eight light infantry/cyclist battalions. The Corps held a 96-kilometre front, while the 1,000 kilometres from Suojärvi to Petsamo was held by Major General Viljo Tuompo's North Finland Group (Pohjois-Suomen Ryhmä) with two small battle groups, totalling seven battalions, three batteries and three road-building companies augmented by Civil Guard units. These forces were deemed adequate because it was anticipated that no more than five Red Army divisions would try to wend their way through the forests.[38] Heiskanen anticipated facing up to three rifle divisions and planned to withdraw to fixed defences running from Lake Syskyjärvi-Kitelä–Lake Ladoga, pin down the enemy then counter-attack from his left, exploiting a branch rail line, to strike across country, isolating and destroying the advance guard.

But during the autumn the Red Army began to build a railway from its supply base at Petrozavodsk to the border on the other side of the Finnish town of Suojärvi (defended by two regiments of Twelfth Division with some medium guns and an armoured train). Although not completed until April, it doubled the number of troops the Russians could put into the region. Khabarov's 8th Army deployed six rifle divisions and a tank brigade – 130,000 men and 400 tanks (26 per cent of Meretskov's forces) – whose task was to advance on a 380-kilometre front to seize eastern Viipuri and Kuopio provinces, cut the railway which ran parallel with the border down to Sortavala on the northern shores of Lake Ladoga, then to strike westwards, advancing at 10 kilometres per day.

On Khabarov's right was 1st Rifle Corps, under Kombrig Roman Panin, which would advance to Ilomantsi (155th Division) and Tolvajärvi (139th Division) and take Suojärvi, covering Khabarov's right and the left of 9th Army. Khabarov's left consisted of 56th Rifle Corps (Komdiv Ivan Cherepanov) which would advance towards Sortavala, 56th Division driving down the Suvilahti branch line, while 18th and 168th Divisions separately cleared the north-eastern shores of Lake Ladoga and met up on the shoreline at Kitelä. They would then drive behind Finland's Isthmus defences. Khabarov assumed he would meet little resistance and left only Cherepanov's two southern divisions capable of supporting each other in the event of a counter-attack.[39] His plans quickly collapsed however, for although he was usually able to brush aside the covering units, progress along the narrow roads was impeded by obstacles such as felled trees, blown bridges and minefields, as well as Finnish raids. Panin also suffered the total absence of any intelligence on enemy forces. The Finnish commanders, who knew the terrain intimately, planned a series of attacks on the roads from the woods, but on 3 December Mannerheim's headquarters demanded a conventional counter-attack. The order arrived only five hours before H-Hour as winter equipment arrived and with the men tired and hungry. Reluctantly, Heiskanen obeyed, but the appearance of Russian armour quickly stopped the Finns, causing panic and flight.

Neither side was pleased with its commander's performance and on 4 December they acted. Mannerheim replaced Heiskanen with Major General Johan Hägglund, a Jäger veteran who had studied in the Swedish Military Academy and who was three years younger than his predecessor, while Khabarov was replaced by Komkor Vladimir Kurdiumov.[40] Meretskov also ordered Kurdiumov and 9th Army to make greater use of the bombers of the VVS to help speed their advance, but strictly forbade the bombing of population centres, a belated recognition of the political fall-out from the first day's bombing campaign.

Cherepanov made slow progress around Lake Ladoga: his 168th Division advanced northward along the eastern bank, while Kombrig Stepan Kondratiev's 34th Tank Brigade reached the outskirts of Kitelä on 10 December, but coast defence batteries on Mantsinsaari Island interdicted Russian communications. The army's right flank was covered by the 18th Division (Kombrig Grigori Kondrashev), part of the Soviet Karelia garrison, whose spearhead on 11 December linked up with the 168th Rifle Division at Uomo, but in doing so Kondrashev stretched his communications to breaking point and exhausted his troops, bringing a halt to his advance by mid-December.

There was further good news for the Finns on Hägglund's northern flank after Heiskanen's plans had unravelled. His northern covering force, under Lieutenant Colonel V. Räsänen, was quickly brought to the edge of disintegration by tanks of 56th Rifle Division, partly because Räsänen spent almost all his time in his command post at Äglÿjärvi some 10 kilometres in the rear. Luckily the enemy's advance was glacially slow, it being only halfway to its initial objective by dusk of the first day. However, the Finns failed to hold the Russians at pre-prepared defences at Piitsoinoja which were abandoned on 7 December for the secondary defensive line at Kollaa on the Kollaa River – a frozen stream where the foxholes and wire entanglements proved enough to hold the Russian advance and were later strengthened with bunkers and dugouts. The line came under severe pressure throughout January, Russian guns turning the battlefield into a moonscape of overlapping craters and tree stumps, but it held and at one point Hägglund asked, 'Will Kollaa hold?' Lieutenant Aarne Juutilainen famously replied: 'Yes, it will hold – unless we are told to run'. By showing 'sisu' ('guts'), the defenders made possible significant victories to the north and the south, but at terrible cost, with the defending regiment suffering 56 per cent casualties (1,665 men).

His left now secure, Hägglund could act more aggressively in his centre and right, but his initial attempts on 12-13 December were a dismal failure in the face of enemy firepower. Another assault on 17 December also failed, but did draw in Cherepanov's reserves as his units were increasingly strung out along roads which were under threat and protected by tank patrols. Irritated by Kurdiumov's lack of progress, Moscow sent Kulik to 8th Army headquarters at Petrozavodsk to investigate. He reported, on 19 December, that Cherepanov had taken heavy losses and needed 20,000 replacements immediately. At this, Moscow merely sent a staff officer, Colonel Raevskii. He warned that with the Red Army road-bound and with deep snow blocking the road, the Finns were now in a position to annihilate Cherepanov's units. Only by sending masses of ski-equipped troops to comb the forests could this be avoided. Moscow ignored Raevskii and responded by bringing

Shtern from the Far East to replace Kurdiumov on 10 January, but he arrived to find an alarming situation.

Mannerheim had been constantly demanding action from Hägglund and sent his operations chief, Colonel Valo Nihtilä, to look over the General's shoulder.[41] Ignoring this crude hint, Hägglund organised two battle groups under Colonels Pietari Autti and Esa Hannukselka to complete the isolation of 18th Division along a 15-kilometre section of the Uoma road, and to then drive south-west to isolate 168th Rifle Division and the 34th Tank Brigade. Kurdiumov ordered his divisions to continue their offensive, but this was impossible and by the time the Finns launched their offensive, massive snowstorms had created drifts across the Lake Ladoga road, further restricting enemy movement. In a series of jabs from the night of 5/6 January and in rapid succession, Autti and Hannukselka isolated 168th and 18th Divisions as well as 34th Tank Brigade which Kondrashev could not relieve because he lacked reserves. Stalin promised Shtern replacements but made it clear that his mission was to divert enemy forces from the Karelian Front.

The Finns had expected the Russians to retreat and were unhappy when they organised all-round defence based on artillery with dug-in tanks reinforcing the perimeters, one of the largest and strongest being around Lemetti where 5,000 men from 18th Division and 34th Tank Brigade headquarters held an area 2 kilometres long but less than half-a-kilometre wide. Many Finnish troops had been lumberjacks who called these isolated units 'mottis' (sliced tree trunks). Because forests in Finland lacked roads, it was difficult to move complete trees through the wilderness, so the trunks were cut into 'mottis' which were easier to transport, a lumberjack being paid by the number of mottis cut.[42] For the Finns the mottis were a tactical success and a strategic disaster, for they had either to be stormed with little artillery support, or invested, consuming scarce manpower. The mottis, which often had plenty of ammunition but little food, faced starvation, for the besieged were forced to kill and eat many horses, resulting in them becoming immobile.

The situation in the Lemetti motti deteriorated as the Finnish siege lines contracted; Kondrashev complained about the lack of food and on 29 January moaned: 'Hunger, sickness and death are here.' The VVS tried to help by dropping supplies, but Kondratiev reported on 9 February that his men had received only 644 kilogrammes of supplies and 18 emergency ration packs. Messages from Kondratiev, a veteran of Spain, became more plaintive and on 25 February he begged: 'Come and help us or we will all die here.' The motti was now only a kilometre long, but the deep snow thwarted relief attempts by the newly-arrived 8th Rifle Corps (Komdiv Iosif Rubin) which was able to advance barely a kilometre. Shtern received two divisions (11th and 60th Rifle) and three airborne brigades, which were assigned to Panin. He tried desperately to relieve the pockets, advancing from Salmi in the south (11th Division) and Käsnäselkä (60th Division) in the east, but Hägglund held him back. To improve command and control on

12 February, Cherepanov (including the newly-arrived 25th Motor-Cavalry Division) was transferred to the newly-formed 15th Army under Kovalev, fresh from Poland, who also received three more divisions (37th Motor, 87th and 128th Rifle Divisions) and Rubin's 8th Corps. Even with some 100,000 men, however, he achieved nothing and on 25 February was relieved by Kurdiumov, with Cherepanov being relieved three days later by Kombrig Konstantin Korotiev.[43]

Kurdiumov arrived as the Lemetti crisis reached decision point. The pocket demanded permission for a breakout and this was given on the night 28/29 February, being implemented immediately. The operation was badly organised with the 3,261 troops striking out in two groups led by Kondratiev and the 18th Division chief-of-staff, Colonel Z.N. Alekseyev, Kondrashev having been wounded three days earlier. Kondratiev's group was intercepted and wiped out, all the officers shooting themselves, but Alekseyev reached safety with 1,237 men, including 900 wounded. They left a tremendous amount of booty behind them: 128 tanks, 98 guns and nearly 400 vehicles, as well as large amounts of weapons and supplies.

Ironically, the 168th Division, formed only in August from reservists and short of both artillery and motor transport, survived the war around Kitelä at a cost of 7,000 men and 60 per cent of its horses, because it was concentrated and could be supplied by horse-drawn sledge with tank escort along a road built upon the frozen Lake Ladoga. The Finns interdicted communications from Koiranoja Island and used Mantsinsaari's coast defence batteries, but the former was taken between 3-6 March by 37th Rifle Division and 204th Airborne Brigade and the latter were stormed a week before the war ended.[44] This was part of an advance by 11th and 37th Rifle Divisions which commenced up the eastern side of Lake Ladoga and which discovered, on 10 March, that the Finns were retreating. Kurdiumov's hopes of exploiting this by committing 25th Motor-Cavalry Division and 201st Airborne Brigade, however, were dashed by fierce Finnish resistance. The survival of 168th Division was little conciliation for the decimation of Cherepanov's corps. Kondrashev's 18th Division lost 12,000 men and the survivors merged with 111th Division in June, while Kondratiev's tank brigade lost 1,800 men. The NKVD arrived; Kondrashev was arrested in hospital on 4 March, tried and shot, while Cherepanov was shot on 8 March.

The 8th Army's butcher's bill for the war was 44,887 including 13,071 dead and missing, while 15th Army suffered 49,787 casualties, including 18,065 dead and missing. Of 320 field and heavy guns in both armies, 49 were lost together with 46 of 452 infantry and anti-tank guns. The 56th Rifle Corps estimated casualties as 6,742 for 168th Division, 8,754 for 18th Division and more than 1,800 for 34th Tank Brigade, plus 143 tanks. The 15th Army suffered 239,555 casualties including 18,065 dead and missing and 217,231 injured.[45] Nor did the Fourth Corps escape unscathed, suffering 13,948 casualties including 3,725 dead and 572 missing; it had been so closely engaged that Mannerheim could not milk it for troops.

Yet Hägglund's successes were overshadowed by triumphs in the north, a region where Mannerheim had anticipated the least Red Army activity.[46] Although the forested wilderness of Oulu Province and the neighbouring Petsamo territory had mineral riches, the Finnish General Staff saw little strategic advantage in holding them and assigned their defence to Tuompo's seven battalions and three batteries of obsolete guns. Moscow thought otherwise and secretly built a network of roads which allowed them to deploy Komkor Mikhail Dukhanov's 9th Army, which was to occupy central Finland. Within the Arctic Circle, Komdiv Valerian Frolov's 14th Army was ready to secure the coast. These armies' total strength amounted to 140,000 men and 150 tanks. Meanwhile, Panin's 1st Corps supported Dukhanov's left.[47]

Dukhanov had Komdiv Ivan Dashichev's 47th Rifle Corps (122nd and 163rd Rifle Divisions) and Komdiv Maksim Shmyrov's Special Corps (reinforced 54th Mountain Rifle Division), and also received the 44th Rifle Division from the Ukraine. He was to advance to the northern end of the Gulf of Bothnia, isolating Finland while also preventing any potential Anglo-French intervention. Frolov's three rifle divisions (104th Mountain, 14th and newly-arrived 52nd Rifle Divisions) were to seize Petsamo then drive down from there along the Arctic Highway to the Gulf of Bothnia. Dukhanov, who had 91 tanks and 100 field guns, anticipated no serious resistance and an advance of 22 kilometres a day. But his divisions would be scattered over a 400-kilometre front, with gaps of 85-250 kilometres between them, preventing mutual support. Having examined the terrain and knowing the anticipated weather conditions, Dukhanov asked the Leningrad District's operations department on 27 November to advance more slowly, but this was rejected.[48]

At first the orders seemed justified with Panin's 139th and 155th Divisions brushing aside Tuompo's four battalions defending Tolvajärvi and Ilomantsi. By 5 December Kombrig Nikolai Belyaev's 139th Division was just outside Tolvajärvi but both sides were exhausted and the Russian advance ground to a halt. The Finns rushed a regiment from their strategic reserve to the town and the defenders were placed under Colonel Paavo Talvela whose detachment became Group Talvela on 19 December when he was promoted to Major General. Vain, petulant, but aggressive, Talvela was a former border guard commander and president of the State Liquor Board who would prove a difficult subordinate, but a skilful independent leader. His forces stopped the 155th Division short of its Ilomantsi objective and a counter-attack on 10 December enveloped and destroyed a Red Army battalion to end, permanently, the Russian advance in this sector which remained quiet until the end of the war.[49] At Tolvajärvi, from 8 December, Talvela's troops exploited the dense forests to raid Belyaev's communications and demoralise his men who were not acclimatised to the severe cold of minus 40°F, 500 of them being arrested for desertion by 11 December. Panin recognised the seriousness of the situation only when he visited Belyaev to demand a renewed assault upon Tolvajärvi, but when he informed Khabarov he simply passed the telephone to Kulik who obstinately demanded an attack. As the NKVD would later observe: 'On 12 December 1939 the division ceased to exist. It became a crowd of men who had lost the will to fight.'[50]

Two days later, a new Finnish attack drove back Belyaev, forcing Kurdiumov to commit his reserve 75th Rifle Division (Kombrig Aleksandr Stepanov) as a prop, but an attempt to rally at strongly fortified Äglajärvi failed on 22 December and the two divisions were pushed back to the Aitto-joki River where they remained on the defensive until the end of the war. By now Nomonhan veteran, Ponedelin (now 1st Rifle Corps chief-of-staff), had relieved Belyaev and imposed strict discipline, while on 29 December, when the new line was secure, Panin was relieved by Komkor Dimitri Kozlov. Belyaev and Stepanov were both investigated by the NKVD who wanted to arrest them, but they appear to have escaped this fate, the former becoming a corps and then army chief-of-staff, and the latter commanding a rifle division against the Germans until he was killed in August 1941.[51] Tolvajärvi was a remarkable Finnish success, but there was a high price: a quarter of Talvela's troops and a third of his officers and non-commissioned officers – 630 dead, 1,320 wounded; indeed, the casualties were so high that Mannerheim had wanted to break off the battle, but Talvela persuaded him to wait until his victory was complete.

Panin's defeat was an embarrassment, but worse was to befall Dukhanov who had achieved total surprise; the Finns had only a few covering battalions and the civilian population had to be hastily evacuated on 30 November at great human cost, some children being bussed out from their schools, and there was much economic loss. Dashichev's 47th Rifle Corps made slow progress: his 163rd Division made for the village of Suomussalmi, while to the north his 122nd Division in Lappland drove a battalion out of Salla on 9 December, opening the road to Kemijärvi and Pelkosenniemi so as to clear the way for an advance north- and south-west in order to link up with columns from Petsamo, Suomussalmi and Kuhmo.

Suomussalmi is a major crossroads with routes from Juntusranta in the north and Raate in the south while the road to the east crosses the highway and railway leading to Oulo, Tornio and the Swedish border. The village was the heart of a left-wing area where Communist agents had been active before the war and Leningrad anticipated that the region would rally to the Communist cause. Many trucks followed the 163rd Division (Kombrig Andrei Zelentsov) carrying propaganda material, printing presses and even sacks of gifts for the workers. The division was formed from Leningrad District reservists in late August, and 'stiffened' by exchanging a regiment with the 54th Mountain Rifle Division, but it suffered major supply problems, with Zelentsov complaining about the lack of camouflage clothing and skis.[52]

Zelentsov took Suomussalmi on 7 December, but the next day the defenders were reinforced by Colonel Hjalmar Siilasvuo, the opinionated and cunning commander of the Ninth Division's last regiment, Twenty-Seventh Jägers, who established his headquarters in Hyrynsalmi, a village at the head of a branch line, the existence of which was apparently unknown to the Russians. Despite a delay due to a rail collision, the rest of the regiment arrived the following day and in

Two Red Army scouts clad in snow capes are briefed by a junior officer prior to a mission behind Finnish lines in the winter of 1939-40. The soldier to the left is armed with a Simonov AVS 36 automatic rifle. (Courtesy of the Central Museum of the Armed Forces, Moscow, via Stavka)

anticipation of a counter-attack, Siilasvuo created an ice road network which allowed him to move his few guns rapidly in 'shoot and scoot' operations. His attacks began from the south on 10 December and began cutting the Suomussalmi road, creating mottis and reaching the village outskirts within three days.

The village had been burned by the retreating Finns, but was hastily fortified and the first Finnish assault, on 14 December, was beaten back but it was isolated from the north. Renewed assaults also failed, machine-gunners whom the Finns had not mopped up firing from their rear. Exhaustion, together with casualties, caused Siilasvuo to abandon his attacks after four days. They were renewed after a brief pause supported by two batteries and two anti-tank guns, but again without success as the trapped Russians fought desperately in the hope of relief.

With Zelentsov under growing pressure, Dukhanov ordered his reserve, Kombrig Alexei Vinogradov's 44th Rifle Division, to relieve him, but Vinogradov detrained on 14 December to discover there were not enough vehicles to move the whole division. He decided to hasten to Zelentsov's aid on foot with support units following in what vehicles were available, but Dukhanov's headquarters radioed his orders *en clair* and these were picked up by Finnish comint. A small force was hastily despatched to block the Raate road about a dozen kilometres east of Suomussalmi, between Lakes Kuomas and Kuivas on 23 December. They held the

Russians for a fortnight leaving Vinogradov's division strung out along some 30 kilometres of road all the way to the border. Komkor Vasilii Chuikov, like Rubin fresh from China, replaced Dukhanov on 22 December and he immediately recommended that Vinogradov secure his communications. He was ignored.[53]

Siilasvuo was reinforced and on 22 December his forces, 11,500 strong, were redesignated Ninth Division. Two days later he was ordered to retake Suomussalmi which he planned to envelop from east and west and, after engulfing it, he would slice up 163rd Division into more digestible pieces. The attack was delayed a day on 24-25 December by furious Russian efforts, with air support, to relieve Zelentsov. All failed however and on 27 December the Finns struck from the west, taking Hulkonniemi across the frozen Lake Kianta from Suomussalmi, driving the demoralised survivors across the ice. The following day the remaining 163rd Division mottis were also attacked and destroyed, despite numerous Russian attempts to break out. By dusk the 163rd Division had been destroyed, Russian records showing 11,601 casualties or 70 per cent of the men including 1,043 dead and missing, of whom 500 were captured with a dozen tanks, two dozen guns, 150 trucks, 250 horses and large amounts of weapons, ammunition and equipment.[54]

After giving his tired troops a brief rest, Siilasvuo sent them against the 44th Division. The Russians had created strongpoints based upon trenches straddling the road and had cleared a 50-metre area of trees to provide open fields of fire, while armoured patrols attempted to keep open the roads. They largely remained in their defences due to psychological feelings of claustrophobia within the forests and their lack of patrols meant they had little idea of the Finns' intentions. Indeed, they believed the 163rd Division was pinning down substantial Finnish forces. Chuikov did seek another rifle division and ski troops only for Moscow to tell him to create his own ski troops!

Siilasvuo's troops, by contrast, did have skis and they exploited a frozen lake south of the Raate road to move, unobserved, striking northwards to cut the road from 31 December, and by 2 January had isolated Vinogradov. The Russian general's men had always been short of food and fodder, while most had not received their winter uniforms with padded jackets and felt boots. Vinogradov's request for 50 tonnes of food was impossible to meet because the VVS was grounded by bad weather so he had to butcher most of his horses. Assaulted from all directions on 4 January, the 44th Division was shattered into a series of exposed mottis.

Vinogradov was beginning to lose control of his demoralised men and sought permission for a breakout. Chuikov was sympathetic, warning Moscow that evening of the dangers, and recommending authorisation if the situation did not improve. But Moscow insisted the division stand its ground. Only after Chuikov's attempt to relieve the pocket was thwarted and as the garrisons panicked, was Vinogradov given permission on the evening of 6 January to act on his own initiative. His breakout was disastrous with many men throwing away their weapons and others dying in blizzards. The survivors, including Vinogradov in a tank, reached Russian lines, but in the abandoned mottis the Finns discovered a cornucopia from which they took 1,300 prisoners. The division recorded its losses as 4,674, including 1,001 dead and 2,243 missing (40 per cent of its strength), while materiel losses were reported as 37 tanks, 47 field guns and howitzers, 350 automatic weapons, 4,340 rifles and 150 brand PPD sub-machine guns. Total Finnish casualties at Suomussalmi and the Raate road were 900 killed and 1,770 wounded with 30 missing, but the Finns had captured 85 tanks, 437 trucks, 1,620 horses, 92 artillery, 78 anti-tank guns, more than 6,000 rifles and an enormous amount of ammunition.

As disaster loomed Moscow despatched Mekhlis to sort out the mess and he became Chuikov's commissar on 9 January, Voroshilov having warned: 'I regard a radical purge…as essential.'[55] Mekhlis immediately selected the hapless Vinogradov, his commissar and chief-of-staff as the scapegoats, arresting them for wilfully ignoring orders, abandoning war materiel and failing to secure their lines of communications. They were shot in front of the surviving staff officers on 11 January as were the commanding officer and commissar of 662nd Rifles/163rd Division, who had the misfortune to survive the disaster. They were accused of 'wrecking'. But as Chuikov reported to Voroshilov, the problem was that the divisions were road-bound and incapable of manoeuvring in the woods. Indeed, the men had been 'frightened by the forest'.

Mekhlis widened his net and on 12 January included Dashichev, Zelentsov and the 9th Army operations chief, Ermolaev, the last being arrested on 30 January.[56] Mekhlis and the NKVD were constantly looking over Chuikov's shoulder and 'monitoring' his staff, Mekhlis reporting that he slept for only two or three hours a day. It is claimed he rallied fleeing troops and led them back to the front. It was not only in the front line that he faced danger, for on 10 December Mekhlis's car had been ambushed and he had a lucky escape. From late February he sought the use of chemical weapons in retaliation for their alleged use against Kombrig Nikolai Gusev's 54th Mountain Rifle Division, but was stopped in his attempts by Shaposhnikov.[57]

This division was part of the pre-war regional garrison which meant the men were acclimatised and its leaders familiar with the terrain, although it had few ski-trained troops and was some 80 kilometres south of Suomussalmi and Dukhanov's units. As Shmyrov's spearhead, it advanced steadily upon the rail junction at Kuhmo, harassed by the single battalion of defenders whose flank attacks kept it some 20 kilometres from the town. On 5 December, the defenders were reinforced to become Lieutenant Colonel Aksel Vuokko's independent brigade and they immediately began more flank attacks. On 8 December, Vuokko cut the Kuhmo road into several mottis, isolating the 54th Division's spearhead and driving one regiment back across the border, leaving Gusev to dig in to await relief, harassed by the Finns' ability to move rapidly through the forest on skis and to strike at will.

Vuokko lacked the men and heavy weapons to storm the mottis, but in late January Siilasvuo arrived with part of Ninth Division. Exploiting a secretly built road north of the Russian-held route, Siilasvuo established not only supply dumps but also insulated tents which allowed the weary troops a few hours of sleep in comfort. His attacks began on 28 January and while they split Gusev's division into 10 mottis and used captured anti-tank guns against bunkers, he found the Russians alert and determined, while he lacked the strength to reduce the mottis. He was further hampered in early February by raids upon his own communications by Colonel V.D. Dolinin's Ski Brigade which included some of the Soviet Union's best skiers. On 14 February Dolinin cut the Finnish road, but was then defeated by an enemy ski company which inflicted heavy losses – 3,083 casualties including 1,274 killed and 583 missing.[58]

Finnish attempts to destroy Gusev from 25 February failed due to the absence of artillery, air and armoured support, but they did compress the 54th Division into two large mottis. Their survival owed much to Gusev's dynamic defence, whereby he cut a 100-metre open zone and used the timber to create bunkers, then built a landing ground to fly in supplies, while more were dropped by low-flying aircraft into the snow. The Finns also had to take account of efforts by Gusev's 337th Rifles (the only regiment to escape encirclement) to relieve the Kuhmo defenders from 4 March, as well as Gusev's attempts to breakout. The Finns succeeded in maintaining the siege until the end of the war, but suffered heavier losses proportionately than in any other sector, especially in officers leading attacks, while Gusev's division recorded 6,423 casualties, 60 per cent of divisional strength, of whom 2,691 were dead or missing.[59]

On Dukhanov's northern flank was Kombrig Petr Shevchenko's 122nd Division which had arrived in October from the Belorussian Front and whose headquarters, evaluating the terrain and weather, had sought vainly to equip some troops with skis.[60] They faced the Lappland Group led by the right-wing demagogue, Colonel (later Major General) Wallenius, whose two battalions also faced the whole of Frolov's 14th Army. Wallenius had been a close friend of Mannerheim until he tried to kidnap the president, yet he would briefly regain his reputation because he was a great tactical improviser who exploited terrain he knew intimately. Wallenius demolished everything of value to the invader and in the perpetual Arctic night his troops braved blizzards and temperatures down to minus 35°F to harass enemy communications until Fortieth Jägers arrived to underpin the defence of the river Kemi.

The approaches to the river were controlled by the small town of Salla, some 80 kilometres to the east, and Shevchenko took this on 10 December and approached the river at Kermijärvi. He then tried to outflank Wallenius from the north, by sending a battle group based upon 596th Rifles which marched on Pelkosenniemi. A counter-attack on 18 December drove back the Russians 14 kilometres with much equipment abandoned, forcing Dukhanov to commit a coastal defence formation formed at Arkhangelsk in September, 88th Rifle Division, north-west of Salla but it too was driven back.

Wallenius's men were exhausted and confined themselves to harassing enemy communications, although they were able to drive back 122nd Division to Märkäjärvi. With 88th Division covering the right, the Russians fortified a bridgehead which was too strong to storm, even if Wallenius had possessed sufficient manpower. Russian communications were secured by roving tank patrols, but from mid-January all major operations on this front ceased and most of Shevchenko's artillery was withdrawn into army reserve. The 9th Army suffered 46,109 casualties in the campaign, including 13,536 dead and missing, while the number of wounded, at 17,674, was almost matched by the numbers who suffered sickness or frostbite – nearly 14,900.[61]

In February Linder's Swedish SFK volunteers arrived and took over part of the Lappland Front between 22-26 February, releasing Wallenius's five Finnish battalions and some batteries which were sucked into the Karelia maelstrom. Linder acted as a shield for the deployment of Sweden's Second Corps whose ground forces would suffer 213 casualties including 33 killed and 130 frostbitten. A Swedish air squadron (F 19) was also deployed, with 250 men and two women, and three of its pilots would be killed.[62]

In the Arctic Circle to defend ice-free Petsamo, 400 kilometres from the nearest railway and with a narrow, gravel-covered road to the south, Wallenius had only a rifle company with a battery of guns dating back to 1887 and unreliable ammunition. Soviet intelligence grossly overestimated the size of the defenders opposite Frolov's 14th Army, with the NKVD claiming there were 12 border battalions when actually there were two companies. Frolov's role was less to invade Finland and more to defend the north against any Anglo-French landing. His men were instructed to 'Greet Norwegian and Swedish border guards when meeting them at the border but avoid conversations.'[63]

Against light resistance Frolov's 104th Mountain Rifle Division occupied the Rybachi Peninsula on the first day and Petsamo on 2 December then, harassed by Finnish guerrilla attacks, moved down the Arctic Highway towards Rovaniemi, the capital of Lappland. It was stopped by a counter-attack mounted by the reinforced defenders at Nautsi (also Rovaniemskogo) on 21 December, which forced the division onto the defensive. The emphasis upon preventing an Anglo-French invasion meant that, on 3 December, the 95th Rifles/14th Rifle Division was detached to garrison the Rybachi Peninsula, while the 52nd Rifle Division was brought up to hold the Petsamo area in the face of guerrilla tactics – although the cold proved even deadlier and six men were killed and 22 injured when fires lit in huts to warm the frozen troops set ablaze the whole structure. Frolov had the lightest losses of the Winter War with 585 men, including 183 killed and missing and 402 wounded, and also had the greatest success, securing his communications using bunkers at 4-5 kilometre intervals with armoured patrols between.[64]

Valentin Drozd's Northern Fleet had been formed in 1933 from three pre-Great War destroyers which were gradually reinforced from the Baltic, bringing his strength to nine destroyers and torpedo boats with 18 submarines. The Fleet helped to secure the coast and throughout the war its submarines patrolled off the Norwegian coast but made no attempt to intercept shipping, for it was more concerned by Norway's reaction, with its submarines monitoring Norwegian naval activity. On 27 November one spotted the torpedo boats KNM *Aegir* and *Sleilner* and the coastguard cutter KV *Fridtof Nansen* sailing toward Varanger Fjord, leading to the despatch of more boats the following day.[65]

Across the border in Norway the outbreak of hostilities had seen a partial mobilisation of the forces in the northern province of Finnmark. Four battalions of the Sixth Division with two field batteries and support troops were rotated in the north, a total of some 2,000–3,000 men with unarmed De Havilland Tiger Moth trainers and, because Oslo regarded the region as volatile, they would remain deployed even after the German invasion in April. The Royal Norwegian Navy had two or three destroyers and two submarines operating in northern waters and reinforced them with the pre-dreadnought coast-defence battleships, KNM *Norge* and *Eidsvold*, which were transferred to Narvik where they were sunk treacherously by German destroyers during negotiations at the time of the Nazi invasion on 9 April.[66]

The wilderness north of Lake Ladoga saw the Red Army suffer severe casualties as its reputation was buried in the snow. To add salt to the wounds, the Finns secured a vast amount of war materiel to sustain their struggle, much of it immediately turned against its former owners. The impact of this unanticipated booty of 164 field guns and howitzers as well as 14 heavy pieces, 1,768 heavy and 3,076 light machine guns, 36,737 rifles and 239 sub-machine guns was to boost the Finnish Army, which also received 125 anti-tank guns and 94 mortars.[67] With Finnish war production of 105 anti-tank guns, 272 mortars, 605 light- and 960 heavy machine guns, 82,570 rifles and 1,265 sub-machine guns, it is clear that the Red Army provided more than half Finland's field artillery, a third of its anti-tank guns, 60 per cent of its heavy and 17 per cent of its light machine guns, as well as 15 per cent of its rifles.[68] In addition the Finns captured and used 167 tracked vehicles, including T-28, T-26, OT-26/130, T-37/38 and 56 T-20 'Komsomolets' gun tractors of which the Red Army recaptured six.[69]

The disasters stunned the Soviet leadership, with Kulik complaining on 19 December that '…rigidity and bureaucracy are everywhere.' Stalin became depressed and, as usual when he was under stress, developed tonsillitis with a high temperature and very sore throat and did not begin to show signs of recovery until 1 February, by which time a major blow was being prepared on the Karelian Isthmus.[70]

Soviet air power was also humiliated over Finland despite starting the war with overwhelming numerical and qualitative superiority – some 2,000 Russian aircraft deployed against 119 Finnish machines, with VVS Frontal and Long-Range

Aviation supported by some 500 naval aircraft. Yet the VVS totally failed to establish air superiority and had limited influence on the ground battles. In striking enemy cities and inflicting 2,796 civilian casualties (956 dead), it failed to cow Finnish or foreign public opinion, rallied Finnish domestic support and demonstrated the weaknesses of Soviet air power, because the cities were not reduced to bomb sites and public fear of air attacks gradually diminished.[71]

The air offensive against Finnish towns and ports was conducted by the Navy's 8th Brigade (which flew 387 sorties and dropped 64.5 tonnes of bombs) and three long-range bomber regiments of the 27th Long-Range Bomber Brigade of the 1 AON, with some 300 aircraft, mostly Ilyushin DB-3s whose prototype had circled Red Square during the 1936 May Day Parade. They flew 2,129 sorties from Estonian bases, some 75 kilometres across the Gulf of Finland from their targets, but were plagued by bad weather and inexperienced crews, the latter reflected in frequent accidents, poor navigation and inaccurate bombing.[72] On 26 December three DBs of the 21st Long-Range Bomber Regiment got lost and bombed their own lines, causing no significant damage, while the previous day aircraft from 6th Long-Range Bomber Regiment were unable to engage enemy fighters because their machine guns would not work; they were still in their storage grease and the gunners had failed to test-fire their weapons after take-off.

The Baltic Fleet lost three DBs in the first two days – one to Finnish anti-aircraft fire, one crashed on take-off and a third in an accident after the pilot became disorientated in dense cloud.[73] The accident involved a bomber from the 1st Mine-Torpedo Regiment crashing into a bomb dump, leading to 32 groundcrew casualties and the damaging of seven other aircraft. This reduced the regiment's operations for a fortnight. Yet the DBs proved to be reliable and robust aircraft, well able to take care of themselves, although on 6 January a pair of Finnish fighters shot down seven. Up to five aircraft which came down in Finland were later used by the Finns.

After the first attacks upon Helsinki, Moscow restricted further raids although the capital was attacked on another seven occasions to mid-January and the historian A.B. Shirokorad notes 70 sorties against the city.[74] Some 35 sorties were flown against Helsinki on the first day with most of the bombs delivered by naval aircraft which had been seeking Finland's two coast-defence battleships and whose crews, rather than land with their deadly loads, decided to use them on a target of opportunity. Subsequently, Meretskov ordered the VVS to avoid bombing population centres. The main targets were the port of Turku, the defence centre of Tampere – strategic targets which attracted 700 sorties. The Finnish rail system saw 243 locomotives and some 2,000 rolling stock destroyed or damaged.

Finland had only 46 fighters at the start of the war (see Table 4-1) and bombers were their prime targets. They had to defend not only the urban centres, but also the army, and consequently were overstretched. The urban centres were largely defended at the start of the war by 38 heavy and 87 medium- and light anti-aircraft guns, with 141 anti-aircraft machine guns. However, there was limited ammunition and a severe shortage of range-finding and fire control equipment, including only eight acoustic detectors and eight searchlights. The small bomber force attacked Estonian air bases in December and January, but heavy losses and the need to be ready to support the army ended these missions.

Table 4-1: Finnish Air Force strength

	Dec 1	Jan 15	Feb 1	Feb 15	Mar 1	Mar 15
Fighters	46	37 (2)	45 (1)	55 (5)	67 (22)	87 (19)
Bombers	17	11 (3)	19 (3)	18 (8)	25 (3)	20 (9)
Army and Navy co-operation	58	49 (8)	45 (6)	49 (6)	48 (8)	48 (7)
Swedish F 19	-	-	-	12 (3)	12 (3)	11 (3)
Total	**121**	**97 (13)**	**109 (10)**	**134 (22)**	**152 (36)**	**166 (38)**

Source: Keskinen & Stenman p.145. Note: figures in parentheses non-operational.

The Russians' ageing four-engined TB heavy bombers could be committed safely only at night loaded with 2-tonne bombs. Ordinarily they operated in flight strength at 1,500-2,000 metres with 500 and 250 kilogramme bombs, against major targets behind enemy lines, although in February they were used occasionally against the defences of the Mannerheim Line. However, their load-carrying abilities meant that they were diverted increasingly to the air ambulance and air transport role, one squadron being formed to feed the front with essential supplies. The transport missions were often flown in daylight and at least two aircraft of the 7th Heavy Bomber Regiment were shot down on them. In December, half of the regiment was used for urgent transport missions in support of the Leningrad District/North West Front, moving 946 men, 85 tonnes of fuel and 145 tonnes of spares, during which only one squadron was used for bombing, flying 85 night sorties and dropping 123 tonnes of bombs, its total losses being six aircraft.

The AON was disbanded on about 12 January and replaced by Dalne-Bombardirovochnaya Aviatsiya (Long-Range Aviation). However, the 27th Brigade was joined in late January by the newly-created 85th Special Purpose Regiment which went into action from 1 February using a squadron of DBs for precision attacks using experienced, instrument-trained crews and two Ar-2/SB squadrons for dive- and glide-bombing. It would fly 203 of its 454 sorties at night and 208 in cloud, while flying 19 dive-bombing sorties.

The bulk of the VVS supported the army, with the 7th Army having the lion's share of the support of some 700 aircraft. There was considerable emphasis upon the strike arm, with bombers operating in squadron or demi-squadron formations, but for many weeks they were rarely escorted, making them vulnerable to the small Finnish fighter force whose 46 fighters claimed 36 victories in the first month. But the 2nd Fast-Bomber Regiment which supported 7th Army from the outset lost only one SB to fighters and five to anti-aircraft fire.

The absence of co-ordination notable in the Red Army was also all too apparent in the VVS; there was little attempt to incorporate timely reconnaissance or intelligence information into bomber missions, and where escorts were scheduled they often did not materialise. Air operations often had little to do with the situation on the ground. Soviet fighter tactics were also clumsy, being based upon three-aircraft vics which reacted slowly to threats.

The Finnish Air Force (Ilmavoimat) suffered minimal losses on the ground due to the dispersal of squadrons onto well-concealed airfields, and it sometimes used frozen lakes. The greatest loss was suffered by the Swedish F 19 volunteer squadron when three of its four Hart light bombers were destroyed in a surprise attack on 12 January, the day after it arrived with 12 Gladiator fighters and the four Harts. The Swedes would claim three victories for the loss of six aircraft and three men.

The Finns were never troubled by fuel shortages, importing 3,500 tonnes through Sweden, while munitions came from manufacturers and friendly states, but there were serious shortages of spares aggravated by a doubling of the number of combat aircraft models. Two squadrons with 24 Fokker C-V and C-X army-co-operation aircraft were used for tactical and photographic reconnaissance and as light bombers and ground-attack aircraft. While they were robust, they were still vulnerable to ground fire and five aircraft were lost in December, one squadron later augmenting its strength with Gladiator fighters.

Poor weather until mid-December restricted VVS operations: indeed, of the 25 Frontal Aviation regiments available, some 20 per cent saw no operational flying on the first day. The pace of operations increased after 19 December as the advance ground to a halt almost everywhere. Poor navigation and communication meant that during December there were six 'friendly fire' incidents involving the VVS on the 7th Army Front while the 4th Rifle Division managed to shoot down two I-16s of the 68th Fighter Regiment. The VVS struck almost randomly and with little effect, although on 5 January 40 bombers struck Mikkeli where the Finnish General Headquarters was located, inflicting considerable damage and forcing the headquarters to move to Otava.

There were major problems: Komkor Petr Shelukhin of the North West Front wrote to Voroshilov complaining about air support. He noted that the effectiveness of the Finnish fighters was magnified by poor Russian combat training, with crews unable to take evasive manoeuvres and bomber gunners unable to operate as a team.[75] The high losses even in poor weather were due partly to poor navigation training; this was the responsibility of observers and pilots were not consulted about the route. There was a shortage of spares which kept many aircraft on the ground, demoralising crews, but this did not prevent airmen from landing alongside downed aircraft to rescue comrades on 11 occasions, seven involving fighters.

Many of these problems were overcome from January as Moscow prepared for a major new offensive and it despatched substantial VVS reinforcements and materiel: seven-and-a-half regiments during December and the first half of January, and 16 from the second half of January, bringing total strength to 2,200 on 10 February and 3,100 by the end of the war (see Table 4-2). This was reflected in the rise in reconnaissance missions, as bombers were increasingly active against Finnish communications centres. They were increasingly escorted and there was a greater emphasis upon night attacks; most of the 2,300 sorties flown against Viipuri and Sortavala were during this period. Fighter and bomber bases were moved forward, often onto iced lakes, and the fighter squadrons ranged deeper into Finland, attacking some airfields and railways, while fitted with auxiliary fuel tanks; some fighters escorted the bombers as far as Tampere. To help artillery fire direction, observation balloons were brought forward, providing valuable information on the defences.

Table 4-2: Number of Soviet planes deployed against Finland at the end of the war

Group	Bombers	Fighters	Recon	Total
Front	430	275	-	705
Special Group	179	95	-	274
7th Army	260	294	115	669
13th Army	200	101	106	407
15th Army	179	127	78	384
8th Army	92	97	83	272
9th Army	162	167	33	362
14th Army	111	83	10	204
Baltic Fleet	109	290	149	548
Arctic Fleet	10	30	20	60
Total	**1,732**	**1,559**	**594**	**3,885**

Source: Winter War website.

In January the VVS flew 7,532 sorties (4,087 bomber, 3,445 fighter) and this rose to 20,500 during the first half of February when 6,200 tonnes of bombs were dropped.[76] During the first ten days of February, 7th Army aviation began pounding the rear of the Mannerheim Line from a kilometre behind the Finnish forward line up to eight kilometres. The air units flew 653 strike sorties including 306 mounted by long-range bombers which focused upon headquarters and communications nodes. On 6 February some 250 Russian bombers were used against the Mannerheim Line. Later, bombers sometimes flew in formations of 100 aircraft to disrupt communications and to decapitate the enemy command. The obsolescence of the I-15 became obvious and increasingly they were diverted from combat air patrol and escort duties to ground-attack missions. The Finns' similar Gloster Gladiator fighters also proved disappointingly obsolete and suffered heavy losses with 14 destroyed and five damaged.

From mid-February until the end of the war the VVS would fly 45,000 sorties and drop 15,000 tonnes of bombs, aided by improvements in the weather which

permitted several sorties a day. The offensive began on the Karelian Isthmus from
12 February, the 7th Army supported by ten aviation regiments and the 13th Army
by five. The ground troops received direct support from a third of the fighters, a
quarter of the bombers and three-quarters of the attack- and light bombers.[77]
During the month improved weather permitted up to 1,000 sorties per day, but this
was more sound than substance, although Viipuri came under increasing attack from
17 February as sunny skies allowed the VVS to play a major role for the first time in
this operation. When Russian forces tried to envelop the city across the ice of Viipurii
Bay they came under sustained attack from Finnish fighters and bombers which were
making an all-out effort at maximum strength and regardless of losses. The bombers
flew some 30 sorties from 11 March and included naval co-operation aircraft but,
while they inflicted casualties, they were unable on their own to stem the tide.

The 1st Light Bomber Brigade's 7th Assault Aviation Regiment, with
32 R-5SSS and 63 R-Z, flew 795 sorties from 11-27 February, despite transferring
a squadron to 8th Army on 22 February. These aircraft dropped 274 tonnes of
bombs while the brigade's 5th Fast Bomber Regiment from 14 February flew 402
sorties and dropped almost 279 tonnes of bombs. The 4th Fighter Regiment, which
joined the battle from 14 February with 18 I-153 and 46 I-15bis, flew 2,590 sorties
including 1,340 ground-attack (nearly 74 tonnes of bombs), 334 bomber escort
and 216 reconnaissance, dropping 462 supply packages to forward troops.
The 148th Fighter Regiment, with 60 I-153, joined the offensive from
27 February and flew 1,120 sorties, claiming three victories.

While the Russian effort was focused upon the Karelian Isthmus, the air forces
supporting the 8th, 9th and 15th Armies flew 4,073 operational sorties (1,059 fighter)
excluding aerial supply missions which were a major element. The 80th Mixed
Aviation Regiment, which had three bomber squadrons with DBs and
SBs, flew 4,769 of its 4,935 sorties supporting 54th Division, its DB squadron
becoming part of an instrument-flying air group under Kombrig Ivan Spirin.
The division was also aided by 91 sorties from 16th Fast Bomber Regiment.
The 8th Army's 72nd Mixed Aviation Regiment's two SB squadrons dropped 120
packages of food and medicines to the 56th Rifle Corps, but most of its missions
were combat and in 1,308 sorties it dropped 650 tonnes of bombs. The 145th Fighter
Regiment, initially with 14th Army, reinforced by half the 48th Fighter Regiment
from 16 February, was the Swedish F 19's prime opponent and flew 1,125 combat
sorties, losing five pilots – two to ground fire. It would transfer to 9th Army.
The 147th Fighter Regiment, which also operated in the north, flew 830 sorties of
which 136 were reconnaissance, 269 were ground-attack and 68 were bomber escort.
The 9th Army's 152nd Fighter Regiment flew 1,435 sorties from 9 January including
608 ground-attack and 108 supply drops. From 23 January, the 16th Fast Bomber
Regiment flew 382 sorties against communications (208 tonnes of bombs),
436 against troops (59 tonnes) and 141 against enemy bases and supply dumps (151.5
tonnes). This regiment flew 12 photographic reconnaissance, 43 meteorological and
nine fighter sorties leading bomber formations and a total of 50 sorties were aborted.

Table 4-3: Soviet air losses

Type	Destroyed		Badly damaged	Total
	Enemy action	Accident		
Fighters	89	70	40	**199**
Fast Bombers	143	60	41	**244**
Light Bombers/Assault	23	18	13	**54**
Heavy Bombers	6	1	7	**14**
LR Bombers	39	18	19	**76**
Unknown	14	15	4	**33**
Navy	17	???	???	**17**
Total	**331**	**182**	**124**	**637**

Based upon war diaries published in Appendix 3 in Pavel Aptekar's article 'Falcons or Hawks' on rkka website. Missing 3rd Heavy Bomber, 1st, 5th Long-Range Bomber, 9th, 16th, 39th Fast Bomber, 5th Mixed and 14th Reconnaissance Regiments.

Table 4-4: Sample VVS regimental activity and losses

Regiment	Sorties	Destroyed		Badly damaged
		Enemy action	Accident	
2nd Fast Bomber	2,237	8	5	-
4th Fighter	2,590	6	2	-
5th Fast Bomber	402	7	2	-
19th Fighter	3,412	1	5	-
35th Fast Bomber	1,358	12	1	-
50th Fast Bomber	2,321	9	6	-
72nd Mixed	1,308	5	2	-
80th Mixed	4,935	9	13	4
85th Mixed	454	4	4	1
145th Fighter	1,564	5	7	-
147th Fighter	830	6	6	5
148th Fighter	1,120	-	-	-
152nd Fighter	1,435	13	12	-

Russian sources state that the VVS flew 84,307 sorties, more than 47 per cent (40,266) by fighters, while the bombers dropped 23,146 tonnes of bombs. The 'bomber sortie' figure includes everything from heavy to light bombers and, probably, reconnaissance, and it is claimed combat losses were 261 aircraft and 321 aircrew. However, the figure certainly excludes accidental losses and even the Soviet historian, Shirokorad, is sceptical of the accuracy of these statistics.[78] The Baltic Fleet started the war with exactly 450 aircraft: 111 bombers (60 DB-3 and 51 SB), 214 fighter (124 I-16, 70 I-15, 20 I-153), 115 MBR-2 flying boats, and 10 R-5 land-based reconnaissance aircraft. They flew 16,663 sorties (21,425 hours) including 881 (1,377 hours) at night, dropped 2,600 tonnes of bombs and took 12,637 photographs.[79]

Soviet losses, based upon war diaries, (see Table 4–3), indicate that at least 513 aircraft were destroyed during the war and 124 badly damaged, with accidents accounting for at least a third of the aircraft lost, while 362 victories were claimed. Details of individual regimental activity and losses are shown in Table 4–4 to provide fragmentary information on VVS activity.

By contrast the Ilmavoimat flew 5,900 combat sorties of which 3,900 were by fighters. Of 800 bomber sorties involving 208 tonnes of ordnance, the Blenheims flew 423 to deliver 113 tonnes with the rest by the Fokker C-V and Fokker C-X, which also flew most of the 70 photographic reconnaissance sorties. There were claims for 190 victories while 62 aircraft were destroyed (see Table 4–5) of which 47 (including Swedish) fell to enemy action, 35 to fighters and eight to ground fire, 77 aircrew being killed or missing.

Table 4-5: Finnish losses (includes accidents)

Month	Fighters		Bombers		Co-operation		Total	
	Dest	Dam	Dest	Dam	Dest	Dam	Dest	Dam
December 1939	1	4	-	2	10	6	11	12
January 1940	3	1	7	3	4	2	14	6
February 1940	20	8	4	3	2	7	26	18
March 1940	5	3	2	2	4	5	11	10
Total	29	16	13	10	20	20	62	46

Source: Keskinen & Stenman pp.152-154.
Dest = Destroyed. Dam = Damaged.

Like the Red Army, the VVS was found wanting in almost every department. The conflict confirmed the need for new high-performance combat aircraft, already under development following experience in Spain, and especially a new ground-attack aircraft. It was also clear that a new high-speed photographic reconnaissance aircraft was needed, but it is reported that the VVS commander, Smushkevich, was so concerned about the failure of command and control that he recommended the diversification of Soviet Air Power into Frontal Aviation, Long-Range Aviation, and Naval Aviation. Homeland Defence was to be scrapped and replaced with a unitary one. This was not accepted, probably through opposition from the conservatives and the services themselves, and may help to explain why he was replaced by Rychagov in the spring of 1940.

ENDNOTES

1. Goltz became a Freikorps condottierre in Latvia in 1919.
2. For background see Condon p.11; Dyke pp.1-4; Shirokorad pp.542-549; Trotter pp.5-12.
3. He would play a key role in normalising relations with the West after 1941.

4. Condon pp.11-13, 15; Shirokorad p.545; Trotter pp.12-14. Yartsev, who discussed progress with Stalin on 7 April 1938, held senior positions in the NKVD until 1947 when he was killed in a car crash in Czechoslovakia.

5. For the Soviet negotiations see Condon pp.15-21; Erickson pp.541-542; Trotter pp.15-18. Paasikivi had striven in vain to get closer military co-operation with Sweden. A major problem was the perception of many Swedish politicians that Finland's President, Pehr Svinhufvud, (1931–1937), was autocratic. His more liberal successor, Kyösti Kallio, failed to overcome earlier Swedish prejudices.

6. A commission led by Kuznetsov recommended in October that, even if Finland was neutral in a war, the Soviet Navy needed coast defence positions on Finland's southern coast, including Hango, to secure the Gulf of Finland. It was concerned about the threat of air attack from Finland's extensive network of air bases. Dyke pp.13-14.

7. Crankshaw, Edward (ed), *Khrushchev Remembers*, Little, Brown, Boston, 1970, p.152.

8. For the pre-war period see Condon pp.19-21; Dyke pp.14-27; Trotter pp.18-22.

9. Meltyuhov p.141.

10. For Soviet planning see Crankshaw p.301; Dyke pp.8-9, 19; Irincheev, Mannerheim Line p.5; Meretskov pp.172, 174, 178-180, 178-179, 183; Shukman p.128; Trotter pp.34-37, 66; Voronov pp.134-136.

11. For Zhdanov see Montefiore pp.122-123.

12. See Meretskov's complaints about GRU failures pp.178, 183. Two photographs are shown in Irincheev, Mannerheim Line, p.5.

13. Dyke pp.22-24, 26.

14. Voronov p.136.

15. The two regions had 72 guns over 100 mm calibre including eight 305 mm, twelve 203 mm and twenty-nine 152 mm.

16. Ramishvili had served with Kuznetsov in Spain and would become the wartime Director of Training.

17. Ries, Tomas (1988). *Cold Will: The Defense of Finland* pp.77-78. Russian records indicate there were no casualties from this 'provocation'. See Shirokorad p.547.

18. After the Winter War, Tuominen split with the Communists, became a Social Democrat and died in his homeland while Kuusinen continued working for the Soviet Communist Party, becoming Secretary of the Central Committee under Khrushchev. Realising he was terminally ill, he requested Helsinki's permission to die in the land of his birth, but this was rejected. It was poetic justice. For the Finnish Communists see Condon p.36; Trotter pp.58-61.

19. Dyke pp.2, 57-59; Shirokorad p.549.

20. Dyke pp.26-27. Drozd, another Spanish Civil War veteran, was one of the best Soviet Navy commanders and would distinguish himself with the Baltic Fleet. He died in a bizarre accident when his car fell through a hole in ice in 1943.

21. Montefiore p.291. Yet Mekhlis would later observe that many of the rank and file regarded the attack upon Finland as an unjust war. See Van Dyke, The Timoshenko Reforms.

22. Dyke pp.39-40, 68.

23. Trotter pp.48-50.

24. Condon pp.36-37, 47. Trotter pp.50-51, 61.

25. Data from Winter War website based upon official histories.

26. Shirokorad pp.663-664.

27. Swedish coast defence mines sank three merchantmen between December 1939 and February 1940.

28. For the Russian blockade see Dyke pp.22-24, 26, 52-53, 55, 63-64, 67-68, 89-9; Shirokorad pp.661-663; Chronik des Seekriegs website.

29. Dyke pp.67-68.

30. Information provided by aviation historian, Mr Adrian English.

31. Second Corps was disbanded on 13 March. I would like to express my debt to Mr Thomas Roth, Senior Curator at the Armémuseum in Stockholm, for information on Swedish Army mobilisation and the SFK. Also see the Swedish Army in World War II by Ingulfur Bjørgvinsson. Website: solar.mcs.st-and.ac.uk/~aaron.sweeds.html.

32. For the background to Finnish defence, see Condon pp.25, 28-30, 71; Irincheev, *White Death* pp.7-9; Salo p.50; Trotter pp.41-46 and for the Finnish Army, as well as many more details of battles and forces see The Battles of the Winter War website.

33. Vihavainen in the Civil Guard of Finland website notes that 20 per cent (6,000) of new recruits trained during the Winter War, and 16 per cent (49,000) of the reservists were Suojeluskunta members. Total Finnish mobilised strength was 337,000.

34. Shirokorad p.565. Lovta Svärd was a literary heroine, a soldier's widow who became a Florence Nightingale.

35. Shirokorad pp.559-560.

36. A sub-machine gun is a fully automatic pistol and allowed officers to augment unit firepower. The Russians tested it before the war and Kulik dismissed it as a 'police' weapon, but it influenced development of the Red Army's PPsh 41 or Shpagin. Voronov p.137.

37. Trotter p.152.

38. For the situation at the outbreak of war north of Lake Ladoga see Condon pp.32, 34, Trotter pp.38, 47, 52, 69, 99.

39. For Fourth Corps' battles see Condon pp.34-36, 57, 59, 62-64, 66-69; Dyke pp.39, 47, 49, 51, 68-69, 71, 80-82, 84-86, 164, 167-168, 176, 178; Irincheev, *White Death*, pp.77-103; Shirokorad pp.580-616; Trotter pp.52, 93-99, 100-140. See also Tragediya okrushennyikh website. Panin had just returned from acting as an advisor in China.

40. In the second war against the Russians, the Continuation War, Heiskanen became first commandant of Viipuri and later General Inspector of Military Training. Khabarov was arrested by the NKVD which recommended his dismissal and arrest, but he would later become the West Front's assistant commander for training at the outbreak of war with Germany. He subsequently held insignificant commands during and after the war. Parrish p.156. Irincheev, *White Death* suggests he became the 1st Rifle Corps commander, but this does not appear to be so. Kurdiumov became a Lieutenant General, but spent most of his later career in military districts, apart from briefly commanding 66th Army in 1942.

41. Nihtilä had been lecturer in tactics at the military academy and would be a distinguished staff officer in the Continuation War.

42. For Mottis see Trotter pp.132-133.

43. Rubin would become the GRU's deputy head in 1941 and spent the rest of his career in intelligence.

44. Shirokorad pp.609-612.

45. Shirokorad pp.613-614; Tragediya okrushennyikh website article.

46. Trotter pp.143-149.

47. For operations in the north see Condon pp.34-36; 57, 81-82, 84-86, 88-89, 91-94, 97-99, 101, 103; Dyke pp.40, 51-52, 68-69, 71, 80-82, 84-89, 177: Erickson pp.544-547; Irincheev, White Death, pp.104-123; Shirokorad pp.576-595; Trotter pp.52, 54, 150-184, 257. See also Tragediya okrushennyikh, Aptakar and Svintsobyii Shkval web articles.

48. Tragediya okrushennyikh website article.

49. This reserve division had no training, lacked winter clothing and the oppressive silence of the forest demoralised the men. Between 12-15 December, it suffered 1,097 casualties including 387 killed and missing. Aptakar website article.

50. Irincheev, *White Death* p.101.

51. The 139th Division suffered 2,377 casualties, including 1,807 dead and missing while losing 13 anti-tank and nine other pieces of ordnance, 2,247 rifles, 165 heavy- and 240 light machine guns. The 75th Division suffered 3,102 casualties, including 2,573 dead and missing, while losing 12 tanks, five 76 mm and eight anti-tank guns, 1,196 rifles, 133 light- and 103 heavy machine guns. Aptakar website article.

52. Tragediya okrushennyikh website article.
53. Dukhanov appears to have escaped the odium of defeat and commanded 22nd (Estonian) Rifle Corps from 1940 and his 2nd Shock Army would play a key role in relieving the siege of Leningrad in 1943.
54. Shirokorad p.592.
55. Montefiore p.292.
56. Dashichev would command armies against the Germans, but the 1942 defeat at Kerch cost him (and Kulik) his career. He appears to have been publicly critical of the leadership and was arrested twice in 1942, spending the rest of the war in prison camps. Zelentsov appears to have escaped the fate of his division, became acting commander of Arkhangelsk District. He was killed in August 1941.
57. Dyke p.177. Montefiore pp.292-293 .
58. Shirokorad p.592.
59. Shirokorad p.592. Special Corps commander Shmyrov became an instructor at the Frunze Academy but died in 1940.
60. Tragediya okrushennyikh website article.
61. Shirokorad p.595.
62. Data from Mr Thomas Roth.
63. Irincheev, p.104.
64. Shirokorad pp.579-580. The 104th Division was formed in the summer and most of the conscripts were nearing the end of their service. They were not pleased to have the service extended for another year and there was a shortage of junior officers and NCOs. Aptakar website article.
65. Dyke p.26.
66. I am indebted to Mr Ivar Kraglund, Senior Researcher at Norway's Resistance Museum, for providing me with information on Norway's military response to the Winter War.
67. See Winter War website.
68. Shirokorad p.604.
69. Op. cit. pp.566-567.
70. Montefiore p.293.
71. For the air war see Dyke p.67; Shirokorad pp.676-681 Aptekar, article, '*Falcons or kites? Through Wars into a Superpower*' Air Force website.
72. Bochkarev & Parygin p.18.
73. Shirokorad p.678.
74. Dyke pp.55-56, 96 f/n 60; Shirokorad p.681.
75. On 10 February 1939 the VVS had 7,885 aircraft but the average pilot had only 16 hours' operational flying. Elisseva article.
76. Shirokorad p.629.
77. Dyke pp.179-180 f/n 37. Svintsobyii Shkval web article.
78. Shirokorad p.676.
79. Op. cit. pp.679-680.

CHAPTER FIVE

THE WINTER WAR:
VICTORY WITHOUT TRIUMPH

'The authority of the Red Army is a guarantee of the USSR's national security.'
IOSEF STALIN TO KIRILL AFANASIEVICH MERETSKOV, 1940

'It's a terrible poker we're playing here.'
GENERAL HARALD ÖHQUIST, FEBRUARY 1940

THE victories north of Lake Ladoga helped avert the destruction of Finland, but the main struggle between the Russians and Finns was on the road across the Karelian Isthmus to Helsinki which was firmly barred to the Russians by the Mannerheim Line. From the beginning of 1940 this line came under mounting pressure, leading to a Russian breakthrough which the Red Army was unable fully to exploit.

The Isthmus is formed of gently undulating and relatively open terrain dotted with woods with long, narrow lakes and swamps in the east. There are few natural obstacles and few heights are more than 40 metres. In 1940 there was a relatively good road and railway network. Both sides began fortifying the border soon after the Treaty of Dorpat, the Russians creating the Karelian Fortified Region, while the Finns created the 135 kilometre-long Pääpulustusasema, or more simply Pääsema (Main Defensive Position), some 20-50 kilometres from the frontier.[1]

The Mannerheim Line exploited the few natural barriers such as the rivers Vuoksi and Suvanto, and the marshes west of Lake Muolaa, through which the railway ran. Both were obstacles through which to channel an attacker and were at their most challenging east of Viipuri (Vyborg) in the Vyborg Gateway where two major roads passed through the villages of Summa and Lähde. The original positions followed a trace suggested by German Army experts in 1918 and work was directed by the first Chief-of-Staff, Major General Oscar Enckell, covering the area west of the Vuoski.

Initially, the Finns built a large number of concrete bunkers to defend key communications and made no attempt to conceal them. They were generally cheap to build, some being made of unreinforced concrete and were vulnerable to shell fire, but six forts were also built along the northern bank of the Vuoksi River and Lake Suvanto equipped with light artillery and good fields of fire. Two coastal defence forts on Lake Ladoga and five on the Gulf of Finland underpinned the rickety defences.[2]

A second construction phase began in 1934 and most of the 14,520 cubic metres of concrete in the fortifications was poured in this period, with two or three bunkers completed per year, with some bunkers modernised to provide flanking and frontal fire. This work continued until the Russians attacked.[3] Upgrading the fortifications helped provide work for some 100,000 unemployed and from the summer of 1939, 60,000 volunteers, many of them Civil Guards, strengthened the defences by building field fortifications, the work focusing upon anti-tank obstacles then dugouts. As the 'Ylimääräiset harjoitukset' (YH) mobilisation (see Chapter Four) was implemented the troops' initial task was to build positions for automatic weapons, then communications and firing trenches. But the war began before work on most communication trenches had started.

The field fortifications consisted of trenches forming platoon strongpoints capable of all-round defence, although in swampy areas the trenches were made from earthen walls contained in logs. The concrete bunkers were augmented by wooden ones, which covered gaps in the line, while barbed wire obstacles were also erected, often covered by snow during the winter, with several woven around trees in woods.[4]

The defences had seven gun-equipped forts, 132 concrete bunkers (60 per cent of them featuring the old design) and 49 concrete shelters (43 of the old design). In addition, around Viipuri there was the rear position (Taka asema or T-Line) with 21 old bunkers and three shelters, while an Intermediate position (Väli aema or V-Line) would be created from some of the poorly-placed original Mannerheim Line bunkers augmented with field fortifications.[5]

The defences had little depth: the gun line was up to 4 kilometres behind in fixed positions (by comparison, in the First World War, the German 'Siegfriedstellung' was some 10 kilometres deep). There was only one concrete bunker for every 0.3 kilometres, compared with 10 in the Maginot Line's weaker extension which covered Belgium, and the 15 in the West Wall. These were supplemented by 606 wooden bunkers and 804 wooden shelters, as well as extensive trench systems.[6]

This lack of depth was recognised before the war and Mannerheim sought to incorporate older fortifications and to bend the line at Summa, but Österman, the former commander of the Kannaksen Armeija, (abbreviated to KannA - the Karelian Army or Army of the Karelian Isthmus), preferred to abandon some older positions and support the others with more field fortification earthworks. Mannerheim objected, but he was unable to provide an alternative because the Finns lacked men and materiel for defence in depth.[7]

This meant the Finns had to hold every position to the last man or last round, relying upon their soldiers' stoicism and skill or bravery, as well as their extensive knowledge of the terrain. Since units were raised provincially, the men were known to each other and mutual confidence aided unit cohesion, which was boosted by intensive training during YH. The Finns would allow the enemy to enter the

Finnish troops watch warily for Soviet troop movements from their positions deep within a frozen forest during the Winter War of 1939-40. (Getty Images)

defences, then engage them with flanking fire, separating enemy riflemen from their supporting tanks, which were then destroyed piecemeal with lost ground regained through platoon or company counter-attacks, usually at night. With limited ammunition the artillery had carefully identified every potential route to the battlefield and marked up every metre of it, but if the battle became mobile it would lose this advantage.[8]

The line's biggest weakness was anti-tank defence: Finland started the war with only 98 Bofors 37 mm guns, two prototype 20 mm anti-tank rifles and six 13 mm machine guns.[9] Lack of money reduced the number of concrete anti-tank obstacles and granite boulder replacements were usually so small that Russian tanks easily passed over them. These obstacles were not covered with fire either. There were few anti-personnel mines, although anti-tank mines were extemporised from wooden boxes, and in one sector 1-tonne naval mines were used.[10]

The Finns anticipated no more than seven enemy divisions along the Karelian Isthmus and to meet them there was the Karelian Army under the tough-minded, intelligent Österman, with his headquarters at Imatra. Nominally, he had six divisions with 133,000 men, but this included the under-strength Sixth Division in Mannerheim's strategic reserve which was west of Viipuri, ready to repel any attempt at a landing between that city and Kotka, a town situated west along the northern coast of the Gulf of Finland. The five remaining divisions, each of 14,200 men, were split between Major General Harald Öhquist's Second Corps (65,400 men) with Fourth, Fifth and Eleventh Divisions and three groups of covering troops, and Major General Erik Heinrichs' Third Corps (45,600 men) with Ninth and Tenth Divisions and one group of covering troops. The battalions moved into the Mannerheim Line in October and had two months to prepare for their ordeal with 20 per cent being deployed as screening forces.[11]

In many respects Mannerheim, Finland's Commander-in-Chief, was at odds with his subordinates, but he would turn this to his advantage. While most Finnish Army leaders had served in the Imperial German Army on the Russian Front during the Great War, Mannerheim served in the Imperial Russian Army, retiring as a Lieutenant General rather than joining the Red Army. He would lead the Finnish White Army from January 1918, roundly defeating the Red forces. Yet it was only after returning to his homeland that he learned to speak Finnish; he would speak it badly, preferring to speak Swedish, and although of German descent, he disliked the Germans.[12]

The son of Swedish-Finnish aristocrats, by inclination Mannerheim was a monarchist and briefly Finland's Regent, yet he remained in the country when it became a republic after voters rejected him as the first president. Noblesse oblige meant he devoted his post-war life to charitable works until appointed Chairman of the Defence Council and de facto commander-in-chief in 1931. Two years later he was promoted to Field Marshal. He doggedly fought to strengthen national defence, sending promising officers to study in German and French military schools.

Mannerheim was a deeply reserved man whom subordinates found it difficult to approach and he was reluctant to delegate authority. He was aware of these weaknesses and at conferences would allow officer subordinates to speak before revealing his own views, but to middle and lower ranks he was courteous and even fatherly. His senior commanders found him more difficult; Österman described him as cold, imperious and unreasonable while Öhquist, despite having a high regard for his tactical abilities, felt he was a harsh man to work for and one who was impossible to please.[13]

He re-established his Civil War headquarters at Mikkeli, which was equidistant from the three front line corps, but made many trips to the front. His chief-of-staff was Lieutenant General Aksel Airo, the Defence Council's secretary who had qualified from the French Military Academy at St Cyr, making him one of the few senior officers who had not served with the Germans. He would be responsible for operational planning and, while they had their differences, theirs would be a good military 'marriage'.[14]

The line was at the heart of the VK 2 strategy (see Chapter Four) which implied a gruelling war of attrition to force Stalin to the negotiating table, but such a strategy would have a greater impact upon tiny Finland than the huge Soviet Union. Although Ambassador Derevyanski reported on 11 October that the Finns were mobilising, the implications were ignored by the Red Army which deployed 43 per cent of the Leningrad District's resources in Yakovlev's 7th Army in the Karelian Isthmus. Yakovlev could boast 200,000 men, 1,569 tanks and 720 guns (480 heavy) excluding infantry, as well as anti-tank pieces organised into a tank corps, 14 rifle divisions and four tank brigades. His left was to take Viipuri, then to drive into the heartland, while the right took the Kemi-Sortavia-Leningrad railway. To support Yakovlev the Russians had expanded the road network to the frontier before hostilities and built up large stocks of supplies.[15]

Yakovlev was to crush the Finnish Army by advancing on a 110-kilometre front with Komdiv Filip Starikov's 19th Rifle Corps on the left driving up the Leningrad-Viipuri railway, spearheaded by Komdiv Mikhail Kirponos's 70th Rifle Division, and Kombrig Filip Gorelenko's 50th Rifle Corps on the right.[16] Yakovlev was to reach the Mannerheim Line in two days, prepare for three days, then assault the line, breaking through it in four to five days and advancing at a daily average rate of up to 10 kilometres.

The offensive began with a bombardment which hit little of significance, the Red Army crossing the border at 08.30 hrs, while border guards took bridges and frontier posts in actions which lasted until noon. They advanced under overcast skies with visibility down to a kilometre. The snow was 30-40 centimetres deep; it hindered movement on foot and confined vehicles to a few roads, although the frozen swamps and lakes had ice thick enough for men and vehicles to cross. During October and November, the civilian population resident between the Mannerheim Line and the border with the Soviet Union was systematically evacuated together with its possessions. The Finns made no attempt to hold their national frontier: instead 21,000 screening troops slowly withdrew to the line, destroying roads and burning every building, leaving booby traps in the ruins, mining roads and their verges, and poisoning wells.

The First Division remained forward of the line between Lakes Suulajärvi and Valkjärvi to support the covering detachments which Mannerheim hoped would pin down and maul at least one Russian division. Österman was always sceptical, recognising that the Russians would deploy large numbers of tanks for which his troops were not prepared. He planned a slow withdrawal covered by screening forces, allowing him to man the line which would be the backbone of his defensive strategy.[17] The Finns manoeuvred in the Isthmus every summer, but this had led to over-confidence. Covering forces sometimes tried to stand up to the advancing Russian columns without success, although they did slow the advance.

The Red Army's road-bound columns made glacial progress, lashed by sporadic but heavy snowstorms, their progress further impeded by demolitions, mines and booby traps which left them almost bumper-to-bumper. They advanced at dawn but withdrew a couple of kilometres towards dusk, with the vehicles circling into laagers, while the men built huge bonfires to keep warm. The massed ranks were vulnerable to ambushes and snipers, whom the Russians called 'cuckoos'.[18] The Russians also developed a 'phobia' about mines, especially as ever more minefields were discovered. Meretskov asked engineers, augmented by Professor N.M. Izyumov's team from the Military Academy of Communications, to create mine detectors and the academics astonished the soldiers by producing a prototype within 24 hours.[19]

Progress was so bad on the first day that Yakovlev, looking anxiously over his shoulder to Moscow, urgently sought answers. He concluded that the problem lay with poor troop control at all levels and he ordered his spearhead regiments to advance behind a broad covering screen while the remainder stayed on the roads. Yet there was no significant improvement in the pace. During the evening of 2 December Österman received false reports of an enemy landing behind the covering force and a breakthrough in the centre, but the army's lack of signalling equipment made this difficult to verify. The Finns withdrew several kilometres, but by the time Österman learned the reports were false, it was too late to recover the ground. Mannerheim reprimanded both Österman and Öhquist the following day and demanded that Second Corps regain the lost ground. Öhquist refused, saying his men were too tired and confused.

Mannerheim, who appears to have underestimated the impact of tanks upon morale due to the lack of anti-tank weapons (the Russians termed it 'tank fright'), backed down for a short time. The Finns quickly extemporised a formidable anti-tank weapon using incendiary devices: they became known as Molotov Cocktails and consisted of a bottle filled with kerosene and potassium chloride which was triggered by novlen and an ampoule of sulphuric acid at the mouth. They could often ignite the tank's petrol tanks.[20]

Within two days Mannerheim returned like a Fury. On 4 December Starikov had created the first crisis for the Finnish Army on the Viipuri-Leningrad road and railway when a tank brigade drove deep into Second Corps, forcing Öhquist to make another hasty withdrawal. Mannerheim stormed into Imatra, summoned Öhquist for a tongue-lashing and then turned on Österman whom he accused of abandoning the forward zone. This led to both men threatening resignation before tempers cooled. The following day Starikov's advance threatened to encircle Fifth Division, the appearance of a single Finnish armoured car panicking the defenders who abandoned weapons, equipment and even field kitchens. That evening Second Corps staged raids, but during the following day the covering forces joined the main body of the field army in the line, their total losses being 400, including 100 dead.

In the east Gorelenko's corps was moved to the centre of the Isthmus while on 4 December his right, formed of 49th and 150th Rifle Divisions, 39th Tank Brigade and eight heavy batteries, was placed under a Group led by Komkor Vladimir Grendal, former Deputy Head of the Main Artillery Directorate. Grendal reached the south bank of the Vuoski by the evening of 6 December and established bridgeheads at Kiviniemi and south of Taipale on Heinrichs's Third Corps Front, bringing them up to the Mannerheim Line's main defences.[21] Yakovlev stridently urged Grendal on, who tried to comply with his task but he lacked bridging and artillery support, while his T-37 amphibious tanks were carried away by the current, leading to the loss of the bridgeheads the following day. Yakovlev and Grendal appear to have been at daggers drawn, with Grendal overruling orders for a new crossing.

The Russians closed with the line but needed eight days' preparation, not three, leaving Moscow displeased, especially when Yakovlev lost contact for a day. Shaposhnikov, who could see the plan collapsing, vented his spleen on both Meretskov and Yakovlev, especially the latter. Ordering Yakovlev to submit a detailed report of his operations, Shaposhnikov admonished him: 'You are a front line commander and do not have the right to leave command of your army for an entire 24-hour period.'

Stalin opted to make significant changes and established a supreme command on 9 December made up of himself, Voroshilov, Shaposhnikov, Kuznetsov and Molotov. Yakovlev was given an administrative assignment in Leningrad District whose commander, Meretskov, replaced him at 7th Army – a subtle hint to restore his reputation. However Shaposhnikov took a hands-on approach and within three days was urging Meretskov to improve command and control, reconnaissance and inter-arm co-operation, the *bête noir* of the Red Army. Shaposhnikov ordered more detailed preparatory work from staffs; in his view, this was the key to reducing concrete fortifications, known to the Russians as Dolgovremennnye Ognevye Tochki (DOT or permanent fire points). Failure to effect co-ordinated efforts would result in severe punishment to those involved.

Neutralisation of the DOTs was vital for the new twin-blow offensive Meretskov was hastily planning. First a diversion would be staged against Third Corps in the east around Taipale, because the road network in that part of Karelia made it easier to assemble the assault force. Once this had attracted the enemy reserves, the main blow would be launched a few days later against the western and central sections which had some of the strongest defences. The DOTs were to be pounded by artillery, isolated and stormed and, once a hole had been punched in the defence, Starikov and Gorelenko would envelop the enemy around Lake Summa, destroy the bulk of the Karelia Army and open the road for the 10th Tank Corps to Viipuri, the gateway to the Finnish heartland. However, Meretskov was all too aware that his men were demoralised by the lack of progress and that discipline was weakening.

The Red Army brought up reinforcements, reorganised forces, ranged guns and launched raids to find information and prisoners ('mouths'). It took some divisions up to two days to reach the line because they refused to go beyond the range of their own batteries. The lull gave the nervous defenders time to settle down and strengthen defences, but it also gave the Russians the opportunity to cut wire and, because they were not covered with fire, to drag away boulders used as anti-tank barriers.

Early on the morning of 15 December Grendal, reinforced by 4th and 142nd Divisions, struck Tenth Division at Taipale after an eight-hour bombardment. This included shelling from a score of heavy artillery batteries to which the Finns, with only nine field batteries, could not reply as they were short of shell. But when the assault waves lumbered across the snow and ice, Finnish guns opened up at close range, breaking up every attack both then and when it was repeated two days later. The Finns allowed the enemy infantry to approach to within 50 metres before opening fire. There was another pause, then a brief flare-up, without effect, on 25 December as Grendal's Operational Group became 13th Army based upon 3rd Rifle Corps' headquarters. However, while the Russians destroyed or overran the old bunkers, the Third Corps' field fortifications prevented them making any significant gains until the armistice, the Tenth Division suffering 2,250 casualties.

Meretskov's main blow fell on 17 December – upon Fifth Division which lacked reserves, artillery and shell, while the reserve Sixth Division was held too far back. Both rifle corps used two divisions with Starikov attacking on a 12-kilometre front supported by 216 tanks and 192 guns. The line was battered for an hour, while Gorelenko struck the main blow on a 6-kilometre front supported by 300 tanks and 306 guns following a five-hour bombardment. The attack was 'compromised by organisational incompetence at every level': units milled around, uncertain about their objectives or how to reach them and, because their tractors lacked fuel, five heavy artillery battalions failed to arrive in time.[22]

Tanks crossing iced lakes found few suitable exit points, and exploited the defenders' lack of anti-tank guns to penetrate the defences, while the Finns were frequently unable to get close enough to throw their Molotov Cocktails. Instead, they focused upon the riflemen, who were caught in murderous crossfire and artillery fire and they fell in heaps. The defence was hampered by communication problems, however, because the bombardment cut telephone communications, while the few radios that there were, were unreliable. At dusk the Russian guns stopped firing, telephone wires were repaired and Finnish commanders discussed the situation using a jargon of Finnish, Swedish and nicknames for people and places. The fighting had cost Second Corps 2,082 casualties including 857 killed and missing.

Despite Meretskov's positive spin, the attack and the following day's assault were a disaster which, despite his orders, were conducted with patchy artillery or engineer support in some sectors. Accurate Finnish artillery fire stopped the armoured spearhead and effectively ended the assault, although Russian guns continued to rain down shells. On 18 December the Russians also struck at Lähde, their KV, SMK, and T-100 experimental heavy tanks making their debut. However, Finnish artillery picked off many of the light tanks before they even reached the defences.

The heavy tanks were designed as replacements for the triple-turreted, 45-tonne, petrol-engined T-35 and included the petrol-engined 58-tonne T-100, as well as the diesel-engined 55-tonne SMK, updated with turrets for a 76 mm and a 45 mm gun, while a derivative of the latter, the 43-tonne KV (Kliment Voroshilov) had only a single turret with 76 mm gun. Their thick armour resisted shell fire, the lone KV taking 43 hits of which one damaged the gun, but the

following day the individual SMK was mined and damaged beyond repair.[23]
By now the Russian guns were also running short of ammunition, having fired a
total of 398,600 rounds by 25 December – 172,600 by heavy artillery, including
6,000 by 203 mm howitzers. Infantry and anti-tank guns fired another 116,500.[24]

Six divisions with air support launched the heaviest attack on 19 December,
focused upon Summa village. The tanks broke through the bunker line but were
stopped by Finnish artillery and only the following night did the survivors escape
to their own lines. At Lähde there was a fierce battle around the 'Poppius' bunker
(officially the 'Summa-Lähde Sector Bunker No 4' or Sj4) which was overrun,
but the garrison there held out for 48 hours, calling down artillery fire upon its
own positions.[25] Where the Russians broke through the lines, they were ejected by
prompt counter-attacks.

From 20-23 December the Russian assaults eased and then ceased, Meretskov
blaming the weather and the tenacity of the defenders, although Gorelenko rightly
concluded the failure was the Red Army's inability to co-ordinate operations
within the services.[26] A feature of this battle was the growing effectiveness of
Russian artillery fire which was better co-ordinated, with tank and infantry assaults.
In a letter to Stalin and Molotov on 21 December, Voroshilov blamed Meretskov
for repeating Yakovlev's mistakes and proposed purging every level of 7th Army to
replace 'cowards and laggards (there are also swine).'[27]

Stalin ignored him and ordered a new 7th Army offensive – Operation 'Ladoga'
– with massive air and artillery support against Viipuri, which was to start on
26 December and to be exploited by 10th Tank Corps the following day. Engineers
were to complete building forward command and observation posts by
23 December, together with jump-off and reserve assembly positions. Two days
before the main assault, as staffs at all levels completed detailed planning, each
division would launch a battalion-strong attack to take damaged defences and
establish bridgeheads in the line for the coming main offensive. Enemy Operational
and Strategic reserves were to have been disrupted by air strikes, but the weather
grounded most of the VVS and Meretskov had to borrow a number of heavy coast
defence rail batteries to do the job. The Red Army had twenty-four 305 mm rail
howitzers and twenty-five 280 mm 'mortars' but only six of the latter were
committed. They supported 8th Army but were later transferred to 7th Army.
A dozen would be deployed in 1940 with the 34th and 316th High Power
Independent Artillery Battalions.[28]

'Ladoga' was never executed, for on the morning of 23 December the Finns
launched an offensive which totally disrupted Russian preparations. With the
VK 1 plan in mind, Öhquist had long wanted to stage a counter-offensive,
but Mannerheim refused his request because he considered it to be too risky
until the enemy was held. The Russians were now in a salient and intelligence
reports claimed their morale was poor while supplies were not getting through.
Öhquist proposed a counter-offensive which would involve Mannerheim's reserve
– the under-strength Sixth Division working on the V- and T-Lines – which

Mannerheim was reluctant to commit, approving only on 22 December, 18 hours before the attack was scheduled to begin.

Öhquist's ambitious plan involved an attack on a 25-kilometre front between Lakes Muola and Kuolema, and was intended to envelop Starikov's 19th Corps using Sixth Division in the west and First Division in the east, although all the divisions in the line would support them. The Finnish leaders did not anticipate a major victory, but hoped to inflict a sharp defeat which would bring Moscow to the negotiating table. However they lacked everything needed for success: armour, artillery support and communications, with most divisions having only 36 hours to prepare, while the Sixth Division entered the front line late and vainly sought a delay. Snow was falling at Zero Hour (06.30 hrs) and the temperature was minus 20°F with a breeze adding wind chill as a brief 10-minute barrage involving only 1,100 rounds fell on the Russian lines. There were too many vehicles in the Finnish rear bringing up reserves and these were still being transferred hours before the attack. Worse, the Finns, like the Russians earlier, failed to carry out adequate tactical reconnaissance and had no idea where the enemy concentrations were. Indeed, overall planning was slipshod and amateurish.

Facing little initial resistance, Sixth Division advanced two kilometres but then encountered enemy armour and heavy artillery fire which stopped it by 10.00 hrs as Meretskov fed in his reserves to strengthen the line. The other divisions encountered the same problems and by mid-afternoon the offensive had ground to a halt as Finnish communications again collapsed while their artillery failed to move forward or learn to react to fluid battle. After eight hours Österman cancelled the offensive and the Finns withdrew unopposed, their morale high despite the failure and 1,600 casualties, including 630 dead and 200 cases of frostbite, these including 30 per cent of the officers. Proportionally, as a month-long lull began, the losses were the heaviest suffered by the Finnish Army to date.

A month's fighting had cost the Red Army in the Isthmus 69,986 men, including 11,676 dead and 5,965 missing, while materiel losses were 67 guns including eight heavy. Tank losses are more difficult to calculate, but until the end of January the 7th Army had 395 tanks damaged but only 62 were total losses, 13 of which sank through the ice. During December the 7th Army's 35th Tank Brigade lost 97 out of 217 tanks, of which 40 were total losses, while 40th Tank Brigade lost 94 out of 219 tanks.[29]

The failures were due to poor planning and inflexible execution, possibly the result of the overwhelming influence of the political officers in the wake of the Purges. The Red Army's endemic failures continued: poor combined arms operations, lack of reconnaissance and targeting, which wasted most shells and, as exercises in previous years had shown, there was the failure to support tanks even when they made a breakthrough. Few leaders displayed tactical initiative and Russian troops were thrown away in bloody and futile frontal attacks with only their instinctive defensive capabilities shining. The troops were not used to fighting in forests or in the depths of winter; indeed both men and equipment were in olive drab and there was no winter camouflage. By contrast the Finns had shown resilience, fortified by nationalism, but their counter-offensive failed because it was short of men and artillery as well as poor communications, so never had a chance. Yet the Russians failed to exploit the situation and for weeks afterwards there were only skirmishes and occasional bombardments.

Stalin was furious with the failure to occupy Finland and his anger focused upon both Zhdanov and Voroshilov. Khrushchev later described a scene at a party in late December when Stalin suddenly began berating Voroshilov who, red-faced, shouted back: 'You have only yourself to blame for all this! You're the one who annihilated the old guard. You had our best generals killed!' then threw a plate of suckling pig at him.[30]

Having vented their spleens the Soviet leadership pondered the future. Recognising that national prestige prevented a peaceful solution, it determined upon victory based upon a well-organised set-piece battle. As a foundation, Stalin gave the Glavnyi Voennyi Soviet (Main Military Soviet) executive functions to oversee operations. The Main Military Soviet included Voroshilov, Mekhlis, Zhdanov, Budenny, Kulik, Pavlov, Shchadenko (Red Army personnel head), Ivan Proskurov, Grigorii Savchenko (Deputy Head of the Main Artillery Directorate), together with Loktionov and Smushkevich from the VVS and, most importantly,

Stalin and Voroshilov exchange a joke. Stalin regarded Voroshilov as an artillery expert and the two were as near friends as Stalin permitted. Yet during the Winter War, when the Red Army's performance was criticised 'Klim' would throw a suckling pig at The Boss and shout, 'You have only yourself to blame for all this! You're the one who annihilated the old guard. You had our best generals killed!' (Hulton-Deutsch Collection/Corbis)

Shaposhnikov and Komandarm I Rank Timoshenko. Joint sessions were held with the Central Committee from January. Shaposhnikov had previously monitored the situation and was now given a more active role. It was apparently at his suggestion that major offensive operations in Karelia ceased from 28 December.[31]

Simultaneously, the Main Military Soviet, augmented by representatives from the Defence Commissariat and the western districts, began analysing the failed campaign, with Meretskov heavily criticised by the General Staff Operations Branch for advancing on a broad front and underestimating the Mannerheim Line. Additionally, there had been poor command and inadequate combined arms execution. Meretskov was recalled to Moscow at this time and faced Stalin's fury for undermining Soviet prestige through his defeats. Stalin told him: 'The authority of the Red Army is a guarantee of the USSR's national security.'[32]

The Red Army's leadership now began preparing for a thorough and steady assault on the Mannerheim Line and recommended a reorganisation of the command structure by establishing a front headquarters. Stalin reluctantly accepted its recommendations and asked for volunteers. One of the few competent senior commanders left, Kiev District commander Timoshenko, stepped forward. He demanded all the resources of Shaposhnikov's plan and received Stalin's carte blanche on the understanding there would be a long butcher's bill.[33]

On 7 January the Leningrad District ceased to have control of operations and was replaced by the North West Front. Timoshenko's chief-of-staff was Komandarm II Rank Ivan Smorodinov, while Zhdanov, having been Meretskov's Political Officer, now assumed the same task for the front. In this, at least, he distinguished himself. Shchadenko was given the task of touring the districts and press-ganging their best troops for the new enterprise. Timoshenko left nothing to chance and brought in staff from the Kiev and Belorussian Districts, the Frunze Academy and even students from the Staff Academy.[34] He began systematic preparations for renewing the offensive with new divisions brought in, and oversaw the assembly of vast stocks of weapons and supplies, while the communications network in the Isthmus was substantially improved. Simultaneously, the troops conducted extensive training exercises designed to prepare them for the assault with greater emphasis upon all-arms co-ordination as well as fire and movement, with mini battle groups intended to destroy specific fortifications.

Detailed planning began on 18 January. The Russians quickly recognised that the Finns were overstretched and that a breakthrough would force them to abandon the line. After considering two options in the east of the line, it was decided that Meretskov's 7th Army would deliver the main blow on a 16-kilometre section of the line between Summa and the Munasuo Swamp, using 75 per cent of his forces. The Summa-Lähde Sector defences were the hardest of the line with 17 concrete bunkers, including the strongest two: Sj5 'Miljoonalinnake' ('Millionaire Fort') and Sj4 'Poppiuslinnake' ('Poppius Fort') which anchored the Lähde defences where most bunkers dated to the 1920s.[35]

Timoshenko aimed to 'gnaw through' the defences over a five-day period using tanks as wedges to pierce the line and infantry to widen the gap, allowing an advance on Viipuri. He offered no hostages to fortune in predicting a breakthrough, merely commenting: 'The armies' missions are to develop the offensive with the goal of encircling and destroying the main enemy group on the Karelian Isthmus.'[36] Meanwhile, 13th Army would launch diversions at the other end of the line and once the Mannerheim Line was pierced Pavlov would launch an enveloping offensive across Viipuri Bay which, hopefully, would help complete the campaign within a fortnight. The plans emphasised delegation and individual initiative as well as the mantra of combined arms operations at every level. They were discussed by the Main Military Soviet and then during a dinner with Stalin, who commented on details and indicated where changes were to be made, but they were finally approved on 3 February.

Timoshenko quickly established a special group to study tactics for 'gnawing through' the defences. The group concluded that there should be a greater concentration, with divisional fronts no more than 2.5 kilometres and, of course, all-arm co-operation. There was also considerable emphasis placed upon reconnaissance to discover every last detail of the defences and for this purpose ski brigades were created (some from cavalry units). Despite having inferior equipment to the Finns they did much useful work. Forward observation posts and even observation balloons used cameras with telephoto lenses, while the VVS used a new Semenov camera which replaced plates with film. However, the conservatism of the VVS photographic reconnaissance department meant production was delayed and only a few were available.[37]

Engineers began removing anti-tank obstacles, only to see them replaced, so the Russians began covering channels through the obstacles with fire. So many batteries were deployed that it proved impossible to conceal them all. The engineers also created assembly and jump-off positions in the frozen earth, some only 100 metres from the defences, as well as a network of roads to aid artillery mobility, which was also helped by assembling 4,519 tractors.

Artillery was the key to success and Timoshenko demanded that the gunners provide more accurate and responsive fire. Units were to create forward observation posts equipped with new lightweight radios to pinpoint bunkers since experience had shown that up to one hundred 203 mm shells were needed to destroy a single bunker. Indeed, Meretskov would despatch a sample of bunker concrete to Moscow for analysis. There was greater emphasis upon using mortars but some divisional commanders, notably Kombrig Pantelemon Zaitsev (90th Rifle Division), were reluctant to use these weapons in the bombardment and did so only under pressure from Voronov and Meretskov.[38]

The riflemen would begin their assault only after a thorough bombardment and behind a creeping barrage following 'fire raids' (artillery sweeps) lasting two or three hours, day and night, and intended to interdict communications, prevent repairs to defences, kill exposed troops and deprive the remainder of sleep.

Voroshilov authorised the use of coastal defence rail batteries with four 180 mm being supplemented from 6 February by three 305 mm guns supporting Meretskov, while two 356 mm guns supported Grendal. To improve fire support for the infantry, Timoshenko created trench mortar units and would deploy five hundred 82 mm and 120 mm tubes, while fifteen anti-aircraft batteries would boost the bombardment.

A surprising aspect of the planning, given the legendary ferocity of Russian winters, was an examination of the way troops could overcome the bitter conditions on the Finnish Front. Frostbite was a major problem with nearly 13,400 casualties due to a shortage of winter clothing and accommodation but, like the Germans two winters later, the Russians had made few preparations for dealing with ice-bound engines and aircraft hydraulic systems. Clothing was rushed in, while vehicle and aircraft mechanics introduced maintenance procedures such as running engines regularly to ensure they would work.

Meanwhile, men and materiel flooded northwards raising North West Front's strength from 400,000 on 10 January to 705,360 by 10 February including 30 artillery regiments. The Motor Highways and Motor Transport Service (Avtotransportnaya I dorozhnaya sluzhba) organised convoys of up to 100 trucks to move supplies on a route running from Gorkii to Moscow to Kalinin to Leningrad. Movement was hindered by ice and snow, inexperienced drivers and a lack of spares, with many vehicles going off the roads. To overcome the problems, dumps with spares were organised together with hot water to de-ice the vehicles, while tow-truck detachments drove along the road providing emergency recovery.[39] Within the Leningrad District, hundreds of armoured sleighs were built to move infantry rapidly and safely, each being towed by a tank and carrying a rifle squad with heavy weapons. There were 2,313 tanks including 492 T-37/38, 1,149 T-26, 570 BT and 99 T-28, with the front armour of the last being increased from 30 to 80 mm, while side and rear armour was doubled to 40 mm and the engines protected from Molotov Cocktails.

Zhdanov improved political work and Party members were expected to show both bravery and discipline by example, but also be ready to follow the example of non-Party members. Interestingly, patriotism rather than socialism was emphasised and helped boost morale, but if enthusiasm should wilt in the face of enemy fire, and following the annihilation of 44th Rifle Division, the NKVD created 27 company-size kontrol'zagraditel'nye otriiady ('control-preventative detachments') on 24 January. These were both to prevent desertion and to secure the front's rear areas, the largest number operated in 8th Army and the next largest in 7th Army, attached to, but independent of, army headquarters.[40]

During January, the Isthmus forces received nine rifle/motorised-rifle divisions while the Karelian Fortified Region was reorganised into 42nd Light Rifle Division so that, by 10 February, the North West Front had 50 rifle/motorised-rifle and one dismounted motor-cavalry divisions, eight tank, three airborne and one rifle-machine gun brigades, 41 artillery regiments and nearly 30 ski battalions supported by 35,546 motor vehicles and 109,739 horses. But apart from 37th Rifle and 91st Motorised Rifle Divisions from the Siberian District, and 128th Rifle Division from Urals District, few had experience of operating in severe winter conditions. The 7th and 44th Rifle and 95th Motorised Rifle Divisions from the Ukrainian District lacked any troops familiar with skis, while skis ordered by Leningrad District failed to reach many units. Others, including Kirponos's 70th Rifle Division, lacked winter clothing and Kirponos had to insist that his men should receive it.

By late January Timoshenko had assembled on the Isthmus 26 rifle/motorised-rifle divisions together with seven tank brigades and 31 artillery regiments for his set-piece offensive. There were 14 rifle divisions in the first echelon, two in the second echelon, three (50th Rifle Corps) in the third echelon and two (with a nominal two Finnish) in the fourth echelon. To improve troop control, Meretskov had earlier reinforced 7th Army with Komdiv Ivan Davidovskii's 10th Rifle Corps, and now Timoshenko brought in Komdiv Vasilii Gonin's 34th Rifle Corps, while Grendal's 13th Army received Komdiv Mikhail Korolev's 15th Rifle Corps and Komdiv Stepan Akimov's 23rd Rifle Corps.[41]

The Finns used the lull to reorganise their forces in the line, but to confuse the enemy they renamed three divisions on 1 January: the Sixth Division became the Third, Eleventh Division became the Second and Tenth Division became the Seventh. Between 2-5 January the Third Division relieved Fifth Division which became the main reserve behind Second Corps holding the V- and T-Lines anchored on Viipuri. At the time of the Russian offensive the Second Corps had from the Gulf of Finland to Vuoksi the Fourth, Third, First and Second Divisions, while Third Corps had Eighth Division on its right and Seventh Division holding the left to Lake Ladoga.[42] Mannerheim had created two replacement/training divisions, the Twenty-First and Twenty-Third, and in late January attached them to the field army because they could be more useful as reserves than training units. Both were weak formations; 60 per cent of the men lacked uniforms, they were short of both automatic weapons and artillery, while mortars were received only as they moved forward. The Twenty-First Division was put into the V-Line behind Third Corps while Twenty-Third Division went to support Fourth Corps.

From late January the Finns came under increasing pressure from fire from an artillery train. By 8 February Russian gun strength had grown to 1,851 guns (728 heavy and 19 very heavy) augmented by 432 regimental and 876 anti-tank guns, as well as 60 anti-aircraft guns, with 87 per cent of the heavy guns on the 45-kilometre front. The navy added four 180 mm, three 305 mm and two 356 mm.[43] With Voronov as advisor, the guns began ranging with destructive fire and numerous brief halts to catch the unwary, the field artillery being used to blast earth and camouflage off the bunkers, exposing them to the heavy artillery. To deceive the enemy, radio stations were scattered along the front while the main batteries, but not the secondary sites, were camouflaged, with little attempt to conceal vehicle movements to them.

The bombardment began on 1 February but Timoshenko left nothing to chance and to ensure the army had absorbed the new ideas needed for a breakthrough, he demanded five division-size 'demonstrations' along the line starting on the same day. Three would be launched by 7th Army (42nd, 100th, 113th Rifle Divisions) and the others by 13th Army's 50th and 150th Rifle Divisions with each division commander selecting his own objectives and making his own preparations.

After air and artillery bombardments the assaults began, but only that of 100th Rifle Division in the Summa sector proved a success. The attacks were supported by engineer tanks, some with rollers to create passages through minefields and others with flame-throwers, while battle tanks dragged armoured sleds with infantry. Behind them came more infantry, often behind armoured shields and covered by smokescreens as the tanks crushed wire entanglements and tried to blow apart anti-tank obstacles before driving up to the bunkers, which they either shelled or blocked their apertures. From the Finnish side, machine guns mowed down the Russian assault waves and the defenders destroyed tanks in a battle which raged into the night. Only one of the five bunkers targeted was destroyed. The 'demonstrations' failed almost everywhere with heavy losses and the successive failures of 113th Rifle Division saw the commander, Colonel A.N. Nechaev, relieved on 6 February by Kombrig Khristofor Alaverdov.[44]

Attacks on the Summa sector were renewed from 5 February and were gradually extended along the whole line, but the Finns stubbornly held their positions. Yet support was uneven, with bombardments ranging from 35 to 75 minutes, and it was obvious that heavy shells were needed to destroy the concrete bunkers. Even with a 203 mm howitzer firing from as close as 7 kilometres they needed up to 35 rounds. Some weapons were, therefore, deployed almost until the gunners could see the whites of the enemies' eyes – 1.5 kilometres for 152 mm howitzers and 4 kilometres for 203 mm. Yet even for the 152 mm guns it might take 200 rounds to destroy a bunker with only one hit for up to eight rounds, although this dropped to one in up to five at ranges of about half a kilometre. Timoshenko was profoundly disappointed and commented publicly on 9 February that standards for inter-arm co-operation were still abysmally low. Nevertheless, he set D-Day for the offensive as 11 February with H-Hour at 12.00 hrs.

On 8 February Öhquist realised the Third Division urgently needed relief and wanted it replaced by the Fifth Division but Mannerheim, who underestimated the seriousness of the situation, refused. His determination to retain control of the situation meant that any reports about an enemy breakthrough had to be double-checked by his staff before he would act, thus slowing response times. On the same day Öhquist ordered his gunners to conserve ammunition and use it only when a senior officer judged that infantry weapons alone would not contain a situation.

The bombardments continued off and on for days, with 7th Army gunners firing up to 10,000 rounds per day.[45] Earth was blasted off dugouts and bunkers whose concrete cracked, some bunkers being undermined and leaning over, while dugouts caved in and buried telephone cables were cut. All resupply was done at night and in temperatures of minus 22°F; dugouts and bunkers froze because the slightest trace of smoke from their stoves proved a shell magnet. Deprived of food and rest the defenders were stretched to breaking point by the strain and the need to repair defences during the night, one division reporting that its exhausted men were sleeping through the bombardments and even when enemy tanks crossed their trenches. Others went literally mad with shell shock.

The night of 10/11 February was cold but clear as the Russians moved up their infantry guns to disguised positions. But as Timoshenko, Meretskov and Voronov (acting as Stalin's representative) arrived at Kombrig Arkadii Ermakov's 100th Rifle Division command post, a dense fog settled on the Isthmus, forcing the abandonment of air strikes. Gorelenko added an hour to the artillery bombardment, increasing Timoshenko's nervousness and leading him to mark time checking details. Ironically, he was not the only one, for at this time Stalin saw a flare-up of his chronic tonsillitis, accompanied by a high temperature, and his doctor was summoned.[46]

The bombardment began at 10.40 hrs and could be heard 160 kilometres away in Helsinki, Russian gunners soon becoming so hot working their guns that they stripped to the waist and still dripped with sweat during the winter morning. The bombardment smashed defences, filled trenches and destroyed anti-tank guns. Divisional artillery focused upon field fortifications and obstacles with three or four pauses to entice the surviving defenders into the open. Corps artillery conducted counter-battery work and sought enemy headquarters, while the very heavy artillery concentrated upon the concrete bunkers. In some cases the Russians brought 152 mm guns forward to engage the most troublesome bunkers, such as the 'Poppius Bunker' (Sj4), over open sights, or their super-heavy artillery struck bunkers such as the 'Millionaire's Bunker' (Sj5). The bombardment was made even more demoralising for the defenders due to the absence of counter-battery fire as Finnish gunners conserved ammunition for the assault.[47]

Meretskov had, from left to right, the 10th, 34th and 50th Rifle Corps, each of two rifle divisions, in first echelon and one in second echelon. All of Starikov's 19th Corps (also three divisions) was in second echelon and a third echelon of five rifle divisions (four motorised) was placed under Meretskov, Romanenko's 10th Tank Corps having fallen victim to the new conservatism and disbanded on 17 January. This gave Meretskov five tank brigades including the 20th Heavy whose 91st Tank Battalion had a company with the T-100 and two KV prototypes, four independent tank battalions and 11 heavy artillery regiments plus two battalions.[48]

The main blow would be launched by Meretskov's right and centre which comprised Gorelenko's 50th Corps and Davidovskii's 10th Corps respectively, while Gonin's 34th Corps, which had taken over the left facing Fourth Division on 3 February, would support them.[49] Gorelenko's 100th and 123rd Divisions, as well as Davidovskii's 138th Division, struck at some of the strongest defences around Summa which were held by Colonel Paavo Paalu's Third Division, with

First Division on its left and Fifth Division in reserve. They had 76.6 guns and 36 tanks per kilometre (the Finns having only 25 guns and 12 anti-tank guns in all) using the 100th and 123rd Rifle Divisions to break through and exploiting their success with 7th Rifle Division and the 20th Heavy Tank Brigade. The neighbouring 10th Corps was also to break through in its sectors. Air support included a third of the front's fighters, a quarter of the bombers and three-quarters of the ground-attack aircraft. Grendal's 13th Army attack was intended to help stretch the Finns to breaking point and was made with nine rifle divisions, a tank brigade and nine heavy artillery regiments as well as two very heavy ('high power') battalions, one armed with the latest BR 5 280 mm mortars and the other with British-made 234 mm mortars.

Grendal's assault began at 11.50 hrs supported by 500 guns and 238 tanks in temperatures of minus 7°F and was followed 10 minutes later by Meretskov, who was able to call upon 430 guns and 200 tanks. Both attacks were mounted behind rolling barrages, the former extending a kilometre behind the enemy defences, while the latter struck twice as deep.[50] Yet the first day's assault largely proved a disappointment, meeting intense machine gun fire, with Grendal making little progress, while Meretskov's troops experienced mixed fortunes. The 100th Division was actually forced back into its jump-off positions, but to everyone's surprise Kombrig Filip Aliabushev's 123rd Rifle Division, supported by 35th Light Tank Brigade including 34 OT 26 flame-thrower tanks, advanced some 1.5 kilometres with the tanks pulling armoured sleds of infantry who debarked. Their success owed much to good reconnaissance and good co-ordination as well as to skilled artillery support which destroyed many anti-tank guns, cut the defenders' telephone network and killed many defenders enticed from their dugouts by temporary pauses in artillery fire.[51]

Öhquist had few reserves and on that day noted in his diary: 'It's a terrible poker we're playing here.' At 13.00 hrs, the 'Poppius' Bunker fell and around it the defences were steadily destroyed or neutralised piecemeal. Since the bunkers were rarely designed to provide mutual covering fire, they could be taken individually, although when some of them were entered, the garrison was found to have been annihilated, having been killed by the concussion of shells. The Russians began widening the breach, pushing back the defenders up to a kilometre. With his reserves being consumed rapidly, Paalu asked Öhquist to commit Colonel Selim Isaksson's Fifth Division, but both corps, and Mannerheim, wished to keep this division as a reserve for as long as possible. At dusk the 'Millionaire's Bunker' just about remained in Finnish hands, but could clearly not be held for long and at 19.00 hrs enemy armour broke through. Within half-an-hour the Russians were pouring through the gap, Isaksson telephoning Öhquist to tell him: 'This is it, they've broken through.'

The Russians did not break off the attack at dusk but fought on through the night, a weak counter-attack being thrown back. The problem for Finnish commanders was that with their communications collapsing they could not accurately gauge the situation and tended to ignore frequent (and usually unfounded) claims of Russian breakthroughs. Elsewhere counter-attacks by local reserves 'hammered out' other dents in the line. But the situation was clearly serious and the Russians were reorganising for a renewed assault the following day. The 34th Rifle Corps tried to outflank the defences with attacks across the frozen Baltic, but the coastal defences under Fourth Division's operational control, especially the Koivisto Sub-Sector with six 254 mm and twelve 152 mm guns, stopped these attacks.

As his tanks broke through, Timoshenko reviewed the day's results and ordered Baltic Fleet heavy coastal defence guns forward to neutralise Koivisto's guns. The 10th Rifle Corps' 138th Rifle Division had also had some success west of Summa, as had the 15th Rifle Corps, but the greatest success was Aliabushev's which Timoshenko and Meretskov decided to exploit, using Gorelenko's corps' reserve, the 27th Rifles/7th Rifle Division, reinforced with part of 95th Tank Brigade which would attack along the eastern shores of Lake Summa to threaten the rear of the Finnish defences.

Aliabushev made slower progress on 12 February pushing forward only 600 metres, but at dusk he was reinforced by armour and artillery which, paradoxically, had failed to help 100th Rifle Division make any progress. During the morning Mannerheim released Fifth Division for a counter-attack at Lähde, but Öhquist had to use two regiments to patch up his defences, leaving only one for a counter-attack, which took the rest of the day to organise. At noon, however, the Finns finally abandoned the 'Millionaire's Bunker' and the Lähde sector as the Russians penetrated the Second Division in three places, although these breaches were all sealed in a day which cost Österman 1,200 casualties.

By now all the Finnish front line strongpoints in the Summa-Lähde sectors had been lost and the Russians were almost a kilometre north of the line's bunkers. Using night counter-attacks in temperatures of at least minus 25°C, the Finns managed to regain some of the strongpoints, but were finally forced back due to the overwhelming superiority of the Soviet artillery and air force, and the improved co-operation between Soviet infantry, armour and artillery. The Taipale sector held out until the end of the war, but with heavy losses for the defenders.[52]

At Lähde on 13 February Russian infantry secured a passage which had been blasted by sappers across an anti-tank ditch, allowing tanks to cross and advance 1.5 kilometres, and in the process overrunning 11 Finnish 150 mm guns, a significant part of the Finn's heavy artillery. Many anti-tank guns were also destroyed. The Russians then secured a bridgehead across the V-Line anti-tank ditch and by dusk Aliabushev, who had created a 4-kilometre gap, ordered his men to dig in to secure it. The Finns were exhausted; indeed, the Third Division's troops who had been in the line for a month, could barely keep open their eyes, even in the face of approaching Russian tanks. That day the division was relieved by the Fifth Division, depriving the Finns of their 'Operational Level' reserve behind the Summa section. Timoshenko was understandably ecstatic and so was Stalin, who was still suffering from stress-induced tonsillitis. When his doctor, Professor Vladimir Valedinsky, visited him that morning a map of Finland was spread out on Stalin's desk and he explained the military operation to the Professor, tapping the table with a pencil and saying: 'Any day now Vyborg will be taken.'[53]

Timoshenko sought further exploitation of Aliabushev's success: on the evening of 13/14 February he ordered Meretskov to bring up the 84th Motorised Rifle Division to the left of 19th Rifle Corps in order to support renewed efforts by 123rd Rifle Division, while 7th Rifle Division tried to roll up the Mannerheim Line defences. The 84th Division was supposed to attack at 10.00 hrs on 14 February, but the snow-bound road was blocked by Aliabushev's transport and knocked-out tanks, so movement was slow. Finnish machine gun fire prevented the division from reaching its jump-off positions. The day proved a disappointment for Gorelenko with only minor progress being made by 7th Rifle Division and none by the exposed 123rd Rifle Division, which could not bring up its batteries. The same applied to 100th Rifle Division which confined its activities to shelling Summa where the defences were finally outflanked. The defenders were driven into the V-Line. The Finns managed to break contact with the enemy which launched a set-piece assault on their old positions.

But the Finns' position was becoming hourly more desperate and with the threat to Viipuri growing, Mannerheim drove to Österman's headquarters to discuss the situation with the army and corps commanders. Österman wanted to withdraw to the T-Line, anchored on Viipuri, using the V-Line for a delaying action while Öhquist, prodded by Mannerheim, wanted to use the V-Line as the main line of resistance. By the end of the conference Mannerheim was pointedly snubbing Österman but departed without leaving any orders. He was probably checking the diplomatic situation before he gave the order to withdraw, in the hopes that the strong resistance of the Finnish troops would persuade the Russians to make concessions.

The well of Finnish manpower was running dry; the navy provided two regiments of raw troops, Third Corps provided a regiment of Twenty-First Division which set out by train and truck on 13 February to move to the other end of the line, while a Defence Corps battalion composed largely of 16-year-old boys was sent forward in automobiles but it did not arrive until after the withdrawal. The Finns were mobilising 50-year-old reservists and convicts serving short sentences to flesh out their battalions, while the Twenty-Third Division, which had just been sent north to the Kollaa Front, was ordered back to the Isthmus.

On the morning of 15 February, and a day late, the 84th Division finally launched its attack and Meretskov filtered two mobile groups under Colonel Vladimir Baranov (commander of 13th Tank Brigade) and Major Boris Vershinin (the 7th Army tank commander) through Aliabushev's positions in order to exploit the success and to push the enemy beyond Lähde. But Aliabushev persuaded them to support his tired infantry in a day-long assault upon Lähde which fell only when the garrison ran out of ammunition in the evening. Only then did the two groups begin driving deep into Finnish territory. At 16.00 hrs Mannerheim reluctantly sanctioned the abandonment of the remaining Mannerheim Line defences and withdrawal to the V-Line by which time Second Corps had suffered 6,400 casualties including 1,976 dead and missing.

Simultaneously Ermakov's 100th Rifle Division finally broke through the defences at Summa, having switched his thrust north-westwards with tractors being driven noisily to conceal any sounds of movement. The attack overcame fierce resistance and Summa was taken at 18.40 hrs and then advanced a further 1.5 kilometres. The fall of the village had been announced prematurely on Moscow Radio some days earlier, to Voroshilov's chagrin. When Meretskov reported it the second time, the Defence Commissar did not believe him and demanded confirmation from Voronov.[54] By the evening of 16 February Meretskov had penetrated up to 11 kilometres on a front of almost 12 kilometres. Carrying infantry and engineers on its tanks, Baranov's Group was joined by the 84th Division but the Finns generally broke contact and left rearguards to slow the advancing Russians, who were unable to overcome the deep snow which slowed 123rd and 7th Divisions' advance to a snail's pace.[55]

Gorelenko's 100th Rifle Division, aided by 10th Rifle Corps' 138th Division, broke out of the Summa defences and Ermakov's division was relieved for a short rest the following day. By the evening Timoshenko was convinced he was about to annihilate the Finnish Army and ordered Meretskov to give 50th Rifle Corps another mobile group from army reserves to help the drive up the railway to Viipuri. Gorelenko, who had already advanced 10 kilometres, did not begin his attack until the afternoon of 17 February. However, he lacked reconnaissance or adequate artillery support and was driven back to his jump-off positions. Moscow was unaware of the setback due to a breakdown in communications with Timoshenko's headquarters and, quite separately, repeated the instructions the front had already given Gorelenko, who now received them directly from Timoshenko.[56]

Again Gorelenko made no attempt to conduct reconnaissance and, with roads jammed preventing the movement of supplies, reinforcements and artillery, on 18 February the advance by the now exhausted 7th, 84th, 100th and 123rd Divisions proved a disaster. They ran into the fully-manned Intermediate V-Line whose artillery had registered the battlefield, while a collective amnesia seemed to fall upon Russian tank leaders who drove beyond the support of other arms and suffered accordingly. The assault was quickly stopped, leaving Meretskov and Timoshenko facing another time-consuming set-piece attack. Opposite Third Corps, Grendal suffered frequent command and control failures to make so little progress and was no doubt glad to be relieved on 2 March by Komkor Filip Parusinov to become front artillery advisor.

The Finnish defence line now ran from Viipuri Bay east to the railway, then swung south-east to the northern end of Lake Muola, and then along the Suvanto. The V-Line, anchored on Viipuri, varied from sector to sector; the eastern section between Lake Muolaanjärvi and the Vuoski had once been part of the Mannerheim

Line and was almost as strong, but around Viipuri there were scattered, obsolete fortifications linked to the eastern section by hastily dug field fortifications with barbed wire entanglements. It lacked depth and the exhausted troops who filed into it immediately had to strengthen it. The question now was how long the weary and outnumbered troops could last. The abandonment of most of the coast defences, apart from Koivisto, brought the prospect of an outflanking attack across the ice-bound sea and, to delay this, a regiment briefly reinforced the nearby islands, but was withdrawn on 21 February leaving Koivisto to act as a breakwater.

Österman had clearly lost Mannerheim's confidence and the strain upon him was increased by the news that his wife had been severely injured in an air raid; he resigned on 19 February citing ill health. Mannerheim did not appoint Öhquist, who had seniority but whose corps was fully engaged. Instead he selected Third Corps' commander, Heinrichs, as the army commander and replaced him with Talvela. To ease Öhquist's burden a First Corps was created from his left (First and Second Divisions) under Major General Taavetti 'Pappa' Laatikainen, intended to hold the centre from the railway to the waterway and allowing Second Corps to shield Viipuri with Third, Fourth, Fifth and Twenty-Third Divisions. The Viipuri defences were expanded with civilian labour while the old stone fortifications of the city with their moat would also be difficult to storm and the Finnish High Command hoped they could be held until an armistice was agreed.

Russian preparations for assaulting the V-Line were delayed by blizzards which lasted until 23 February – Red Army Day. That night there was a celebratory feast in the Kremlin at which Budenny provided music, but Shaposhnikov was absent making plans. Shortly afterwards, Grendal and Meretskov were given 26 and 27 February to complete their preparations. But they continued to maintain pressure on the Finns and after the arrival of heavy artillery on 20 February, Gorelenko again attacked to secure some minor footholds in the defences. The attack was renewed the next day with less success while Baranov advanced too far and was isolated by a counter-attack. Timoshenko was now paying the price of his success; his advance had depended upon the weight of numbers and materiel – thousands of vehicles. These vehicles jammed the few roads and became trapped on them by the snow, forcing Timoshenko to inform Meretskov on 22 February that his subordinates would have to place greater reliance upon brains than brawn. In a Parthian shot, Aliabushev secured a foothold in the V-Line on 23 February while 84th Division relieved Baranov.

Yet Timoshenko was planning a bold move to outflank the whole of the Karelian Army in a move emulating the feat of Peter the Great in 1710 when he had advanced across the ice of Viipuri Bay. Pavlov was assigned the task with three of Meretskov's motorised rifle divisions and 29th Tank Brigade, aided by the formation, on 29 February, of Komdiv Vasilii Popov's 28th Rifle Corps. This was a gamble for it was unclear whether or not the ice would be thick enough to carry the troops and there were doubts whether the Russian supply network would be able to support a thrust of some 50 kilometres which might be interdicted from Koivisto.[57]

Pavlov's first step, on 16 February, was to order the Baltic Fleet to construct a road across the ice; 23 MBR-2 flying boats dropped 7 tonnes of paint to mark the route which was then smoothed to create a road 4-6 metres wide, marked with flashers every 2 kilometres. The work was completed by 19 February and tested personally by Pavlov in a T-26 tank, but when Popov's troops began their crossing the next day the weight of traffic proved too much, the ice cracked, and three tanks fell through it. Another two roads had to be built to distribute the weight and these were used from 22 February, the three routes carrying some 40,000 troops and 10,000 vehicles by 8 March.[58]

In an effort to secure Pavlov's right, the Russians began driving along the coast to secure the southern shore of Viipuri Bay and by 19 February the Finns had only a toehold on the shore. This allowed the Russians to engage Koivisto from the east. The garrison, which no longer served any useful purpose, fired off all its ammunition on 23 February, spiked its guns and marched 40 kilometres northwards across Viipuri Bay in a snowstorm, arriving unscathed on the southern coast the following day. The island was occupied by 34th Corps' 43rd Division while the Russians completed the occupation of Viipuri Bay's southern shore.

Meanwhile, Gorelenko 'gnawed through' the V-Line from 17 February, driving a wedge through the Fifth and Twenty-Third Divisions on the route to Viipuri between the main road and the railway, a region of small hills and swamps. Gradually, this advance widened and on 25 February Gorelenko exploited gaps in the defences to punch a hole through the V-Line and threatened to outflank Fifth Division's rear. Moscow immediately ordered him to encircle Viipuri with Pavlov's forces.

Neither Österman nor Heinrichs had been optimistic about holding the V-Line, but Mannerheim demanded they hang on as long as possible, for every day gained improved Helsinki's negotiating position. But Mannerheim did not explain his reasons to his commanders, who grew angry because they felt he was out of touch. But they obeyed his orders and held on. However, during the February and March battles the Finns would lose 20 per cent of their army and received only 25,400 replacements together with 14 battalions of recruits.

In an attempt to stop Gorelenko, the Finns launched a counter-attack on 26 February with 15 Vickers Mk E tanks, the presence of which caused confusion and alarm, especially among the support and supply troops. The tanks had difficulty in the snow and were no match for the Russian armour (many lacked cannon armament) and only half returned to their lines – seven tanks were destroyed and one badly damaged vehicle was recovered.[59]

The following day the Red Army prepared for the final assault on the V-Line with average concentrations of up to 82 barrels per kilometre (including mortars and anti-aircraft guns). Pavlov would advance to the northern shore of Viipuri Bay while Meretskov advanced upon Viipuri, with the 10th and 34th Corps coming up from the south. Gorelenko's 50th Corps swept in from the east and Grendal would pin down the Third Finnish Corps.[60] But Meretskov's usual problems of poor traffic control and the resultant traffic jams made movement glacial and some batteries took three days to move a mere eight kilometres, while supplies came in a trickle.

On 27 February the Finns decided to abandon the V-Line in favour of the Rear or T-Line just outside Viipuri, which extended to Tali to Vuosalmi to the Vuoski Waterway. The retreat was hasty with frequent engagement with the Russians, but it was carried out in gradual phases with rearguards inflicting heavy losses on the pursuing Russians. The V-Line fell to Meretskov's renewed attack on 28 February after an intense 30-minute bombardment which proved less effective than anticipated due to poor reconnaissance and communications. There was bloody fighting and many positions had to be reduced by heavy artillery at point-blank range. Once again Gorelenko's forces led the way, the 51st Division distinguishing itself to accelerate the enemy's withdrawal to the T-Line; but, in the east, the attack was less successful, despite the 23rd Corps' 136th Rifle Division, which was covering Meretskov's right, having support from no fewer than 135 barrels per kilometre, as well as Colonel Dimitrii Leliushenko's mobile group based on 39th Tank Brigade.[61]

Gorelenko's fortunes did not improve on 29 February as he tried to exploit his success; the 51st Division was slow to send forward a mobile detachment and then ran short of supplies, but the reliable Aliabushev finished off enemy defences in its sector before a well-deserved four-day rest. A new problem for the Russians was metre-deep inundations of Viipuri's north-eastern approaches. This was caused by the Finns opening sluices to dams to prevent a wider encirclement and channelling the Red Army, as the defenders occupied the T-Line by 1 March and used guns captured at Suomussalmi to hold their pursuers.

South of Viipuri, Davidovskii's 10th Corps pushed back the Third Division remorselessly, crossed the coastal railway near Nuorra on 29 February and, the following morning, the 138th Division crossed the ice of Viipuri Bay to isolate the city from the west. The coldest winter of the 20th century, which had often been Finland's ally, now became its enemy, for the sea ice did not melt as usual in late February but remained many metres thick, allowing even tanks to cross.

With Viipuri threatened with envelopment, Mannerheim hastily organised a new command: Coastal Group, under Wallenius, to contain the threat along the northern shore of Viipuri Bay using Fourth Division from Second Corps, five battalions from the Salla Front and three coastal battalions, many of the last partly trained and poorly equipped. Wallenius reacted to the situation by turning to drink and was often barely able to stand during conferences. A furious Mannerheim relieved him on 3 March, forbade him ever to serve in the Finnish Army, and replaced him with the Chief of the General Staff, Lieutenant General Karl Oesch, who would achieve miracles.

The failure of Meretskov's attacks led to Grendal's appointment as Front Chief of Artillery by which time the ordnance on the Isthmus totalled 3,419 artillery tubes, 1,911 anti-tank guns and 1,045 trench mortars as well as 2,620 tanks, while Timoshenko's total strength had risen to 760,578 men.[62] The 10th and 34th Corps were putting the T-Line under great pressure as Second Corps' Third and Fifth Divisions struggled to hold their main line of resistance, part of which was on bare, rocky ground where it was difficult to dig trenches, while exploding shells sent granite splinters through the air.[63] From 5 March Davidovskii's 10th Corps began reducing the fortifications shielding Viipuri's inner harbour, but the Finns retained two outposts in the bay: Tuppura and the Uuras Islands at the mouth. Anticipating the inevitable, on 2 March the Finns evacuated 80,000 of Viipuri's 83,000 residents.

As Meretskov hastily reorganised his forces, Stalin decided to ratchet up the pressure since a Finnish delegation was due to arrive in Moscow to discuss terms. Military defeat and the erosion of Red Army prestige had eroded Russian intransigence, while intelligence reports from London and Paris indicated that the allies were preparing to despatch an expeditionary force to aid the Finns – Moscow had long feared the presence of major powers in neighbouring countries. Negotiations opened on 29 January and, on the eve of the Russian offensive, Tanner and Ryti met Mannerheim who advised them to give priority to a negotiated settlement. He pledged to buy as much time as he could but Helsinki's position was undermined when Stockholm not only turned down requests for military aid on 13 February, but also leaked the news. On 5 March the Finns accepted a summons to negotiate, but Molotov refused to accept an immediate ceasefire asking rhetorically: 'Why stop the fighting if one cannot rule out the possibility of having to resume it over a difference?'[64]

It was no coincidence that 5 March saw Timoshenko order attacks along the whole Finnish Front while Meretskov was to complete the encirclement and capture of Viipuri. The 34th and 50th Corps were to break through south and east of the city, with the latter swinging into it from the east, then storming it. The 10th Corps, straddling Viipuri Bay, was to strike northwards and, with 28th Corps, swing eastwards from its bridgeheads to isolate the city from the north. To do this they would have to cross the 43-kilometre-long, Tsarist-built, Saimaa Canal which ran due south from Lake Saimaa at Lappeenranta through Nuijamaa to enter Viipuri Bay north of Viipuri. That day, as Mannerheim succumbed to influenza, Gorelenko pushed through Second Corps' Twenty-Third Division and broke through south-west of Tali. The gap was widened the following day and when Oesch asked his neighbour Öhquist for shells, he was told that Second Corps had only 600 left.

Timoshenko was determined to take Viipuri by 7 March and demanded that Meretskov accelerate his advance. Gorelenko's men overcame the enormous problems facing them and, after infantry had secured bridgeheads beyond the rivers and inundations, were reinforced over wooden assault bridges hastily built by the engineers. On the night of 7/8 March, the Twenty-Third Division broke; one battalion fled the field while the men of another walked away when ordered to retake ground, pointing their rifles at their officers. The division was pulled into reserve, but the Russian success brought nearer the isolation of Viipuri just as the Finnish delegation in Moscow learned that the Russians were demanding large swathes of Finnish territory.

Morale within Second Corps was cracking and rumours of a Russian tank breakthrough during the night 8/9 March caused a battalion in the line to flee. The rot spread along the line. It took hours to rally the men and to persuade them to return to their lines. The Finns were fortunate that the Russians did not exploit the situation. By now Meretskov's envelopment of Viipuri was falling further and further behind schedule due to the rising flood waters, now up to six metres. Even when Meretskov's men waded through, sometimes up to their necks in freezing water, in temperatures of -10 to -15° C, they had to dry out and warm up or suffer frostbite while facing fierce counter-attacks, which were often held only with artillery fire.

The Finns were running short of manpower and ammunition, however, and the only silver lining was the strengthening of their anti-tank defences with captured Russian 45 mm guns and newly-arrived French 25 mm guns. The Second Corps had committed almost all its reserves and had also sent in construction and supply troops, and although every available unit had been despatched to Viipuri by First Corps, it would be some time before they arrived. On 10 March Timoshenko repeated his order to storm Viipuri, his men reaching the southern shores of Lake Leitmo. With tank support they punched three holes in the Finnish line as the 34th Corps south of Viipuri and the 50th Corps to the east destroyed the last line of defence, but Meretskov's men advanced less than half a kilometre. The following day Davidovskii cracked Third Division's line in two places but when Heinrichs ordered its withdrawal, Mannerheim countermanded the order and demanded that it hold its positions for another day for political reasons.

Meanwhile, by crossing the outer Bay of Viipuri, Pavlov opened a new front which extended the Finn's defensive line by some 30 kilometres. Firstly, however, he had to clear Tuppura and the Uuras Islands to secure his communications. Tuppura was attacked first, from 2 March, by 86th Motorised Rifles. As the unit moved forward it came under fire from the heavy coast defence guns, including the two 305 mm at Ristaniemi and four 155 mm at Sataniemi, which tore great gaps in the ice to swallow four tanks and many men before blizzards stopped the advance, giving the Russians time to build another ice road to disperse their forces.

On the evening of 3 March, Timoshenko ordered 28th Corps to cross the ice and strike the Finns' soft underbelly by establishing beachheads around Vilajoki and Häränpääniemi. They were then to drive towards the Saimaa Canal to isolate the Karelian Army aided by Komdiv Iakov Cherevichenko's 3rd Cavalry Corps which was en route from Poland. It arrived on 10 March. Dense fog delayed Pavlov on 4 March but, when it cleared, the 86th Division on the left, supported by three artillery regiments, stormed Tuppura only to discover the garrison had slipped away. It then continued marching northward to the Vilajoki Peninsula, while on the right 70th Rifle Division (supported by a heavy artillery regiment) leapfrogged Uuras then the Suoni Islands before striking out towards the Finnish coast despite air and artillery attack.

The following day the Russians established beachheads but the 43rd Division had great difficulty securing 70th Division's left in the face of fire from coastal batteries and resistance from the Hamina Group, which was formed from two dismounted cavalry regiments at Häränpääniemi. The Russians were hindered by a lack of armoured support because the coastal terrain, with large granite outcroppings on the shore and steep slopes from the beaches, made it difficult for the tanks to get off the ice onto land. Where low and relatively level slopes were discovered, deep snowdrifts hindered the passage of the tanks, but their drivers gradually learned the tricks for getting off the beaches and inland.

The Russian landings on the coast focused upon peninsulas which would be suppressed by tank fire from both sides until the infantry attacked. As the riflemen scrambled up the steep, rocky sides, the tanks would provide fire support until the troops were established, but casualties were heavy. The tanks would then drive to the head of the bay or inlet, where there was usually a village, where they would move off the ice then drive inland to isolate the peninsula defenders before driving deeper inland.

At first, Oesch was able to survive by using the Second Corps' supply depots which were linked to his troops through a good network of roads. But as the battle approached the coast, refugees began to clog the roads, making it difficult for supplies to get through, while air attacks were also a major problem. Meanwhile, 10th Corps' 113th and 138th Divisions drove eastwards up the inner Viipuri Bay on 5 March leaving only a few islands in Finnish hands and helping to secure the eastern flank of Pavlov's beachhead. The latter was reinforced the next day with the fresh 173rd Motorised Rifle Division which was pushed into the breach on 6 March at Vilajoki and cut the Helsinki–Viipuri highway. That night the Fourth Division commander wanted to pull back his left, but this would have exposed the Third Division, weakened by providing forces at Vilaniemi.

The Viipuri Bay Front was clearly in crisis as pressure mounted on communications west of the city, with the Russians cutting the Viipuri–Hamina Road on 7 March, forcing Finnish reserves and supplies to take a circuitous route. By the evening it was obvious the remaining island defences in the Bay were untenable and almost all were abandoned on the night of 7/8 March. Over the next few days, the Russians tightened their grip on the Viipuri–Hamina Road and by 10 March, Popov's 28th Corps had secured a five-kilometre-wide bridgehead. To exploit the situation, Cherevichenko's cavalry began crossing the Viipuri Bay, but progress was slow as the horses slid on the ice because they had been fitted with the wrong horseshoes.[65]

Blizzards on 10 March exacerbated the Red Army's supply problems, slowing the 10th and 28th Corps' advance. However, it quickly recovered the following morning as Meretskov launched his heaviest attack upon Third and Fifth Divisions, holding Viipuri and tearing several gaps in the Finnish lines which Heinrichs was unable to close. Gorelenko was threatening to engulf Third Division, but progress was slow due to a combination of flooding, supply problems, and incessant Finnish counter-assaults. Air attacks were another problem for Meretskov who threatened hysterically to court-martial any anti-aircraft battery commander who failed to respond to such attacks. By dawn of 12 March the Finns had been driven back four kilometres in less than a week, with Oesch's left close to the outskirts of Viipuri. The Red Army was clearly on the verge of rolling up the whole Finnish Army.

While Öhquist considered a retreat, Mannerheim would permit only the withdrawal of Third Division into Viipuri, whose southern outskirts they set ablaze, slowing the advance of 7th Rifle Division. Later that night there was some good news as Fifth Division managed to contain Gorelenko by separating the enemy infantry and armour and it became clear that the Russians had temporarily shot their bolt for there was now a brief lull as they regrouped. By the time they were ready to renew their advance, the armistice came into force.

As the Finnish Army battled desperately, their peace delegation arrived in Moscow on 8 March and was presented with terms which included the loss of virtually all the Karelian Isthmus, the Rybachi Peninsula and the leasing of a base at Hanko Bay. The delegation sought better terms without avail and, reluctantly, the Finnish government accepted the Russian terms on 12 March. A ceasefire was to take effect the following morning at 11.00 hrs (noon Moscow time), Stalin informing Timoshenko that evening but ordering him to continue attacking right up to the ceasefire. If enemy resistance continued he was 'to beat the hell out of him.'[66] News of the ceasefire was a great relief to Timoshenko whose victory was running neck-and-neck with exhaustion, but he continued to maintain pressure.

Throughout Meretskov's attack the 13th Army had also tried, with little success except where its left (23rd Rifle Corps) benefited from Gorelenko's success. Grendal's last act before handing over to Parusinov was to plan a new offensive spearheaded by 15th Rifle Corps under Kombrig Mikhail Korolev. But it was the 23rd Corps which had the greatest success when the attack began on 7 March, when it established a bridgehead two kilometres wide on the north shore of the Vuoksi Waterway. The success was overshadowed, however, by a collapse in morale in Korolev's 4th Rifle Division which managed to establish a regimental-sized bridgehead without artillery preparation; but then, for no apparent reason, its men fled back across the ice. Attempts to repeat their feat the next day saw heavy casualties and panic with men firing upon each other, then retreating again and abandoning many weapons.

Nevertheless Talvela recognised he could not resist indefinitely and ordered the construction of a new defensive system two kilometres behind the existing defences in case of a breakthrough. On the evening of 12 March Third Corps was drafting orders for a withdrawal. They were not executed, but their need was reflected in the heavy losses the corps had suffered: 4,888 casualties, including 1,714 dead and missing from 4 February to 12 March.

In the west of the Isthmus, the morning of 13 March saw the Finns repulse the usual morning attacks, but then the guns suddenly fell silent as word passed down to the front line about the ceasefire. But at 10.45 hrs, the Russians suddenly unleashed a 15-minute bombardment apparently out of pure vindictiveness and when the guns stopped there was a brief eerie silence soon broken by the music of the Red Army bands.[67]

The battles for Viipuri cost the Finns some 5,150 casualties including 1,650 dead and missing – amounting to 8 per cent of total Finnish casualties during the Winter War and bringing the total butcher's bill to 68,480 casualties including 24,923 or 22,849 dead and missing, the figures coming from two sources using official statistics.[68] Finland had retained its independence, but at a terrible cost in the loss of most of eastern Karelia which represented 10 per cent of the country's pre-war territory (35,000 square kilometres) with 422,000 people (12 per cent of the population) losing their homes. Civilian casualties were 2,464 (826 dead) attributable largely to air raids. The Russians claimed the Finns had lost 62 aircraft, 500 guns and mortars, as well as 50 tanks, the latter figure reportedly including static vehicles embedded in the line![69]

The Soviet Union had gained a buffer zone for Leningrad, which was no longer threatened by potential enemy artillery based in Finland but the Red Army had suffered a terrible loss of international prestige and sustained heavy casualties and severe losses of materiel. Metelyakov gave a figure of 7.5 billion roubles which accounted for 653 tanks (at least 113 were reported to have sunk through the ice) as well as 422 guns and mortars. The last figure appears accurate, for artillery losses to the beginning of March were 302 tubes including 124 anti-tank and 67 infantry guns as well as 41 heavy guns.[70]

The human cost was even greater and, while Molotov would publicly acknowledge 48,745 dead and 158,863 wounded, this was a gross underestimate, although historians give widely differing figures from Russian sources. The most comprehensive data (see Table 5-1) indicates that the Red Army suffered 520,500 casualties including 123,848 dead and missing. A total of 305,000 men was injured and the remainder were sick or had frostbite. In addition, the Baltic Fleet suffered 1,600 casualties.[71] It appears that 4,479 Russians (other figures say 5,567) were captured, of whom 99, including eight officers and an NCO, wisely decided to remain with their captors after the war. Few received a heroes' welcome upon their return home and while the details are obscure, it appears they swapped one prison for another and were subject to intensive 'interrogation' as to how they came to be in Finnish hands. Apparently many were shot, including probably most of the 301 officers and 787 NCOs, for 'dereliction of duty', 'cowardice' or 'desertion'. This was an omen for 1945: most prisoners of war were regarded as potential traitors and investigated by the NKVD, with an unknown number of officers and NCOs being shot, while enlisted men were sent to the camps.[72]

Table 5-1: Soviet casualties during the Winter War

	Front	7 Army	13 Army	8 Army	9 Army	14 Army	15 Army	Total	Fleet
Killed	33,720	16,422	16,878	8,100	8,540	181	14,689	98,530	154
Missing	6,110	2,037	3,826	4,971	4,996	2	3,376	25,318	155
Wounded	119,122	61,481	57,271	21,723	17,674	301	27,463	305,035	301
Sick	27,242	19,256	7,986	7,296	12,250	-	4,259	78,289	845
Frostbite	3,922	723	3,199	2,797	2,649	101	-	13,391	145
Total	**190,116**	**99,919**	**89,160**	**44,887**	**46,109**	**585**	**49,787**	**520,563**	**1,600**

Source: Kirovsheev pp.60-80.

The Red Army leadership had failed badly at every level. True, it had victories on the Karelian Peninsula, but these were due more to overwhelming numerical and materiel resources, (the steam hammer to smash a walnut), while north of Lake Ladoga it had been humiliated by 'puny' Finland. Mekhlis noted that many of the rank and file regarded the attack upon Finland as an unjust war.[73] Certainly Stalin recognised the boil could no longer go unlanced and as regiments returned to their barracks, he began analysing the causes of a Pyrrhic victory.

ENDNOTES

[1.] For the Line see Irincheev, *Mannerheim Line* and The Battles of the Winter War website. Finnish official documents do not refer to 'the Mannerheim Line'.
[2.] Irincheev p.9.
[3.] Op. cit. pp.9-13, 24-25.
[4.] For the field fortifications see Irincheev pp.18-23.
[5.] Op. cit. p.63.
[6.] See The Winter War website. Shirokorad, pp.565-566, claims the Finns dug in most of their 32 Renault FT 17 as pillboxes, mostly in Nyaykkiyarvi and Taipale, but this is not confirmed by Finnish sources.
[7.] Trotter pp.65-66.
[8.] Irincheev pp.23-24.
[9.] See Winter War website, Anti-tank weapons.
[10.] Irincheev pp.23-24.
[11.] For the Finnish build-up see Condon pp.32, 34, Trotter pp.47, 52, 69, 99.
[12.] For Mannerheim see Condon p.25 Trotter pp.23-32, 47.
[13.] Trotter p.39.
[14.] For life at Mannerheim's headquarters see op. cit. p.202.
[15.] Condon pp.34-36.
[16.] Kirponos would be killed in late summer 1941 leading South West Front's futile breakout.
[17.] For the 1939 Karelian battles see Condon pp.39-40, 44-47, 71-72,75, 76, 78-79; Dye pp.40, 44-45, 60-61, 63, 72-80, 101 f/n 170; Erickson pp.543-544; Irincheev, *Mannerheim Line* pp.29-34, 36-39, 42-44, 54, 56-58; Trotter pp.37-38, 62-64, 67-72, 74-90, 99; Shirokorad pp.616-627; Voronov pp.137-140.
[18.] Voronov p.137.
[19.] Meretskov p.184. Voronov p.139 says they were developed by the Smolny Institute.
[20.] Condon pp.46-47; Trotter pp.72-73.
[21.] For Grendal see Bellamy pp.94-96. Grendal's work as President of the Artillery Committee in 1938 shaped Red Army equipment during the Second World War. He was promoted to Komandarm II Rank on 16 January 1940.

22. Dye p.74.
23. Shirokorad pp.655–656.
24. Shirokorad pp.626–627. During December Finnish field artillery fired 119,300 rounds, but industry produced only 47,100. Suomen kenttätykistön historia Vol. II, p.551, quoted in Winter War website.
25. Sj4 consisted of two casements and was known to the Russians as DOT 006 or Hill 65.5.
26. Dyke p.76.
27. Op. cit. p.77.
28. Shirokorad pp.619–620.
29. Casualty figures from Kirovsheev pp.60–61. There were 35,800 wounded, 1,164 battle fatigue, 493 from burns and 5,725 with frostbite. Artillery losses from Shirokorad p.683. They are inflated by 28 anti-tank and 17 infantry guns. Tank brigade losses from Aptakar website article.
30. Montefiore p.293.
31. Proskurov played a major role in supplying aircraft to Spain and later became head of the GRU. He was purged and later shot five days after the German invasion. Savchenko was purged on 19 June and, with Rybachov, shot in October 1941.
32. Dyke p.103.
33. For 1940 campaign preparations see Condon pp.105, 107; Dyke pp.88, 101 f/n 173, 103–127, 129 f/n 15, 136–40, 142, 144–145, 147–149, 180 f/n 50; Erickson pp.547–550; Meretskov pp.185–187; Shirokorad pp.627, 629–630, 632–634, 638, 660–661 Table 8; Trotter pp.203–209, 213–214; Voronov pp.140–151.
34. Chuikov and Kovalev arrived from the Belorussian District leading Timoshenko to comment: 'Apparently, everybody from the Belorussian Military District is here at the Front.'
35. Irincheev, Mannerheim Line pp.29, 33.
36. Based on Dyke p.137.
37. Voronov pp.140–144.
38. Op. cit. p.152. Zaitsev was mortally wounded in January 1944.
39. Erickson, Road to Stalingrad p.33.
40. Dyke pp.88, 127.
41. Gonin and Aimov both died in 1941, the former, reportedly, executed for drinking on duty and the latter in a plane crash.
42. For life in the Mannerheim Line see Irincheev, Mannerheim Line pp.24–25.
43. Shirokorad p.638.
44. One unsuccessful 7th Army demonstration saw 20,000 rounds fired. Voronov p.151. Alaverdov was captured in 1941 and executed the following year.
45. Shirokorad p.629.
46. Montefiore p.185.
47. For the assault on the Mannerheim Line see Condon pp.107, 109, 111, 113–115; Dyke pp.117, 145, 147, 149–152, 154–155, 157–159; Erickson Soviet High Command pp.549–550; Irincheev, Mannerheim Line pp.24–26, 28–29, 32–34, 36–39, 40–45, 47–50, 51–54, 57–58; Irincheev White Death pp.124–191; Meretskov pp.187–189; Shirokorad pp.627–639; Trotter pp.215–233; Voronov pp.149–150, 152. See also Aptakar and Svintsobyii Shkval website articles.
48. Four more KVs joined the experimental heavy tank company during the war, three prototype KV-2s with 152 mm guns. Three KVs were hit by anti-tank guns, one 14 times, without effect, but all suffered anti-tank mine damage to their running gear. The brigade also had radio-controlled robot tanks to demolish fortifications.
49. Gorelenko commanded 7th Army at the time of the German invasion and would then command 32nd Army on the same front until the end of the war.
50. That day, the 24th Corps Artillery Regiment supporting 50th Corps fired 14,769 rounds.
51. Aliabushev would be killed within three days of the German invasion while leading 87th Rifle Division.
52. Irincheev Mannerheim Line pp.57–58.
53. Medvedev. & Medvedev, pp.4–5.

[54.] Voronov p.152.

[55.] In the battle to penetrate the Mannerheim Line, 7th Army lost 96 tanks (43 sank through ice and nine disappeared) to 25 February while 264 were damaged by shell fire and 137 by mines.

[56.] For the final battles in southern Finland see Condon pp.115-122, 124, 126-129,132-134, 136-7 Dyke pp.160, 162-169-170, 172, 174-178; Erickson, *Soviet High Command* pp.550-552; Irincheev *White Death* pp.192-204; Meretskov p.189; Shirokorad pp.566, 640-650, 663-664; Trotter pp.242 - 245, 255-261. See also Stalynoii potop website article.

[57.] The ice in the Gulf of Viipuri was 47-70 centimetres thick, which could carry tanks and heavy artillery, while making it impossible for Finland's Navy to intervene. See Nordling's article.

[58.] Dyke p.164, Shirokorad pp.663-664.

[59.] From 1936 the Finns purchased 33 unarmed tanks but in November 1939 only 10 were battleworthy with 47 mm guns and some received 37 mm Bofors guns. No more than 18 tanks were armed during the Winter War.

[60.] In 34th Corps, Gonin was replaced by Meretskov's deputy, Komdiv Konstantin Piadyshev. The following year he would command the Luqa Group, but was arrested in September 1941, jailed and died in prison two years later.

[61.] Lelushenko would be a distinguished tank army commander fighting the Germans.

[62.] Stalynoii potop website article and Kirovsheev p.63.

[63.] The assault on Viipuri was supported by heavy tank prototypes, and two heavy self-propelled gun prototypes – the SU-14 with a 152 mm BR-2 gun and SU-100U with a 130 mm gun on a T-100 chassis.

[64.] For the diplomatic background see Condon pp.139-143, 145-146; Dyke pp.135-136, 161-162, 164-16, 170, 172, 174-175; Trotter pp.234-241, 246-254..

[65.] Meretskov p.189. Popov, who appears to have been wounded or fallen ill, was replaced by Zhukov's former chief-of-staff, Komdiv Pavel Kurochkin, in March and he would rise to front command fighting the Germans. The intensity of Finnish resistance is reflected in the 5,229 casualties, including 1,892 dead and missing, suffered by 86th Division.

[66.] Dyke p.178.

[67.] Russian sources are silent about this bombardment; Irincheev, *White Death*, makes no mention of it, while Voronov (p.156), who was visiting 8th Army, claimed the Finns shelled them heavily in the 15 minutes before the ceasefire took effect. In the final battles, 7th Army lost 61 tanks (37 sank through the ice), but 242 were damaged by shell fire and 82 were mined.

[68.] 820 Finns were taken prisoner during the Winter War.

[69.] For the cost of the war see Condon pp.153-154; Trotter p.263.

[70.] Shirokorad p.683.

[71.] Of those wounded after 7 January 68 per cent were injured by bullets and only 31 per cent by shell or mortar bomb fragments. This was the reverse of First World War figures.

[72.] Shirokorad p.683.

[73.] Van Dyke article, *The Timoshenko Reforms*.

CHAPTER SIX

AWAITING THE WESTERN STORM

'There is no such thing as Blitzkrieg.'
SEMON KONSTANTINOVICH TIMOSHENKO, 25 SEPTEMBER 1940

'Have you come to scare us with war...?'
STALIN TO ZHUKOV, 17 MAY 1941

THE Winter War had barely ended when the first debriefing session was hosted by Stalin in the Kremlin on 14 April 1940 as the Red Army secured the new western frontiers and began to reorganise its forces in the aftermath of the conflict. The disbandment of 7th, 9th, 13th and 15th Armies was ordered on 26 March, while 14th Army became the Arkhangelsk Military District and 8th Army was transferred to Novgorod.[1] Four days of presentations and discussions made depressing listening, even when viewed through rose-tinted spectacles.[2] Technically, Russian equipment was like the curate's egg – good in parts, but it was clear that the Red Army needed tanks with thicker armour, bigger guns and diesel engines, the last items to give greater fuel efficiency and to reduce the risk of fire.

The greatest failures were in staff work at all levels, and at the Strategic-Operational Level planning had been slapdash and inadequate, although Stalin clearly recognised his own contribution in encouraging too hasty decision-making (see Chapter Four). The absence of reconnaissance plagued Operational and Tactical-Level planning before Timoshenko arrived in January and there remained the chronic problem of combined arms operations, which even he could not overcome, and even when practised at Tactical Level, it was sometimes forgotten in the heat of battle. The ghost at the feast was the impact of the Purges which, with the associated dual command system, had created a layer of inexperienced leaders, most of whom were reluctant to display operational initiative for fear of arrest.

Timoshenko was one of the few deemed to emerge with any credit and for this, as well as loyalty to Stalin during the Purges, he was promoted on 7 May to Marshal of the Soviet Union together with Shaposhnikov, whom Stalin now recognised had given sound advice, and Kulik – who had not. Kulik's joy was tempered by the disappearance of his beloved wife, Kira, two days earlier. Officially, this remained a mystery even after Kulik was shot in 1950. In fact Beria had arrested her on Stalin's orders because she was too interfering and, unusually, she was shot out of hand.[3]

The sacrificial goat was Voroshilov who was kicked upstairs on 8 May to become Deputy Chairman of the Defence Committee of the Council of People's Commissars (Komitet Oborony pri Soviet Narodnykh Kommissarov). He was replaced as Defence Commissar by Timoshenko, Mekhlis's attempts to become Timoshenko's deputy failing, no doubt to the Marshal's relief.[4] Timoshenko attempted a root and branch reform of the Red Army and one of his initiatives was to return to active service as many purged officers as possible to improve overall experience.

In the autumn of 1940 the Inspector General of Infantry noted that, of 225 regimental commanders, none had attended a full course at the military academy, 25 had completed courses at a military school and the only military education of the remainder was a junior lieutenant's course.[5] This offered Timoshenko and Shaposhnikov the opportunity to prise thousands of officers from the clutches of the NKVD and 11,178 of them would return to the colours during May, including Rokossovsky and Gorbatov, with others following later. Indeed, on 20 June Timoshenko successfully secured the release of former 1st Army commander, Kuzma Podlas, who had been jailed in March 1939. Others who had been under a cloud and been placed on the reserve list also rejoined at this point.[6]

The framework of Timoshenko's 'reforms' was a Defence Commissariat Order, issued on 16 May, listing the Red Army's faults and how they would be corrected. This was largely concerned with operational training in difficult terrain, the avoidance of piecemeal attacks and in the all-important use of combined arms, while there was a greater emphasis at staff-level on what would be known half a century later as 'information management'.[7] During the year there was a succession of conferences and meetings to examine the Red Army's problems, with dozens of discussion papers looking at almost every aspect of recent operations.

Timoshenko's task was eased slightly by his predecessor who had introduced a Law on Universal Military Duty at the end of August 1939 during which he noted to the Supreme Soviet: 'Neither an illiterate, nor even a well-educated person, can nowadays effectively exercise even the functions of a simple communications operator without having undergone basic training, let alone (fulfil the responsibilities of) the junior officer corps.' The law therefore increased the training period for junior commanders to three years and in the aftermath of the Poland campaign, command and control were supposed to be effected not through rigid orders, but through guidelines ('nastavlenie'), allowing greater subordinate initiative.[8] The Winter War had shown a lack of initiative at all levels and there was clearly a fine boundary between achieving this and retaining military-political discipline in the Red Army.

A reflection of the changes came in June 1940 when the Red Army introduced the rank of General to replace that of Kommander, a decision which apparently dated from a meeting between Voroshilov and Shaposhnikov on 16 March. The details were hammered out and presented to Stalin and Molotov on the evening of 18 March. The Presidium of the Supreme Soviet drafted a decree on 11 April on the subject, but it was not published immediately because the generals were squabbling over details, especially whether or not each branch should have its dedicated rank, a view finally accepted on 7 May. The following day a committee led by Voroshilov and including Budenny, Kulik, Mekhlis, Pavlov, Timoshenko and Shaposhnikov, perused the officers' list and assigned the new ranks. Most Kombrigs became Colonels, Komdivs became Major Generals, Komkor became Lieutenant Generals, Komandarm II Rank usually became full Generals, while Komandarm I Rank received the newly-devised rank of Colonel General. Within the navy 74 officers became Admirals.

The changes were not always straightforward and of the 914 officers promoted to General, three Komkors, 71 Komdivs and 71 Kombrigs became Major Generals; 11 Komandarm II Rank, 32 Komkors and 20 Komdivs became Lieutenant Generals. Not all received the new ranks and at the time of the German invasion there remained at least one Komkor, 15 Komdivs and 196 Kombrigs, the failure to update their ranks apparently being a combination of questions over their professional competence or political reliability with 60 per cent of the Komdivs and 21 per cent of the Kombrigs having been 'repressed'. During 1940 and early 1941 many of the most senior officers were upgraded, but an unknown number of Kombrigs still held their old title when the Germans invaded. The downside to the new titles was the introduction of a stricter disciplinary code in July, but in August 'unitary command' (see Chapter One) was restored.

Yet the 'Timoshenko reforms' proved to be more style than substance.[9] The debates led to few decisions and the training programme failed to resolve the long-term problems. Timoshenko went as far as he could, but he was all too aware that former Red Army Marshals were rotting in their graves after opposing 'The Boss'. While Beria may have been reined in, he could still ride down victims with Stalin's approval and 29 generals were 'repressed' in 1939 and 1940 (see Table 6-1), while the Military Collegium of the Supreme Court of the USSR tried 7,826 officers in 1939 and 38,527 in 1940.[10]

Table 6-1: Generals purged 1939 – 1940

Year	Komkor	Komdiv	Kombrig	Korkom	Divkom	Brigkom	Total
1939	1	4	4 *	2	7	5	**23**
1940	1	-	2	-	-	3	**6**
Total	**2**	**4**	**6**	**2**	**7**	**8**	**29**

* Excludes Vinogradov in Finland.

The generals arrested during 1939 included Komkor Aleksandr Todovsky, a member of the Main Military Council while of four Komdivs arrested, A.G. Orlov, head of the Artillery Academy's foreign languages facility, was shot in January 1940 but the others (including Podlas) were reinstated. Five Kombrigs, including the luckless Vinogradov in Finland, were arrested of whom only the chief-of-staff of the 57th Rifle Corps, Aleksandr Kushchev, was reinstated. Of the commissars arrested, both Korkoms died in prison and two of the Divkoms are known to have been shot, as were at least two Kombrigs.

In 1940 the unfortunate Komkor Ya.Z. Pokus, who had been arrested in the Far East in February 1938 and released two years later, enjoyed exactly eight months of freedom before he was rearrested while a lecturer at the General Staff Academy. He would die in prison. One Kombrig, Gregorii Kondrashev, commanding 18th Rifle Division, was shot in August 1940, but Kombrig Ivan Sukhov was reinstated. The commissars of the Central Asian District, and 2nd Aviation Brigade, were both arrested in April with the latter, Fedor Zolotilovskii, shot in July 1941. Only intelligence operative Yakov Bronin was reinstated, but he would be arrested again in 1949.

A similar fate befell Komkor Maksim Stepanov, head of the Red Army Chemical Department (responsible for chemical and pyrotechnic weapons, as well as fuel transport and delivery), who had been arrested on 9 December 1938: he was apparently released shortly afterwards. On 30 March 1939 he wrote a letter to Voroshilov complaining that the NKVD had arrested 40-45 per cent of the chemical officers in the districts and 60-65 per cent of those in the corps and divisions. Voroshilov forwarded this to the NKVD and on 31 May 1939 Stepanov was sentenced to 20 years and died in the camps on 24 September 1945.[11]

But the full fury of Beria's Purge would fall on the unfortunate inhabitants whose territory was grabbed by the Soviet Union. In Poland, a kilometre-long strip of land along the new frontier with the Generalgouvernement (the German occupation zone) was depopulated, and within 30 kilometres of this zone fortifications began to be built. The relative prosperity of Poland 'B' evaporated rapidly as the Russians shaped it into their own image by buying goods at favourable exchange rates, stealing or 'requisitioning' property and, when billeted on the wealthier Polish citizens, quickly taking over their homes.[12]

The Red Army's 'requisitions' were from all but the poorest peasants (who had nothing), but the army helped remould the new territory into the Soviet form. The army had encouraged the creation of local administrations and militias, sometimes using Communists to do this, and on 4 October the front military councils (ostensibly) called for local elections to take place on 22 October, setting the scene for the Soviet Union's formal absorption of Poland 'B'. The army organised public meetings to 'select' candidates, all Soviet-approved and often from poor and the least educated peasants, while society itself was 're-educated' and land redistributed. With the NKVD supervising the voting, the result of the election was a foregone conclusion and the new representatives of the people promptly asked for Poland 'B' to be absorbed into the Soviet Union, which occurred on 28 November.

On 10 February 1940 130,000 'counter-revolutionary' elements – real and imagined – were deported to Siberia. Further round-ups followed so that by November 1940 1.17 million people, 10 per cent of the population of Poland 'B', had been herded into the cattle trucks. By the time of the German invasion, the figure had risen to some 1.25 million people but conditions in their new homes were so harsh that about a third died of neglect. Meanwhile some 110,000 Poles had been flung into the NKVD's dungeons by June 1941 and many executed.[13]

Although the Polish Army began organising resistance networks from the moment of the Soviet invasion, they were ineffective, suffering from lack of central organisation or funding, with most networks disrupted from January 1940 when the NKVD arrested their designated commanders. The commander of the Lwow District, however, Colonel Emil Macielinski, was reportedly an NKVD informer. Civilian networks proliferated and occasionally attacked Russians and supplies, but were easily penetrated by the NKVD and also rolled up.[14] An uprising organised by high school pupils at Czortkow on 21 January 1940 was quickly suppressed. The students attacked a barracks and armouries, but the latter were found to be empty and a train-load of Russian troops who, by not so happy coincidence, were waiting at the station, quickly crushed resistance.[15]

Perhaps this incident focused NKVD attention upon its thousands of Polish officer prisoners. With the conclusion of the Polish campaign some 250,000 Poles were in Russian custody including soldiers, landowners, officials, doctors, lawyers, writers and academics. There were 14,735 Polish officers as well as the aviatrix, Janina Lewandowska, together with 11,000 other prisoners including police and civilians. On 3 October 1939, Beria ordered 4,000 officers to be transferred to Starobelsk near Kharkov, 6,000 gendarmes and police to Oshtakov in Kalinin and NCOs plus privates to Kozelsk and Putivl, the transfers being completed by 8 October. Most of the last category was released during the autumn through Kulik's intervention, while later some 10,000 officers were transferred to Kozelsk, south-east of Smolensk. From the end of October NKVD investigators interviewed prisoners to see whether or not they would be willing to co-operate with their new masters. Some 400 officers indicated they would accept the new regime. But as early as 1 December, the majority were regarded as 'counter-revolutionaries' destined for the prison camps, a view apparently supported by Kulik.[16]

With the prisons overflowing, Beria proposed executing certain categories of prisoners, including 295 generals and 2,080 majors and captains, but on 5 March Stalin, Molotov and Mikoyan went further, signing an order to execute the 'troublemakers' at Kozelsk. Some 15,000 officers and senior police, as well as Janina Lewandowska, returned to the cattle trucks believing they were going to a labour camp, but instead they ended up in the woods near Katyn not far from Smolensk. They were then taken in trucks to the execution ground and shot through the back of the head with German-made Walther automatics, which were more reliable than Russian Tokarev and Korovin pistols. Others were executed in prison in the same manner, one executioner claiming 250 victims a night for 28 successive nights. The awful process was completed by 20 May with 21,857 dead, including 7,000 civilians.

The removal of the Poles was aimed at securing the region in the event of an attack, the prospect of which rose sharply during the summer. Anticipating this in July 1940 and because of the poor work of Glavnoye Razvedyvatel'noye Upravleniye (Military Intelligence), Timoshenko fired Lieutenant General Ivan Proskurov as its head and replaced him with Filip Golikov, a man with no intelligence experience. The decision was also payback for the arrogant Proskurov who, while representing Voroshilov during the Winter War, loudly complained when Timoshenko did not meet him personally.[17] Sadly, Golikov proved a slender reed and his reports to Stalin were written with a courtier's eye because the new GRU head recognised that 'The Boss' did not wish to hear too much about the German build-up.

Another member of Stalin's court who remained a thorn in Timoshenko's side was Kulik. As Head of Nachalnik Artillerii RKKA (Red Army Artillery), he split the responsibilities of his triumvirate of deputies, Voronov, Grendal and Savchenko, to give himself supreme control over weapons programmes by preventing co-ordinated development, which eroded the army's scientific research. Grendal, who had a distinguished career as a gunner and was a prolific writer, publishing some 300 works which laid the foundations for Russian artillery success in the Second World War, was a major opponent of the idea and twice tried in vain to persuade Kulik to change his mind. But by the summer it was clear that Grendal was dying of lung cancer and he finally succumbed in November 1940.[18]

The question of the Red Army's motor-mechanised forces dramatically resurfaced during the summer of 1940, less than five months after Kulik and his friend Pavlov had disbanded the tank corps. German motor-mechanised forces had conquered vast areas of western Europe in a six-week campaign, making advances of 200-300 kilometres, just as the Red Army's dead visionaries had anticipated, because the Wehrmacht had solved the problems of command and communication, all-arms co-ordination, and supply. The rapid German success was a severe shock to the Kremlin which had confidently anticipated the Reich being involved in a prolonged and debilitating conflict. It now had to reassess the future of its own armoured forces.

In one of his last decisions before taking command of Belorussian District, Pavlov caused the disbandment of the Avtotransportnaya i Dorozhnaya Sluzhba (Motor Transport and Motor Highway Service) and its absorption by the new Glavnoe Upravlenie Bronetankovykh Voisk (Main Armoured Forces Administration) which would soon be fully committed to reorganising the armoured forces.[19] As the Germans struck in the West, the Red Army was planning to create 15 motorised rifle divisions, but the Defence Ministry and Shaposhnikov were also working on plans for a tank division with 385 tanks, similar to the old tank-heavy mechanised/tank corps. Pavlov disagreed and, having analysed experience in Finland, his directorate concluded on 22 April that tanks should still be used to support infantry, but that rifle divisions should lose the independent tank battalions which should be grouped into tank brigades.[20]

However, the directorate also concluded it was possible to use tanks independently to exploit successes when the army broke through enemy defences. With this apparent meeting of the minds on 27 May, Timoshenko and Shaposhnikov proposed combining two of these tank divisions and a motorised rifle division into a tank corps for 'exploitation during offensive operations' or for counter-attacks operating with the support of a three-regiment aviation brigade. There would be six tank corps created from two cavalry and four rifle corps, with two each in the Belorussian and Kiev Districts and one each in the Odessa and Trans-Baikal Districts, with the Leningrad and Moscow Districts having one tank and one motorised rifle division respectively. The total tank strength of the Red Army would be 18,349 tanks excluding T-37/T-38 light, but including 1,260 heavy and 1,140 flame-thrower. However, on 1 April 1940 total tank strength was 20,008 including 468 heavy and 1,027 flame-thrower.

The German victories showed these proposals were not ambitious enough — even for Stalin — so Timoshenko and Shaposhnikov submitted a more ambitious plan on 2 June calling for eight tank corps and two independent tank divisions (Trans-Caucasus and Central Asian Districts), exploiting the fact that half the motorised rifle divisions required already existed. But there was no public return to the damned radical ideas of Tukhachevskii and his friends; indeed, as late as 25 September 1940 Timoshenko claimed: 'There is no such thing as Blitzkrieg.'[21] The new plans, approved on 9 June, meant the Leningrad and Moscow District would now also receive a tank corps, giving the Red Army 177 divisions (including 11 motorised rifle and 92 rifle) together with 25 tank brigades (see Table 6-2 for distribution of the Red Army in the west). But work on creating the new formations was disrupted because, with the fall of France, clearly Stalin wanted to strengthen the Soviet Union's defences, actions which would actually stimulate German plans to destroy his country.

Table 6-2: Distribution of forces in West, 1 April 1940

District	Corps		Divisions		Tank Brigades
	Rifle	Cavalry	Rifle	Cavalry	
Leningrad	6	1	21	-	8
Belorussian	6	2	16	7	12 (1 heavy)
Ukrainian	9	3	24	9	14 (2 heavy)
Odessa	2	-	10	-	2
Total	**23**	**6**	**71**	**16**	**36**

Based on data by Alexander Kiyan in Divisions Section website rkka.ru.

He began by completing the occupation of the Baltic States, Russian suspicions of an anti-Soviet plot being aroused when the Baltic Entente held a conference at Tallinn from 14–16 March. The Russians had three rifle divisions, three tank brigades and four aviation regiments plus communications and anti-aircraft units totalling 75,000 men, 1,000 tanks and 600 aircraft deployed in the States.[22] On 23 April Voroshilov had proposed 'reorganising' these forces during the first half of July, but Timoshenko was drafting more radical plans and on 2 May Voroshilov agreed that the rotation should be 'postponed'.[23] On 5 May Mekhlis ordered the districts bordering on the Baltic States to begin immediately the political education of those scheduled to enter the States and complete it by the beginning of June. Meanwhile the Estonians sought unsuccessfully to renegotiate the occupation agreement to end with the conclusion of the European war, but Moscow refused.

Pressure on Lithuania began from 24 May when the Soviet Ambassador demanded the return of two missing soldiers. Molotov claimed the next day that they had been kidnapped by the Lithuanian government, which made a conciliatory reply. The Russians refused offers of a joint investigation and there appears no evidence of any disappearances; but from 30 May Moscow began a propaganda campaign against the Lithuanian government and there were soon dark murmurs of Kaunus encouraging an incursion from neighbouring Germany. The stakes were raised on 3 June when Vladimir Semyonov, the Soviet Chargé in Lithuania, claimed the Lithuanian government was preparing for a German takeover and aiding a Fifth Column.

The same day Timoshenko informed former VVS commander, Komandarm II Rank Loktionov, that he would be commanding all forces in the Baltic States in two days' time. Simultaneously, a decree was published retaining recruits for a third year to New Year's Day 1941 'due to the difficult international situation'. The following day troops of the Leningrad, Kalinin and Belarus Districts were alerted and began concentrating on the borders. Their air defence forces were ordered to establish an aerial blockade, all under the guise of exercises as the units in the States were placed on alert.[24]

On 7 June Lithuanian Premier, Antanas Merkys, arrived in Moscow in a vain attempt to defuse the situation, but was accused of a disloyal attitude toward the Soviet Union. Within two days it was clear the Soviet Union wished to control his country – indeed the day he arrived, Eremenko's 3rd Cavalry Corps was alerted to be ready to occupy Lithuania within two days. On 8 June, as tension increased, Timoshenko warned Loktionov to prepare to protect air bases which might be used to bring in troops. That evening (a Saturday) at a secret meeting of Belorussian District commanders in Lida, the District's deputy commander (and 11th Army commander), Lieutenant General Fedor Kuznetsov, warned of 'possible actions against Lithuania'. The Kalinin and Baltic Districts received 1st Motorised, 17th and 84th Rifle Divisions, 39th and 55th Tank Brigades from the Moscow District, the 128th Motorised Rifle Division from the Arkhangelsk District and the 55th Rifle Division from the Orel District.

By 9 June the NKVD reported that it had prepared eight camps capable of taking 48,000 prisoners (later 70,000), some of these already holding Polish prisoners who were to be transferred, while another was established for those who faced 'special isolation'. Two further camps were set up for officers, gendarmes and identified agents. The NKVD also provided an operational regiment and three border guard detachments which began conducting cross-border reconnaissance. The same day, as the scale of the threat became more apparent, the Lithuanians began to take defensive measures by moving up an infantry and a cavalry regiment with some armour and anti-tank guns.

By 10 June Pavlov had assembled 3rd Army north of 11th Army and assigned it the 4th, 24th Rifle and 3rd Cavalry Corps, while Soviet military bases in Estonia declared they were ready for combat. In some cases these were more expressions of hope; when the 33rd Rifle Division joined Eremenko on 10 June its artillery regiments were short of shells while 400 of its horses lacked shoes, forcing Eremenko's blacksmiths to save the situation. Each army had seven rifle and two cavalry divisions and three or four tank brigades, totalling 221,000 troops supported by 513 tanks and 1,140 aircraft. Meretskov's Leningrad District assembled 8th Army with six rifle divisions and a tank brigade for operations against both Estonia and Latvia, together with the Kalinin District's 65th Special Rifle Corps (one rifle division and a tank brigade). The 11th Rifle Division was to strike independently along the Gulf of Finland coast into Estonia. The two districts had a total of 139,000 men, 1,508 tanks and 855 aircraft, and were ordered to complete preparations by 16 June.[25]

Molotov summoned Merkys on 11 June and while speaking darkly of the Baltic States forming an anti-Soviet alliance, informed him he must dismiss his Interior Minister Karzys Skucas, and the Director of State Security, Augustinas Povilaitis. That afternoon, in a three-hour conference at the Grodno artillery barracks, Pavlov, the Belorussian District's new commander, outlined plans to seize Lithuania and prevent its army from escaping into neighbouring East Prussia in an operation expected to take no more than four days.[26] The plan drafted the next day involved 11th Army with elements of the 16th Special Rifle Corps enveloping Kaunus, while the 214th Airborne Brigade dropped 935 men to seize key bridges across Neman and Neris. The brigade would also airlift some 475 troops to Kaunus and Pavlov. Detailed planning was to be concluded by the morning of 15 June and would include the garrisons within the States, whose radio operators were put on listening watch to await orders.

Pressure on the Lithuanian government increased with the disappearance on 12 June of an officer of the 5th Rifle Division, Senior Lieutenant Vladimir Golovin, who had attempted to desert but was soon arrested by the Lithuanian police. The Red Army invaded before he could be handed over, and Golovin was sentenced to death on 21 June. Meanwhile, Semyonov loudly denounced the 'provocation' and claimed the Lithuanian government was isolating the Soviet garrisons while police investigated Soviet supporters. More active Russian preparations were made on 13 June when seven soldiers were secretly parachuted into the country to prepare a landing site near Gayzhun station.

The following day Moscow denounced the Baltic States for being anti-Soviet and claimed they were breaking the terms of the October treaties. Shortly before midnight on 14/15 June, the Lithuanian Ambassador was called to Molotov and handed an ultimatum which would expire at 10.00 hrs the following morning. It demanded the immediate arrest of Interior Minister, Karzys Skucas, and the Director of State Security, the anti-Communist Augustinas Povilaitis. It also sought the formation of a government which would implement the October treaty 'fairly' and an increase in the garrison up to 12 divisions. Molotov added ironically that if these measures were implemented, the Soviet Union would not interfere with Lithuania's internal affairs!

The Russians also began an air and sea blockade of all the Baltic States, the seriousness of which was underlined when two fighters shot down a Finnish airliner flying from Tallinn to Helsinki. The passengers included a US embassy courier with diplomatic pouches.

The Baltic Fleet had received its orders on 9 June to capture all warships and merchantmen belonging to the Baltic States and it deployed 120 vessels, including the battleship *Oktiabrskaya Revolutsiya*, the cruiser *Kirov*, nine destroyers, 17 submarines and 10 motor-torpedo boats, as well as 144 aircraft and the specially-formed 1st Special Marine Rifle Brigade with four battalions.

On hearing the news of the ultimatum, President Antanas Smetona urged resistance to the occupation but failed to find support, either among the government or the armed forces. The Armed Forces Commander-in-Chief, Divisional General Vincas Vitkauskas, appointed only on 22 April, refused to sanction what he regarded as a suicidal order. Smetona and his family promptly fled to East Prussia and then went to live in exile, initially in Switzerland and from 1941 in the United States, where Smetona died in a fire in January 1944. Merkys announced he had dismissed Smetona and assumed the presidency himself and the government accepted the Russian ultimatum some 15 minutes before it was due to expire.

The Russian armies learned almost at the last minute that their mission had become an occupation, but the NKVD had already struck Lithuanian border guard outposts before dawn on 15 June to capture not only a dozen men, but also six women and a child! The Red Army did not follow until the afternoon, with the 16th Special Rifle Corps sending spearheads to take the key bridge near Kaunus. Despite an agreement between Vitkauskas and Pavlov, in which the former ordered his men to offer no resistance to 3rd and 11th Armies, there were occasional minor clashes with Lithuanian troops who were determined to offer token resistance. For the most part, however, they reluctantly surrendered. Eremenko's cavalry was on the extreme left wing, swimming the Neman River then sweeping parallel with the East Prussian border on the extreme left. Before they entered Kaunus, and on Eremenko's instructions, the cavalrymen changed into parade dress to emphasise that this was an occupation. On 20 June, NKVD border guards assumed responsibility for the Lithuanian-German border as Vladimir Dekanozov became

Stalin's Pro-Consul in the country, while across the border in East Prussia the Germans briefly alerted their forces.[27]

Estonia and Latvia also came under pressure and received ultimata within half-an-hour of each other on the afternoon of 16 June. Molotov again claimed that Russian reinforcements would be despatched as 'a temporary measure'. Both countries were informed they must form new governments with Moscow's viceroys and when Berlin refused Latvia permission to evacuate its government and army to Germany, Riga capitulated at 19.45 hrs having learned that Andrei Vyshinsky, Stalin's feared prosecutor at the Moscow show trials, was being sent as Stalin's representative. Estonia, which would host Zhdanov, followed suit with an hour to spare at 23.00 hrs.

The ultimata were received as Pavlov signed an agreement with the Latvians covering the support of nine divisions in Latvia, while Meretskov did the same for 12 divisions in Estonia. The following morning, at 05.00 hrs, 8th Army crossed the border, although the occupying 65th Corps did not begin operations until 13.15 hrs. The occupation went so smoothly that a planned major amphibious operation was cancelled, although two airborne operations went ahead. A force of 63 TB-3 brought in 720 paratroops of 214th Airborne Brigade to Latvia's Siauliai airfield, while another force of paratroops dropped near Riga, a day after Captain Starchak had been dropped to check the site, but the city itself was captured by 4th Rifle Corps.

There were some minor amphibious operations in Estonia whose capital, Tallinn, was occupied by the 65th Special Rifle Corps after encountering resistance from a signal battalion on 21 June which was battered into submission by Red Army troops and Communist militia supported by armour. Two Estonians were killed. By then Zhdanov had entered his new capital, arriving in a tank escorted by two armoured cars, and the Soviet occupation of the Baltic States was complete.

BT-7 tanks of the 27th Tank Brigade taking part in the celebratory parade in Riga on 7 November 1940 to mark the anniversary of the October Revolution. (Nik Cornish at www.Stavka.org.uk)

Yet despite the general absence of resistance – apart from occasional protests – the Red Army lost 58 killed (including 15 suicides) and 158 wounded.[28] The 8th Army headquarters moved to Tartu (also known as Dorpat) in Estonia, the 3rd Army to Riga and the 11th Army to Kaunus, while the reinforcements returned to their former barracks from 26 June, the airborne brigade going to the Kiev District. The Baltic Fleet was also involved in seizing bases and 52 merchantmen, sometimes having to fire warning shots to stop ships at sea. Within three days the Fleet was instructed to produce a comprehensive defensive plan using the new facilities, as well as those at Hanko in Finland, and to establish new coast defences.

Timoshenko had suggested the despatch of an NKVD regiment to each state 'to protect internal order'. It cut the usual bloody swathe through the 'counter-revolutionary' elements to deport or execute 34,250 Latvians, 75,000 Lithuanians and almost 60,000 Estonians by the time of the German invasion. Soviet-style administrations and elections were quickly organised and the 'popular' governments in all three states sought to join the Soviet Union as Soviet 'socialist republics' between 3-6 August.

Surprisingly, the Baltic States' armed forces were not scrapped but rather thrown into the revolutionary furnace for reforging, with the Estonian, Latvian and Lithuanian Armies emerging as the 22nd Rifle Corps (180th, 182nd Rifle Divisions), 24th Rifle Corps (181st, 183rd Rifle Divisions) and 29th Rifle Corps (179th, 184th Rifle Divisions) respectively, while their ships augmented the Baltic Fleet's patrol and training organisations and a few aircraft were transferred to VVS training units.[29] The forces were purged and some Estonian officers were shot, but 20 generals transferred to the Red Army with their old ranks. These included Jonas Cernius (referred to by Soviet sources as I.K. Chernius), Albinas Cepas-Cepaukas (Ch.A. Chapauskas), Jonas Juodisius (I.V Iodishus), August Kasekamp (A.A. Kazekamp), Vlades Karvelis, Robert Klavins (R.Iu Kliavnsh), Andrejs Krustins (A.N. Krustynsh), Janis Liepens (Ia. P. Liepinsh), Richard Tomberg (R.I. Temberg or R.I. Tomberg), Johans Voldemars and Vincas Vitkauskas (V.I Zhilis), the majority of whom were arrested in 1941-1942.[30]

Several Lithuanian Army officers would have distinguished careers in the Red Army; Feliks Baltusis-Zemaitis and Vitkauskas both served as instructors in the General Staff Academy, the latter after enduring some months in NKVD custody. A similar fate befell Cepas-Cepaukas who later became a Red Army instructor. Karvelis would later follow Baltusis-Zemaitis as commander of the distinguished Lithuanian 16th Rifle Division, fighting the Germans, and he became head of the Military Faculty of Vilnius University after the war until 1961. The former Estonian Deputy Defence Minister, Tonis Rotberg (Tu.I. Rotberg), who had fought the Soviets after the Great War, became head of the 22nd Rifle Corps supply organisation. He would be taken prisoner by the Germans and released, but refused to join the Communist resistance. When the Red Army retook Tallinn in 1944, Rotberg was arrested and jailed for 25 years. He died in prison.[31] By contrast, Voldemars soon retired after briefly commanding 24th Rifle Corps.

He was in Lithuania when the Germans invaded. He would join the Waffen-SS and become a divisional commander, ending his days in Western Europe.

When the invasion began, Timoshenko proposed creating a Baltic Military District with headquarters in Riga as well as a start on the construction of fortifications, improved communications and the stockpiling of materiel. By 21 June the nascent military district had 11 corps headquarters with 24 rifle and four cavalry divisions, supported by 11 tank brigades. Already work had begun to produce 'popular' governments. Initially Pavlov was responsible for the new garrisons, but Stalin had no intention of allowing even a loyal general like Pavlov to have too much military power. The Leningrad District was given Estonia, creating 3rd Rifle Brigade to defend Estonia's Muhumaa (Moon Island).

On 11 July, even before the Baltic States were formally absorbed by the Soviet Union, the Baltic District was created under Loktionov, now a Colonel General, while General Tyurin (the former 65th Special Rifle Corps commander) was given command of 8th Army. The district returned some divisions to Pavlov, but was swiftly expanded from 15 divisions and 173,014 troops on 1 August to 23 divisions with 295,907 men on 20 October. Armour and air support rose from 1,025 tanks and 675 aircraft to 1,558 tanks and 1,316 aircraft in the same period. Appropriately, Loktionov's command, now consisting of Latvia, Lithuania and the western parts of the disbanded Kalinin District, was upgraded to Special Military District status on 17 August, bringing it into line with the other districts on the western border, the Belorussian being renamed the Western Special Military District on 11 July.

Moscow also decided to adjust its southern border, with Molotov serving notice in a speech to the Supreme Soviet on 29 March by pointing out there was no non-aggression pact with Rumania, which had seized Bessarabia from the Soviet Union in March 1918. The following day the Rumanians sought German support for their army, but they were informed coldly this would depend upon their economic performance to the Reich. In April the Russians complained that the Rumanians had shelled their territory and mined the Dneister bridges, which Bucharest denied. By mid-April Rumania was seeking closer relations with Germany and seriously thinking of resisting any Red Army attacks upon its territory.[32]

Stalin needed to tread carefully: Rumania was vital to the Reich. A quarter of the oil from its wells in 1939 went to Germany, although this dropped in 1940 to 22 per cent, leading Berlin to sign a trade agreement on 28 May in which Bucharest agreed to a 30 per cent increase in oil exports. Yet when Bucharest sought Berlin's response to any Russian aggression two days later, it was clear that Germany would do nothing. A Rumanian attempt to improve relations with Moscow, using trade relations as an excuse, failed and, ominously, in May, Zhukov, the much vaunted victor at Khalkin Gol, was quietly appointed commander of the Kiev District, meeting Stalin for the first time.[33]

Rumanian anxiety had increased after the Winter War due to the steady strengthening of the Soviet southern districts. Indeed, on 14 May, the Kiev

District's operations division ordered maps of the border with Rumania, while on 1 June the first Russian reconnaissance aircraft flew 62 kilometres into Rumanian air space. But it was not until 9 June that the Kiev and Odessa Districts were ordered to begin planning to take Bessarabia. The Kiev District became Southern Front under Zhukov for this operation. Zhukov would have his own two army headquarters: the 5th under Lieutenant General Vasilii Gerasimenko, and the 12th under Major General Filip Parusinov, together with the Odessa District's 9th Army under Lieutenant-General Ivan Boldin, who had commanded the Southern Cavalry Mechanised group during the Poland campaign. Training began on 10 June while the operation's parameters were defined at an hour-long meeting at the Kremlin on the afternoon of 13 June, attended by Stalin, Molotov, Timoshenko, Shaposhnikov, Mekhlis and the navy's most senior representatives, including the minister, Admiral Kuznetsov, the chief-of-staff, Admiral Galler, and Rear Admiral Filip Oktyabrskii, the commander of the Black Sea Fleet since March 1939.

Rumania's traditional guarantor, France, was tottering on the edge of defeat and it was obvious that the Reich would not intervene if the Russians sought to retake Bessarabia at bayonet point, a goal the Red Army could easily achieve. As late as 19 April, in a meeting with his Prime Minister, Gheorghe Tatarescu, and Foreign Minister, Grigore Gafencu, King Carol decided to resist any military action by either Germany or the Soviet Union, but the day after the trade agreement with the Reich he decided, despite close relations with Italy, to transfer the country's traditional allegiance from France to Germany. This message underlined advice received by the Chief of the General Staff, General Florea Ţenescu, who had earlier sought government intentions and was informed, on 22 May, that the Rumanian Army was to hold the eastern frontier with all its strength.

Tenescu's army, equipped largely with French and Czech military equipment, had 210,000 men during the winter of 1939-1940 but had been steadily expanded; by 15 June 1940 it had 1,067,671 men, 2,109 guns, 200 tanks organised into four armies, 13 corps (one cavalry and one mountain), 24 infantry (plus eight reserve) and three cavalry divisions (plus one reserve), and four mountain, two fortress, one cavalry and one motorised brigades. Tensions with neighbouring Hungary and Bulgaria required the deployment on their borders of 10 infantry and two cavalry divisions and five brigades, plus another of frontier guards. There was no significant strategic reserve while the reserve infantry divisions had little military capability.[34]

Much of the 500-kilometre eastern border ran along the river Dniester which had numerous fords all the way towards Moghilev and naturally Bucharest had decided to secure the frontier with fortifications. Work on what was called the Carol Line had begun in the late 1920s. This was limited to a small number of bunkers behind the Dniester and received lower priority from 1938 when the emphasis was upon fortifying the frontier with Hungary. With the fall of Poland some 100,000 civilians were brought in to improve the eastern defences, but it seems likely there were less than 100 bunkers covering a water-filled ditch known as 'Carol's Ditch', which could be covered with oil and ignited.[35]

Wary neighbours: A Rumanian soldier on the left and a Soviet soldier on the right glance at each other across the Rumanian-Soviet border in early 1940. (Nik Cornish at www.Stavka.org.uk)

The Third Army, which included a fortress regiment in the Carol Line, was traditionally responsible for Bessarabia. But when the Soviet invasion of Poland brought the Red Banner to the border of North Bukovina, the Rumanian leadership moved the Fourth Army there. Both armies were reinforced during the spring and early summer, receiving four infantry divisions, bringing the total to 20. Additionally, there was a cavalry division (bringing the total to three), plus a mountain brigade, and they were expecting the Cavalry and Mountain Corps – but this would be a slender reed to face the might of the Red Army, estimated by Rumanian intelligence at 40-50 rifle and 12 cavalry divisions, 15 motorised and mechanised brigades and 20 aviation brigades.

Zhukov, with his customary efficiency, produced an operational plan within four days of it being requested. On the afternoon of 13 June a 70-minute meeting attended by all interested parties produced a strategic directive. The Operational-Level plan was completed four days later and, on 19 June, the army and corps commanders were briefed. Three days later Timoshenko received the final presentation and approved the plans, allowing Zhukov to begin detailed preparations, with the armies ordered to concentrate immediately along the frontier within two days under the guise of training exercises. The 12th Army headquarters in the Carpathians moved its headquarters from Stanislav to Kolomiya and took over 8th, 13th, 15th and 17th Rifle Corps with Cherevichenko's Cavalry Mechanised Group (2nd and 4th Cavalry Corps). The 5th Army headquarters moved from Lutsk to Dunaevcy and part of its forces was assigned to 6th and 12th Armies, leaving it with 36th and 49th Rifle Corps, while the Odessa District's 9th Army, with headquarters at Grossulovo, had 7th, 35th, 37th and 55th Rifle Corps and 5th Cavalry Corps.

Zhukov envisaged enveloping the enemy with Parusinov's 12th Army (12 divisions), striking from Kamenets Podolski, down the Pruth and Sirit valleys to Iasi (Jassy), where it would meet Boldin's 9th Army (15 divisions including two cavalry) advancing from Tirasopol along the railway through Chinesnau (Kishinev). Gerasimenko's 5th Army would act as the anvil, pinning the enemy to the Dneister with five divisions. The isolation of the enemy would be completed by the use of a cavalry mechanised group (four cavalry divisions) under Cherevichenko, Zhukov's deputy commander, supported by three airborne brigades with 2,040 troops who would be dropped by 120 TB-3 of 29th Heavy Bomber Brigade, covered by 300 fighters, around Targu Frumos (also Tirgu, Tirgul or Targul Frumos), 40 kilometres west of Iasi. Oktyabrskii's fleet would keep watch on the small Rumanian fleet of seven destroyers and fleet torpedo-boats as well as a submarine.

Zhukov intended to commit 30 rifle and six cavalry divisions supported by 11 tank brigades and to keep five rifle divisions and the airborne force, bringing his total to 460,000 men. They would have overwhelming support which included 14 corps artillery regiments, 16 artillery reserve regiments and four high-power batteries – a total of some 12,000 guns and mortars. The VVS had assembled 2,160 aircraft in 21 fighter, 12 fast-, four light- and four heavy-bomber regiments, supported by another four Long-Range Aviation regiments. Mekhlis's Political Administration cranked up the propaganda machine from 21 June under the mixed slogans of 'Liberation' and 'Revenge'. However, some troops complained that they were once again being sent to war, leading to some desertion – 138 personnel in 12th Army alone, with five of them shot.

Four years later a similar operation, under Malinovsky and Tolbukhin, and on a larger scale, would tear apart the southern flank of the Eastern Front, but Zhukov's plans were undermined by a shortage of support troops. The Red Army's and NKVD's rail troops organisations were involved late in the planning process, the Military Transport Directorate being informed only on the evening of 12 June, which meant only 480 trains were provided instead of the 709 required. Medical reservists were called up and some 35,000 men from combat units were drafted to solve the support problem, but preparations were further hampered by a shortage of vehicles, leading to a three-day delay before deployment was completed on 27 June. Fortunately, the Red Army's experience in the Baltic States led Zhukov to draft an alternate plan assuming a Rumanian withdrawal and here the mechanised and cavalry forces would simply move rapidly to the new frontier in the west.

For Rumania there was a brief burst of hope with Italy's entry into the war as Germany's ally on 10 June, but Mussolini was in a conciliatory mood with Moscow and his ambassador made this clear in a meeting with Molotov ten days later at which the Russian hinted that the Soviet Union was seeking a rapid solution to the Bessarabia issue. Three days later, Molotov ran the matter before the German Ambassador, Schulenburg, who pointed out that the Reich had significant economic interests in Rumania. Yet despite France's capitulation on 22 June, German troops were fully committed in the West and Ribbentrop said (no doubt through gritted teeth) that he would support the Russian claim and Italy quickly agreed.

On 24 June Germany stated publicly that it had no interest in Bessarabia. The following day the NKVD frontier guards were ordered to seize bridges and support the passage of spies into Rumania. In the next few days, the Russians claimed that Rumanian aircraft were strafing their border posts and on the evening of 26 June Molotov handed the Rumanian Ambassador an ultimatum, demanding the return to Russian control within four days of Bessarabia and neighbouring north Bukovina so as to push the frontier back to the river Prut.

The following morning the Rumanians began to mobilise, but it quickly became clear they would receive no support from the Pact of Steel. That night the Royal Council considered the situation and by 27:11 voted to cede the territories, announcing the decision on the morning of 28 June as Bucharest sought vainly an extension of Molotov's four-day evacuation period. Zhukov now switched to his back-up plan; Parusinov committed four rifle divisions (one mountain) and four tank brigades, as well as Cherevichenko's group; Boldin committed his cavalry corps and five rifle divisions (one motorised); while Gerasimenko provided two of his rifle divisions and two tank brigades. The airborne force was held in reserve. These forces began crossing the frontier on the afternoon of 28 June, often overtaking the retreating Rumanian troops, although Boldin was hampered by a shortage of pontoon bridges.

To secure facilities and materiel, on 29 June 1,372 men of 204th Airborne Brigade were dropped at Bolgrad (also Bolhrad) on the railway leading to Galati (Galatz). The following morning an airborne landing was planned to take the airfield at Ismail in the Danube estuary with 809 troops of 201st Brigade in 44 TB-3. But the airfield was too small to take more than a dozen aircraft and 240 troops, so the remaining troops were dropped by parachute. There were 35 casualties as a result of the drop, three fatal. The head of Red Army combat training, Lieutenant General Kurdiumov (who commanded 15th Army in Finland), later complained the airborne operations were poorly executed because of an absence of preparation. Despite these setbacks the new frontier was reached by dusk on 1 July and sealed two days later, Southern Front being disbanded on 7 July followed by 9th Army three days later.

Moscow had gained 50,762 square kilometres of territory and netted 3.7 million people, and with the Rumanian Army more concerned with flight than resistance, there was little opposition. Total Soviet casualties were 119, including 44 dead (12 by suicide and three by drowning), but the impact upon the Rumanian Army was tremendous; nearly 378,000 troops came from these territories, and 62,500 of them deserted to stay with their families. The Rumanians suffered nine dead and five wounded, but the army lost four divisional depots with their materiel, causing the disbandment of three corps and six divisions, half of them reserve units, while other divisions lost up to three battalions. A new 80-kilometre-long line of fortification, the Focsani - Namoloasa - Braila (or FNB) Line, had to be built hastily. Equipment was abandoned by fleeing Rumanian troops which the Russians refused to return, claiming it had been stolen by deserters; the haul included 52,796 rifles and carbines, 1,071 light and 326 heavy machine guns, 40 mortars, 258 guns and six anti-aircraft guns as well as hundreds of tonnes of ammunition.[36] The Russians also seized 545 tonnes of fuel, plus horses, cattle and sheep as well as canned food and forage, but to rub salt into Bucharest's wounds, Moscow also demanded the 'return' of 175 locomotives and 4,375 wagons, although they could not fit on the broader gauge Russian track.

But the Russians had overplayed their hand. In the aftermath of their occupation of Bessarabia, the Luftwaffe despatched its strongest paratroop regiment to secure the Ploesti oilfields. During a conference about the campaign against Great Britain on 18 July, Hitler observed that as a result of the Russian action: 'Thoughtful preparations must be made.' Within hours the Führer began planning for a campaign against the Soviet Union. He also supported Hungarian territorial claims against Rumania, which was forced to concede substantial parts of its territory on 30 August but, despite the Molotov–Ribbentrop Pact, Berlin deliberately snubbed Moscow on the issue.

This helped to fuel concerns within the Soviet leadership about German 'friendship'; although, officially, the leaders remained confident, they were also desperate to avoid the moment of truth and so Stalin began strengthening the nation's defences. In August Shaposhnikov's declining health led to his resignation as chief-of-staff and his replacement on 25 August by Meretskov, who was in turn replaced in Leningrad by Kirponos.[37] Yet Shaposhnikov remained in harness, becoming Inspector of Combat Training and helping to draw up new field service regulations.

Securing the new frontier 200-400 kilometres to the west was the prime concern, and with the experience of fighting on the Mannerheim Line, there was consensus on underpinning the defence with fortifications. But should these be the existing fortifications on the old frontier, providing defence in real depth or a new defensive belt on, or set back from, the new frontier? Shaposhnikov proposed building new positions some distance from the frontiers but keeping the bulk of the Red Army behind the existing fortified regions, the so-called Stalin Line, leaving a screening force between the two sets of fortifications as security against a surprise attack.[38] As usual, Stalin rejected this excellent advice and demanded fortifications along the frontier, these being nicknamed the 'Molotov Line', with the bulk of the Red Army behind them to deter a German attack. Colonel General Arkadii Khrenov, head of the Main Military Engineering Directorate (Glavnoe Voenno-inzeneroe Upravleniia), proposed that the new defences initially be based upon field fortifications rather than concrete bunkers which could be built in a second phase, but this idea too was rejected.

Work on the Molotov Line's first four Fortified Regions (UR) began in the Baltic District, but during the summer of 1940 the focus was the Western and Kiev Districts. In the former work started on the Grodno and Brest UR to shield the Bialystok salient, while in the latter the Vladimir-Volynski, Strumilov, Rava-Russkaia and Przemsyl URs were to cover the rolling plains between the Pripet Marshes and the Carpathians. But plans for two URs along the river Prut were never implemented. The following spring the Western District began to plug the gap between the two URs with the Osovets and Zambruv UR, while the Kiev District started work on extending its defences northwards with the Kovel UR, and along north Rumania's new frontiers with the Verkhne Prut and Nizhne Prut URs. Also, during the spring of 1941, the Odessa District began preparatory work for the Chernovtsy, Dunayskiy (Danube) and Odessa URs.

Preparatory work on the Western and Kiev District fortifications began in the winter of 1939/40, but the harsh weather slowed progress which was described in May 1940 as 'extremely poor in all respects'. Voroshilov, an advocate of fortifying the new frontiers, reported to Stalin and Molotov on 25 June that 1,295 positions had been built in the Stalin Line since the previous year and that it was planned to build another 3,802 in the new defences. Work on the new defences was placed under the Directorate of Defensive Construction (Upravleniia Oboronitelnogo Stroitelstva) under Khrenov's Directorate and allotted 84 construction battalions and 25 companies, as well as 25 motor transport battalions supported by an unknown number of civilians. Yet there was little serious study of defence at the Strategic and Operational Levels. As early as March 1930, Professor Aleksandr Svechin, a senior lecturer in tactics at the Frunze Academy, warned Voroshilov about the lack of respect for defence and general over-confidence. Shortly afterwards, and despite Tukhachevskii's intervention, Svechin was reassigned and it was not until 1938 that a study, 'The Army on the Defensive', was produced.[39]

Yet there was a growing realisation that the backbone of the defence needed to be large motor-mechanised forces which was signified not only by Pavlov's transfer to the Western District, but the reorganisation of armoured forces under the Main Armoured Forces Administration led by his successor, Lieutenant General Takov Fedorenko. Authority to create mechanised corps was given on 9 June, the first being formed in the Leningrad and Baltic Districts as the 1st and 3rd respectively, the former from the headquarters of 20th Heavy Tank Brigade which absorbed two light tank brigades and a motorised rifle division, the latter (intended for the Western District) from 84th Motorised Division headquarters, absorbing that division, 7th Cavalry Division and a tank brigade.

From these disparate sources another seven mechanised corps were cobbled together during 1940 (see Table 6-3) in the Western, Kiev (two), Odessa, Moscow and Trans-Baikal Districts, while tank divisions were created in the Trans-Caucasus and Central Asia Districts from a tank brigade and a cavalry division respectively. This took the Red Army right back to where it had been a year earlier, absorbing 19 tank brigades (four heavy and three flame-thrower), two regiments of T-26s and almost all the independent tank battalions allocated to rifle divisions, apart from those in the Far East. To aid expansion of the mechanised force, the three Chemical Tank (flame-thrower) brigades were disbanded between 2 June and 12 August 1940 and their vehicles distributed among the new corps, while the next step towards expansion was taken with the creation in November 1940 of 20 tank and 20 artillery-machine gun brigades as cadres for new tank and motor-rifle divisions respectively.

Table 6-3: New Mechanised Corps

Corps	Divisions		Formed	District	Corps headquarters
	Tank	Motor			
1	1, 3	163	Jun 1940	Leningrad	From 20 Heavy Tk Bde
2	11, 16	15	Oct 1940	Odessa	From 15 Mot Rifle Div
3	2, 5	84	Jun 1940	Baltic	From 84 Mot Rifle Div
4	8, 32	81	Jul 1940	Kiev	-
5	13, 17	109	Jul 1940	Trans-Baikal	From 51 Rifle Corps
6	4, 7	29	Jul 1940	West	From 3 Cav Corps
7	14, 18	1	Aug 1940	West	-
8	12, 34	7	Jul 1940	Kiev	From 4 Cav Corps
9	20, 35	131	Nov 1940	Kiev	-
10	21, 24	198	Mar 1941	Leningrad	-
11	29, 33	204	Mar 1941	West	-
12	23, 28	202	Feb 1941	Baltic	-
13	25, 31	208	Mar 1941	Leningrad	-
14	22, 30	205	Mar 1941	West	-
15	10, 37	212	Mar 1941	Kiev	-
16	15, 39	240	Mar 1941	Kiev	-
17	27, 36	209	Mar 1941	West	-
18	44, 47	218	Mar 1941	Odessa	-
19	40, 43	213	Mar 1941	Kiev	-
20	26, 38	210	Mar 1941	West	-
21	42, 46	185	Mar 1941	Moscow	-
22	19, 41	215	Mar 1941	Kiev	-
23	48, 51	220	Mar 1941	Orel	-
24	45, 49	216	Mar 1941	Kiev	-
25	50, 55	219	Mar 1941	Kharkov	-
26	52, 56	103	Mar 1941	North Caucasus	From 10 and 12 Cav Div
27	9, 53	221	Jun 1940	Central Asia	From 25 Cav Div
28	6, 54	236	Jul 1940	Trans-Caucasus	From 16 Cav Div
29	57, 61	82	Mar 1941	Trans-Baikal	-
30	58, 60	239	Mar 1941	Far East Front	-

Source: Mechanizirovannieye Korpusa RKKA website.

But did this reorganisation go far enough? Work on revising PU 39 began soon after the end of the Winter War with a draft completed by August 1940. It was then submitted at the end of October to a special panel under Budenny for refining. Some of the stars who would emerge in the war against Germany were involved in this process including Lieutenant General Vatutin (Meretskov's deputy), Colonel General Voronov (Kulik's deputy), Major General Leonid Govorov (Deputy Inspector General of Artillery) and Lieutenant General Dimitrii Karbyshev (a senior lecturer at the General Staff Academy), but they were still discussing the regulations when the Germans attacked.[40] During September 1940 almost every Red Army district began a series of exercises, but the focus was upon individual soldier skills and none appears to have lasted more than four days. The most significant exception was a war game supervised by Timoshenko involving 6th Rifle Corps breaking through a fortified area with subsequent exploitation by mechanised forces.[41]

Even as the results were analysed there was ominous activity on the German side of the frontier. On 10 October, a Luftwaffe mission arrived in Rumania to train its hosts' air force and to strengthen the defence of the Ploesti oilfields, while shortly afterwards the German 12th Army joined it in preparation for operations against Greece (Unternehmen 'Marita'). Molotov sought to discover German intentions, but encountered little more

Marshal Semon Budenny (centre), then Deputy People's Commissar for Defence, with Lieutenant General Vladimir Kurdiumov (right) and Captain P. Pavliuchenko, a battalion commander, in an observation post during exercises in the Odessa Military District during the autumn of 1940. Budenny was another military conservative who was obsessed with cavalry. (Bettmann/Corbis)

than a smokescreen from Ribbentrop and Hitler about new spheres of interest, while on 18 December Hitler issued Directive 21 calling for an invasion of the Soviet Union the following summer as Unternehmen 'Barbarossa'.

It was something the Red Army was anticipating, but determining where the main blow would land was more perplexing. In the aftermath of the Munich Crisis in November 1938, Shaposhnikov laid the foundation with plans based upon threats both north and south of the Pripet Marshes. In July 1940 the plan came under Stalin's scrutiny and while Shaposhnikov concluded that the Germans would strike into the Baltic States and Belorussia, Stalin believed their main blow would be the Ukraine in order to acquire the region's mineral and agricultural wealth. According to Pleshakov it was Shaposhnikov's obstinate insistence that the main blow would be north of the Marshes that was as much a factor as his health in the decision to replace him as chief-of-staff but, if so, this was very much out of character for the man.[42]

In July 1940 Shaposhnikov's protégé, the deputy Operations Chief, Major General Vasilevsky, began the first revision of Shaposhnikov's plan and agreed the main blow would come into Belorussia along the Minsk-Smolensk axis, but he included a second blow in the Ukraine when presenting the plan to Stalin on 18 September. Under Meretskov the plans were further revised to fit Stalin's concerns about a threat to the Ukraine, a concern shared by Timoshenko, a former Kiev District commander, and Zhukov the current District commander. Given the uncertainty, both options were covered with versions designed to meet whichever was the more serious threat.[43]

The revised plan was presented on 5 October to Stalin whose only comment was that Hitler's most likely objectives were to seize the grain and minerals of the Ukraine. Ever the courtier, Meretskov promptly adapted the plan emphasising the defence of the Ukraine and this was adopted on 14 October, becoming the basis for the 1941 mobilisation plan which envisaged a first Strategic echelon subdivided into three echelons: 57 rifle divisions holding the frontier, with 52 rifle divisions and 62 rifle divisions together with the mechanised corps behind them. Behind this would be a second strategic echelon along the rivers Dvina and Dnepr. While these discussions were under way the Red Army held its first major exercises in December, the usual drills having been disrupted by the summer land grabs. The war games were designed to test the October plan. Stalin was alarmed to discover that they demonstrated that a German mechanised thrust would stab through the defences and plunge deep into the Soviet Union.[44]

Senior Red Army commanders assembled in Moscow in December for an enlarged meeting of the Main Military Soviet. They discussed a Central Committee report on the state of the Defence Commissariat which included scathing comments upon the lack of uniformity on the use of modern forces and the poor quality of the Soviet armoured forces.[45] Over the next month the commanders tried to hammer out a training plan for the following year, as well as uniform operational doctrines. Nearly 30 generals made presentations and, in a frank exchange of views, it was confirmed that mechanised forces with powerful air support could smash through fortified defences and have great Operational-Level success. They also discussed how they could replicate the Germans' success and Lieutenant General Eremenko, commanding 3rd Mechanised Corps, pointed out the need to address supply problems and recommended the building of fuel tanker vehicles.

Many of the participants departed at the end of the conference in which Timoshenko gave vague résumés, but the senior officers remained for two days of war games in the New Year to test the theories. They began on 8 January and examined the threat of mechanised forces against the western districts, with teams led by Pavlov and Zhukov who later swapped roles. However, things were unrealistic, with an allowance of ample time to ponder moves. Zhukov's forces punched through the defences of the Bialystok salient to encircle Pavlov's forces in Belorussia, raising serious questions about the wisdom of the new fortification policy and the need for defence in Operational-Strategic-Level depth. Just as the participants were about to depart they were summoned suddenly by Stalin to present their conclusions.

This meeting, on 13 January, saw Meretskov mishandle the General Staff's carefully produced evaluation of the war games, as he lost the script and floundered under Stalin's questioning. Kulik fired Parthian shots on behalf of the military reactionaries, advocating an 18,000-man rifle division with horse transport. He claimed artillery would stop any tank breakthrough. Fedorenko took the opportunity to raise the dangerous question about re-equipping the tank units with the new T-34 medium and KV heavy tanks – a dangerous move because it implied criticism of Stalin who had established a special procurement commission, led by Kulik with Mekhlis and Army Commissar I Rank Efim Shchadenko (a fool and two ignorant political officers), effectively putting a key element of Soviet defence under three blind mice.[46] Kulik proposed cutting the allocation of 76 mm guns to the artillery in favour of the new tanks, but Kulik was having none of this, leading one participant to quote sarcastically the Russian proverb, 'Each snipe (Kulik) praises his own marsh.' Stalin asked how many mechanised corps the army wanted. Timoshenko told him the district commanders wanted 13–17.

Although it was clear which way the Red Army's Young Turks wished to go, the conference ended inconclusively. Shaposhnikov was especially annoyed with Meretskov and made little contribution to the proceedings, often staring ahead but occasionally expressing his feelings with disapproving looks or slight shakes of the head. Stalin was also unhappy and decided to replace Meretskov with Zhukov and to reshuffle the leadership. Meretskov became head of training while Zhukov was replaced in the Kiev District by Kirponos, who was in turn replaced in Leningrad by Lieutenant General Markian Popov, the 1st Red Banner Army commander. The last change reflected a major reshuffle of commands in the Far East from February 1941 onwards; Shtern returned from the Far Eastern Front and in February became commander of the Air Defence force. He was replaced by

Eremenko. Lieutenant General Pavel Kurochkin became commander of the Trans-Baikal District with the 16th Army (formed in July 1940) and the 17th Army (formerly 57th Special Rifle Corps) in Mongolia. To the east, the 1st and 2nd Red Banner Armies were split to ease command and control; the left of the former became 25th Army in late March, while the latter's Amur sector became the 15th Army in February.[47]

In the aftermath of the Kremlin conference the Soviet armed forces resembled a swan, serene above the water, but paddling strongly below it. During the spring of 1941 there was gradual awareness that Germany was preparing to attack the Soviet Union, but Stalin appeared in denial. He was actually seeking to delay such an attack as long as possible by appeasing the Reich's demands for food and minerals while simultaneously authorising a frantic expansion of the Red Army. On 12 February Timoshenko presented a new mobilisation plan which included 30 mechanised corps and within weeks work had begun to create a score of the new formations. The process began in the Baltic District when 12th Mechanised Corps was created in February. The following month another 19 corps were created, mostly west of the Urals, while the tank divisions in the Central Asian and Trans-Caucasus Districts were expanded into mechanised corps.

While corps were created at the stroke of a pen, it was more difficult to turn them into effective formations. Commanders had to organise their forces then ensure that they followed a uniform doctrine with which their unit commanders were only partly familiar. There were also major problems with equipment; by the time of the German invasion, the western districts had received only 1,475 of the superb new medium T-34 and heavy KV tanks, scattered among the forces like pepper on a meal. The tank fleet was substantial but obsolete and in a society obsessed with impressive statistics it was more style than substance – a giant with feet of clay. Even the best-equipped corps had only half its official establishment of 1,003 tanks, while the 13th, 17th, 20th and 24th Corps had hardly any (see Table 6-4). Their drivers rarely had more than an hour a day in their vehicles which were poorly maintained, partly due to a shortage of spares. By the time of the German invasion on 22 June, 29 per cent of the tanks required major overhaul while 44 per cent required some form of maintenance.

There were major problems finding motor vehicles to support the new divisions. Until 1939 the Red Army had assumed it could commandeer civilian vehicles to make up any shortages, but the campaign in Poland had shown this was not feasible due to a shortage of such vehicles and the fact that they were poorly maintained. When the Germans invaded, motorised rifle divisions had only 39 per cent of their authorised trucks and 44 per cent of their tractors because the motor-transport troops had only 27,000 trucks.[48]

The quality of the officer corps was more worrying, many having been promoted too quickly and without sufficient experience or education to plug gaps caused by the Purges. At the beginning of 1941, barely 7 per cent of commanders had received a higher military education, nearly 56 per cent had received a

Table 6-4: Mechanised Corps Tank Strengths

Corps	District	1940		1941	
		Aug 25	Oct 1	Feb 20	Jun 22
1	Leningrad	924	926	1011	1039
2	Odessa	414	435	456	527
3	Baltic	547	635	640	672
4	Kiev	797	856	632	979
5	Trans-Baikal	823	889	1011	1070
6	Western	276	682	707	1131
7	Moscow	305	743	792	959
8	Kiev	768	623	818	899
9	Kiev	-	-	94	316
10	Leningrad	-	-	540	469
11	Western	-	-	241	414
12	Baltic	-	-	589	730
13	Western	-	-	32	282
14	Western	-	-	513	518
15	Kiev	-	-	707	749
16	Kiev	-	-	372	478
17	Western	-	-	182	63
18	Odessa	-	-	235	282
19	Kiev	-	-	274	453
20	Western	-	-	16	94
21	Moscow	-	-	120	175
22	Kiev	-	-	527	712
23	Orel	-	-	161	413
24	Kiev	-	-	56	222
25	Kharkov	-	-	163	300
26	North Caucasus	-	-	125	184
27	Central Asia	-	-	308	356
28	Trans-Caucasus	-	-	710	859
29	Trans Baikal	-	-	1011	????
30	Far East	-	-	U/K	U/K

Source: Mechanizirovannieye Korpusa RKKA website.

secondary one, just over 24 per cent had been through accelerated courses and the remainder had received none at all. The 15th, 16th, 19th and 22nd Mechanised Corps could not find enough officers to create either an operations section or an intelligence section and there was little time to gain experience in post for, by the summer of 1941, 75 per cent of officers and 70 per cent of commissars had been in their posts less than a year.[49]

The twin problems of inadequate modern equipment and a technically inept leadership were reflected in the key element of communications. From the start, the Red Army had failed to make adequate preparations for command and control, a hurdle not surmounted by the original mechanised corps, and although lip service was paid to faster communications in increasingly mobile battles, there was a great gap in capability. The western districts suffered a desperate shortage of radio transmitters: Pavlov's Western District had only 27 per cent of its requirement, Kirponos's Kiev District 30 per cent, while Fedor Kuznetsov's Baltic District had 52 per cent.[50] Many generals regarded radios as insecure and preferred wire communications, ignoring their vulnerability to enemy fire or sabotage, and during the disastrous summer and autumn of 1941 they would rapidly lose control of the battlefield due to poor communications.

Given the problems, much faith was being placed in the Molotov Line, but progress was inevitably slow, with work dogged by the long, harsh winter of 1940–41. In places the defences were no more than 20 kilometres behind the frontier.[51] The construction effort was also diluted by the need to create an infrastructure, including converting the railways to broad gauge, with new barracks having a low priority which led to a shortage of accommodation, with many troops in tents and the lucky ones in peasant cottages. Most of the roads in the west were dirt tracks with bumps and potholes and many bridges were too weak to take a tank, or even a gun. As a result of the land grab in the west, the VVS alone required more than 200 new airfields. But during the spring of 1941 many airfields were closed for the construction of concrete runways and the remainder were overcrowded, some with 100 aircraft. The Herculean effort was poorly supported by the rail network, with the Russians running 84 trains per day to their new western frontiers; by comparison, the German build-up involved 220 trains a day.[52]

Khrenov became the scapegoat and was demoted in the spring of 1941 to command the Moscow District's engineers. Shaposhnikov was given added responsibility as head of Military Fortification and Supervisor of Engineer Troops.[53] Another 41 engineer battalions were assigned, while 160 engineer battalions in the districts were also ordered to assist and 136,000 workers were drafted. But engineers and construction workers were also required to move the Red Army's infrastructure westward, building communications, accommodation, storage facilities and airfields and, with motor vehicles in desperately short supply, the trucks and tractors of the artillery units were pressed into service. By June 1941 only 2,500 positions had been completed, with less than 1,000 being fully equipped, while in the Stalin Line a German 1942 survey of the URs between the Baltic and the Black Sea noted that of nearly 3,330 positions, nearly 230 were incomplete.[54]

As he appointed Zhukov, Stalin also took the fatal decision to cease work on the Stalin Line, with the exception of the Kamenets–Podolski UR on the Dneister. The decision was so sudden that the Kiev District's operations chief learned of it only when he visited the Slutsk UR and discovered its construction units had been transferred to Brest. The decision was recognition that the Soviet Union lacked the resources to build two fortification systems simultaneously. Nevertheless, in April 1941, Zhukov ordered the Stalin Line prepared for war and in June he would divert some troops into the old positions.

While attention was focused upon the mechanised forces, the traditional formations were not neglected as the Red Army expanded, although horse cavalry units declined, often being converted into motor-mechanised units. The numbers of rifle divisions expanded (see Tables 6-5 and 6-6): between 2 September 1939 and 1 December 1940 the number rose from 173 to 188, although many existed only in cadre or low establishment form (3,000-6,000 men). In part, this reflected a downgrading of motorised-rifle divisions which declined from a peak of 15 on New Year's Day 1940 to nine by the end of the year, largely due to the shortage of motor transport and the priority given to the mechanised corps, which often received the small numbers of vehicles when motorised divisions reverted to foot soldiers.

Table 6-5: Rifle divisions 2 September 1939 – 1 December 1940

Type	Sept 2, 39	Jan 1, 40	Feb 1, 40	May 1, 40	Aug 1, 40	Dec 1, 40
Motorised	-	15	11	4	8	9
Rifle	160	134	136	147	164	169
Mountain	13	11	13	10	10	10
Total	**173**	**160**	**160**	**161**	**182**	**188**

Table 6-6: Red Army expansion February 1940 – June 1941

Formations	1 February 1940	22 June 1941
Rifle corps	30	62
Regular rifle divisions	152	198
Motorised rifle divisions	11	31
Tank divisions	-	61
Cavalry corps	4	4
Cavalry divisions	26	13
Rifle brigades	5	3
Airborne brigades	6	6
Strength	4,207,000	4,800,000

Source: Based on Glantz 'Soviet Mobilisation in Peace and War' Table 2.

However the numbers fluctuated, with 30 being formed in 1940, 23 following an order of 8 July, and six from the rump of the Baltic States' armies. In April 1941 11 were disbanded, possibly to provide manpower for new motorised divisions. In the months leading up to the war, 10 more rifle and mountain rifle divisions were added together with 20 motorised, the majority of the latter by cobbling together the recently raised artillery-machine gun brigades with tank brigades. On 23 April, the Central Committee authorised the creation of 10 brigades of anti-tank artillery with men and materiel from the Trans-Baikal's recently raised 29th Mechanised Corps, and also the reorganisation of the airborne brigades into five division-strength corps by the beginning of June under a dedicated directorate created on 12 June.[55]

To provide strategic defensive depth, from March onwards the Red Army began moving troops from rear, or less threatened, districts west of the Urals, behind the frontier armies, and from 26 April-10 May, the Trans-Baikal, Urals and Siberian Districts as well as the Far Eastern Front also began to contribute to the western defensive shield by creating new armies. On 13 May, the General Staff ordered the 16th Army (Lukin) from Trans-Baikal, the 19th Army (Konev) from the North Caucasus, 20th Army (Lieutenant General Fedor Remezov) from Orel, 21st Army (Efremov) from the Volga and 22nd Army (Ershakov) from the Urals Armies, with 28 rifle divisions to move from the interior to the west. A fifth army assembled in the Moscow District. Ershakov was to prop up the Baltic District, the 20th Army would be behind the Western District and the 16th, 19th and 21st Armies behind the Kiev District by 10 July. Movement was slow, however, and the armies were still assembling some 300 miles behind the frontiers when the Germans struck. They would become part of the High Command reserve under Budenny on 21 June.

On 24 May Stalin met Timoshenko, Zhukov, the new VVS commander, Lieutenant General Pavel Zhigarev, as well as all the district military, air and political chiefs. The meeting lasted 150 minutes, but its purpose is unknown and it has been suggested that Stalin briefed them on a plan for an offensive. A month earlier Stalin had authorised preparations for the Red Army to be ready if war was imminent and from late May to early June 800,000 reservists were called up to fill out 100 divisions and many fortified regions so that, by the summer of 1941, 2.9 million of the Red Army's 4.8 million men were in the western districts supported by 14,200 tanks. But nowhere was the Red Army prepared and, thanks to the 'three blind mice', there was a desperate shortage of anti-tank guns and artillery ammunition.[56]

From the spring of 1941 there were ominous signs of increasing activity on the German side of the frontier, yet Stalin refused obstinately to react to what he described as 'provocations'. In February 1940, Moscow and Berlin had signed a new trade pact and within a year the Reich received some 4 million tonnes of minerals and foodstuffs; indeed, the last grain shipment rolled westward only hours before the German invasion. In return, Russia received examples of military equipment together with diesel engines, turbines, electrical equipment and machine tools and Stalin desperately hoped this would appease Hitler long enough for him to strengthen his defences, although he told his inner circle in May 1941: 'The conflict is inevitable, perhaps in May next year.'

Yet that month alone the NKVD captured 353 German agents trying to cross the border and by 10 June another 108. German aircraft were blatantly carrying out reconnaissance missions. Even when one accidentally came down in Soviet territory and its camera film provided incriminating evidence, Stalin refused the PVO permission to intercept the aircraft. He also countermanded Kuznetsov's partial blackout of airfields and naval bases. The only glimmer of hope was the signing of a treaty between Moscow and Tokyo on 13 April guaranteeing the neutrality of each if attacked by a third party. Tokyo had sought the agreement because relations with the United States were worsening. It secured the borders of Manchukuo while Moscow was able to focus upon defending the west.[57]

Stalin recognised the Soviet Union's military weaknesses and Golikov's GRU reports pandered to his desire for good news, while bad news provoked an hysterical reaction. When Vsevolod Merkulev, head of the NKVD Foreign Department, passed a report to Stalin on 16 June from his agent 'Starshina' in Luftwaffe headquarters to the effect that the final decision had been made to attack the Soviet Union, Stalin scrawled on the report: 'Tell the "source" in the German Air Force Staff to fuck his mother.'[58] Ironically, his paranoia was already laying the foundation for the Luftwaffe's greatest victory through another savage purge which would focus upon Soviet air power and which would continue even as German bombs were falling. This little known event undoubtedly influenced the senior Red Army leadership and, perhaps, it was one reason why it was launched.

Concern about national air power had been growing and it blossomed during the Winter War when the weaknesses and inability of the air force to neutralise the tiny Finnish Air Force became all too apparent. Immediately after the Winter War ended, the 38-year-old commander of the VVS, Komkor Smushkevich, was replaced by 29-year-old Lieutenant General Rychagov, a brave and talented fighter pilot but a man with no senior command experience.[59] On 25 February 1941, the Central Committee approved a plan to reorganise and to expand the VVS with new regiments and a broader support infrastructure, as well as improved training. The most significant change was the replacement of the aviation brigade by the aviation division of three to five regiments, while long-range bomber divisions were grouped into air corps. The rear services were reorganised on a regional basis from April 1941 with the work scheduled for completion in August.[60]

Yet there remained serious problems and on 12 April 1941, Timoshenko and Zhukov presented a report stating that poor aircrew discipline and maintenance meant that every day the VVS had two or three fatal accidents, with up to 900 aircraft being lost per year. In the first quarter of the year there had been 156 crashes and 71 'breakdowns' leading to the loss of 138 aircraft and 141 aircrew. It was possibly during this meeting that, when asked by Stalin to comment on the high accident rate, a frustrated Rychagov retorted: 'Of course we will continue to have many accidents as long as you keep making flying coffins.' Stalin ominously replied: 'You should not have said that.' About this time Timoshenko and Zhukov had sought Rychagov's removal and the court-martialling of a number of officers. Stalin approved this, but added air staff members, including the head of Long-Range Aviation, Proskurov, to the list of those to be court-martialled, adding sanctimoniously: 'That would be the honest and just thing to do.'[61]

Rychagov was replaced by 41-year-old Pavel Zhigarev, a former head of combat training and the former First Deputy Head of the VVS Main Directorate, his positions giving him maturity and experience.[62] Rychagov's lack of interest in training was displayed when Stalin's personal pilot, Lieutenant Colonel Aleksandr Golovanov, had used his personal contacts to establish an instrument training unit in 1940 using civil pilots and VVS navigators to develop a training and equipment programme. Golovanov was told he was wasting his time, but by March 1941 the Russians were beginning to establish a network of navigation aids and to supply multi-engine aircraft with navigation systems.[63]

Even basic flying experience was at a premium and by April 1941 the average pilot in the Baltic District had only 15½ hours (less than one a week). Things went literally south, with 9 hours in the Western District and 4 in the Kiev District, made up of little more than taking off, a quick circuit and then landing. Although 72 per cent of Pe 2 pilots, 80 per cent of MiG 3 and 32 per cent of LaGG 3 pilots were officially qualified on their new aircraft, this meant little. Transition training was extremely slow for fear of accidents in which pilots might be accused of sabotage. The malaise was exacerbated by the inexperience of the front line leadership, with 91 per cent of VVS major unit commanders having held their posts for less than six months.[64]

New aircraft were slow to reach the front and by 1 June 1941, of the Western District's 7,864 aircraft (855 unserviceable), only 1,749 (192 unserviceable) were modern, including the inadequate Su 2 and Yak 2/4. The re-equipment programme was also bungled, and instead of withdrawing units to exchange new aircraft for old, the administrators had simply sent a number of fighter regiments their full quota, while a few bomber regiments received the Su 2, and others small numbers of the Pe 2 twin-engined dive-bomber. There was no systematic attempt to train the crews with the result that barely 500 aircrew were rated as combat ready on new aircraft.[65] Even in formations with a large number of new aircraft, such as Major General Sergei Chernykh's 9th Mixed Air Division whose fighter regiments had 276 fighters (39 unserviceable), only 64 of its pilots were rated combat ready, and inevitably the division was rapidly annihilated at the beginning of 'Barbarossa', leading to the general's arrest and execution in July.[66]

Stalin's dissatisfaction with, and suspicions of, his 'Eagles' were fed by an incident which occurred on 15 May. At the beginning of 1941 the Air Defence Organisation (PVO) was reorganised into zones which fitted into the district structure and, in February, Shtern was recalled from the Far East to become its commander. But his forces suffered from a shortage of guns and modern interceptors, although up to 30 Rus 1 radars had been deployed west of the Urals, the fighters being under district command and isolated from the remainder of the

PVO forces.[67] None of this explained the fact that, through an oversight, a Lufthansa transport on a regular run to Moscow, managed to land without its flight having been cleared by the PVO. Stalin's wrath waxed great when he was informed.

Like sharks, Beria's men were prowling the defence industry and the lower echelons of the armed forces. They arrested Colonel F.T. Kovalev, a department head at the VVS Navigation Academy, who implicated an instructor of the Frunze Academy, Major General Sila Mishchenko, leading to his arrest on 21 April 1941 and execution on 16 October. A professor at the Frunze, Major General Georgii Sokolov, was arrested on 26 May 1941 and died in a Gulag in July 1943, while Lieutenant General Aleksandr Filin, head of the VVS Scientific Research Institute, was arrested on 23 May. The NKVD was already looking at the VVS and on 30 May it arrested Lieutenant General Ernest Schakht, the Orel District air commander and former Moscow District aviation training chief and, the following day, Lieutenant General Petr Pumpur, the Moscow District aviation commander. Pumpur, a former head of training, had been arrested and then released in 1938. The Leningrad District aviation commander, Major General Aleksandr Levine, was relieved on 10 March and an investigation report was submitted to Timoshenko on 8 June, although he was not arrested until 7 July when his interrogation damned Loktionov, Rychagov, Smushkevich and Schakht.

Beria's men now ran riot through the PVO organisation, arresting Shtern on 7 June, although he had apparently been under investigation since March for 'associating with known enemies of the people'. The 'investigation' grew, being extended into the VVS leadership after 'confessions' were beaten out of the unfortunates.[68] Smushkevich, who had been Assistant Chief of the VVS General Staff and was now Inspector General of the VVS, was in hospital for an operation on his leg, but was arrested either on 8 or 14 June; Lieutenant General Pavel Alekseev, the former commander of VVS supplies, was arrested on 18 June, the day after Lieutenant General Pavel Yusupov, the VVS deputy chief-of-staff. On the eve of war, Loktionov, Smushkevich's predecessor as commander of the VVS was arrested and, as the Germans drove deep into Belorussia, Rychagov too was picked up on 24 June followed by the VVS chief-of-staff, Major General Pavel Volodin, on 27 June. Loktionov, Smushkevich, Rychagov (and his wife), as well as Shtern and Volodin would be shot without trial outside Moscow on 28 October 1941 with seven other generals and 13 other individuals in what appears to have been an act of NKVD house-cleaning. Pumpur, Levine, Filin, Schakht and Yusupov lived on until 23 February 1942 when they all felt the fatal pistol against the back of their necks.[69]

Aware of these events, but also from their own observations of German preparations, the frontier district commanders sought to warn Moscow and to mobilise their forces. They were told repeatedly: 'There will be no war.' When Kirponos, on his own initiative, moved some of his troops into positions best suited for defence, he was ordered in no uncertain terms to move them back.

Increasingly depressed, Timoshenko, with the bewildered Zhukov and the General Staff, tried to make Stalin face reality. During the spring of 1941, they began to prepare plans for defence in the west, although they were hamstrung by 'The Boss's' demands for forward defence.[70]

Zhukov sought a more dynamic defence and proposed an offensive in the west with 152 divisions, a plan he persuaded Timoshenko to rubber-stamp then present to Stalin with the State Frontier Defence Plan on 15 May (the day of the Lufthansa incident). Stalin ignored their suggestions and brushed off attempts to put the Western District forces on alert. The new defence plan, distributed five days later, was little more than a statement of intentions with individual armies receiving their deployment plans, but no overall operational context. The enemy was to be confined in the frontier defences using the mechanised forces to crush any which broke through, although there was no provision to co-ordinate their operations with those of the frontier forces, while operations into enemy territory would be conducted only upon special instructions.

Two days later Timoshenko and Zhukov again tried to get Stalin to permit border forces to go on the alert. Stalin leapt to his feet and asked Zhukov: 'Have you come to scare us with war, or do you want a war because you're not sufficiently decorated or your rank isn't high enough?' Stalin believed the Germans had missed the boat and that they would not attack until the following year, and although Beria forwarded to Stalin a warning from the Russian embassy in Berlin, he added that he believed in Stalin's predictions that the Germans would not attack in 1941. On the evening of 21 June there were further indications of an attack, including desertions, but all that Stalin would permit in response was a vague alert that something might happen and that the forces were to 'refrain from any kind of provocative action'. Surprisingly, Stalin told Budenny that war would probably start the following day, yet he could not bring himself to believe it. He then left for his dacha at Kuntsevo. In the early morning Zhukov tried to telephone Stalin to tell him the attack had begun, but the secret police denied he was there and hung up.[71]

On the morning of 22 June, the Western District's deputy commander, Boldin, informed Timoshenko that the Germans had invaded, but was told Stalin believed this was a provocation. Paralysed with fear, Timoshenko contacted Budenny and told him: 'The Germans are bombing Sebastopol. Should I or shouldn't I tell Stalin?'

'Inform him immediately,' Budenny replied.

Timoshenko responded: 'You call him. I'm afraid.'

Budenny retorted: 'No, you call him. You're the Defence Commissar.'

Eventually Budenny agreed to call Kuntsevo himself while Timoshenko ordered Zhukov to do the same. Zhukov succeeded in contacting 'The Boss' who was roused from his bed and heard the news in silence. He then ordered Zhukov to bring Timoshenko to the Kremlin and ordered the Politburo to be summoned, but by then the atheist socialist state was well on the road to Calvary.[72]

This conversation illustrates the impact of the Purges upon the Soviet forces as much as the plaintive exchange of messages intercepted by Germany's Heeresgruppe Mitte:

'We are being fired on. What shall we do?'
The response: 'You are mad. And why is your signal not in code?'

It was fear, induced by the Purges, which permeated every level of the Red Army, for no one was safe. Even those closest to 'The Boss' were likely to face arrest if they were so much as suspected of disloyalty. Indeed, in mid-July, the NKVD sent a long report to Timoshenko and Beria denouncing Budenny, and another report to Malenkov denouncing Timoshenko and Kulik. Both reports were ignored.[73]

When the German invasion came, the NKVD continued to pose a threat. Hundreds of Soviet officers and men would be executed or imprisoned in the coming months because the Red Army was unable to stop the invaders. Meretskov, appointed front co-ordinator in the north on 22 June following an inspection of the frontier districts, was arrested on suspicion within 48 hours of his assignment and savagely beaten. With 40 prisoners implicating him in treason, he confessed to plotting with Loktionov but, unlike him, was miraculously spared, possibly due to Beria's intervention and he would lead fronts against both the Germans and Japanese.[74] Pavlov was less fortunate and became the scapegoat for Western District/Front's defeat, being dismissed on 30 June, interrogated (he too implicated Meretskov), court-martialled and shot on 22 July. Dozens more followed.[75]

The paralysis of will was one legacy the Red Army inherited from the Purges, the other was the inexperience of the surviving officers who filled gaps but were promoted beyond their level of professional competence, with inadequate training and preparation. This combination of factors almost destroyed the Red Army in 1941's summer of catastrophe, yet it is worth remembering that the purged generals such as Tukhachevskii, Uborevich and Yakir, had failed to solve the army's chronic problem of combined arms warfare, let alone those of controlling and supplying the big new mechanised formations to whose masts they had nailed their colours.

While the Purges undoubtedly hamstrung Red Army operations, they were also the alibi for failure. The loss of so many experienced officers struck inevitably at the roots of the army's capabilities, together with the promotion of the survivors to positions for which they were totally unsuited through lack of training or experience. Yet this lack of senior officer capability is also true of those who were purged, as is demonstrated by the state of the Red Army when Tukhachevskii attended his last May Day Parade.

The leaders who had been promoted after the Revolution were often good 'regimental' officers who knew their men and could inspire them with personal leadership. In the less demanding environment of the Russian Civil War these men had proved capable, but traditional war was becoming more complex with more demanded of a leader. Battles were becoming as complex as a mechanical watch and commanders had to ensure that the activities of all the arms were co-ordinated and supported with engineering, signals, transport and medical services, as well as supplies of all sorts throughout an operation. This required a willingness to face the drudgery of prolonged administrative and bureaucratic work to produce detailed plans, with leaders from division to front ensuring that their intentions were understood, executed and supported.

Civil War-generation leaders promoted in the 1920s and 1930s tried to meet their ever more arduous duties aided by relatively short higher command courses at the Frunze Academy. But this merely added a veneer of expertise and it remained hard for them to grasp the greater responsibilities of higher command, while many potential staff officers, even in the mid-1930s, were reluctant to become what they saw as military bureaucrats. Consequently, the performance of the Red Army leaders in both peace and war during the 1930s and early 1940s reflected these problems in terms of failing to make realistic evaluations of the situation, often through the absence of reconnaissance, poor all-arms co-ordination and the frequent collapse of the supply organisation.

With properly trained staff, many of the Civil War-generation leaders might have been more effective, and it seems that Shaposhnikov perceived the problem in the 1920s but had to overcome the Party's traditional objections to military elites.

He made it his life's work to create a new generation of staff officers through the founding of the General Staff Academy in 1936, but its impact may have been greater than even its most strident supporters recognised, for the Red Army's ultimate victory owed almost everything to the first generation of staff officers who emerged from its earliest courses – men such as Zhukov, Vasilevsky and Sokolovsky. These were men who not only escaped the clutches of the NKVD, but saw their experience and staff training forged into a sword which disembowelled the Third Reich and provided Imperial Japan's *coup de grâce*.

ENDNOTES

1.   7th Army disbanded immediately, 9th and 13th Armies on 5 April and 15th Army on 28 March.
2.   For this conference see Kulkov and Rzheshevsky.
3.   Montefiore pp.290, 295-296.
4.   Op. cit. p.295.
5.   Erickson, *Road to Stalingrad* pp.19-20.
6.   Montefiore pp.294, 623 f/n 3. Podlas would prove a capable commander in Ukrainian operations, but was killed in May 1942 during the abortive Kharkov offensive. Parrish, *Sacrifice* p.294. In May 1940, Red Army personnel records showed 6,742 purged officers had still not been reinstated.
7.   For the Red Army reforms see Erickson, *Soviet High Command* pp.552-555, *Road to Stalingrad* pp.16-24. Van Dyke's article.
8.   Dyke pp.43-44.
9.   Erickson, *Road to Stalingrad* p.20.
10. Parrish, *Lesser Terror* p.32. The figures probably include all ranks.
11. Parrish, *Lesser Terror* pp.26-27, 38. Also Parrish, *Officers* p.380.
12. For the Soviet occupation see Gross pp.18, 50-138,144-224; Rees pp.27-29, 38-41, 47-51, 58-64.

13. Gross pp.187-224; Montefiore pp.277-278.
14. Gross pp.138-143.
15. Op. cit. pp.139-140.
16. For the murder of Polish officers see Montefiore pp.296-297; Parrish, *Lesser Terror* pp.53-67; Rees pp.51-58.
17. See biography of Golikov in Shukman p.79. In October Proskurov became head of Long-Range Aviation.
18. Erickson, *Road to Stalingrad* pp.17-18. For Grendal see Bellamy pp.94-96; Parrish p.126.
19. Erickson, *Road to Stalingrad* p.34.
20. Habeck pp.290-291.
21. Gerard's article.
22. The Red Army forces were Divkom Tyurin's 65th Special Rifle Corps in Estonia, Divkom Morozov's 2nd Rifle Corps in Latvia and Divkom Korobkov's 16th Special Rifle Corps in Lithuania. The Baltic States had 65,000 troops.
23. For the occupation of the Baltic States see Eremenko pp.29-30; Metelyukhov pp.195-208; Montefiore p.297; Extracts from Eremenko's diary are on the rkka website. See the Eesti Sõjaveteranide Liit (Estonian Sub-Branch, returned and Services League of Australia) website for Baltic Fleet operations and also Documents of the Soviet Military Occupation.
24. VVS units were not alerted until 8 June.
25. Meretskov became Deputy Defence Commissar on 9 June.
26. Parrish, *Sacrifice of the Generals* p.282 says Pavlov was appointed on 7 July.
27. Merkys was arrested, deported to Russia and died there in 1955, while Povilaitis and Skucas were arrested by Lithuanian police at his instigation, taken to Moscow and executed in July 1941.
28. There were both pro- and anti-Russian demonstrations in the Baltic State following the occupation.
29. The Germans would capture 94 aircraft in flying condition when they invaded. See Kopanski pp.12-13.
30. Parrish, *Lesser Terror* pp.85, 94 and *Sacrifice of the Generals* pp.64, 68, 137-138, 156, 169, 199-200, 229, 390-391, 440. See also Maslov's article. Cernius was the 29th Rifle Corps chief-of-staff, Cepas-Cepaukas commanded 179th Rifle Division, Juodisius was artillery commander of the 179th Rifle Division, Kasekamp was 180th Rifle Division chief-of-staff, Klavins was Latvia's pre-war Army Commander and became commander of 24th Rifle Corps after Voldemars, Karvelis, Krustins, Liepens and Tomberg commanded the 184th, 183rd, 183rd and 180th Rifle Divisions respectively, while Vitkauskas commanded the 29th Rifle Corps artillery. Details taken from Generals of World War II website.
31. See Parish, *Sacrifice of the Generals* pp.324-325. Rotberg was not the War Minister.
32. For Bessarabia see Axworthy et al pp.17-18; Metelyukhov pp.217-235. Midan pp.241-320. See Piskunov in website Preparations for the campaign of Bessarabia.
33. Zhukov pp.184-186.
34. For the Rumanian Army during this period see Axworthy pp.12, 28-31, 40 and Statiev's article. The army had 15 types of rifles and carbines and nine of machine guns while the officer corps' training emphasised the academic over the practical.
35. For the defences see Kaufmann & Jurga pp.306-307, 313. See also Statiev. Of 312 bunkers planned along all the frontiers only 267 had been completed by July 1940.
36. The Rumanians give figures of 67,079 rifles and carbine, 1,080 light and 277 heavy machine guns, 43 mortars and 147 guns.
37. Erickson, *Road to Stalingrad*, p.24.
38. For fortifications see Short pp.12-15, 37-39. Erickson, *Road to Stalingrad*, pp.68-71.
39. Articles by Aptekat & Dudorova as well as Gerard.
40. Erickson, *Road to Stalingrad* p.30.
41. Op. cit. pp.37-38.
42. Pleshakov pp.56-57.
43. For planning see Erickson, *Road to Stalingrad* pp.37-38; Glantz & House pp.25-26, 39; Pleshakov op. cit. pp.56-57: Glantz '*Soviet Mobilisation in Peace and War*'.

44. Glantz & House p.26.
45. For the events in December 1940 and January 1941, see Erickson, *Road to Stalingrad* pp.40–46, 49–54. Pleshakov pp.22–23, 46–52, 58.
46. Erickson, *Road to Stalingrad* pp.31–32.
47. Op. cit. pp.54–57.
48. Tyushkevich pp.239–240.
49. Erickson, *Road to Stalingrad*, p.63; Volkogonov p.369.
50. Pleshakov p.65. Kuznetsov appears to have taken over the district from Loktionov on 25 December 1940 after the first round of December conferences, probably because the latter had come into the NKVD's sights.
51. Tarleton.
52. Erickson, *Road to Stalingrad*, p.70; Higham, Greenwood, Hardesty pp.55–56; Pleshakov p.65.
53. Khrenov had been an advocate of landmines but could not overcome Kulik's dismissal of these as 'weapons of the weak' so that by the beginning of 1941, the Red Army had only a million anti-tank mines in its supply dumps when the total requirement was 7.25 million anti-tank and anti-personnel mines. Erickson, *Road to Stalingrad*, p.72.
54. Kaufmann and Jurga p.366.
55. Tyushkevich p.239.
56. Erickson, *Road to Stalingrad*, p.63; Glantz & House pp.26–27; Pleshakov pp.81–83, 94.
57. See Erickson, *Road to Stalingrad*, pp.58–59, 65, 73–76, 87–89, 92–97; Pleshakov pp.69–75, 86–92; Volkogonov p.393.
58. Montefiore p.313. The source was the famous Rote Kapelle spy ring. See Hooton, *Phoenix Triumphant* p.113.
59. Some sources say the change occurred on 28 August 1940.
60. Erickson, *Road to Stalingrad*, p.64; Higham, Greenwood, Hardesty pp.54–55.
61. Higham, Greenwood, Hardesty p.56; Pleshakov pp.65, 72; Volkogonov p.375.
62. He would become a post-war Marshal of Aviation and help to create the Soviet strategic bomber force. Parrish, *Sacrifice of the Generals* p.331 says Rychagov was relieved on 9 April.
63. Golovanov, who had flown Blyukher and other Far Eastern leaders to the NKVD's torture chambers, would bomb Berlin and ultimately command 18th Air Army, the Soviet long-range bombing force. Higham, Greenwood, Hardesty pp.58–59; Parrish p.120.
64. Higham, Greenwood, Hardesty pp.56–57.
65. Details from Soviet Aviation in the Greater Patriotic War by the Soviet Aviation in the Greater Patriotic War website, Table 2.1 based upon File Arkhiv MO folio 35 op 107559ss.D.5 (T.1) pp.116–153, 170–207.
66. Parrish, *Sacrifice* p.69.
67. Erickson, *Road to Stalingrad*, pp.37 f/n, 65–66.
68. Parrish, *Lesser Terror* p.29 who claims Shtern was arrested on 18 June. Voronov replaced Shtern on 19 June.
69. For the October 1941 massacres see Parrish, *Lesser Terror* pp.79–94.
70. For Red Army planning see Erickson, *Road to Stalingrad*, pp.68–70, 80–81, 90–92, 101–103; Glantz & House p.41; Pleshakov pp.2–3, 76–81, 89.
71. Montefiore pp.309–321.
72. Op. cit. p.322.
73. Parrish, *Lesser Terror* p.29.
74. Parrish, *Sacrifice* pp.246–249; Pleshakov pp.157, 186, 221.
75. Parrish, *Sacrifice* pp.282–284.

APPENDICES

Appendix 1
Soviet Order of Battle in Lake Khasan Battles

1 RED BANNER ARMY

5 Aviation Brigade
    10 Heavy Bomber Regiment
    14 Heavy Bomber Regiment
    45 Heavy Bomber Squadron
12 Aviation Brigade
    59 High-speed Bomber Regiment
    57 High-speed Bomber Regiment
25 Aviation Brigade
    36 Light Bomber Regiment
    55 Light Bomber Regiment
53 Aviation Brigade
    2 Assault Regiment
    40 Fighter Regiment
    59 Aviation Squadron
61 Aviation Brigade
    8 Assault Regiment
    47 Fighter Regiment
    48 Fighter Regiment
    69 Light Bomber Squadron
    21 Long Range Reconnaissance Squadron
72 Aviation Brigade
    71 Mixed Aviation Regiment
    79 Mixed Aviation Regiment
    143 Mixed Aviation Regiment

39 Rifle Corps
(Komkorps G.N. Stern from 2 August?)
32 Rifle Division (Colonel N.E. Berzarin)
    17, 113, 322 Rifles
    133 Light Artillery; 154 Heavy Artillery
    303 Tank Battalion
    12 Reconnaissance Battalion
    30 Engineer Battalion
    65 Anti-Tank Battery
    53 Anti-Aircraft Battery
    74 Anti-Aircraft Battery
40 Rifle Division (Colonel V.K. Bazarov)
    118, 119, 120 Rifles
    40 Light Artillery, 107 Heavy Artillery
    302 Tank Battalion
    5 Reconnaissance Battalion
    5 Engineer Battalion
    52 Anti-Tank Battery

2 Mechanised Brigade (Colonel A.P. Panfilov)
    2 Tank, 42 Mechanised Regiments
Corps troops
    115 Rifles/39 Rifle Division
    118 Rifles/40 Rifle Division
    304 (ex 65) Rifles/43 Rifle Division
    121 Cavalry
    39 Corps Artillery Regiment
    21 Independent Mortar Battalion
    1 Battery/182 Artillery (22 Division)
    37 Anti-Aircraft Battery/39 Division
    39 Corps, 43 Corps Anti-Aircraft Batteries
    11 Signal Regiment
    32 Engineer Battalion
    63 Bridging Battalion
    Bridging Battalion, 43 Rifle Corps
    47, 49, 87, 91, 94, 104, 121 Construction Battalions

Appendix 2
Soviet Order of Battle at Khalkin Gol:
20 August 1939

1st ARMY GROUP

1st Rifle Regiment/152nd Rifle Division (To Southern Group, 25 August)
212th Airborne Brigade (To Northern Group, 25 August)
11th Tank Brigade
    16th, 24th, 45th Tank Battalions
    354th Artillery Battalion
    210th Reconnaissance Battalion
9th Motor-Mechanised Brigade (To Northern Group 21 August)
    241st Motor-Mechanised Battalion
    196th Rifle Machine Gun Battalion
    240th Reconnaissance Battalion
Tank Battalion, 6th Tank Brigade
I/126th Gun Artillery Regiment RGK
155th Artillery Regiment RGK
85th Anti-Tank Battalion
85th, 191st Anti-Aircraft Regiments
63rd, 66th Anti-Aircraft Battalions
24th, 42nd, 46th, 123rd Bridging Battalions
6th, 10th, 189th, 190th, 229th, 230th Construction Battalions

Aviation

22nd Fighter Regiment

56th Fighter Regiment

70th Fighter Regiment

38th, 56th, 150th Fast Bomber Regiments

Heavy Bomber Detachment

Mongolian Squadron

Northern Group (Colonel I.P. Alekseenko)

82nd Rifle Division: 601st Rifles

              82nd Howitzer Artillery

6th Mongolian Cavalry Division

              15th, 17th Mongolian Cavalry

Two tank battalions,11th Tank Brigade

7th Motor-Mechanised Brigade

              247th Motor-Mechanised Battalion

              161st Rifle Machine Gun Battalion

              204th Reconnaissance Battalion

87th Anti-Tank Battalion

Central Group (Kombrig D.E.Petrov)

36th Motorised Rifle Division (Petrov)

              24th, 76th, 149th Motorised Rifles

              175th Gun Artillery Regiment

              175th Howitzer Artillery Regiment

              133rd Reconnaissance Battalion

              67th Anti-Tank Battalion

              252nd Engineer Battalion

82nd Rifle Division (Colonel F.F. Posya)

              602nd, 603rd Rifles

              82nd Gun Artillery

              94th Reconnaissance Battalion

              146th Anti-Tank Battalion

              123rd Engineer Battalion

5th Motor Machine Gun Brigade

              162nd, 165th, 169th Rifle Machine Gun Battalions

              356th Artillery Battalion

Southern Group (Colonel M.I. Potapov)

57th Rifle Division (Colonel I.V. Galanin)

              80th, 127th, 293rd Rifles

              57th (later 105th) Gun Artillery

              57th (later 234th) Howitzer Artillery

              15th Reconnaissance Battalion

              180th Anti-Tank Battalion

              24th Engineer Battalion

8th Mongolian Cavalry Division (Colonel G. Erendo)

              16th, 18th Mongolian Cavalry

6th Tank Brigade (minus one tank battalion)

              Two tank battalions

              Rifle Machine Gun Battalion

8th Motor-Mechanised Brigade (Colonel V.A. Mishulin)

              234th Motor-Mechanised Battalion

              171st Rifle Machine Gun Battalion

              223rd Reconnaissance Battalion

185th Artillery Regiment

Self-propelled gun Battalion (equipped with SU-1-12)

175th Rifle Machine Gun Battalion,11th Tank Brigade

37th Anti-Tank Battalion

Flame-thrower Tank Company (equipped with HT-26)

Two Frontier Guards Companies (From 25 August)

Appendix 3
Soviet Orders of Battle in Poland:
17 September 1939

BELORUSSIAN FRONT
(Komandarm II Rank M.P. Kovalev)

23rd Independent Rifle Corps: 52nd Rifle Division

Dvinsk Flotilla: Monitors Flyagin, Levachov,
Martynov, Rostovtsev, Udarnyy,
Zheleznyakov, Zhemchuzhin

3rd Army (Komkor V.I. Kuznetsov)

4th Rifle Corps: 27th, 50th Rifle Divisions

Lepel Group: 5th Rifle Division

              24th Cavalry Division

              22nd, 25th Light Tank Brigades

4th Army (Komdiv V.I. Chuikov)

29th, 32nd Light Tank Brigades

25th Rifle Corps: 8th, 143rd Rifle Divisions

10th Army (Komkor I.G. Zakharin)

3rd Rifle Corps: 33rd, 113th Rifle Divisions

11th Rifle Corps: 6th, 121st Rifle Divisions

11th Army (Komkor N. Medvedev)

16th Rifle Corps: 2nd, 100th Rifle Divisions

              (Later plus 55th Rifle Division)

24th Rifle Corps (II Echelon): 139th, 145th Rifle Divisions

3rd Cavalry Corps: 7th, 36th Cavalry Divisions

              6th Light Tank Brigade

**Dzherzhinsk Cavalry Mechanised Group
(Komkor I.V. Boldin)**

5th Rifle Corps: 4th, 13th Rifle Divisions
6th Cavalry Corps: 4th, 6th, 11th Cavalry Divisions
15th Tank Corps: 2nd, 27th Light Tank Brigades
     20th Rifle Machine Gun Brigade
Attached: 21st Medium Tank Brigade

**Ukrainian Front (Komandarm I Rank
S.K. Timoshenko)**

36th Rifle Corps: 7th, 25th, 131st Rifle Divisions
    156th, 187th Rifle Divisions

5th Army (Komdiv I. Sovetnikov)

38th Light Tank Brigade
8th Rifle Corps: 44th, 81st Rifle Divisions

36th Light Tank Brigade

15th Rifle Corps: 45th, 60th, 87th Rifle Divisions

6th Army (Komkor F. Golikov)

17th Rifle Corps: 96th, 97th Rifle Divisions
    10th Medium Tank Brigade
    10th, 38th Light Tank Brigades
2nd Cavalry Corps: 3rd, 5th, 14th Cavalry Divisions
    24th Light Tank Brigade

12th Army (Komandarm II Tank I. Tyuleniev)

13th Rifle Corps: 72nd, 99th, 124th, 146th Rifle
Divisions
4th Cavalry Corps: 32nd, 34th Cavalry Divisions
    26th Light Tank Brigade
5th Cavalry Corps: 9th, 16th Cavalry Division
    23rd Light Tank Brigade
25th Tank Corps: 4th, 5th Light Tank Brigades
    1st Rifle Machine Gun Brigade

VVS-RKKA

Belorussian Front

8th Air Brigade: 3rd Heavy Bomber Regiment
16th Fast Bomber Brigade: 13th, 54th Fast Bomber
Regiments
Attached: 18th Fast Bomber Regiment
18th Fighter Brigade: 20th Fighter Regiment
56th Fighter Brigade: 35th Fighter Regiment
65th Air Brigade: 46th Fighter Regiment
    8th Light Bomber Regiment
    40th, 49th Independent Reconnaissance
    Squadrons
40th Fast Bomber Regiment/58th Air Brigade

6th Light Bomber Regiment/ 70th Light Bomber Brigade
4th Independent Fighter Squadron
8th Independent Long-Range Reconnaissance Squadron
30th, 40th, 43rd, 46th, 57th Independent
Reconnaissance Squadrons
Attached 3rd Army
70th Light Bomber Brigade: 43rd Light Bomber Regiment
    15th Fighter Regiment
10th Independent Fighter Squadron
41st Independent Air Squadron
4th Independent Long-Range Reconnaissance Squadron
38th Independent Reconnaissance Squadron/
65th Air Brigade

Attached 4th Army
4th Fighter Regiment

Attached 10th Army
10th Fighter Regiment/56th Fighter Brigade

Attached 11th Army
58th Fighter Brigade: 21st, 31st Fighter Regiments
    Attached: 31st Fast Bomber Regiment/
    18th Brigade

1st Light Bomber Regiment
5th Assault Regiment/8th Air Brigade

Cavalry Mechanised Group
66th Fighter Brigade: 33rd, 41st Fighter Regiments
    Attached: 39th Fast Bomber Regiment/
    70th Light Bomber Brigade
    14th Assault Regiment/8th Air Brigade
    43rd Independent Reconnaissance
    Squadron

Ukrainian Front

1st Light Bomber Brigade: 5th, 44th, 52nd Light
Bomber Regiments
22nd Fighter Brigade: 55th Fighter Regiment
10th Fast Bomber Aviation Brigade: 33rd, 52nd, 58th
Fast Bomber Regiments
51st Assault Brigade: 3rd, 7th Assault Regiments
69th Fighter Brigade: 12th, 17th, 19th, 23rd, 46th
Fighter Regiments
55th Fast Bomber Brigade: 5th, 24th, 48th Fast
Bomber Regiments
2nd Fighter Regiment
14th Heavy Bomber Regiment
45th Fast Bomber Regiment

5th, 8th Independent Fighter Squadrons
10th Independent Long-Range Reconnaissance Squadron,
47th, 52nd Independent Reconnaissance Squadrons

Attached 5th Army
41st Independent Reconnaissance Squadron

Attached 6th Army
69th Fighter Regiment/69th Fighter Brigade
62nd Light Bomber Brigade: 2nd, 11th Light Bomber
Regiments
36th, 44th Independent Reconnaissance Squadrons

Attached 12th Army
59th Fighter Brigade: 25th, 28th Fighter Regiments
34th Independent Reconnaissance Squadron
Corps Aviation Squadron, 13th Rifle Corps

2 October 1939
LENINGRAD DISTRICT
(Komandarm II Rank K.A. Meretskov)

7th Army (Komandarm II Rank V.F. Yakolev)
24th Cavalry Division
39th Light Tank Brigade
4th Rifle Corps: 10th, 84th, 126th Rifle Divisions

Belorussian Front (Komandarm II Rank M.P. Kovalev)

3rd Army (Komkor V.I. Kuznetsov)
25th Light Tank Brigade
3rd Rifle Corps: 139th, 150th Rifle Divisions
10th Rifle Corps: 5th,10th,115th Rifle Divisions
3rd Cavalry Corps: 7th, 36th Cavalry Divisions
15th Tank Corps: 2nd, 27th Light Tank Brigades
            20th Rifle Machine Gun Brigade

10th Army (Komkor I.G. Zakharin)
4th Cavalry Division
113th Rifle Division
29th, 32nd Light Tank Brigade
5th Rifle Corps: 4th, 13th, 121st Rifle Divisions
        11th Rifle Corps: 29th, 64th,145th Rifle
        Divisions
6th Cavalry Corps: 6th, 11th Cavalry Divisions

11th Army (Komkor N. Medvedev)
22nd Light Tank Brigade
16th Rifle Corps: 2nd, 27th,100th,164th Rifle Divisions

**Ukrainian Front (Komandarm I Rank
S.K. Timoshenko)**
13th Rifle Corps: 58th, 72nd, 146th Rifle Divisions
27th Rifle Corps: 25th, 131st, 141st Rifle Divisions
36th Rifle Corps: 135th, 169th, 176th Rifle Divisions
37th Rifle Corps: 124th, 130th, 187th Rifle Divisions
30th Rifle Division
10th Medium Tank Brigade,
14th, 49th Light Tank Brigades

5th Army (Komdiv I. Sovetnikov)
60th Rifle Division
36th, 38th Light Tank Brigades
8th Rifle Corps: 44th, 81st Rifle Divisions
15th Rifle Corps: 45th, 52nd, 87th Rifle Divisions

6th Army (Komkor F. Golikov)
26th Light Tank Brigade
6th Rifle Corps: 7th, 41st, 140th Rifle Divisions
17th Rifle Corps: 96th, 97th, 99th Rifle Divisions
2nd Cavalry Corps: 3rd, 5th, 14th Cavalry Divisions
24th Light Tank Brigade

12th Army (Komandarm II Tank I. Tyuleniev)
80th Rifle Division
23rd Tank Brigade
49th Rifle Corps: 23rd, 62nd Rifle Divisions
4th Cavalry Corps: 32nd, 34th Cavalry Divisions

Cavalry Group
5th Cavalry Corps: 9th, 16th Cavalry Divisions
25th Tank Corps: 4th, 5th Tank Brigades
1st Rifle Machine Gun Brigade

Appendix 4
**Soviet Order of Battle, occupation of
Baltic States: October 1939**

LENINGRAD MILITARY DISTRICT
Independent Rifle Corps: 11th, 16th Rifle Divisions
35th Light Tank Brigade

8th Army
16th, 123rd Rifle Divisions
25th Cavalry Division

1st, 40th Light Tank Brigades
1st Rifle Corps: 49th, 56th, 75th Rifle Divisions
10th Tank Corps: 13th, 18th Light Tank Brigades
       15th Rifle Machine Gun Brigade
Kalinin Military District
7th Army
2nd Rifle Corps: 48th, 67th, 155th Rifle Divisions
       34th Light Tank Brigade
4th Rifle Corps: 10th, 84th, 126th Rifle Divisions
       24th Cavalry Division
47th Rifle Corps: 138th, 163rd Rifle Divisions
       39th Light Tank Brigade

Belorussian Special Military District
3rd Army
3rd Rifle Corps: 139th, 150th Rifle Divisions
10th Rifle Corps: 5th, 50th, 115th Rifle Divisions
       25th Light Tank Brigade
3rd Cavalry Corps: 7th, 36th Cavalry Divisions
15th Tank Corps: 2nd, 27th Light Tank Brigades
       20th Rifle Machine Gun Brigade

Based upon Meltyuhov Table 12

Appendix 5
Soviet Orders of Battle during Winter War
30 November 1939

LENINGRAD MILITARY DISTRICT
(Komandarm II K.A. Meretskov)

7th Army: Komandarm 2nd Class V.F. Yakovlev
136th, 138th, 150th Rifle Divisions
20th Heavy Tank Brigade
436th, 442nd Independent Tank Battalions
447th Corps Artillery Regiment
402nd (RGK) High-Power Howitzer Artillery Regiment
311th (RGK) Anti-Tank Artillery Regiment
Karelian Fortified Region
19th Rifle Corps (Komdiv F.N. Starikov)
       24th, 43rd, 70th Rifle Divisions
       40th Light Tank Brigade
    315th, 368th, 369th Independent Tank Battalions
    28th, 43rd, 455th Corps Artillery Regiments
    101st, 301st, 320th (RGK) Howitzer Artillery
    Regiments
50th Rifle Corps (Komdiv F.D. Gorelenko)
       49th, 90th, 142nd Rifle Divisions
       35th Light Tank Brigade

339th, 391st, 445th Independent Tank
Battalions
       21st, 24th Corps Artillery Regiment
       302nd (RGK) Howitzer Artillery Regiment
       136th, 402nd (RGK) High-Power
       Howitzer Artillery Regiments
10th Tank Corps (Komdiv P.L. Romanenko)
       1st, 13th Light Tank Brigades
       15th Rifle Machine Gun Brigade

8th Army (Komdiv I.N. Khabarov)
       75th Rifle Division
111th Tank Battalion/35th Light Tank Brigade
       21st, 368th, 381st Independent Tank
       Battalions
111th Tank Battalion/35th Light Tank Brigade
201st, 218th Chemical Tank Battalions
       31st Artillery Regiment/49th Rifle
       Division
       73rd Gun Artillery Regiment
       10th (RGK) Howitzer Artillery Regiment
315th (RGK) High-Power Artillery Battalion
1st Rifle Corps (Kombrig R.I. Panin)
       139th, 155th Rifle Divisions
       421st Independent Tank Battalion
       47th Corps Artillery Regiment
56th Rifle Corps (Komdiv A.I. Cherepanov)
       18th, 56th, 168th Rifle Divisions
       381st, 410th, 456th Independent Tank
       Battalions
       49th, 467th Corps Artillery Regiments

9th Army (Komkor M.P. Dukhanov)
44th Rifle Division (Arrived 4 December)
312th Independent Tank Battalion
47th Rifle Corps (Komdiv I.F. Dashichev)
       122nd, 163rd Rifle Divisions
       365th Independent Tank Battalion
       100th Tank Battalion/39th Light Tank
       Brigade
       51st Corps Artillery Regiment
Special Corps (Komdiv M.S. Shmyrov)
       54th Rifle Division
       97th Independent Tank Battalion

14th Army (Komdiv V.A. Frolov)
349th, 411th Independent Tank Battalions
150th Corps Artillery Regiment

104th (RGK) Gun Artillery Regiment
208th, 241st (RGK) Howitzer Artillery Regiments
14th, 52nd Rifle, 104th Mountain Rifle Divisions

12 February 1940

NORTH WEST FRONT
(Komandarm I S.K. Timoshenko)

95th Rifle Division
13th Light Tank Brigade
15th Rifle Machine Gun Brigade
6th NKVD Border Guard Regiment

7th Army (Komandarm II K.A. Meretskov)
84th, 86th, 91st Motorised Rifle Divisions
42nd Light Rifle Division
18th, 38th, 355th Independent Tank Battalions
165th Artillery Regiment
207th Corps Artillery Regiment
124th, 378th, 530th (RGK) Howitzer Artillery Regiments
6th, 7th NKVD Border Guard Regiment

19th Rifle Corps (Komdiv F.N. Starikov)
    80th, 90th Rifle Divisions
    20th Heavy Tank Brigade
    40th Light Tank Brigade
        217th, 307th, 339th Independent Tank
        Battalions
        28th, 43rd, 455th Corps Artillery Regiments
        301st, 320th (RGK) Howitzer Artillery
        Regiments
        168th (RGK) High-Power Artillery Howitzer
        Regiment
8th Armoured Train Division

50th Rifle Corps (Komdiv F.D. Gorelenko)
        7th, 24th, 100th,123rd Rifle Divisions
35th Light Tank Brigade
        315th, 317th, 405th Independent Tank
        Battalions
        210th Chemical Tank Battalion
21st, 24th, 471st Corps Artillery Regiments
302nd (RGK) Howitzer Artillery Regiment
136th, 402nd (RGK) High-Power Howitzer Artillery
Regiments
34th, 316th, 317th (RGK) High-Power Artillery Battalions

10th Rifle Corps (Komdiv I.E. Davidovskii)
        51st, 113th, 138th Rifle Divisions
        1st Light Tank Brigade
        393rd, 436th Independent Tank Battalions
        322nd Howitzer Artillery Regiment
34th Rifle Corps (Komdiv V.M. Gonin)
        43rd, 70th Rifle Divisions
        29th Light Tank Brigade
        28th Tank Regiment
        361st, 369th Independent Tank Battalions
        447th Corps Artillery Regiment

13th Army (Komandarm 2nd Class V.D. Grendal)
49th, 62nd, 150th Rifle Divisions
39th Light Tank Brigade
14th, 368th, 391st, 442nd Independent Tank Battalions
204th Chemical Tank Battalion
28th Cavalry Regiment
116th, 375th, 495th (RGK) Howitzer Artillery
Regiments
211th (RGK) High-Power Gun Artillery Regiment
40th, 317th (RGK) High-Power Artillery Battalion
311th (RGK) Anti-Tank Artillery Regiment

15th Rifle Corps (Komdiv M.F. Korolev)
    4th, 50th, 142nd Rifle Divisions
    17th Motorised Rifle Division
    81st, 320th, 350th, 445th Independent Tank
    Battalions
    47th, 49th Corps Artillery Regiments
    116th (RGK) Howitzer Artillery Regiment

23rd Rifle Corps (Komdiv S.D. Akimov)
    8th, 97th, 136th Rifle Divisions
    41st, 377th Independent Tank Battalions
    101st, 376th (RGK) Howitzer Artillery Regiment
    137th (RGK) High-Power Howitzer Artillery
    Regiment
    55th Corps Artillery Regiment

8th Army (Komandarm 2nd Class G.M. Shtern)
75th Rifle Division
21st, 368th, 381st Independent Tank Battalions
111th Tank Battalion/35th Tank Brigade
201st, 218th Chemical Tank Battalions
31st Artillery Regiment/49th Rifle Division
73rd Gun Artillery Regiment
10th (RGK) Howitzer Artillery Regiment
315th (RGK) High-Power Artillery Battalion
73rd Anti-Tank Artillery Regiment
1st, 8th NKVD Border Guard Regiments

1st Rifle Corps (Kombrig R.I. Panin)
      56th, 139th, 155th, 164th Rifle Divisions
      135th, 410th, 421st Independent Tank
      Battalions
      7th NKVD Border Guard Regiment

14th Rifle Corps (Komdiv G.F. Vorontsov)
      87th Rifle Division
      128th Motorised Rifle Division
      383rd, 437th Independent Tank Battalions

15th Army (Komandarm II V.N. Kurdyumov)

119th Motorised Rifle Division
168th Rifle Division
Kombrig Koroteev's Composite Unit (I & II/219th Rifles;
I/620th Rifles)
653rd, 657th Independent Rifle Regiments
34th Light Tank Brigade
456th Independent Tank Battalion
      4th NKVD Border Guard Regiment

8th Rifle Corps (Komdiv I.G. Rubin)
      11th, 18th, 72nd Rifle Divisions
      37th Motorised Rifle Division
      25th Motor-Cavalry Division
      201st, 204th, 214th Airborne Brigades
      (From 13 February)
      23rd Tank Regiment
      357th, 381st, 394th Independent Tank Battalions

56th Rifle Corps (Komdiv A.I. Cherepanov)
      60th, 168th Rifle Divisions
      367th, 456th Independent Tank Battalions
4th NKVD Border Guard Regiment
108th (RGK) High-Power Howitzer Artillery
Regiment
467th Corps Artillery Regiment

9th Army (Komkor V.I. Chuikov)
      2nd, 5th NKVD Border Guard Regiments

47th Rifle Corps (Komdiv I.F. Dashichev)
      122nd, 163rd Rifle Divisions
      9th, 79th, 100th, 365th Independent Tank
      Battalions
      100th Tank Battalion/39th Light Tank
      Brigade
      51st Corps Artillery Regiment
      3rd NKVD Border Guard Regiment

Special Corps (Komdiv M.S.Shmyrov)
      44th, 54th, 88th Rifle Divisions
      97th, 312th, 502nd Independent Tank
      Battalions

14th Army (Komdiv V.A. Frolov)

86th Tank Battalion/34th Light Tank Brigade
96th, 349th, 411th Independent Tank Battalions
150th Corps Artillery Regiment
104th (RGK) Gun Artillery Regiment
208th, 241st (RGK) Howitzer Artillery Regiments
14th, 52nd, 131st Rifle Divisions
104th Mountain Rifle Division

North West Front Aviation

1st, 32nd Reconnaissance Squadrons
38th Transport Squadron

7th Army

15th, 43rd Fighter Regiments
45th, 53rd Fast Bomber Regiments
1st Squadron/9th Assault Regiment
1st Light Bomber Brigade
      5th Fast Bomber Regiment
      7th Assault Regiment
      43rd Light Bomber Regiments
18th Fast Bomber Brigade
      48th, 50th Fast Bomber Regiments
54th Fighter Brigade
      19th, 26th, 44th Fighter Regiments
55th Fast Bomber Brigade
      44th, 58th Fast Bomber Regiments
59th Fighter Brigade
      7th, 23rd, 25th, 38th, 148th Fighter
      Regiments
68th Bomber Brigade
      3rd, 4th Light Bomber Regiments
      10th, 60th Fast Bomber Regiments

13th Army

3rd, 4th Squadrons/27th Fighter Regiment
1st, 13th Fast Bomber Regiments
15th Fast Bomber Brigade
      2nd, 24th Fast Bomber Regiments
      68th Fighter Regiment

8th Army
4th Fighter Regiment
11th Light Bomber Regiment
72nd Mixed Regiment
13th Fast Bomber Brigade
        18th, 36th Fast Bomber Regiments
        39th Light Bomber Regiment
14th Mixed Brigade
        49th Fighter Regiment
        13th Fast Bomber Regiment
29th Bomber Brigade
        7th Heavy Bomber Regiment
        9th Fast Bomber Regiment

9th Army
80th Mixed Regiment
10th Fast Bomber Brigade
        16th, 41st, 80th Fast Bomber Regiments
        145th Fighter Regiment
13th Mixed Brigade
        152nd, 153rd Fighter Regiments
        41st Fast Bomber Regiment
        9th Assault Regiment

15th Army
153rd Fighter Regiment
        3rd Heavy Bomber Regiment

14th Army
Murmansk Aviation Brigade
        5th Mixed Aviation Regiment
        146th, 147th Fighter Regiments
        3rd, 4th Squadrons/20th Fighter Regiment
        33rd Fast Bomber Regiment

Long-Range Aviation
1st Long-Range Bomber Regiment
149th Fighter Regiment
9th Attack Regiment
16th Fast Bomber Brigade
        31st, 54th Fast Bomber Regiments
27th Long-Range Bomber Brigade
        5th, 6th, 21st, 42nd Long-Range Bomber
        Regiments
        85th Special Aviation Regiment
Independent Aviation Brigade
        7th, 51st, 53rd Long-Range Bomber
        Regiments
        35th Fast Bomber Regiment

Naval Aviation

Baltic Fleet
14th Naval Reconnaissance Regiment
15th Naval Reconnaissance Regiment
8th Naval Bomber Brigade
        1st Mine-Torpedo Regiment
        57th Naval Fast Bomber Regiment

10th Naval Mixed Brigade
        71st Naval Fighter Regiment
        73rd Naval Fast Bomber Regiment
        80th Naval Assault Regiment
        12th, 43rd and 44th Naval
Reconnaissance Squadrons
61st Naval Fighter Brigade
        5th, 13th Naval Fighter Regiments
        12th, 13th Independent Naval Fighter
        Squadrons

Northern Fleet
72nd Naval Mixed Regiment
118th Naval Reconnaissance Regiment

Appendix 6
Soviet Order of Battle for Invasion of the Baltic States: June 1940

LENINGRAD MILITARY DISTRICT
11th Rifle Division
8th Army
        128th Motorised Rifle Division
        13th Light Tank Brigade
1st Rifle Corps: 24th, 56th Rifle Divisions
19th Rifle Corps: 42nd, 49th, 90th Rifle Divisions

KALININ MILITARY DISTRICT
65th Special Rifle Corps: 48th Rifle Division
49th Light Tank Brigade

BELORUSSIAN SPECIAL MILITARY DISTRICT
214th Airborne Brigade
3rd Army
23rd Rifle Division
4th Rifle Corps: 121st, 126th Rifle Divisions
        25th Light Tank Brigade
24th Rifle Corps:10th, 55th, 113th Rifle Divisions
        55th Light Tank Brigade

3rd Cavalry Corps: 7th, 36th Cavalry Divisions
            1st Motorised Rifle Division
            27th Light Tank Brigade

11th Army

10th Rifle Corps: 84th, 143rd, 185th Rifle Divisions
            21st Light Tank Brigade
11th Rifle Corps: 29th, 115th, 125th Rifle Divisions
            32nd Light Tank Brigade
6th Cavalry Corps: 4th, 6th Cavalry Divisions
            33rd Rifle Division
            22nd, 29th Light Tank Brigades

Source: Meltyuhov Table 17

9th Army

140th Rifle Division
7th Rifle Corps: 51st, 74th Rifle Divisions
            15th Motorised Rifle Division
            14th Light Tank Brigade
35th Rifle Corps: 25th, 95th, 173rd Rifle Divisions
37th Rifle Corps: 30th, 147th, 176th Rifle Divisions
55th Rifle Corps: 116th, 150th, 164th Rifle Divisions
5th Cavalry Corps: 9th, 32nd Cavalry Divisions
            4th Light Tank Brigade

Source: Meltyuhov Table 19

Appendix 7

Soviet Order of Battle for occupation of Bessarabia and Bukovina: June 1940

SOUTHERN FRONT
8th, 17th, 86th, 100th Rifle Divisions
201st, 204th, 214th Airborne Brigades

12th Army

8th Rifle Corps: 72nd, 124th, 146th Rifle Divisions
            10th, 26th Light Tank Brigades
13th Rifle Corps: 60th, 62nd, 139th Rifle Divisions
            192nd Mountain Rifle Division
            24th Light Tank Brigade
15th Rifle Corps: 7th, 141st Rifle Divisions
            38th Light Tank Brigade
17th Rifle Corps: 58th, 131st Rifle Divisions
            81st Motorised Rifle Division
            13th Light Tank Brigade
2nd Cavalry Corps: 3rd, 5th Cavalry Divisions
            5th Light Tank Brigade
4th Cavalry Corps: 16th, 34th Cavalry Divisions
            23rd Light Tank Brigade

5th Army

36th Rifle Corps: 130th, 169th Rifle Divisions
            49th Light Tank Brigade
49th Rifle Corps: 44th, 80th, 135th Rifle Divisions
            36th Light Tank Brigade

BIBLIOGRAPHY

BOOKS

Anderson, Dr Edgar *Latvijas bru otie sp kium to prieksvesture* Daugavas Vanagi, Toronto, 1983

Axworth, Mark, Scafe   Cornel, Craciunoiu Cristian *Third Axis, Fourth Ally: Romanian Armed Forces in the European War 1941–1945* Arms and Armour Press, London, 1995

Bellamy, Chris *Red God of War: Soviet artillery and rocket forces* Brassey's Defence Publishers, London, 1986

Condon, Richard W. *The Winter War: Russia against Finland* Ballantine Books, London, 1972

Coox, Alvin *The Anatomy of a Small War: The Soviet-Japanese struggle for Changkufeng/Khasan 1938* Greenwood Press, London, 1977

Coox, Alvin *Nomonhan: Japan against Russia* (two volumes) University Press, Stanford, California, 1985

Czesław Grzelak *Kampania polska 1939 roku : poczatek II wojny swiatowej* RYTM Agencja, Warsaw, 2008

Czesław Grzelak *Wilno-Grodno-Kodziowce 1939* Dom Wydawniczy Bellona, Warsaw 2002

Doughty, Robert Allan *The Seeds of Disaster: The development of French Army doctrine 1919–1939* Archon Books, Hamden, Connecticut, 1985

Eremenko, A.I. *V Nachale Voinyi* Nauka, Moscow, 1965

Erickson, John *The Soviet High Command: A military-political history 1918–1941* (Third Edition) Frank Cass, London, 2001

Erickson, John *The Road to Stalingrad: Stalin's War with Germany Volume 1* Weidenfeld and Nicolson, London, 1977

Getty, J. Arch and Naumov, Olga *The Road to Terror: Stalin and the Self Destruction of the Bolsheviks 1932–1939* Yale University Press, 2010

Glantz, David M. *Soviet Military Operational Art: In Pursuit of Deep Battle* Frank Cass and Company, London, 1991

Glantz, David M. and House, Jonathan *When Titans Clashed: How the Red Army stopped Hitler* University Press of Kansas, Lawrence, 1995

Gorbatov, A.V. *Gody I Voiny* Voenizda, Moscow, 1989

Gross, Jan T. *Revolution From Abroad: The Soviet conquest of Poland's Western Ukraine and Western Belorussia* Princeton University Press, Princeton, 1988

Habeck, Mary R. *Storm of Steel: The development of armor doctrine in Germany and the Soviet Union, 1919–1939* Cornell University Press, London, 2003

Higham, Robin, Greenwood, John T. and Hardesty, Von (Editors) *Russian Aviation and Air Power in the Twentieth Century* Frank Cass Publishers, London, 1988

Hooton, E.R. *Phoenix Triumphant: The Rise and Rise of the Luftwaffe* Arms and Armour Press, London, 1994

Irincheev, Bair *The Mannerheim Line 1920-39: Finnish fortifications of the Winter War* (Osprey Fortress 88) Osprey Publishing, Botley, 2009

Irincheev, Bair *War of the White Death: Finland against the Soviet Union 1939–1945* Pen & Sword Military, Barnsley, 2011

Kaufmann, J.K and Jurga, Robert. M (trs H.W. Kaufmann) *Fortress Europe: European Fortifications of World War II* Greenhill Books, London, 1999

Kirosheev, Colonel General G.F. (editor) *Soviet Casualties and Combat Losses in the Twentieth Century* Greenhill Books, London, 1997

Kondratyev, Vyacheslav *Khalkin Gol: Voina v Vozdukhe* Tekhniki-Molodeshi Moscow, 2002

Kopanski, Tomasz J. *Barbarossa Victims: Luftwaffe kills in the East* Mushroom Model Publications, Redbourn, 2001

Kozlov, A.I. *Finskaya Voina, Veglyad 's toi storonyi'* Riga, 1997

Kulkov, E.N. and Rzheshevsky, O.A. (Editors), Shukman, Harold (English Editor) *Stalin and the Soviet-Finnish War 1939–1940* Frank Cass Publishers, London, 2002

Medvedev, Zhores A. & Medvedev, Roy A. *The Unknown Stalin* I.B. Tauris & Co, London, 2003

Meister, Jürg *Soviet Warships of the Second World War* Macdonald and Jane's, London, 1977

Meretskov K.A. *Na Sluzhbe Narodu* Politizdat, Moscow, 1968

Midan, Christophe *Carol al II-lea i teroarea istoriei 1930–1940* Editura militar, Bucharest, 2008

Montefiore, Simon Sebag *Stalin: The Court of the Red Tsar* Weidenfeld & Nicolson, London, 2003

Novikov, M.V. *Pobeda na Khalkhin-Gole* Politizdat, Moscow, 1971

Parrish, Michael *Sacrifice of the Generals: Soviet Senior Officer Losses 1939–1953* The Scarecrow Press, Oxford, 2004

Parrish, Michael *The Lesser Terror: Soviet State Security 1939–1953* Praeger Westport, London, 1996

Pleshakov, Constantine *Stalin's Folly: The tragic first ten days of WW II on the Eastern Front* Houghton Mifflin Company, New York, 2005

Porter, David *Soviet Tank Units 1939–1945* Amber Books, London, 2009

Ragsdale, Hugh *The Soviets, the Munich Crisis and the Coming of World War II* University Press, Cambridge, 2004

Rayfield, Donald *Stalin and his Hangmen: An Authoritative Portrait of a Tyrant and Those Who Served Him* Viking Press, New York, 2004

Rees, Laurence *World War Two Behind Closed Doors: Stalin, the Nazis and the West* BBC Books, London, 2008

Service, Robert *Stalin: A Biography* Pan Books, London, 2005

Shagdariin Sandag, Harry H. Kendall *Poisoned Arrow: The Stalin-Choibalsin Mongolian Massacres 1921–1941* Weetview Press, Boulder, Colorado, 2000

Shirokorad, A.B. *Severnyie Voyennoi* Kharvest, Moscow, 2001

Shishov, Aleksei *Rossiya i Yaponiya. Istoriya voennyikh konfliktov* Veche, Moscow, 2001

Short, Neil *The Stalin and Molotov Lines: Soviet Western defences 1928-41* (Osprey Fortress 77) Osprey Publishing, Botley, 2008

Shukman, Harold (editor) *Stalin's Generals* Weidenfeld & Nicolson, London, 1993

Simpkin, Richard (in association with Erickson, John) *Deep Battle: The Brainchild of Marshal Tukhachevskii* Brassey's Defence Publishers, London, 1987

Szubanski, Rajmund *Plan operacyjny 'Wschód'* Wydawnictwo Bellona, Warsaw, 1994

Trotter, William R. *A Frozen Hell: The Russo-Finnish Winter War of 1939-40* Algonquin Books of Chapel Hill, Chapel Hill, North Carolina, 1991

Tyushkevich, S.A. *The Soviet Armed Forces: A History of their Organisational Development* Superintendent of Documents, US Government Printing Office, Washington, 1978

Van Dyke, Carl *The Soviet Invasion of Finland 1939–1940* Frank Cass Publishers, London, 1997

Voronov N.N. *Na sluzhbe Voyennoi* Voyenzdat, Moscow, 1963

Vorotnikov M.F. *G.K. Zhukov na Khalinh-Gole* Knizhnoe Izdatelystvo Publishing House Omsk, 1989

Wawrzynski, Miroslaw *Czerwone Gwiazdy: Sojusznik czarnych krzyzy nad Polska* Agencja Wydawnicza, Warsaw, 2008

Zaloga, Steven J. *Spanish Civil War Tanks: The Proving Ground for Blitzkrieg* Osprey Publishing, Botley, Oxford, 2010

Zhukov, G.K. *Vospominaniya i. Razmyshleniya Vol I* Olma Press, Moscow, 2002

ARTICLES

Anderson, Edgar *Military Policies and plans of the Baltic States on the Eve of World War II* Lithuanian Quarterly Journal of Arts and Sciences, Vol 20 No 2 (Summer 1974)

Aptekat, Pavel & Dudorova, Olga (Translated by Dr Harold S.Orenstein) *The Unheeded Warning and the Winter War 1939–1940,* Journal of Slavic Military Studies Vol 10 No 1 (March 1997)

Coox, Alvin D. *The Lesser of Two Hells: NKVD General G.S.Lyushkov's Defection to Japan 1938–1945 Part I,* Journal of Slavic Military Studies Vol 11 No 3 (September 1998)

Van Dyke, Carl *The Timoshenko Reforms: March-July 1940,* Journal of Slavic Military Studies Vol 9 No 1 (March 1996)

Elisseva, N.E. (translated by David M.Glantz) *Plans for the development of the Workers' and Peasants' Red Army (RKKA) on the Eve of War,* Journal of Slavic Military Studies Vol 8 No 2 (June 1995)

Gerard, Beth M. *Mistakes in Force Structure and Strategy on the Eve of the Great Patriotic War,* Journal of Soviet Military Studies Vol 4 No 3 (September 1991)

Glantz, David M. *Motormechanisation,* Armies and Motorisation Interwar Documents-Combined Arms Research Library website

Glantz, David M. *Soviet Mobilisation in Peace and War: A Survey,* Journal of Soviet Military Studies, Vol 5 No 3 (September 1992)

Kaplowski, Christopher *Prelude to Violence: Show Trials and State Power in 1930s Mongolia,* American Ethnologist Vol 35 No 2 (May 2008)

Kipp, Dr. Jacob W. *Mass, Mobility, And The Red Army's Road To Operational Art 1918–1936* Foreign Military Studies Office, Fort Leavenworth, KS. 1988, Foreign Military Studies Office Publications-Mass, Mobility Website
www:fmso.leavenworth.army.mil/documents/redopart.htm

Kolomiets, M. *Istoriya Tanka KV,* Frontovaya Illyustratsia, Strategiya KM, Moscow, 2001

Kuznetsov, Ilya I. *The Soviet Military Advisors in Mongolia 1921–1939,* Journal of Slavic Military Studies Vol 12 No 4 (December 1999)

Lukinov, M.I. (Translated by Oleg Sheremet) *Notes on the Polish Campaign (1939) and the War with Finland (1939–1940),* Journal of Slavic Military Studies Vol 14 No 3 (September 2001)

Main, Steven J. *The Arrest and 'Testimony' of Marshal of the Soviet Union M.N.Tukhachevsky,* Journal of Slavic Military Studies Vol 10 No 1 (March 1997)

Mazlov A.A. *General Officer Victims of the Baltic: Concerning the Scale of Political Repression among leading Soviet Generals from the Baltic Region,* Journal of Slavic Military Studies Vol 9 No 1 (March 1996)

Mil'bakh, Vladimir S. *Repression in the 57th Special Corps (Mongolian People's Republic),* Journal of Slavic Military Studies Vol 15 No 1 (March 2002)

Mil'bakh, V.S. (Translated by Dr Harold S. Orenstein) *Repression in the Red Army in the Far East 1936–1938,* Journal of Slavic Military Studies Vol 16 No 4 (December 2003)

Mil'bakh, Vladimir S. *Red Army Artillery in the Armed Conflict on the Khalkin-Gol River,* Journal of Slavic Military Studies Vol 15 No 4 (December 2002)

Nordling, Carl O. *Sacrificing Men or Machines?: The Soviet 1940 Over-Sea Invasion of Finland: Why did General Pavlov's ice-borne attack succeed?* Journal of Slavic Military Studies Vol 14 No 4 (December 2001)

Parrish, Michael *The Downfall of the 'Iron Commissar' N.I. Eshev 1938–1940,* Journal of Slavic Military Studies Vol 14 No 2 (June 2001)

RKKA PU 36, Interwar Documents-Combined Arms Research Library website

Rukkas, Andriy *The Red Army's Troop Mobilization in the Kiev Special Military District during September 1939,* Journal of Slavic Military Studies Vol 16 No 1 (March 2003)

Searle, Alaric *J.F.C. Fuller, Tukhachevsky and the Red Army 1923–1941: The question of the reception of Fuller's military writings in the Soviet Union,* Journal of Slavic Military Studies Vol 9 No 4 (December 1996)

Šèerbinskis Valters *Intensions and reality: Latvian-Finnish military co-operation in the 1920s and 1930s,* Baltic Defence Review 2/1999

Sekigawa, Eiichiro *The Undeclared Air War,* Air Enthusiast, May 1973 (Part 1), June 1973 (Part 2), July 1973 (Part 3)

Shpakovskyy, Vyacheslav; Saneev, Sergei *Bronyetehnika i tankovye voyska Polshi 1919–1939,* Tankomaster 6/2005

Statiev, Alexander *When an Army Becomes 'Merely a Burden': Rumanian defence policy and strategy 1918–1941,* Journal of Slavic Military Studies Vol 13 No 2 (June 2000)

Tarleton, Robert E. *What Really Happened to the Stalin Line? Part 1,* Journal of Soviet Military Studies, Vol 5 No 2 (June 1992)

Tereshkin Petr *First combat in Khasan lake,* RKKA website

Urbšys Juozas *Memoirs of Juozas Urbšys (edited by Sigita Naujokaitis)* Lithuanian Quarterly Journal of Arts and Science, Volume 34 No 2 (Summer 1989)

Watt, Donald Cameron *Who plotted Against Whom? Stalin's Purge of the Soviet High Command Revisited,* Journal of Soviet Military Studies Vol 3 No 1

WEBSITES

Aptakar website. See Pervyii mesyats voinyi

Assorted information on Soviet RKKA-H0I2

www.paradoxian.org/.../Assorted_information_on_Soviet_RKKA
Axis History Forum – www.forum.axishistory.com

Battles for Khalkin Gol

http:en.wikipedia.org/wiki/Battles_for_Khalkin_Gol
cgsc.edit/carl/resources/biblio/interwar.asp

Documents on the Soviet Military Occupation of Estonia in 1940

Tonu Tannberg and Enn Travel: www.kirj.ee/public/trames/trames-2006-1-6.pdf

Excerpts from the Report on 21 June 1940 of the Commander of the Red Banner Baltic Fleet, Vice Admiral V. Tributs

Eesti Sõjaveteranide Liit (Estonian Sub-Branch, returned and Services

Finnish-Estonian defence co-operation

Website http: en.wikipedia.org/wiki/Finnish– Estonian_defense_cooperation

Fortifications with underground passages in Polesie
www.forteca.w.activ.pl/polesiee.html

Generals of World War II
www.generals.dk

Hronos
www.hrono.ru /sobyt/1900war/1939pol.html)

Interwar Documents–Combined Arms Research Library
Website (www):cgsc.contentcdm,oclc.org

Kavaleriiskie Korpusa RKKA
Website http: rkka.ru/Cavalry

League of Australia
http:veterans.eesti.org.au/history/soviet-russia-occupies-estonia/1a-supplement-excerpts- from - the-report-of-the-commander-of-the-red-banner-fleetvice-admiral-vtrubuts

History, Soviet Union occupies Estonia. Supplement 1b Mechanizirovannieye **Korpusa RKKA (Eugene Drig)**
http:mechcorps.rkka.ru

Regional History Association 'Karelia'(PPI "Karelia") – Eugene A. Balashov
http:kannas.nm.ru/rkka.htm

RKKA in World War II
www.armchairgeneral.com/rkkaww2/

Soviet invasion of Poland 1939
Written by Henrik Krog with information from Oleg Sheremet and William Wilson
http: info-poland.buffalo.edu/web/history/WWII/soviet/link.shtml

Stalinist Purges in Mongolia
http: wn.com/Stalinist_purges_in_Mongolia

Stalinist Repressions in Mongolia
http: en.wikipedia.org/wika/Stalinist_repressions_in_Mongolia

Documents on the Soviet Military Occupation of Estonia in 1940
Tannberg, Tõnu & Tarvel, Enn. Dissertation for Tartu University
www.kirj.ee/publictrames/trames-2006-1-6.pdf

The coming of the war and Eastern Europe in World War II (Anna M.Cienciala)
http:web.ku.edu/~eceurope/hist557/lect16.htm

Estimation of security threats and Estonian defence planning in the 1930s
Urmas Salo doctoral dissertation
www.kirj.ee/public/Acta_hist/2008/issue_1/acta-2008-1-3.pdf

Workers' and Peasants' Red Army (RKKA) (Aleksandr Kiyan)
www.rkka.ru

The Civil Guard of Finland by Jarkko Vihavainen
www.moisinnagant.net/finland/The CivilGuard Of Finland.asp

The Battles of the Winter War by Sami Korhonen
www.winterwar.com
Posle vuri, pered Schtormom by Pavel Anmekary RKKA website
http.rkka.ru/ibib/1.htm
Pervyii mesyats voinyi by Pavel Aptakar RKKA website. http.rkka.ru/ibib/1.htm

Preparations for the campaign of Bessarabia by Sergei Piskunov
www.hrono.ru/sobyt/1900war/1940prut.php

Polesie
http:forteca.w.activ.pl/polesiee.html

RKKA handbook
www: rkka.ru/handbook

Soviet Aviation in the Greater Patriotic War
http:ilpilot.narod.ru/vvs_tsifra/index.htm
Svintsobyii Shkval RKKA website
http.rkka.ru/ibib/1.htm
Stalynoii potop RKKA website
http:rkka.ru/ibib/1.htm

Target Is to Destroy the Baltic Fleet
Amosov, Igor, Pochtarev, Andrei Nikolayevich
http:rusnavy.com/history/events/collaboration.htm

Tragediya okrushennyikh RKKA website
http:rkka.ru/ibib/1.htm

INDEX